Rwanda

the Bradt Travel Guide

Philip Briggs
Janice Booth

edition
3

www.bradtguides.com

Bradt Travel Guides Ltd, UK
The Globe Pequot Press Inc, USA

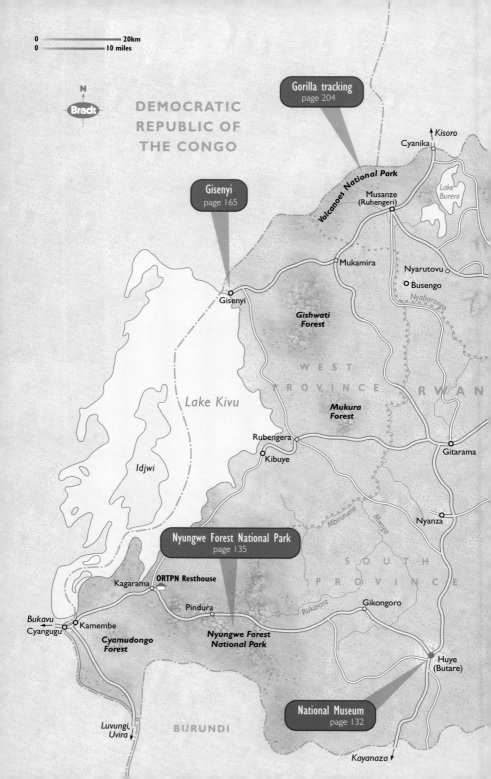

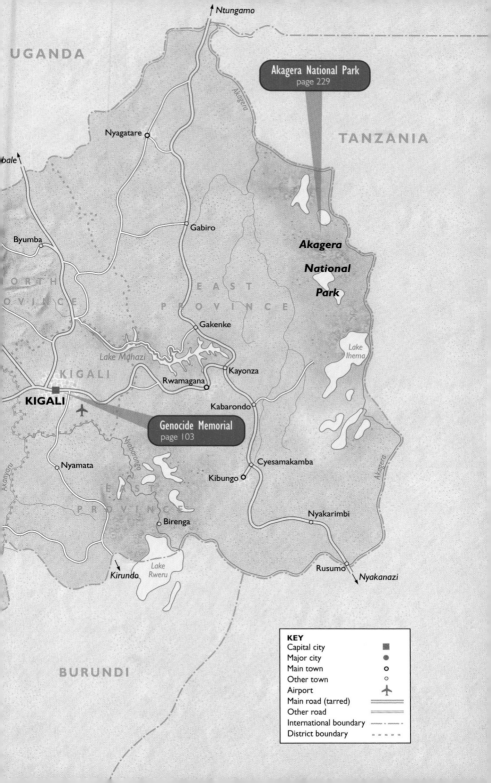

Rwanda
Don't
miss…

Gorillas
Mountain gorilla, *Gorilla gorilla berengi*,
Volcanoes National Park
(TC/IA) page 206

Intore dancing
(AZ) page 29

National parks
Tea plantations on
fringe of Nyungwe
Forest National Park
(AZ) page 135

Wildlife
Young African elephant
Loxodonta africana
(AZ) page 233

**People and
culture**
Village scene
(AZ) page 25

"NYIRAMACHABELLI"
DIAN FOSSEY
1932 — 1985
NO ONE LOVED GORILLAS MORE
REST IN PEACE, DEAR FRIEND
ETERNALLY PROTECTED
IN THIS SACRED GROUND
FOR YOU ARE HOME
WHERE YOU BELONG

previous page **Nyungwe Forest National Park — a montane rainforest** (AZ) page 135

top & above left **Mountain gorillas**
Gorilla gorilla berengi (AZ) page 206

above right **Dian Fossey's grave next to gorilla graveyard, Karisoke Research Centre** (AZ) page 199

right **Mother with young, Volcanoes National Park**
(TC/IA) page 199

top   **Outskirts of Musanze (Ruhengeri), outside Volcanoes National Park**
(AZ) page 177

centre **Silhouette of boys in Mokoro** (TC/IA)

left   **Tea picker in estate, Byumba**
(AZ/IA) page 216

top Rural homestead, near Musanze (Ruhengeri) (AZ/IA) page 177

centre King's Palace (traditional ancient palace of the Mwami) — now a museum (AZ/IA)

right Woman in her home, Kigali (RH) page 83

top **Hippopotamus bulls fighting**
Hippopotamus amphibius (AZ)

centre **Buffalo** *Syncerus caffer* (AZ)

below **Warthog** *Phacochoerus aethiopicus* (AZ)

top   **Burchell's zebra** *Equus burchelli* (AZ)

above   **Ankole bull** (AZ)

left page

top left   **Bushbuck** *Tragelaphus scriptus* (AZ)

top right   **Male defassa waterbuck**
         Kobus ellipsiprymrus defassa (AZ)

bottom   **Impala**, *Aepyceros melampus*, **Akagera**
         National Park (AZ)

right page

top   **Lake Burera, near Musanze (Ruhengeri)**
         (AZ) page 189

above   **Red-throated alethe**, *Alethe poliophrys*,
         Nyungwe Forest National Park (AZ)

right   **Grey-crowned crane** *Balearica regulorum* (AZ)

previous page   **Waterfall, Nyungwe Forest National Park** (AZ) page 135
top   **Golden monkey** *Cercopithecus kandti* (AZ)
above left   **L'Hoest's monkey, yawning** *Cercopithecus l'hoesti* (AZ)
above right   **Olive baboon with young** *Papio cynocephalus anubis* (AZ)
below   **Red-tailed monkey** *Cercopithecus ascinius* (AZ)

above **Intore dancing** (AZ) page 29

left **Intore traditional drummers**
(AZ/IA) page 29

Authors

Philip Briggs is a travel writer and tour leader specialising in East and southern Africa. Born in Britain and raised in South Africa, he started travelling in East Africa in 1986, and his first book guide to South Africa was published by Bradt in 1991. Since then, Philip has divided his time between exploring and writing about the highways and byways of Africa. In addition to authoring the Bradt travel guides to Tanzania, Uganda, Ghana, Ethiopia, Malawi, Mozambique and East & southern Africa, he has contributed to numerous other books and contributes regularly to various travel and wildlife magazines.

Janice Booth's career has encompassed professional stage management, amateur archaeology, charity work, writing, selling haberdashery in Harrods, translating documents about African agriculture, travelling whenever possible, and compiling logic problems for puzzle magazines. She started editing Bradt travel guides after meeting Hilary Bradt on a bus in the Seychelles in 1996, and since first visiting Rwanda in 2000 – and co-writing the first edition of this guide – has lectured on Rwanda, led tours there and contributed articles to various magazines and websites.

PUBLISHER'S FOREWORD
Hilary Bradt

The first Bradt travel guide was written in 1974 by George and Hilary Bradt on a river barge floating down a tributary of the Amazon. In the 1980s and '90s the focus shifted away from hiking to broader-based guides covering new destinations – usually the first to be published about these places. In the 21st century Bradt continues to publish such ground-breaking guides, as well as others to established holiday destinations, incorporating in-depth information on culture and natural history with the nuts and bolts of where to stay and what to see.

Bradt authors support responsible travel, and provide advice not only on minimum impact but also on how to give something back through local charities. In this way a true synergy is achieved between the traveller and local communities.

* * *

What a lot has changed in Rwanda since we launched the first edition in Kigali in 2000! During that visit I was the only tourist in the small group visiting the gorillas, the roads through the beguiling countryside were full of potholes, and accommodation outside Kigali was fairly basic. Now the new Rwanda has embraced tourism with the far-sighted view of the importance of sustainability and conservation that is a model for Africa. This remains the guidebook to the country and I am happy that it remains in the hands of the original authors whose enthusiasm for Rwanda is shared by all visitors.

Reprinted November 2008
Third edition August 2006   First published 2001

Bradt Travel Guides Ltd
23 High Street, Chalfont St Peter, Bucks SL9 9QE, England; www.bradtguides.com
Published in the USA by The Globe Pequot Press Inc, 246 Goose Lane,
PO Box 480, Guilford, Connecticut 06475-0480

Text copyright © 2006 Philip Briggs and Janice Booth
Maps copyright © 2006 Bradt Travel Guides Ltd
Illustrations © 2006 individual photographers and artists

British Library Cataloguing in Publication Data
A catalogue record for this book is available from the British Library
ISBN-10: 1 84162 180 3   ISBN-13: 978 1 84162 180 7

Photographs *Text* Ariadne Van Zandbergen (AZ), Richard Human (RH), Images of Africa (IA)
Front cover Intore dancer (AZ)
Back cover Lake Burera (AZ), Mountain gorilla (AZ)
Title page Silverback mountain gorilla (AZ), Lake Burera (AZ), Young girl (IA)

Illustrations Annabel Milne
Maps Alan Whitaker

Typeset from the authors' disc by Wakewing
Printed and bound in India by Nutech Photolithographers

Acknowledgements

JANICE BOOTH As I won't be involved with subsequent editions of this guide (see my *Introduction* on page VII), I'd like to recall and thank some of the people in Rwanda who were so supportive of the first edition back in 2000, at a time when the media had nothing good to say about the country and tourists hesitated to return. The late and much-missed Florence Nkera was an inspiration throughout, with her enthusiasm and energy, and Patricia Kanyiginya has always been a steady source of help. Rosemary Museminali, then Rwandan Ambassador in London, patiently read and corrected the proofs of the first edition, working late into the night; Théogène Rudasingwa in the President's Office checked the History section; and Claver Gatete (now Ambassador in London) gave me information on investment and the country in general. Rwanda's First Lady and the Minister for Tourism demonstrated their support by attending the guide's official launch in Kigali. They all had confidence in us, just as we had confidence in Rwanda. Zac Nsenga, now Rwandan Ambassador in Washington, reminded me on my first visit not to miss the mountain gorillas (I hadn't realised they were accessible) and thereby introduced me to Rwanda's biggest tourist attraction! Beth Payne, Liz Williamson and Marie Chantal Uwimana all provided useful information. Many other Rwandans helped with smiles and friendship as I travelled round their country – and of course I have thanks also for my co-author Philip, whose input has been essential and who is always a pleasure to work with. Finally, if Protais Rwihimba, who died in the genocide, had not written to me in 1978 and launched a friendship that lasted 16 years, I would never have come to Rwanda to look for his family and this book would not have been written; so in the end his has been the greatest contribution.

PHILIP BRIGGS & ARIADNE VAN ZANDBERGEN The successful research of this third edition at monumentally short notice is largely thanks to the generous support of the following tourist-related individuals and institutions: Rosette Rugamba, Rica Rwigamba and Emmanuel Werabe of ORTPN; Praveen Moman and Yusuf Mulima Mubiru of Volcanoes Safaris, as well as our enthusiastic driver (and apprentice mapmaker) Paul Ruganintwali and the staff of Virunga Lodge; Manzi Kayihura, Flora Butamire and Dirk Nel of Rwandair; André Tanner of the Motel le Garni du Centre Kigali; and Basha of the Gorillas Hotel in Kigali. I remain indebted to my co-author Janice Booth for her hard work compiling earlier versions of this guide and her unstinting support and advice during the research and writing of the present edition. And, like Janice, we greatly missed the enthusiastic involvement of Florence Nkera, who gave us such a positive introduction to Rwanda.

Contents

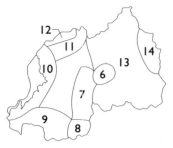

	Introduction	VII

PART ONE   **GENERAL INFORMATION**   **I**

Chapter I   **Background Information**   **3**
Natural history 3, History 6

Chapter 2   **People and Culture**   **25**
People 25, Religion 25, Education 27, Culture 29

Chapter 3   **Planning and Preparation**   **35**
When to visit 35, Getting there and away 35, Red tape 39,
Packing 40, Money 43, Itinerary planning 46

Chapter 4   **Health and Safety**   **47**
Health 47, Safety 58

Chapter 5   **Travelling in Rwanda**   **61**
Tourist information and services 61, Public holidays and
events 61, Money 62, Getting around 62, Accommodation
65, Eating and drinking 66, Language 69, Hassles 70,
Media and communications 73, Shopping 76, Arts and
entertainment 76, Becoming involved 77, Investing in
Rwanda 80

PART TWO   **THE GUIDE**   **81**

Chapter 6   **Kigali**   **83**
Getting there and away 83, Getting around 86, Where to
stay 87, Where to eat and drink 97, Practicalities 100, What
to see an do in Kigali 102, Excursions from Kigali 110

Chapter 7   **The Road to Huye (Butare)**   **115**
Gitarama 115, Ruhango 120, Nyanza 120

Chapter 8   **Huye (Butare)**   **127**
Getting there and away 127, Getting around 128, Where
to stay 128, Where to eat and drink 130, Nightlife 130,
Practicalities 130, What to see and do 131, Excursions
from Huye 133

Chapter 9   **Nyungwe Forest National Park**   **135**
Natural history 138, Getting there and away 143, Where
to stay and eat 143, Activities 144

Chapter 10	**Lake Kivu**	153
	Cyangugu 154, Kibuye 161, Gisenyi 165	
Chapter 11	**Musanze (Ruhengeri) and the Virunga Foothills**	177
	Getting there and away 177, Where to stay 179, Where to eat and drink 185, Practicalities 186, Excursions from Musanze 188	
Chapter 12	**Volcanoes National Park**	199
	Getting there and away 201, Where to stay and eat 201, Non-gorilla attractions 202, Gorilla tracking 204, Tourism and conservation 211	
Chapter 13	**Eastern Rwanda**	215
	The Byumba Road 215, The Nyagatare Road 217, The Rusumo Road 221	
Chapter 14	**Akagera National Park**	229
	Natural history 231, Further information 238, Getting there and away 238, Where to stay 239, Fees 239, Activities 239	
Appendix 1	**Language**	243
Appendix 2	**Websites**	249
Appendix 3	**Further Reading**	251
	Index	260

LIST OF MAPS

Akagera National Park	230	Kigali city centre	93
Cyangugu & Kamembe	156	Kigali Nyamarambo	96
Eastern Midlands	214	Kigali environs	84–5
Gisenyi	168–9	Lakes Burero & Ruhondo	190
Gitarama	116	Musanze (Ruhengeri)	180–1
Huye (Butare) orientation	126	Nyanza	122
Huye (Butare) town centre	129	Nyagatare	220
Kibungo	224	Nyungwe National Park	136
Kibuye	162	Virunga Foothills	178
Kigali central	88–9	Volcanoes National Park	200

Introduction

Janice Booth

This is both an introduction and a signing-off, because Philip (with my wholehearted approval, and in fact at my suggestion!) is taking over all future editions of this guide. So I'm allowing myself a few paragraphs of reminiscence.

Back in 1978, a young and unknown Rwandan half my age found my address and wrote to me from Uganda, announcing that he had chosen me for a friend. And that friendship endured for 16 years, during which time he returned to Rwanda, found (and lost) various jobs, helped to see his younger siblings through secondary school, was imprisoned and released, fled briefly to an adjoining country, set up a small charity, got married, had a child – and all the time, through his letters, drew me ever more closely into his life and that of his family.

From April 1994 the letters stopped. I waited. I tried to follow up the few contacts I had, but there was no reply. Finally, in February 2000, I came to Rwanda for the first time. I was sure he had died in the genocide, but maybe I could at least trace some surviving relatives.

The international media at that time were portraying a dark and damaged country, still volatile, only semi-functional and filled with memories of death. I didn't expect to enjoy my visit, and the last thing in my mind was tourism or writing a guidebook.

In the event I was captivated. I caught minibus-taxis to all corners of Rwanda, in absolute safety, and was stunned by its beauty. From every road I took, amazing landscapes unfolded. People were friendly, and the infrastructures – although shaken – were operational. Back in Kigali, I faxed Hilary Bradt to say that Rwanda absolutely deserved a travel guide. To my relief and gratitude, she agreed. Philip was available to cover the important wildlife sections – and so the first edition of this book was born.

Seven visits later, I've seen for myself the extraordinary growth of Rwanda's tourism sector, which has bounced back to well above its pre-genocide peak. I've seen a shattered and shell-shocked country transform itself into a vibrant, safe, prosperous and energetic nation, well able to tackle the demands of the 21st century. And I've seen the courage and dignity of the genocide survivors as they rebuild their lives. It is a truly amazing place, this 'land of a thousand hills' deep in the heart of Africa.

Of course the picture isn't all rose-tinted. There is still poverty, and very deep sadness. Not a family was untouched by the genocide, and no-one forgets. Trauma still clouds many minds and survivors still suffer. Memorials honour the dead and underline Rwanda's message to the world, which is 'Never again'. But it is the strength, beauty, bravery, energy and determination of Rwanda and its people that make the greatest impression on the visitor.

As I'd expected, my friend had died, as had his wife, baby, sister, brother, father … and that is how things were, back in 1994. However, I did manage to trace several other members of his family, and we've remained in close and happy contact, so my 'Rwanda story' ends well. I feel privileged to have been involved with this unforgettable country and its even more unforgettable people.

So – *Rwanda: The Bradt Travel Guide* is now in Philip's safe hands. I wish him – and it – well. We know, and it's a source of great pride and satisfaction to all of us who have played a part in it, how important the book has been for the reconstruction of Rwanda's tourist industry. Please send Philip news and updates for subsequent editions. And please – above all – do take the plunge and start planning a visit to Rwanda! You won't be disappointed.

RWANDA UPDATE NEWSLETTER!

An update newsletter for Rwanda, which is regularly revised by Philip Briggs based on feedback from readers and from other local sources, is available online at www.bradtguides.com. A copy may also be obtained by email from info@bradtguides.com.

The newsletter is provided as a free service and without obligation, but if you have benefited from it, we would be grateful if you could return the favour by writing to us on your return with any information that may be of use to future travellers and, if you find the book useful, posting your comments on amazon.com and other online booksellers.

We also believe the newsletter will provide a forum by which visitors to Rwanda can be made aware of any new tourist-related projects, activities and facilities. We therefore extend an invitation to volunteers, hotel owners and ecotourist professionals working in Rwanda to contact us with any information that might be of interest to travellers.

Please also have a look at Philip Briggs's blog at http://philipbriggs.wordpress.com for interactive, regularly updated travel information for Rwanda.

CHANGES AND UPDATES

Tourism in Rwanda is developing very fast, and practical details (prices, hotels, transport, attractions ...) may well alter during the life of this guide. Also the names of some towns are changing: Butare has just become Huye, Ruhengeri is now Musanze, and more seem likely to follow. The Rwanda Tourist Board (see page 61) should have up-to-date information, and periodic updates will also appear on the Bradt website, www.bradtguides.com.

Note: All GPS readings in this guide are taken with Map Datum set to 'Cape'.

Part One

GENERAL INFORMATION

GEOGRAPHY
Land area 26,340km² (less than half that of Scotland)
Location 120km south of the Equator in the Tropic of Capricorn
Capital Kigali
Rainfall Annual average 900–1,600mm; rainy seasons March–May and
October–December
Average temperature 24.6–27.6°C; hottest August and September
Altitude From below 1,000 to above 4,500m above sea level; highest point is
Mt Karisimbi (4,507m)
Terrain Mostly grassy uplands and hills; relief is mountainous with altitude
declining from west to east
Vegetation Ranges from dense equatorial forest in the northwest to tropical
savanna in the east
Land use 47% cropland, 22% forest, 18% pasture, 13% other
Natural resources Some tin, gold and natural gas
Main exports Coffee and tea
National parks Volcanoes (northwest); Nyungwe (southwest); Akagera (east)

HUMAN STATISTICS
Population 8.2 million (2002 census), 8.5 million (2006 estimate); 53.8%
female, 46.2% male
Life expectancy at birth Women 45 years, men 42 years
Religion Roman Catholic (majority), Protestant, Muslim, traditional
Official languages Kinyarwanda, French, English. Swahili is also widely spoken.
Education Primary, secondary, technical/vocational, higher/university
GDP per capita US$220 in 2005

POLITICS/ADMINISTRATION
Government The broad-based Government of National Unity, with three
branches: executive, legislative and judicial.
Ruling Party Rwanda Patriotic Front (RPF)
President Paul Kagame
Prime Minister Bernard Makuza
National flag Blue, yellow and green, with a sun in the top right-hand corner
Administrative divisions 4 provinces plus Kigali City, subdivided into 30
districts and 416 sectors

PRACTICAL DETAILS
Time GMT + 2 hours
Currency Rwandan franc
Main health risk Malaria
Electricity 230/240 volts at 50Hz
International telephone country code 250
Airport Kigali International Airport
Nearest seaports Mombasa (1,760km); Dar es Salaam (1,528km)

1

Background Information

Rwanda is a land-locked country in Central Africa. Also known as the 'Land of a Thousand Hills', Rwanda has five volcanoes, 23 lakes and numerous rivers. The country lies 1,270km west of the Indian Ocean and 2,000km east of the Atlantic – literally in the heart of Africa.

NATURAL HISTORY

GEOGRAPHY Rwanda's mountainous topography is a product of its position on the eastern rim of the Albertine Rift Valley, part of the Great Rift Valley which cuts through Africa from the Red Sea to Mozambique. The country's largest freshwater body, Lake Kivu, which forms the border with the Democratic Republic of the Congo (DRC), is effectively a large sump hemmed in by the Rift Valley walls, while its highest peaks – in the volcanic Virunga chain – are a result of the same geological process which formed the Rift Valley 20 million years ago. The Rift Valley escarpment running through western Rwanda also serves as a watershed between Africa's two largest drainage systems: the Nile and the Congo.

Western and central Rwanda are characterised by a seemingly endless vista of steep mountains, interspersed with several substantial lakes whose irregular shape follows the mountains that surround them. Much of this part of the country lies at elevations of between 1,500 and 2,500m. Only in the far east of the country, along the Tanzania border, do the steep mountains give way to the lower-lying, flatter terrain of the Lake Victoria Basin. The dominant geographical feature of this part of the country is the Kagera River and associated network of swamps and small lakes running along the Tanzania border, eventually to flow into Lake Victoria, making it the most remote source of the world's longest river, the Nile (see box *The Riddle of The Nile* below). Much of this ecosystem is protected within Akagera National Park.

VEGETATION In prehistoric times, as much as a third of what is now Rwanda was covered in montane rainforest, with the remainder of the highlands supporting open grassland. Since the advent of Iron-Age technology and agriculture some 2,000 years ago, much of Rwanda's natural vegetation has been replaced by agriculture, a process that has accelerated dramatically in the last 100 years. The only large stand of forest left in Rwanda today is Nyungwe, in the southwest, though several other small relic forest patches are dotted around the country, notably Cyamudongo and Mukura Forests. Patches of true forest still occur on the Virungas, though most of the natural vegetation on this range consists of bamboo forest and open moorland. Outside of Nyungwe (now designated a national park) and the Virungas, practically no montane grassland is left in Rwanda; the highlands are instead dominated by the terraced agriculture that gives the Rwandan countryside much of its distinctive character. The far east of Rwanda supports an

3

The first European to see Lake Victoria was John Hanning Speke, who marched from Tabora to the site of present-day Mwanza in 1858 following his joint 'discovery' of Lake Tanganyika with Richard Burton the previous year. Speke named the lake for Queen Victoria, but prior to that Arab slave traders called it Ukerewe (still the name of its largest island). It is unclear what name was in local use, since the only one used by Speke is Nyanza, which simply means lake.

A major goal of the Burton-Speke expedition had been to solve the great geographical enigma of the age, the source of the White Nile. Speke, based on his brief glimpse of the southeast corner of Lake Victoria, somewhat whimsically proclaimed his 'discovery' to be the answer to that riddle. Burton, with a comparable lack of compelling evidence, was convinced that the great river flowed out of Lake Tanganyika. The dispute between the former travelling companions erupted bitterly on their return to Britain, where Burton – the more persuasive writer and respected traveller – gained the backing of the scientific establishment.

Over 1862-3, Speke and Captain James Grant returned to Lake Victoria, hoping to prove Speke's theory correct. They looped inland around the western shore of the lake, arriving at the court of King Mutesa of Buganda, then continued east to the site of present-day Jinja, where a substantial river flowed out of the lake after tumbling over a cataract that Speke named Ripon Falls. From here, the two explorers headed north, sporadically crossing paths with the river until they reached Lake Albert, then following the Nile to Khartoum and Cairo. Speke's declaration that 'The Nile is settled' met with mixed support back home. Burton and other sceptics pointed out that Speke had bypassed the entire western shore of his purported great lake, had visited only a couple of points on the northern shore, and had not attempted to explore the east. Nor, for that matter, had he followed the course of the Nile in its entirety. Speke, claimed his detractors, had seen several different lakes and different stretches of river, connected only in his own deluded mind. The sceptics had a point, but Speke had nevertheless gathered sufficient geographical evidence to render his claim highly plausible. His notion of one great lake, far from being mere whimsy, was backed by anecdotal information gathered from local sources along the way.

Matters were scheduled to reach a head on 16 September 1864, when an eagerly awaited debate between Burton and Speke – in the words of the former, 'what silly tongues called the "Nile Duel"' – was due to take place at the Royal Geographic Society (RGS). And reach a head they did, but in circumstances more tragic than anybody could have anticipated. On the afternoon of the debate, Speke went out shooting with a cousin, only to stumble while crossing a wall and in the process discharging a barrel of his shotgun into his heart. The subsequent inquest recorded a verdict of accidental death, but it has often been suggested – purely on the basis of the curious timing – that Speke deliberately took his life rather than face up to Burton in public. Burton, who had seen Speke less than three hours earlier, was by all accounts deeply troubled by Speke's death, and years later he was quoted as stating 'the uncharitable [say] that I shot him' – an accusation that seems to have been aired only in Burton's imagination.

Speke was dead, but the 'Nile debate' would keep kicking for several years. In 1864, Sir Stanley and Lady Baker became the first Europeans to reach Lake Albert and nearby Murchison Falls in present-day Uganda. The Bakers, much to the delight of the anti-Speke lobby, were convinced that this newly named lake was a source of the Nile, though they

altogether different vegetation: the characteristic African 'bush', a mosaic of savanna woodland and grassland dominated by thorny acacia trees.

FAUNA Rwanda naturally supports a widely varied fauna, but the rapid human population growth in recent decades, with its by-products of habitat loss and openly admitted it might not be the only one. Following the Bakers' announcement, Burton put forward a revised theory, namely that the most remote source of the Nile was the Rusizi River, which he believed flowed out of the northern head of Lake Tanganyika and emptied into Lake Albert.

In 1865, the RGS followed up on Burton's theory by sending Dr David Livingstone to Lake Tanganyika. Livingstone, however, was of the opinion that the Nile's source lay further south than Burton supposed, and so he struck out towards the lake along a previously unexplored route. Leaving from Mikindani in the far south of present-day Tanzania, Livingstone followed the Rovuma River inland, continuing westward to the southern tip of Lake Tanganyika. From there, he ranged southward into present-day Zambia, where he came across a new candidate for the source of the Nile: the swampy Lake Bangweulu and its major outlet the Lualaba River. It was only after his famous meeting with Henry Stanley at Ujiji, in November 1871, that Livingstone (in the company of Stanley) visited the north of Lake Tanganyika and Burton's cherished Rusizi River, which, it transpired, flowed *into* the lake. Burton, nevertheless, still regarded Lake Tanganyika to be the most likely source of the Nile, while Livingstone was convinced that the answer lay with the Lualaba River. In August 1872, Livingstone headed back to the Lake Bangweulu region, where he fell ill and died six months later, the great question still unanswered.

In August 1874, ten years after Speke's death, Stanley embarked on a three-year expedition every bit as remarkable and arduous as those undertaken by his predecessors, yet one whose significance is often overlooked. Partly, this is because Stanley cuts such an unsympathetic figure, the grim caricature of the murderous pre-colonial White Man blasting and blustering his way through territories where Burton, Speke and Livingstone had relied largely on diplomacy. It is also the case, however, that Stanley set out with no intention of seeking headline-making fresh discoveries. Instead, he determined to test methodically the theories advocated by Speke, Burton and Livingstone about the Nile's source. First, Stanley sailed around the circumference of Lake Victoria, establishing that it was indeed as vast as Speke had claimed (and, incidentally, crossing the so-called 'Alexandra Nile' (Kagera River) into what is Akagera National Park, where he camped on the shore of Lake Ihema). Stanley's next step was to circumnavigate Lake Tanganyika, which, contrary to Burton's long-held theories, clearly boasted no outlet sufficiently large to be the source of the Nile. Finally, and most remarkably, Stanley took a boat along Livingstone's Lualaba River to its confluence with an even larger river, which he followed for months with no idea as to where he might end up.

When, exactly 999 days after he left Zanzibar, Stanley emerged at the Congo mouth, the shortlist of plausible theories relating to the source of the Nile had been reduced to one. Clearly, the Nile did flow out of Lake Victoria at Ripon Falls, before entering and exiting Lake Albert at its northern tip to start its long course through the sands of the Sahara. Stanley's achievement in putting to rest decades of speculation about how the main rivers and lakes of East Africa linked together is estimable indeed. He was nevertheless generous enough to concede that: 'Speke now has the full glory of having discovered the largest inland sea on the continent of Africa, also its principal affluent as well as its outlet. I must also give him credit for having understood the geography of the countries we travelled through far better than any of us who so persistently opposed his hypothesis'.

poaching, has resulted in the extirpation of most large mammal species outside of a few designated conservation areas. Rwanda today has three main conservation areas: the Volcanoes Park, Akagera Park and Nyungwe Forest. Each of these protects a very different ecosystem and combination of large mammals, for which reason greater detail on the fauna of each reserve is given under the appropriate regional section. Broadly speaking, however, Akagera supports a typical savanna fauna dominated by a variety of antelope, other grazers such as zebra, buffalo and giraffe, the aquatic hippopotamus, and plains predators such as lion, leopard and spotted hyena.

Nyungwe Forest and the Volcanoes Park probably supported a similar range of large mammals 500 years ago. Today, however, the faunas differ, mostly as a result of extensive deforestation on the lower slopes of the Virungas. The volcanoes today support bamboo specialists such as golden monkey and mountain gorilla, as well as relic populations of habitat-tolerant species such as buffalo and elephant. The latter two species are probably extinct in Nyungwe (buffalo were hunted out 25 years ago, while elephant spoor has not been detected since a dead elephant was found in late 1999), but this vast forest still supports one of Africa's richest varieties of forest specialists, ranging from 13 types of primate to golden cat, duiker and giant forest hog. Despite the retreat of most large mammals into reserves, Rwanda remains a rewarding destination for game viewing: the Volcanoes Park is the best place in the world to track mountain gorillas, while Nyungwe offers visitors a good chance of seeing chimpanzees and 400-strong troops of colobus monkeys – the largest arboreal primate troops in Africa today.

Rwanda is a wonderful destination for birdwatchers, with an incredible 670 species recorded in an area which is smaller than Belgium and has less than half the land surface of Scotland. Once again, greater detail is supplied in regional chapters, but prime birdwatching destinations include Nyungwe (280 species including numerous forest rarities and 26 Albertine Rift endemics) and Akagera (savanna birds, raptors and waterbirds). Almost anywhere in the country can, however, prove rewarding to birders: an hour in the garden of one of the capital's larger hotels is likely to throw up a variety of colourful robin-chats, weavers, finches, flycatchers and sunbirds.

HISTORY

EARLIEST TIMES Even back in the **ice age**, Rwanda was showing its typically green and fertile face; a part of the Nyungwe Forest remained uncovered by ice, so that animal and plant life could survive there. Excavations undertaken from the 1940s onwards identified several **early Iron-Age** sites in Rwanda and neighbouring Burundi, yielding fragments of typical 'dimpled' pottery (see *Africa in the Iron Age*, Roland Oliver & Brian M Fagan, Cambridge University Press, 1975). At Nyirankuba in what is now South province, a site of **late Stone-Age** occupation (without pottery) underlay a later occupation level containing both pottery and iron slag. Iron-smelting furnaces at two other sites in southern Rwanda (Ndora and Cyamakusa) gave radio-carbon datings of around AD200–300. Oliver & Fagan (above) describe these furnaces as being some 5ft in diameter, built of wedge-shaped bricks. Other sites in the area of Rwanda, Burundi and Kivu show late Stone-Age occupation sites underlying early Iron-Age occupation. The early Iron-Age pottery was later succeeded by a different and coarser type, apparently made by newcomers from the north who were cattle raisers – but archaeological investigation in Rwanda has been sparse, and there must be much still awaiting discovery. Some artefacts are displayed in the National Museum in Huye (formerly Butare).

Rwanda's earliest inhabitants were pygmoid **hunter-gatherers**, ancestors of the *Twa* (the name means, roughly, 'indigenous hunter-gatherers'), who still form part of the population today and are still known for their skill as potters. Gradually – the dates are uncertain, but probably before about 700BC – they were joined by Bantu-speaking **farmers**, who were spreading throughout Central Africa seeking good land on which to settle. Fertile Rwanda was a promising site. The arrival of these incomers, known as *Hutus,* was bad news for the Twa; now a minority, they saw some of their traditional hunting grounds cleared to make way for farming, and retreated further into the forests. Then Iron-Age technology developed tools – such as hoes – which enabled the farmers to grow more crops than were needed for subsistence and thus to trade.

Next came the **cattle raisers**, taller and lankier people than either the pygmoid Twa or the sturdy farmers, who may have come from either the north or the northeast. With only oral tradition to guide us, there's no hard historic evidence for the timing of their arrival – some say before the 10th century AD, others after the 14th. Gradually, whether by conquest or by natural assimilation, a hierarchy emerged in which the cattle raisers (known as *Tutsis,* meaning 'owners of cattle') were superior to the farmers and a master–client relationship known as *ubuhake* developed. Then most of Rwanda was a monarchy ruled by a Tutsi king or *Mwami* – although there remained outlying areas where the farming groups did not accept his authority.

Note The three groups are more correctly called Batwa, Bahutu and Batutsi, while individuals are a Mutwa, a Muhutu and a Mututsi. However, we have opted for the forms Twa, Hutu and Tutsi because outside Rwanda they are commonly used. The plural of Mwami (sometimes spelt Mwaami) is Bami. The language spoken by all three groups is Kinyarwanda.

THE KINGDOMS OF RWANDA Rwanda has a rich oral history, which was maintained primarily by members of the Rwandan royal court. According to this history the founder of Rwanda's ruling dynasty, Abanyiginya, was not born naturally like other humans, but was born from an earthenware jar of milk. The grandmother of Rwandans lived in heaven with Nkuba (thunder) who was given the secret of creating life. He made a small man out of clay, coated him with his saliva, and placed him in a wooden jar filled with milk and the heart of a slaughtered bull. The jar was constantly refilled with fresh milk. At the end of nine months the man took on the image of Sabizeze. When Sabizeze learned of his origin, he was angry that his mother had revealed the secret and decided to leave heaven and come to earth. He brought with him his sister Nyampundu, his brother Mututsi, and a couple of Batwa. Sabizeze was welcomed by Kabeja who was of the Abazigaba clan and king of the region (in the present-day Akagera National Park). Sabizeze then had a son named Gihanga who was to found the Kingdom of Rwanda. A Rwandan historian, Alexis Kagame, estimates that Gihanga ruled as King of Rwanda in the late 10th or early 11th century.

Before the arrival of Europeans, Rwandans believed they were the centre of the world, with the grandest monarchy, the greatest power and the highest civilisation. Their king or *mwami* was the supreme authority and was magically identified with Rwanda. There was a strong belief that if the ruling monarch was not the true king, the people of Rwanda would be in danger. The well-being of Rwanda was directly linked to the health of the king. When he grew old, Rwanda's prosperity was compromised. Only when the ageing ruler died and a new, stronger king was enthroned did the country re-stabilise.

The centralised control by the king was balanced by a very powerful queen mother and a group of dynastic ritualists: the *abiiru.* Queen mothers could never come from the same family clan as the king and rotated among four different family clans. The *abiiru,* who were also drawn from four different clans, could reverse the king's decisions if they conflicted with the magical Esoteric Code, protected and interpreted by the *abiiru.* They also governed the selection and installation of a new king. Any member of the *abiiru* who forgot any part of his assigned portion of the Esoteric Code was punished severely. Members of the *abiiru* and other custodians of state secrets who revealed the secrets of the royal court were forced to drink *igihango*, a mixture containing a magical power to kill traitors or anyone who failed in his duty. While the king could order the death of a disloyal member of the *abiiru*, he was required to replace the traitor with a member from the same family clan.

Rwanda's dynastic drums, which could be made only by members of one family clan from very specific trees with magical elements, had the same dignity as the king. The genitals of the enemies of Rwanda killed by the king hung from the drum. The capture of a dynastic drum from an enemy country normally signified annexation, with the group whose drum was stolen losing all faith in itself. This tradition is shared among all Bantu-speaking peoples in Africa. When Rwanda's royal drum *Rwoga* was lost to a neighbouring kingdom by King Ndahiro II Cyaamatare in the late 15th century, Rwanda was devastated. *Rwoga* was eventually replaced by *Karinga*, the last dynastic drum, when King Ruganzu II Ndori regained Rwanda's pride through his military exploits. The fate of *Karinga* is unknown. It is reported to have survived the colonial period, but disappeared soon after Rwanda's independence.

The origin of the division between Tutsis and Hutus is still being debated, but oral history portrays a feudal society with one group, the Tutsis or cattle herders, occupying a superior status within the social and political structure, and the other group, the Hutus or peasant farmers, serving as the serfs or clients of a Tutsi chief. The hunter-gatherer Twa were potters and had various functions at the royal court – for example, as dancers and music makers.

The complex system known as *ubuhake* provided for protection by the superior partner in exchange for services from the inferior: *ubuhake* agreements were made either between two Tutsis, or between a Tutsi and a Hutu. While *ubuhake* was a voluntary and revocable private contract between two individuals, with subjects able to switch loyalty from one chief to another, a peasant could not easily survive without a patron. Cattle could be acquired through *ubuhake* as well as by purchase, fighting in a war, or marriage. A Hutu who acquired enough cattle could thus become a Tutsi and might take a Tutsi wife, while a Tutsi who lost his herds or otherwise fell on hard times might become a Hutu and marry accordingly. A patron had no authority over a client who had gained cattle, whether Hutu, Tutsi or Twa. Whereas Hutus and Tutsis could and did sometimes switch status, a Twa seldom became a Tutsi or Hutu. In the rare instances when this did occur, it would be because the king rewarded a Twa for some act of bravery by granting him the status of a Tutsi. He would then be given a Tutsi wife and a political post within the royal court. Meanwhile the three groups spoke the same language (Kinyarwanda, a language in the Bantu group), lived within the same culture and shared the same recent history.

Rwandan nobles were experts in cattle breeding and an entire category of poetry was devoted to the praises of famous cows. Cattle were bred for their beauty, rather than utility. Between AD1000 and 1450 herders in the Great Lakes region invented no fewer than 19 words for the colourful patterns of their animals' hides. As elsewhere in Africa, cattle were closely associated with wealth and status.

AD1000–1894 Whatever the exact timespan may have been, Rwanda (or the larger part of it) was ruled over by a sequence of Tutsi monarchs, each with his various political skirmishes, battles and conquests. Oral tradition shows us a colourful bunch of characters: for example, Ndahiro II Cyaamatare who catastrophically lost the royal drum; Mibambwe II who organised a system of milk distribution to the poor, ordering his chiefs to provide jugs of milk three times a day; and Yuhi III

Mazimpaka, the only king to compose poetry – and to go mad. From the 17th century onwards the rulers seem to have become more organised and ambitious, using their armies to subjugate fringe areas. The royal palace was by then at Nyanza – and can still be seen, carefully reconstructed, today.

The *Mwami* was an absolute monarch, deeply revered and seen to embody Rwanda physically. The hierarchy beneath him was complex and tight-knit, with different categories of chief in charge of different aspects of administration. His power covered most of Rwanda, although some Hutu enclaves in the north, northwest and southwest of the country clung to their independence until the 20th century. The country was divided into a pyramid of administrative areas: in ascending order of size, from base to apex, these were the immediate neighbourhood, the hill, the district and the province. (These are echoed in today's administrative pyramid of Commune, Sector, District and Province.) And through this intricate structure ran the practice and spirit of *ubuhake*, the master–client relationship in which an inferior receives help and protection in return for services and allegiance to a superior.

Beneath the *mwami*, power was exercised by various chiefs, each with specific responsibilities: *land chiefs* (responsible for land allocation, agriculture and agricultural taxation), *cattle chiefs* (stock-raising and associated taxes), *army chiefs* (security) and so on. While Hutus might take charge at neighbourhood level, most of the power at higher administrative levels was in the hands of Tutsis.

Since our only source of information about these early days is oral tradition, which by its nature favours the holders of power, we cannot be certain to what extent the power structure was accepted by those lower down the ladder, to what extent they resented it and to what extent they were exploited by it. But, whether harsh, benevolent or exploitative (or possibly all three), it survived, and is what the Europeans found when they entered this previously unknown country.

Rwanda had remained untouched by events unfolding elsewhere in Africa. Tucked away in the centre of the continent, the tiny kingdom was ignored by slave traders; consequently Rwanda is one of the few African countries that never sold its people, or its enemies, into slavery. There is no record of Arab traders or Asian merchants, numerous in other parts of East and Central Africa, having penetrated its borders, with the result that no written language was introduced and oral tradition remained the norm until the very end of the 19th century.

The Kingdom of Rwanda was isolationist and closed to foreigners (also to many Africans) until the 1890s. The famous American explorer, Henry Stanley, attempted to enter several times and did penetrate as far as Lake Ihema in 1874, but was then forced to retreat under arrow attack. Trade with neighbouring countries was extremely limited and Rwanda had no monetary system.

GERMAN EAST AFRICA Unlike most African states, Rwanda and Burundi were not given artificial borders by their colonisers – they had both been established kingdoms for many centuries. At the Berlin Conference of 1885, they – under the name of Ruanda-Urundi – were assigned to Germany as a part of German East Africa, although at that stage no European had officially set foot there. The first to do so formally was the German Count Gustav Adolf von Götzen on May 4 1894 (an Austrian, Oscar Baumann, had previously entered privately from Burundi in 1892 and spent several days in the south of the country). Von Götzen entered Rwanda by the Rusumo Falls in the southeast and crossed the country to reach the eastern shore of Lake Kivu. En route he stopped off at Nyanza where he met the *mwami*, King Rwabugiri – apparently causing consternation among the watching nobles when he, a mere mortal, shook the sovereign by the hand. They feared that such an affront might cause disaster for the kingdom. At this stage the *mwami* had no idea that his country had officially been under German control for the past nine years.

THE DISCOVERY OF THE MOUNTAIN GORILLA

The mountain gorilla was first discovered on 17 October 1902, on the ridges of the Virunga Mountains, by German explorer Captain Robert von Beringe, then aged 37. Captain von Beringe, together with a physician, Dr Engeland, Corporal Ehrhardt, 20 Askaris, a machine gun and necessary porters set off from Usumbura on August 19 1902 to visit the Sultan Msinga of Rwanda and then proceed north to reach a 'row of volcanoes'. The purpose of the trip was to visit the German outposts in what was then German East Africa in order to keep in touch with local chiefs and to confirm good relations, while strengthening the influence and power of the German Government in these regions. On arriving at the volcanoes, an attempt was made to climb Mount Sabinyo.

Captain von Beringe's report of the expedition (below) is adapted from *In the Heart of Africa* by Duke Adolphus Frederick of Mecklenburg (Cassell, 1910).

From October 16th to 18th, senior physician Dr. Engeland and I together with only a few Askaris and the absolutely necessary baggage attempted to climb the so far unknown Kirunga ya Sabyinyo which, according to my estimation, must have a height of 3,300 metres. At the end of the first day we camped on a plateau at a height of 2,500 metres; the natives climbed up to our campsite to generously supply us with food. We left our camp on October 17th taking with us a tent, eight loads of water, five Askaris and porters as necessary.

After four and a half hours of tracking we reached a height of 3,100 metres and tracked through bamboo forest; although using elephant trails for most of the way, we encountered much undergrowth which had to be cut before we could pass... After two hours we reached a stony area with vegetation consisting mainly of blackberry and blueberry bushes. Step by step we noticed the vegetation becoming poorer and poorer, the ascent became steeper and steeper, and climbing became more difficult – for the last one and a quarter hours we climbed only over rock. After covering the ground with moss we collected, we erected our tent on a ridge at a height of 3,100 metres. The ridge was extremely narrow so that the pegs of the tent had to be secured in the abyss. The Askaris and the porters found shelter in rock caverns, which provided protection against the biting cold wind.

From our campsite we were able to watch a herd of big, black monkeys which tried to climb the crest of the volcano. We succeeded in killing two of these animals, and with a rumbling noise of falling rocks they tumbled into a ravine, which had its opening in a north-easterly direction. After five hours of strenuous work we succeeded in retrieving one of these animals using a rope. It was a big, human-like male monkey of one and a half metres in height and a weight of more than 200 pounds. His chest had no hair, and his hands and feet were of enormous size. Unfortunately I was unable to determine its type; because of its size, it could not very well be a chimpanzee or a gorilla, and in any case the presence of gorillas had not been established in the area around the lakes.

On the journey back to Usumbura, the skin and one of the hands of the animal that von Beringe collected were taken by a hyena but the rest (including the skull) finally arrived safely at the Zoological Museum in Berlin. It was classified as a new form of gorilla and named Gorilla beringei in honour of the Captain. Later it was considered rather to be a subspecies and renamed Gorilla gorilla beringei.

Von Götzen subsequently became Governor of German East Africa, into which Ruanda-Urundi was formally absorbed in 1898; the same year that the mountain gorilla was first recorded by a European (see box above). At this time the kingdom was larger, stretching as far as Lake Edward in the north and beyond

Lake Kivu in the west; it was reduced to its present area at the Conference of Brussels in 1910.

The Germans were surprised to find that their new colony was a highly organised country, with tight, effective power structures and administrative divisions. They left these in place and ruled through them, believing that support for the traditional chiefs would render them and their henchmen loyal to Germany. Meanwhile various religious missions, Roman Catholic at first and then Protestant, began setting up bases in Ruanda-Urundi and establishing schools, farms and medical centres. In 1907 the colonisers opened a 'School for the Sons of Chiefs' in Nyanza, as well as providing military training.

Allowing for the blurring caused by intermarriage and the switching of status between Tutsi and Hutu, the power structures encountered by the colonisers were linked – and this proved to be a matter of great anthropological fascination – to three very visibly different groups of inhabitants: the tall, lanky Tutsi chiefs and nobles; the shorter, stockier Hutu farmers (who formed the majority); and the very much smaller Twa. The Duke of Mecklenburg, visiting the country in 1907, noted:

> The population is divided into three classes – the Watussi, the Wahutu, and a pygmy tribe, the Batwa, who dwell chiefly in the bamboo forests of Bugoie, the swamps of Lake Bolero, and on the island of Kwidschwi on Lake Kiwu.
>
> The Watussi are a tall, well-made people. Heights of 1.80, 2.00 and even 2.20 metres are of quite common occurrence, yet the perfect proportion of their bodies is in no wise detracted from… The primitive inhabitants are the Wahutu, an agricultural Bantu tribe, who look after the digging and tilling and agricultural economy of the country in general. They are a medium-sized type of people…
>
> Ruanda is certainly the most interesting country in the German East African Protectorate – in fact in all Central Africa – chiefly on account of its ethnographical and geographical position. Its interest is further increased by the fact that it is one of the last negro kingdoms governed autocratically by a sovereign sultan, for German supremacy is only recognised to a very limited extent. Added to this, it is a land flowing with milk and honey, where the breeding of cattle and bee-culture flourish, and the cultivated soil bears rich crops of fruit. A hilly country, thickly populated, full of beautiful scenery, and possessing a climate incomparably fresh and healthy; a land of great fertility, with watercourses which might be termed perennial streams; a land which offers the brightest of prospects to the white settler.

In 1911–12 the Germans joined with the Tutsi monarchy to subjugate some independent Hutu principalities in the north of the country which had not previously been dominated. Their inhabitants, who had always been proud of their independence, resisted vigorously, overrunning much of what are now Ruhengeri and Byumba provinces before they were defeated and brought under the *mwami*'s control. Their resentment and deep sense of grievance were to endure for the next half-century.

Germany had little time to make its mark in the colonies; in 1916 Belgium invaded Ruanda-Urundi and occupied the territories until the end of World War I; Belgium was subsequently officially entrusted with their administration under a League of Nations mandate in 1919, to be confirmed in 1923.

THE BELGIAN ERA In its adjoining colony of the Congo, Belgium had full control, but for Ruanda-Urundi it remained responsible first to the League of Nations and then (after 1945) to the United Nations Organisation. Annual reports had to be submitted and no important changes could be made without agreement from above. Despite these constraints, and despite the fact that Ruanda-Urundi had far less potential wealth than the Congo, Belgium took its charge seriously, and by the time of independence some 40 years later its material achievements (in terms of increased production; public services such as roads, schools and hospitals; and buildings and administrative infrastructures) were considerable. In terms of human beings it did far less well, as later events demonstrated.

Priorities Rwanda had always been subject to periodic famines, to such an extent that some were named and absorbed into history as milestones of time: such-and-such a child was born 'just after the Ruyaga famine' (1897), or a man died 'just before the Kimwaramwara famine' (1906). Most had climatic origins, but some which occurred around the time of the Belgian takeover (in 1916/17 and 1917/18) could also be blamed on World War I, as precious foodstuffs were shipped overseas to feed the troops. At the same time the new Belgian authorities commented that the local chiefs made little attempt to prevent the famines recurring, or to get emergency relief to the worst-hit areas. They therefore set about implementing a strict overall food strategy to make supplies less precarious.

The peasant farmers were first of all encouraged (by field workers) to maximise their production using traditional methods. They were then given help to improve their existing techniques, for example by using higher-yielding varieties of their normal crops. From 1924 the cultivation of food crops was made compulsory, including foreign species such as manioc and sweet potatoes. Next the distribution channels were upgraded, with a new road network and the development of markets and co-operatives. Storage facilities were set up; high-grade seed was distributed; the use of manure and fertiliser was promoted; the problem of erosion (caused by overuse of vulnerable land) was tackled; farmers were required to set aside a small emergency hoard of beans, peas or cereals each year; and various new types of stock breeding were initiated. Factories and processing plants were built. Finally, the farmers were encouraged to grow crops (especially coffee) for export, so that they could earn cash with which to buy extra food in times of hardship.

These measures – not easily implemented, because of the farmers' understandable initial resentment and resistance to change – proved more or less successful, helped by a regulated but controversial and sometimes harsh policy of forced labour (*uburetwa*). Famine did recur in 1942–44 and resulted in thousands of deaths, but this could be blamed partly on the appropriation of manpower and the lack of efficient machinery caused by World War II. By the time of independence, large areas of farmland had been better protected against erosion and per-hectare crop yields had risen substantially. The scale of the anti-erosion works was massive, and many remain in the terracing visible today. Horizontal ditches were dug on the hillsides, following the contours; directly below these, hedges were planted. Water running down the slope of the hillside was trapped by the ditch, and then seeped through it to irrigate the hedge on the lower side; while the roots of the hedge contributed by securing the soil and strengthening first the ditch and then the hillside.

The agricultural improvements, together with extensive physical provisions such as roads, schools, hospitals and all the associated construction work, were probably colonisation's most helpful input to Rwanda. Its contribution to the relationship between the country's long-term inhabitants was less positive.

Power structures Like the Germans before them, the Belgians decided to retain and use the existing power structures, but unlike their predecessors they then proceeded to undermine the authority of the *mwami* and his chiefs and to forbid some of their traditional practices, introducing their own Belgian experts and administrators at every level. This interference did not make for easy collaboration. In any case the *mwami* in power at the time of Belgian accession, Mwami Musinga, was hostile to colonisation and also resented the missionaries, since their innovations undermined the established order and worked against the subjugation of Hutus. In 1931 he was forced by the Belgians to abdicate in favour of his son, the more amenable and Westernised Mwami Mutara Rudahigwa. Until well into the 1950s, although the traditional structures keeping them in a subservient position were somewhat weakened, the Hutus still got a bad deal and remained 'second-class citizens' in almost all respects. So both Hutus and Tutsis – and indeed the minority Twas too, because they received virtually no recognition or privilege – reacted to colonisation with varying degrees of grievance.

Education The Germans had established a few government schools in Rwanda and the Belgians followed suit, but the main source of education was always the Church. In the 1930s, the Catholic Bishop Léon Classé, who had arrived in Rwanda almost 30 years earlier as a priest and worked his way up through the hierarchy, entered into an agreement with the Belgian administration by which the Catholic Church took over full responsibility for the educational system. He may not have been entirely without financial motive, since the government then subsidised the church to the tune of 47 francs per pupil and 600 francs per qualified teacher.

The Church broadened its curriculum to cover more secular subjects such as agronomy, medicine and administration; however, the main beneficiaries of the increased educational possibilities were still largely Tutsis, although Hutus were not entirely neglected and many attended primary school. Some did make good use of the limited educational openings available to them but could not easily progress beyond a certain level. Of those who trained in the Catholic seminaries (which they could enter more easily than secular educational institutions) some went on to become priests, while others switched back to secular careers. Less than one-fifth of the students attending the Groupe Scolaire in Butare from 1945 to 1957 – and emerging as agronomists, doctors, vets and administrators – were Hutus. The School for the Sons of Chiefs originally opened by the Germans in Nyanza had a minimum height requirement which effectively reserved it for Tutsis.

In 1955, there were some 2,400 schools of various types and levels (the majority were primary) in Rwanda, with around 215,000 pupils. Of the 5,500-odd teachers, over 5,000 were Rwandan.

Categorisation Size mattered. Like the Germans before them, the Belgians were intrigued by the sharply differing physical characteristics of their colony's inhabitants, and enthusiastically measured, recorded, compared and commented on the facial and bodily proportions of Rwanda's three indigenous groups. For the more timid of the Rwandans, this 'attack' with callipers, measuring tapes, scales and other paraphernalia proved a fearsome ordeal. So man dehumanises his brothers…

Most tellingly, in the early 1930s the Belgians embarked on a census to identify all indigenous inhabitants, on the basis of these physical characteristics, as either Hutu, Tutsi or Twa, and in 1935 issued them with identity cards on which these categories ('ethnic groups' or, in French, 'ethnies', although the accuracy of this term is debatable) were recorded. If, even after strenuous measuring, someone's ethnie was not immediately clear, having been blurred by intermarriage or a change of status, those who were reasonably wealthy and/or had more than ten cattle were generally recorded as Tutsis. Identity cards – and the habit of classification they engendered – were still in use at the time of the genocide in 1994, providing an extra pointer (if one were needed) as to who should or should not die.

In 1945 the United Nations Organisation was created, with its charter promising the colonised peoples of the world justice, protection and freedom. Formerly a League of Nations mandate, Ruanda-Urundi now became a UN Trust Territory and Belgium was responsible to the UN's trusteeship council, which was to preside over all colonies' transition to independence. In 1948 a UN mission visited Ruanda-Urundi, and its report was critical of the administration, particularly regarding the inferior status of the Hutus and Twa by comparison with the Tutsis. All too often, compulsory labour was harshly enforced, and the educational system remained heavily biased in favour of Tutsis, although many priests and missions were starting to veer more towards the Hutus.

At the same time, the observers were surprised by the completeness and intricacy of the social and political hierarchy which, if used properly, would offer a sound framework for democratic development. All the necessary command structures were in place, but badly oriented.

Subsequent visits gave rise to similarly critical reports. The Belgians introduced elections at local and administrative levels – which Tutsis won, except in the far north where resentment still smouldered after the 1912 defeat. Throughout Africa, colonies were becoming restless and the scent of independence was in the air, but in Ruanda-Urundi far too little preparation had yet been made, in terms both of political awareness and practical training. Nothing was ready.

THE RUN-UP TO INDEPENDENCE From about 1950, as the numbers of educated Hutus increased, the Hutu voice grew stronger. Hutu leaders such as Grégoire Kayibanda began to demand recognition for the majority. In 1954 the system of *ubuhake* was officially abolished, although in reality it lingered for a few more years. In 1957 the Superior Council of Rwanda (which had a huge Tutsi majority) called for independence preparations to be speeded up.

In 1956, Mwami Rudahigwa had called for total independence and an end to Belgian occupation. Just before another UN visit in 1957, a *Hutu Manifesto* drawn up by a group of Hutu intellectuals was presented to the Vice Governor General, Jean-Paul Harroy. It challenged the whole structure of Rwanda's administration, called for political power to be placed in the hands of the Hutu majority, pointed out injustices and inequalities, and proposed solutions. Little official action was taken.

The Catholic Church, now pro-Hutu, encouraged Grégoire Kayibanda and his associates to form political parties: APROSOMA (*Association pour la Promotion Sociale des Masses*) was openly sectarian, championing Hutu interests strongly, while RADER (*Rassemblement Démocratique Rwandais*) was more moderate. Whereas Tutsis, comfortably in a position of power, were calling for immediate independence without any changes to the system, Hutus wanted change first (to a more democratic system, recognising the fact that they were the majority) and *then* independence. For whatever reasons and after whatever deliberations, Belgium, having supported the powerful Tutsi minority throughout colonisation, now switched its allegience to the Hutu majority, ostensibly in the name of fairness and democracy.

The wind of independence was blowing strongly in colonial Africa. More political parties sprang up. UNAR (*Union Nationale Rwandaise*) was formed by the proponents of immediate independence under the Rwandan monarchy, while PARMEHUTU (*Parti du Mouvement de l'Emancipation Hutu*) was established under the guidance of the Catholic Church by those favouring delayed independence. MSM (*Mouvement Social Muhutu*) was created by Grégoire Kayibanda to support Hutu interests, while UNAR (*Union Nationale Rwandaise*) was a pro-monarchy and anti-Belgian party.

In July 1959 the Mwami Rudahigwa died in hospital, in circumstances that may or may not have been suspicious. Rumours of Belgian involvement were rife and tension grew. He was succeeded by one of his brothers. There were arrests and some sporadic small-scale violence – which erupted on a larger scale on 1 November, when a Hutu sub-chief belonging to the PARMEHUTU party was attacked and beaten in Gitarama by young members of UNAR. Within 24 hours, highly organised Hutu gangs were out on the streets of towns and villages throughout the country, burning, looting and killing. Then Tutsis began to retaliate. Within about a fortnight things were calm again – around 300 had died, and 1,231 (919 Tutsis and 312 Hutus) were arrested by the Belgian authorities. The country was placed under military rule headed by the Belgian Colonel Guy Logiest, who quickly began replacing Tutsi chiefs with Hutus. He was strongly pro-Hutu, claiming to be righting the injustices of colonisation, and played a virtually unconcealed part in anti-Tutsi attacks.

It is worth remembering that this was the first organised violence between the two groups, and it happened little more than 40 years ago. Those who speak of a long-drawn-out feud originating before colonisation are mistaken. But the revolution had begun, Tutsis started to flee the country in large numbers, and outbursts of violence continued.

The PARMEHUTU party won hastily manipulated elections in 1960. Belgium, the reins of power slipping rapidly from its grasp, organised a referendum on the monarchy under the auspices of the United Nations. In January 1961, Rwanda's elected local administrators were called to a public meeting in Gitarama, Grégoire Kayibanda's birthplace. They and a massed crowd of some 25,000 declared Rwanda a republic – and the United Nations had little option but to accept this ultimatum. However, the 1960 elections were not recognised by the UN so more were held in September 1961, under UN supervision. Again they were won by PARMEHUTU, with Grégoire Kayibanda at its head. Later that year, some 150 Tutsis were killed in the Butare area, 5,000 homes were burned and 22,000 people were displaced. In July 1962 Rwanda's independence was finally confirmed with Kayibanda as its new president, heading a republican government. The university town of Astrida, so named after Queen Astrid of Belgium, reverted to its local name Butare. Violence against Tutsis continued; by now about 135,000 had fled as refugees to neighbouring countries and the number was growing. Among those who left in 1960 was a three-year-old child named Paul Kagame, of whom much more was to be heard later.

It is true that Belgium emerged from the fiasco with little credit. But it is equally true that, even without colonisation, some kind of revolution would inevitably have occurred sooner or later, for the tightly stratified hierarchy of the 19th century could not have held firm indefinitely against the pressures, promises and potentials of the modern world.

The trend today in Rwanda is to hold the colonisers – through their behaviour during colonisation – responsible for the eventual genocide. Indeed, without colonisation the explosion might well, as a Rwandan friend said to me, 'have happened differently', and perhaps after something as inexplicable as a genocide there is a need to apportion blame as part of the recovery process. But to claim – as is also the trend today – that before the arrival of the Europeans all was peace and harmony may simply reflect the fact that oral tradition tends to favour those in power.

1962–1994 The situation became yet more tangled and yet more sensitive. Since this is a guidebook rather than a historical treatise, readers who want a fuller picture than is given below will find several good sources in *Appendix 3*, page 251.

John Reader's *Africa* (Penguin, 1998) is particularly recommended, as is Gérard Prunier's *The Rwanda Crisis – History of a Genocide* (Hurst, 1998). They (among others) have been used as sources in this chapter.

Once in power, the government sought to reinforce its supremacy. 'Quotas' were introduced, giving the Tutsis (who were a minority of about 9% of the population) a right to only 9% of school places, 9% of jobs in the workforce and so on. Small groups of Tutsi exiles in neighbouring countries made sporadic commando-style raids into Rwanda, leading to severe reprisals. In late 1963, up to 10,000 Tutsis were killed. The pattern of violence continued.

In 1964 the Fabian Society (London) published a report entitled *Massacre in Rwanda*, commenting on events since 1959. Also – chillingly, in view of what happened 30 years later – a report entitled *Attempted Genocide in Rwanda* appeared in the March 1964 issue of *The World Today* (vol 20, no 3).

In 1965 Kayibanda was re-elected president and Juvenal Habyarimana was appointed Minister of Defence. In 1969 Kayibanda was again re-elected and PARMEHUTU was renamed the MDR (*Mouvement Démocratique Républicain*). But Kayibanda's regime was becoming increasingly dictatorial and corrupt. The 'quotas' and other 'cleansing' measures began to be enforced so rigidly that even Hutus became uneasy. In 1973, ostensibly to quell violence following a purge of Tutsis from virtually all educational establishments, Major General Juvenal Habyarimana toppled Grégoire Kayibanda in a military coup.

In 1975, a single party, the MRND (*Mouvement Révolutionnaire et National pour le Développement*), was formed. For a while, there were signs of improvement, although this tends to be forgotten in the light of subsequent events. Despite initial optimism and a period of relative stability, however, the regime eventually proved little better than its predecessor. Some educational reforms were undertaken, with the object of 'Rwandanisation' – revaluing Kinyarwanda and Rwandan culture. Habyarimana was reconfirmed as president in 1978, 1983 and 1988 – unsurprisingly, since he was the only candidate. The Hutu–Tutsi conflict was to some extent replaced by conflict between Hutus from the south and those from the north (Habyarimana was a northerner, so was accused of favouring 'his own'). Meanwhile, in the international sphere, rising oil prices and falling commodity prices were bringing the country's economy close to collapse and, among all but the privileged elite, dissatisfaction grew.

In 1979 a group of Rwandan exiles in Uganda established the RRWF (Rwandan Refugee Welfare Foundation) which in 1980 became RANU (Rwandan Alliance for National Unity), whose name explains its aim. In 1981, in Uganda, one Yoweri Museveni, later to become Uganda's president, started a guerrilla war against the oppressive regime of Dr Milton Obote – among his men were two Rwandan refugees, Paul Kagame and Fred Rwigima. Obote was hostile to the Rwandan refugees in Uganda and political youth groups were encouraged to attack them and their property. As a result of such attacks in 1982–83, there was massive displacement of the refugees in southern Uganda and large numbers tried (or were forced) to return to Rwanda. The Rwandan government quickly closed its borders with Uganda and confined those who had already entered to a small and inhospitable area in the north, where many of the young and the old died of hunger and disease.

In 1986, in Uganda, Yoweri Museveni's National Resistance Army (which contained a number of Rwandan refugees) overthrew Obote, and Museveni assumed power. In 1987 RANU was renamed the RPF (Rwandan Patriotic Front), and was supported not only by exiled Tutsis but also by a few prominent Hutus opposed to Habyarimana's regime.

In 1987/8, a military coup in Burundi and consequent ethnic tensions caused a wave of Burundian refugees to flood into Rwanda. In 1989 the price of coffee,

Rwanda's main export, collapsed, causing severe economic problems. Censorship rules were flouted, new politically oriented publications emerged and reports of corruption and mismanagement appeared openly. In July 1990, under pressure from Western aid donors, Habyarimana conceded the principle of multi-party democracy and agreed to allow free debate on the country's future. In practice, little changed.

Then, on 1 October 1990, the RPF (led by Major General Fred Rwigyema), invaded the northeast of Rwanda from Uganda, with the stated objective of ending the political stalemate once and for all and restoring democracy. French, German and Zairean troops were called in to support the Rwandan national army and the incursion was soon suppressed; but the government now took the RPF threat seriously. Habyarimana enlarged the Rwandan army from around 5,000 in 1990 to about 24,000 in 1991 and 35,000 in 1993. Various overseas countries (France, South Africa, the US) provided arms. Additionally, the 1990 RPF invasion was followed by severe reprisals: thousands of Tutsi and southern Hutu were arrested and held in prison for some months. Several were tried and sentenced to death but the sentences were not carried out, although, as one of those arrested later wrote, 'many died of the hunger and the beatings'. Sporadic unrest continued throughout the country.

Political solutions were sought, both nationally and internationally, with several Western countries now involved. In November 1990 Habyarimana agreed to the introduction of multi-partyism and the abolition of 'ethnic' identity cards, but nothing was implemented. The Rwandan army began to train and arm civilian militias known as *interahamwe* ('those who stand together'). It was later estimated that up to 2,000 Rwandans (Tutsis or anti-government Hutus) were killed by their government between October 1990 and December 1992.

The RPF – now led by Major Paul Kagame, since the charismatic Rwigema had died in the October 1990 invasion – continued its guerrilla raids, striking at targets countrywide. By the end of 1992 it had expanded to a force of almost 12,000 and was growing rapidly. Its stated aim was always to bring democracy to Rwanda rather than to claim supremacy. Meanwhile, French troops were supporting the government forces. In the face of increasing violence, international pressure was applied more strongly and the Arusha Agreement (so named because it was drawn up in Arusha, Tanzania) committed Habyarimana to a number of reforms, including the establishment of the rule of law, political power-sharing, the repatriation and resettlement of refugees, and the integration of the armed forces to include the RPF. A 70-member Transitional National Assembly was to be established. The Agreement was signed in August 1993 and should have been implemented within 37 days, overseen by a United Nations force. But the process, unpalatable to both Tutsi and Hutu hardliners, stalled. Hostilities deepened. Radio stations poured forth inflammatory propaganda. Rwanda's *Radio-Télévision Libre des Mille Collines*, in particular, insistently and viciously identified Tutsis as 'the enemy', in dehumanising and vilifying terms. Scattered outbursts of violence rumbled on.

On 21 October, the Hutu president of neighbouring Burundi, Melchior Ndadaye, elected only a few months previously, was killed in a military coup, fuelling ethnic tensions in Rwanda. The UN began sending UNAMIR (UN Assistance Mission for Rwanda) forces to the country. Politics were deadlocked. A sense of impending danger grew and, by March 1994, vulnerable (or well-informed) citizens were starting to evacuate their families from Kigali.

On 6 April 1994, a plane carrying Rwanda's President Habyarimana and Burundi's new President Cyprien Ntaryamira was shot down by rocket fire near Kigali airport. Both men died. The source of the attack has never been confirmed. Within hours, the killing began.

THE GENOCIDE It had been well planned, over a long period. Roadblocks were quickly erected and the army and *interahamwe* went into action, on a rampage of death, torture, looting and destruction. Tutsis and moderate Hutus were targeted. Weapons of every sort were used, from slick, military arms to rustic machetes. Orders were passed briskly downward from *préfecture* to *commune* to *secteur* to *cellule* – and the gist of every order was: 'These are the enemy. Kill.'

A painfully detailed account, which includes many eyewitness testimonies and brings home the full horror of the slaughter, is given in the 1,200 pages of *Rwanda – Death, Despair and Defiance* (African Rights, London, 1995). In *A People Betrayed*, L R Melvern analyses the political and international background (Zed Books, London & New York, 2000), as does Gérard Prunier in *The Rwanda Crisis* (see *Appendix 3*). A condensed overview of events is given below.

In three months, up to a million people were killed, violently and cruelly. Barely a family was untouched. The international media suddenly found Rwanda newsworthy. Chilling images filled our TV screens and the scale of the massacre was too great for many of us to grasp. Amid the immensity came tiny tales of heroism: villagers who flatly disobeyed the order to kill; Hutus who hid their Tutsi neighbours, at great (often fatal) risk to their own lives, or who, while feigning to round them up for the killers, furtively led some to safety. But these glimpses of humanity were engulfed and lost in the great, surging tide of slaughter that spread across the country.

On 8 April, just two days after the plane crash, the Rwandan Patriotic Front (RPF) launched a major offensive to end the genocide. As they advanced, they rescued and liberated Tutsis still hiding in terror from the killers. Meanwhile, however, a new Hutu government, based on the MRND and supporting parties, was formed in Kigali and later shifted to Gitarama.

The United Nations' UNAMIR force was around 2,500 strong at the time. They watched helplessly, technically unable to intervene as this would breach their 'monitoring' mandate. After the murder of ten Belgian soldiers the force was cut to 250. On 30 April the UN Security Council spent eight hours discussing the Rwandan crisis – without ever using the word 'genocide'. Had this term been used, they would have been legally obliged to 'prevent and punish' the perpetrators. Meanwhile tens of thousands of refugees were fleeing the country. In May the UN agreed to send 6,800 troops and police to Rwanda to defend civilians, but implementation was delayed by arguments over who would cover costs and provide equipment. The RPF army had taken control of Kigali airport and Kanombe barracks and was gaining ground elsewhere. In June, France announced that it would deploy 2,500 peacekeeping troops to Rwanda (*Opération Turquoise*) until the UN force arrived. These created a controversial 'safe zone' in the southwest.

On 4 July the RPF captured Kigali and set up an interim government. The remnants of the Hutu government fled to Zaire, followed by a further tide of refugees. The RPF continued its advance westward and northward. Many thousands of refugees streamed into the French 'safe zone' and still more headed towards Zaire, cramming into makeshift camps on the inhospitable terrain around Goma. The humanitarian crisis was acute, later to be exacerbated by disease and a cholera outbreak which claimed tens of thousands of lives.

On 18 July 1994, the RPF announced that the war had been won, declared a ceasefire, established a broad-based Government of National Unity and named Pasteur Bizimungu as president. Faustin Twagiramungu was appointed prime minister. The following day, the new president and prime minister were sworn in, and RPF commander Major General Paul Kagame was appointed defence minister and vice president. By the end of July, the UN Security Council had reached a final agreement about sending an international force to Rwanda. By the end of August

AFTER THE GENOCIDE...

A report produced in July 2000 by the Statistics Department of Rwanda's Ministry of Finance and Economic Planning concludes that the horrors of the 1994 genocide have left large segments of the population with severe mental health problems that cannot in fact be expressed in statistics. Many people have lost family members, and/or have witnessed, experienced (or participated in) massacres or rapes. A National Trauma Survey by UNICEF in 1995, quoted in the same report, estimated the percentages of children affected by the genocide as follows:

- 99.9% witnessed violence
- 79.6% experienced death in the family
- 69.5% witnessed someone being killed or injured
- 61.5% were threatened with death
- 90.6% believed they would die
- 57.7% witnessed killings or injuries with machete
- 31.4% witnessed rape or sexual assault
- 87.5% saw dead bodies or parts of bodies

Does it make you look at the streetkids in Kigali and Huye a little differently?

Opération Turquoise was terminated and UN forces had replaced the French. Internationally, it had now been accepted that a 'genocide' had indeed taken place – and it was over. At sites of some of the worst massacres, memorials now commemorate the dead and remind the world that such an atrocity must never, never be allowed to occur again.

THE AFTERMATH The 70-member Transitional National Assembly provided for in the Arusha Agreement of 1993 finally became operational in December 1994. In November 1994, the UN Security Commission set up the International Criminal Tribunal for Rwanda (ICTR), whose brief is to prosecute those who were guilty, between 1 January and 31 December 1994, of genocide and other violations of international humanitarian law; by the end of 1996 suspects were being brought to trial.

Sporadic bursts of violence were to continue for a further three years or so, with killings on both sides, as tensions in and around refugee settlements persisted and hardline Hutus who had fled across the border mounted guerrilla raids. But the RPF army and the new government remained in control. UN forces left the country in March 1996. Refugees returned home, in massive numbers. Problems of insecurity posed by former Rwanda government forces and *interahamwe* troops caused Rwanda to become militarily involved with the Democratic Republic of the Congo (DRC).

In 1999, local elections were held at sector and cellule level, and the Lusaka Agreement, to end the war in the DRC, was signed.

In March 2000, President Pasteur Bizimungu resigned and in April Major General Paul Kagame was sworn in as the fifth president of Rwanda, exactly four decades after his flight as a three-year-old refugee.

In July 2000, the Organisation of African Unity (OAU) recommended that the international community should make payments to the government and people of Rwanda in reparation for the genocide. Later the same year, the Rwandan government launched a census to determine the true and total number of genocide victims – irrespective of whether they were Hutus, Tutsis, Twa or foreigners.

In June 2002, with some 115,000 genocide suspects still in gaol after eight years

GACACA

The traditional system of 'Gacaca' courts was revived in Rwanda in order to clear the prisons of the throng of genocide suspects who had been held captive (awaiting trial) for up to eight years. It was estimated that the regular justice system, lacking adequate facilities and qualified personnel, could take almost 100 years to clear the backlog – clearly impossible – whereas Gacaca offers the hope of a solution within five years or so. Around 250,000 local judges, men and women, were elected by and within their local communities in 2001 and in 2002 received brief training in such subjects as law, conflict resolution and judicial ethics. They receive no salaries but are entitled to free schooling and medical fees for their families. Throughout Rwanda up to 11,000 Gacaca courts have been set up (with a panel of 19 judges per court, and requiring the presence of at least 15 judges and 100 witnesses to be valid) in different administrative areas.

First, the courts identify victims of the genocide. Next, suspects are identified and categorised, according to the extent of their crime. They attend courts in their home areas, where local witnesses speak for or against them. Suspects who confess fully and plead guilty can expect lighter sentences, as can those who agree to community service in atonement for their crimes. The courts are authorised to try, and then to sentence, anyone suspected of carrying out (or being an accomplice to) killing, serious assault or property crimes during the genocide. The more serious 'Category 1' suspects, those who allegedly organised, instigated, led or played a particularly zealous part in the violence, continue to be tried and sentenced in the formal judicial system. Gacaca courts cannot impose the death penalty, nor can they try army personnel.

For the witnesses, confronting the *génocidaires* and re-living the events of 1994 can be both traumatic and cathartic. No-one claims that the Gacaca courts are a perfect solution, just that they are the best solution under the circumstances – and at least they offer a very visible form of justice in which the villagers have a voice. Observers monitor their progress and so far they seem to be mostly uncorrupt, although there have been several instances of witness intimidation. Once again, as they have done in so many ways since the genocide, Rwandans are playing a very personal role in solving their country's problems.

and the country's regular courts unable to clear the backlog, the *Gacaca* Judicial System was launched. *Gacaca* (pronounced Ga-cha-cha, with a hard g) means 'grass', and is based on the traditional form of Rwandan justice where villagers used to gather together on a patch of grass to resolve conflicts between families, with heads of household acting as judges. See box above.

In the first half of 2003, around 30,000 genocide suspects were released from prison and, after a spell of 're-education', returned to their villages, in an amnesty aimed at those who were aged 14–18 at the time of the genocide, the old and sick, those accused of lesser crimes and those who had already been in gaol for longer than the sentence they would have received. Further releases over the past three years have returned tens of thousands more prisoners to their home villages. In solving one problem (prison overcrowding) it risks creating another, as survivors – many of them still suffering either physically or mentally – find themselves once again living close to the alleged *génocidaires*, and it's a tribute to the extraordinary strength, courage and forbearance of Rwanda's village communities that the situation has so far proved manageable.

In June 2003, Rwanda's new Constitution was signed, marking the end of the transition period that followed the genocide and replacing various documents referred to as the Fundamental Law. The presidential elections held – entirely peacefully – in August 2003 saw Paul Kagame returned as president for a term of seven years, with 3,544,777 votes or 95.05% of the total. Parliamentary elections followed in September 2003 in which women took 48.8% of the seats, making Rwanda the country with the highest number of women in its parliament. (Previously Sweden led with 45.3%, followed by Denmark with 38% and Finland with 37.5%. Britain has only 17.9% and the US House of Representatives a mere 14.3%.)

Rwanda has qualified for debt relief under the Highly Indebted Poor Countries Initiative and had economic reform and development programmes supported by the IMF and the World Bank. Huge amounts of foreign aid have been provided – and the fact that these grants have been ongoing since the genocide demonstrates international satisfaction about how the money is used. Donors renew their contracts. As an example, in September 2003 US$30 million was granted by the World Bank for the HIV/AIDS programme; US$19.9 million by the EU Mission in Rwanda for the repair and rehabilitation of roads; and US$29.9 million by the African Development Bank for the improved supply of water and energy to Kigali, the management of natural resources and, again, HIV/AIDS. The UK's total 2005–06 budget for Rwanda is £47 million. Meanwhile, Rwanda's economy keeps growing, and more children are attending school that at any other time in the country's history.

Rwanda's international links are strengthening. In June 2005, Rwanda's President Paul Kagame took over from Ugandan President Yoweri Museveni as chairman of COMESA (Common Market for Eastern and Southern Africa) and in 2006 his tenure was extended. In July 2005, Rwanda's then finance minister, Dr Donald Kaberuka, was elected president of the African Development Bank group; and in September 2005 Rwanda's ambassador in Switzerland, Valentine Sendanyoye-Rugwabiza, was appointed one of four deputy directors-general of the World Trade Organization – the first woman to hold such a high position.

RWANDA'S NATIONAL SYMBOLS

Rwanda's new flag, coat of arms and national anthem were launched on 31 December 2001, to replace the old ones designed in 1962, at a time when Rwanda was shaken by ethnic violence, human-rights violations and bad governance.

The old flag contained red, symbolising the blood shed for independence, but in today's peaceful Rwanda this is seen as inappropriate. The new flag is blue, yellow and green: blue to signify peace and tranquillity; yellow to signify wealth as the country strives for economic growth; green to symbolise agriculture, productivity and prosperity. There is a sun in the top right-hand corner, against a blue background, representing new hope for the country and its people. The flag was designed by Alphonse Kirimobenecyo, a Rwandan artist and engineer.

The coat of arms consists of a green ring with a knot tied at the upper end, representing industrial development through hard work. Inscriptions read Republika Y'U Rwanda and the national motto Ubumwe, Umurimo, Gukunda Igihugu (Unity, Work, Patriotism). Other features are the sun, sorghum and coffee, a basket, a cog wheel – and two shields, representing defence of national sovereignty and integrity and justice.

The national anthem, Rwanda Nziza, has four verses and highlights heroism, the Rwandan culture and the people's patriotism. The words are by Faustin Murigo of Karubanda prison in South Province. The music is by Captain Jean-Bosco Hashkaimana of the army brass band.

Currently a contingent from the Rwandan army is part of the peace-keeping force in Sudan's troubled Darfur region.

Finally, January 2006 saw the federal map of the country redrawn to merge the 12 former provinces, whose boundaries reflected ethnic distinctions and whose names still held strong associations with the genocide, into five larger and more neutrally named provinces (North, South, East, West and Kigali). In connection with this change, the town of Ruhengeri (access town for the Volcanoes National Park and the mountain gorillas) has been renamed Musanze and Butare (location of the National Museum) has been renamed Huye.

Of course tensions still exist; of course the government has its critics; of course poverty persists; of course there are complaints of 'discrimination'; and of course many Rwandans – particularly in rural areas – still struggle in conditions that are far from ideal. Human rights organisations point to some abuses. The budget is seriously overstretched, the neediest still do not always benefit enough from the reforms, and there's too wide a gap between the 'haves' and the 'have nots'.

But, this is Africa! Considering the size and resources of Rwanda, considering what happened there in 1994 and considering the inherent problems faced by almost all countries in sub-Saharan Africa, even without the aftermath of a genocide, the achievements of the past 12 years have been amazing, and based on a huge amount of energy, courage, goodwill and sheer hard work. Progress has been dramatic and durable. Rwanda today is a vibrant and forward-looking country, well able to cope with the demands and technologies of the 21st century.

It deserves respect.

24

2

People and Culture

PEOPLE

Rwanda today probably contains inhabitants raised in a greater number of countries than most other African nations, as long-term exiles returned after the genocide from Uganda, Kenya, Tanzania, Burundi, Europe, the USA and more. But of course Rwanda is their origin and their home.

Following the disruptive ethnic clashes of the post-colonial years, which culminated in the 1994 genocide, the currently accepted line is to stress Rwandan unity: the fact that before the arrival of the colonisers Rwandans were living together on the same hills, speaking the same language and practising the same culture.

In fact, matters may not be quite so clear-cut and the insistence on 'same-ness' should not be carried to the extent of concealing historical individuality. But there's no doubt that the people of Rwanda in general are committed to overcoming any awkward or damaging differences. There's a story, well known now, about a group of schoolgirls who, during the genocide, were told by the killers to divide up into Hutus and Tutsis (with the implication that the Hutus would be spared). The girls refused, saying that they were all Rwandans. So all of them died. In a different context, a genocide survivor wrote: 'Before the genocide, Hutu and Tutsis lived together. I remember we used to play with Hutu children and share everything. There were even intermarriages. The only time when we felt discriminated against was when a place at school, or a job, was given to a Hutu, even if there was a Tutsi more qualified for it. But this was no reason for hatred between the two groups.'

Of course individual attitudes may vary around the country and from person to person. However, the energetic – and courageous – efforts at reconciliation and peaceful coexistence are visible nationwide, extending from government level down to small rural groups and individuals.

RELIGION

The Christian religions are a powerful force in Rwanda today, as witnessed by the great number of active churches throughout the country. Roman Catholicism leads the field with 65% adherence, followed by 9% for Protestantism. Pope John Paul II visited Rwanda in 1990. Some evangelical sects are now gaining ground. There is a small (1%) Muslim population, leaving a 25% following for minority and traditional beliefs, some of which may have absorbed traces of Christianity.

TRADITIONAL RELIGION AND BELIEFS Rwandans traditionally believe in a supreme being called Imana. While Imana's actions influence the whole world, Rwanda is his home where he comes to spend the night. Individuals hold informal ceremonies imploring Imana's blessing. There is a tradition that, before retiring, a woman may leave a pitcher of water for Imana in the hope he will make her fertile.

Since words can have a magical impact, the name of Imana is often used when naming children, also in words of comfort, warnings against complacency, blessings, salutations, and during rites associated with marriage and death. Oaths take the form of 'May Imana give me a stroke', or 'May I be killed by Imana'. In instances when a long-desired child is born, people say to the new mother, 'Imana has removed your shame.' Tales of Imana granting magical gifts to humans, who then lose these gifts through greed and disloyalty, are common.

There is a special creative act of Imana at the beginning of each person's life. Impregnation in itself would not be sufficient to produce a new human being. This is why the young wife, at evening, leaves a few drops of water in a jar. Imana, as a potter, needs some water to shape the clay into a child in her womb. Then after birth, Imana decides what life is to be for that individual: happy or unhappy. If, later on, a man is miserable, poverty-stricken or in bad health, it is said that he was created by Ruremakwaci, a name given to Imana when he does not create very successfully, when 'he is tired', or, for some inscrutable reason, decides that a certain destiny will be unhappy.

Rwandans traditionally believe that a life force exists in all men and animals. In animals this invisible soul disappears when the creature dies, but in humans it is transformed into *bazimu*, spirits of the dead who live in Ikuzimu, the underworld or the world below the soil. While the deceased kings of Rwanda constitute a kind of governing body in the underworld, there are no social distinctions. Life is neither pleasant nor unhappy. The *bazimu* continue the individuality of living persons and have the same names. Though non-material, they are localised by their activity. They do not drink, eat, or mate but their existence in other respects is similar to that in the world of the living. *Bazimu* return to the world, often to places where they used to live. Some may stay permanently in the hut where their descendants live or in the small huts made for them in the enclosure around the dwelling. *Bazimu* are generally bad. They bring misfortune, sickness, crop failure and cattle epidemics because they envy the living the cherished things they had to leave behind. Their power, actuated by the male spirits, or grandfathers, extends only over their own clan. The living members of a family must consult a diviner to discover the reason for the ancestor's anger. Respect to *bazimu* is shown principally by joining a secret cult group.

The cult of Ryangombe Ryangombe is said to be the chief of the *imandwa*, Rwandans who are initiated into the cult of Ryangombe. According to Rwandan legend, Ryangombe was a great warrior who was accidentally killed by a buffalo during a hunting party. In order not to leave Ryangombe, his friends threw themselves on the bull's horns. Imana gave Ryangombe and his followers a special place, the Karisimbi volcano in the Virunga volcano chain, where they have a notably more agreeable afterlife than the other bazimu. The cult of Ryangombe became an important force of social cohesion, with Tutsi, Hutu and Twa being initiated into the cult. Ryangombe has said himself that he should be called upon by everybody. He is propitiated by the babandwa, a politico-religious fraternity, who perform rituals, chants and dances in his honour. They are not a permanent group and meet only once a year during July, at which time initiation takes place. During their festival the members of the fraternity paint themselves and decorate the spirit huts. A member of the group appears as the personification of the spirit of Ryangombe, carrying his sacred spear. After a ritual is performed, all members purify themselves at the stream. While the cult of Ryangombe is not common today, Rwandans can recall when their grandfathers or fathers participated in the Ryangombe festival and a popular Rwandan song recounts Ryangombe's exploits as a warrior and lover. Also see box on page 195.

More children are attending school in Rwanda today than at any time in the country's history. The education at state schools is free, but pupils from poorer families still find it hard to cover the additional costs of equipment, uniform etc; a number of NGOs and local charities are currently targeting this problem. Many private schools – primary and secondary, some of them church-run – also function throughout the country, but here fees must generally be paid. English and French are included in both the primary and the secondary curriculum, so that children should leave school with at least a working knowledge of the two languages. There are also English-medium and French-medium schools.

A noticeable change over the past few years is that far more girls are now attending primary school and continuing to secondary education (see below). The Rwanda chapter of the Forum for African Women Educationalists (www.fawerwa.org.rw) strongly supports this trend and runs its own girls' school with 800 pupils as well as working with schools throughout the country.

The death of so many professionals during the genocide left the country with a severe shortage of qualified teachers. Organisations such as VSO (Voluntary Service Overseas, *www.vso.org.uk*) helped to fill the gap and gradually the position is improving.

Further education is also well catered for. Apart from the long-established National University in Huye (formerly Butare), the Kigali Institute of Science and Technology (KIST, the Kigali Free University (Université Libre) and the Kigali Institute of Education, there are colleges and training schools throughout the country, several of which have opened or re-opened since the genocide. In some cases distance learning via the internet is possible, enabling students to study in their spare time while holding down a job and just to attend the institute in order to sit exams.

THE LIFE OF A STUDENT AT KIST *Akili Fidèle, October 2004*

KIST (the Kigali Institute of Science and Technology, www.kist.ac.rw) is a governmental body that was set up in 1997, three years after the 1994 genocide, in response to the serious lack of educational establishments at that time: the National University of Rwanda was then the only state body in either the capital or the country as a whole.

The institute offers both full-time and part-time courses. Grant-aided students study from 08.00 to 17.00; those without grants from 17.30 to 20.30. The official language of instruction is English. Previously French was Rwanda's main European language, because of the country's history as a Belgian (thus francophone) Trust Territory. However, in 2002, as a result of Rwanda's growing tendency to set up links with the anglophone countries of East Africa, KIST replaced the French language with English and the old French system of teaching with the English system. Any non-Rwandan lecturers come mostly from anglophone countries such as India, the USA, Uganda, Tanzania, Britain, Kenya etc. English-language classes are available for students who are stronger in French.

As a part-time student, I set off for KIST at 17.00 and arrive there at 17.20, so I've got ten minutes to settle down and get my breath back before the first lesson starts. The lecturer arrives at 17.30 and begins to teach; the students follow his words attentively. At the end of the session the students ask questions, and this develops into an exchange of ideas, so that when they finally leave the lecture room their heads are still buzzing with thoughts.

The lecturers are approachable and understanding. If a student has a problem in any course, he or she can easily discuss it with the lecturer, who will find time to sort out and explain the difficulty outside teaching hours.

Every two weeks, tests are set to check how well the students have assimilated their subject. After three or four months, examinations are held, and preparation for these starts from the very beginning of term. The timetable for the semester – giving the dates of the exams – is displayed on the notice board, as a warning to students to take their work seriously and be ready for them.

Two weeks after the exams, the results are announced. Students who have failed must re-sit the exam. A student who fails again at this second attempt is expelled, no matter how good his/her conduct may have been otherwise, so this is a strong incentive to study hard.

KIST's most important facility for its students is the library, open Monday to Friday from 08.00 to 20.00 and Saturday 08.00 to 13.00. It contains the books necessary for all the courses, and is available to every student who has a 'library card'. It's on the second floor of KIST 2 building, in an airy and comfortable room where one can read and study peacefully. Students have access to a wide range of books, and during the examination period many choose to do their reading in the library.

There is also a cinema, which provides entertainment for students outside teaching hours or at weekends.

The institute's canteen is open to everyone; grant-aided students get their meals free, while others must pay.

Finally, many sporting activities are organised, for example football, basketball and tennis – these help with the physical growth of young students, the strengthening of their muscles and the avoidance of certain illnesses. Thus KIST caters for the body as well as for the mind.

WOMEN'S ACCESS TO EDUCATION *Marie Chantal Uwimana*

After the genocide, with up to a million of its people slaughtered, the political, social and economic structures of Rwanda were at rock bottom. To rehabilitate, reintegrate and reconcile the country was a colossal task for the Government of National Unity. In every sector, they were starting from scratch. Among the priorities, education initially took second place to the more urgent needs of food, clothing and health.

Historically, education – and particularly that of girls – had not been greatly developed in Rwanda before and even after independence. Missionaries did build schools, but they were mainly for the children of chiefs and those in power. The intake of girls was very low.

Before 1994, the low enrolment rate for girls at primary school (and the still lower rate at secondary school and college) was explained by the ignorance of the parents (a belief that girls should not study scientific subjects), by custom (that after primary school girls should stay in the family and work at home or on the land) and by enforced early marriage.

After 1994, their parents now dead, many of these girls had also become single 'parents', head of their household and caring for their younger siblings. Recognising the problem, the government began setting in place mechanisms to support Rwandan women, and particularly to motivate girls to go to school. The statistics began to change rapidly, and by 2003 the number of girls at primary school equalled that of boys. At secondary school, however, girls continued to be oriented towards the more 'feminine' subjects and the drop-out rate for girls was 10.8% versus 9.5% for boys.

Although primary schooling had theoretically been compulsory, the fees were beyond the reach of some parents. Under the new constitution, state primary schools are now free and thus available to all – as long as the law is enforced that defines 'free education' as 'students receiving without payment education provided by the teacher together with learning aids and basic textbooks needed by both the teacher and the students'.

Problems remain, and steps still needing to be taken include:

- Possible sanctions against parents who fail to send their children to school
- Elimination of discriminatory practices against schoolgirls who fall pregnant
- Non-discriminatory guidance for career selection
- Improved access for girls to non-traditional education subjects
- Provision of literacy programmes and literacy trainers
- Grants and scholarships awarded with no bias towards gender
- Information and training in sexually transmissible diseases and HIV/AIDS
- Social integration measures for disadvantaged girls/women

Then, little by little, Rwanda's women can play their full part in rebuilding and running their country.

CULTURE

THE ARTS

Literature A written language was not introduced until the Europeans arrived in Rwanda at the end of the 19th century, so there is no great tradition of written literature. However, there is a wealth of oral literature in the form of myths, folk stories, legends, poetry and proverbs. These have passed on not only stories but also moral values and historical traditions from generation to generation. Before (and to some extent after) the arrival of the Europeans, the Mwami's court was a centre for training young nobles in various art forms, particularly the composition and performance of songs and poems dedicated to valour in warfare and the magnificence of their cattle.

The historian Alexis Kagame wrote extensively about oral poetry and recorded many poems in both Kinyarwanda and French. A display in the National Museum of Rwanda in Huye (see pages 132–3) gives an idea of the intricacy of some poetic structures.

Music Music is of great importance to all Rwandans, with variations of style and subject among the three groups. Traditionally, Tutsi songs praised excellence and valour; Hutu songs were lighter, sometimes humorous and linked to social occasions; Twa songs related more directly to aspects of their original occupation, hunting. During the time of the monarchy, the court was dominated musically by the royal drummers, and drumming is still of great artistic importance.

A full drum ensemble typically consists of either seven or nine drums. The smallest of these, sometimes called the soprano, which is often (but not invariably) played by the director of the orchestra, sets the rhythm for each tune and is backed up by some or all of the following drums: a tenor, a harmonist alto, two baritones, two bass and two double bass. The other widely used musical instrument is the *lulunga*, an eight-stringed instrument somewhat resembling a harp. It is most often played solo, perhaps as the background to singing or dancing, but may also be used to provide a melodic interlude and/or as a counterpoint to drums.

Dance Dance is as instinctive as music in Rwanda and its roots stretch back through the centuries. As with music, there are variations of style and subject among the three groups. Best known today are the **Intore dancers**, based in Nyanza and Huye (Butare), who perform both nationally and internationally. At the time of the monarchy and for centuries before the arrival of the Europeans, the Intore dancers at the royal court were selected young men who had received a

Elaine Gardner

> Sheer delight – and what is particularly appreciable, the authenticity... and to discover a whole aspect of Rwandan culture that I didn't know existed!

So commented a recent visitor at a display of traditional dance organised at a Twa pottery in Kigali – Batwa are, both currently and historically, Rwanda's favourite exponents of this particularly distinctive and highly reputed dance. In olden times, they were dancers and potters at the Royal court.

The Batwa (or Twa) are a pygmy people, comprising Rwanda's third 'ethnic' group – today numbering around 22–25,000. That they are indigenous Rwandans is surprisingly little known; even the recent film *A Hundred Days* mentioned only two groups as making up Rwanda's cultural diversity.

They lived originally as hunter-gatherers in the high mountain forests around Central Africa's Great Lakes. As the forests were felled and national parks established, the Batwa evolved another lifestyle, as potters, using the clay found in the marshes that lie between Rwanda's many hills. They left the forests with virtually no material possessions – and they process the clay with none. They use their feet to trample it into malleability and then their hands to shape cooking pots, stoves, decorative vases, traditional lamps, candle-holders and charming little replicas of local animals, from cattle to gorillas. The pots are fired without kilns, largely in a hollow in the ground, by burning grasses and natural debris, and sealed with earth.

Because of their pygmy origins the Batwa have suffered extreme prejudice over the years; they are socially and economically marginalised and extremely poor. Only 28% of Batwa children attend primary school (and far fewer start secondary school) compared with 88% in the population as a whole. Only 1.6% Batwa have enough land to feed their families. Most survive by begging, working on the land of others in return for food, or carrying loads. An estimated 30% of the Batwa population, as against 14% of the population overall, was lost during the 1994 genocide. So, income-generating schemes are vital – which is where the pottery and dance come into their own.

The UK-based charity, Forest Peoples' Project (*1c Fosseway Centre, Stratford Road, Moreton-in-Marsh, GL56 9NQ, UK;* ✆ *01608 652893;* e *info@fppwrm.gn.apc.org; www.forestpeoples.org*), works in Rwanda in partnership with CAURWA (*Communauté des Autochtones Rwandais* or Community of Indigenous Peoples in Rwanda), which FPP has supported since 1995. In December 2001, the UK Community Fund awarded FPP a three-year grant to start a Pottery Commercialisation Project with the Batwa potters. You can see some of the results if you visit 'Dancing Pots' in Kigali. Directions are on page 107. Items on sale in the pottery-workshop include many traditional designs plus a new range of mugs, bowls, vases and pen pots, as well as terrace stoves for chilly Rwandan evenings; and this is where you can arrange to attend performances of the lively and inventive Twa dances.

privileged education and choreographic training in order to entertain their masters and to perform at special functions. The name *intore* means 'best', signifying that only the best of them were chosen for this honour.

Traditionally their performances consisted mainly of warlike dances, such as the *ikuma* (lance), *umeheto* (bow) and *ingabo* (shield), in which they carried authentic weapons. In the 20th century dummy weapons were substituted, the dances were given more peaceful names and rhythm and movement (rather than warfare) became their main feature. The Intore dancers were divided into two groups. The first group, the *indashyikirwa* or 'unsurpassables', were all Tutsi. The second, the *ishyaka* or 'those who challenge by effort', were Twa led by a Tutsi. A description nearly three-quarters of a century old leads us through a performance:

In the opening movement, the group of Twa advances with measured step. The musicians also are Twa. The dancers form a square or line up in double file. They perform the opening sequence and then a dance representing 'safety'. Next they stand at ease, chanting the exploits of real or imaginary Rwandan heroes. Then come movements representing 'tattooing', 'stability', 'the incomparable' and 'the most difficult case'. At this point the Tutsi dancers leap into the arena, armed, to mingle with the Twa and demonstrate that they deserve the name of 'unsurpassables'. The names of some of their dances translate into English as 'that which puts an end to all discussion', 'the crested crane', 'the exit dance' and 'thanks'.

SOLAR OVENS IN RWANDA

Katot Meyer

Ever since I can remember I have had a heart for renewable energy, especially solar energy. After my studies I joined an overland company in order to see more of Africa without spending too much money. After my first trip I bought a South-African-produced solar oven. I took this oven on all my trips and tested it in many African countries. It performed very well. I mainly used it for baking bread and cakes. The highlight of my oven was baking a chocolate birthday cake in the middle of Botswana's Okavango Delta.

After my overland chapter I started my first real job here in Rwanda. I work as an electrical engineer at a small tin smelter. When I saw how little of Rwanda's forests were left I immediately decided to start a small solar oven project. My oven is based on one produced by a South African company, which shares all its drawings and research with anyone who is interested.

The oven measures about 650mm long, 500mm wide and 500mm high. It is in the shape of a monitor (the speaker you get on a music stage used by the singer/musicians to hear themselves). I constructed it out of a simple wooden frame. The inside and outside are then covered by thin aluminium plates. I get these at the price of scrap aluminium from printing companies (litho plates). The inside layer of plates act as reflectors, reflecting sunlight on a black pot placed inside the oven. The outside layer forms an air insulation between the two sets of plates. I am still experimenting with better insulation material like sawdust. The box has a glass lid to keep the heat inside.

I constructed my first oven for about US$8 (glass US$2, wood US$3, aluminium plates US$2, nails and some silicone US$1). I introduced it to the workers at our factory by heating some water. They did not believe me and said I changed the water with hot water. The next day I arrived with a cup of rice. I let them all inspect the rice and then placed it in the oven with some water. This was at about 9.00am. I placed the oven in a sunny spot near where they were working and only returned at 12 midday. They were all there when I opened the oven and pot. To their amazement – a pot of cooked rice!

The second oven was constructed only recently by one of my workers. I make the aluminium plates available to them at cost price since this is the only unknown item to them. Considering the number of copies of the oven plans I have been asked to make, I believe that many more ovens will be built soon!

Katot is contactable on email kattermaai@yahoo.co.uk.

The costume worn by the Tutsi dancers consists of either a short floral skirt or a leopard skin wound around their legs. Crossed straps decorated with coloured beads are generally worn across the chest. On their heads they wear a fringe of white colobus monkey fur. Depending on the theme of the dance and the region they may carry a bow, a spear or a stick decorated with a long tail of raffia. Around their ankles they wear bells, the sound of which adds to the rhythm of the dance.

The Intore dancers perform regularly today and it's a dramatic spectacle. You may come across them in Kigali, Nyanza, Huye – or abroad, on one of their tours. Ask ORTPN in Kigali (see page 86) for details of any scheduled performances.

Another striking performance of dance – equally traditional – is given by a group of Twa in Kigali – see page 104.

Handicrafts As in other countries, most genuinely traditional handicrafts have a practical use or are decorated forms of everyday objects. An object which gives purely visual pleasure and is unrelated to any function has probably evolved for the tourist market – although it is none the worse for that. In Rwanda the weaving (of bowls, mats, baskets, storage containers, etc) from various natural fibres is particularly fine. The quality of wood-carving is variable, but at best it's excellent. Pottery made by the Twa community is plain but strong and its uncluttered style is attractive. See *Chapter 6* (pages 107–8) for details of where in Kigali to find handicrafts on sale.

SPORT Sport is a passion in Rwanda as it is throughout most of Africa. Football, volleyball, rugby, swimming, cricket (see page 105), tennis, golf, even karate… it's all there, and developing.

Olympic and paralympic games – Athens 2004 It was a tense moment! Nkundabera Jean de Dieu was running strongly in the Paralympic men's 800m, but then so had Nyirabareme Epiphanie in the Olympic women's marathon – for a while she was jogging composedly at the front alongside the UK's Paula Radcliffe – and Disi Dieudonné in the Olympic men's 10,000m, and they eventually fell back to finish 54th (out of 66 finishers) and 17th (of 24) respectively. However Nkundabera held his position, to capture Rwanda's only medal – the bronze – in the 2004 year's games. (The gold went to the UK's Danny Crates.) Another courageous Paralympic competitor was young Akobasenga Olive (women's 200m), but she wasn't among the qualifiers in her heat.

In the Olympic men's marathon, the more experienced Ntawulikura Mathias held his ground among the front runners for a while, but then fell back to 62nd place out of 81 finishers. In the Olympic swimming men's 50m freestyle, Sekamana Léonce successfully made it through to come 4th in the second heats, but sadly this didn't put him among the qualifiers. The other Olympic swimming competitor, Girimbabazi Rugabira Pamela, didn't gain a qualifying place in her heat for the women's 100m breast-stroke.

It was exciting to see Rwanda represented at the Games, but too little money and preparation had been put in beforehand. However, there's always 2008 – and maybe the next edition of this guide will be able to report more spectacular results!

Football
Chris Frean
Two years ago the future looked so exciting; but, since 2004's triumphant appearance at the African Nations Cup and APR's reaching the Semi Finals of the African Cup Winners' Cup, Rwandan football has in fact gone backwards.

COLLEGE OF GISENYI KARATE CLUB FOR GIRLS

Lindsay Hodgson

'They won't come' was the overwhelming consensus from my colleagues. Either that or simply 'Why?' I had spent my lunchtime putting '*Coming soon – karate club for girls*' posters at various vantage points around the school. I don't usually condone discrimination, 'positive' or otherwise, so why did I decide on a girls-only club? I guess it was a question of balance.

During one of my first lessons here as a maths teacher in Rwanda, I showed the pupils photographs from home. A few of them were of me in my karate gear and I explained how I wanted to start a club at the school. At the end of the lesson, one of the girls hung around for a while and when everyone else had left she asked if the club would only be for boys. I was genuinely surprised – I am, after all, female myself – so I asked why she had thought this. She told me that the boys already had a karate club – one of the older pupils was the sensei – but girls weren't allowed. 'Right then', I thought, 'why not have a club just for girls too?' So I set to designing posters.

Initially, admittedly, I was concerned. Virtually every colleague was so sure of a poor turn-out. In addition I was finding it difficult to get the girls to add their names to my list. 'But karate's for boys, teacher, very aggressive' to quote but one girl's opinion. With only three names in as many days I worried that the line 'Limited to 20 places' would come to haunt me. Would I have to invite the boys after all? I set myself a minimum of ten girls to make it worthwhile.

I'm glad I persevered. A week after the posters went up (and several pep talks later) I had 15 names in total. I found that once one girl plucked up the courage to join, her friends usually followed. We had a meeting to discuss logistics and the College of Gisenyi Karate Club for Girls was born!

The first few sessions were rather 'interesting'. It seemed as if every student and his or her goat was trying to sneak a peek! The girls found this, and the karate, difficult at first. Their level of confidence was low and I spent a lot of my time chasing away the spectators!

However, very quickly the girls' style and fitness both improved. Instead of a shy whimper I started getting a veritable roar for each 'KIAI' (the motivational shout used in karate). Soon I had girls coming to see me after classes to ask if there were any places left and, if so, could they join. And so it continued, every Tuesday and Thursday.

Seven months on and our dojo is 25 strong. I had to start turning girls away as the room is too small to accommodate any more. Now, rather than chasing the spectators away, the girls train regardless, with a real sense of pride and achievement – they know they look and feel great.

The girls have demonstrated for delegates at a gender workshop in Kigali, the general public in Gisenyi and, all importantly, for the boys' club at school. It was during this last demonstration that the girls were invited to train with the boys each weekend. The boys were delighted at seeing the girls participate in karate just as enthusiastically and with as much focus as they did.

As for my colleagues, I think the girls' progress and determination has shocked them more than anyone. But they are delighted nonetheless. As for me, if the girls and boys ultimately join into one club, I would be done out of a job. I can honestly say that this would delight me too!

Lindsay was teaching in Rwanda for Voluntary Service Overseas (www.vso.org.uk).

The *Amavubi*, which translates as 'wasps', finished last in their qualifying group for the Nations Cup and World Cup (one group for both) in 2006. Just about the only result of note was a 1-1 home draw to Nigeria. But when Angola beat Nigeria to qualify, it put that into perspective. Rwanda's problems began when they lost their coach to Ghana and replaced him with an unknown Swede. After an early win over Gabon, the side stumbled to the bottom of the group and stayed there. At least one international was picked up in Brussels accused of some Papa Wemba-style illegal racket. The wasps finished below not only Angola and Nigeria but well adrift – in quality if not points – of Algeria, Zimbabwe and Gabon. The Swede, Roger Palmgren, has been demoted to a minor post in the coaching ranks, and at the time of writing the former head of the football association, FERWAFA, Caesar Kayizari of the RDF, is up for re-election.

So the qualification for the Nations Cup in Ghana in 2008 offers them a chance to get their act together. Football matters too, since along with tennis it is one of President Kagame's interests (he has been seen at internationals and APR games). For Ghana, Rwanda have been drawn against George Weah's Liberia, Equatorial Guinea, and Cameroon. One team will qualify. Realistically Rwanda cannot look to finish higher than second. Third behind Cameroon and Liberia might be acceptable. Failure to beat Equatorial Guinea will be a serious embarrassment.

Women's rugby Rwanda has made history here! In February 2005 in the floodlit Amahoro Stadium, the inaugural East African Women's Rugby International was held. Rwandan women hosted their Ugandan counterparts. Despite there being no dedicated rugby pitches in the country, there's huge enthusiasm nationwide and already the first steps have been taken.

3

Planning and Preparation

WHEN TO VISIT

Rwanda can be visited at any time of year. The long dry season, June to September, is the best time for tracking gorillas in the Volcanoes Park and hiking in Nyungwe Forest, since the ground should be dry underfoot and the odds of being drenched are minimal, but this should not be a major consideration for any reasonably fit and agile traveller. The dry season is also the best time for travelling on dirt roads, and is when the risk of malaria should be lowest.

There are two annual rainy seasons: the big rains which last from mid-February to the beginning of June, and the small rains from mid-September to mid-December. Rainfall, especially over the mountains, can be heavy during these two periods – particularly from March to May, although it is still perfectly feasible to travel at these times of year.

As for the two dry seasons, the major one lasts from June to September and the shorter from December to February. However, the climate is not uniform throughout the country: it is generally drier in the east than in the west and north. On occasion, the volcanoes of the north may be capped by snow, and evenings in Kigali can call for a sweater – as do days anywhere in the highlands should you happen to hit a cold snap! Nevertheless, every season is good for swimming and tanning on the banks of Lake Kivu.

An advantage of travelling during the rainy season is that the scenery is greener, and the sky less hazy (at least when it isn't overcast), a factor that will be of particular significance to photographers. The wet season is also the best time to track chimps in Nyungwe (in the dry season they may wander further off in search of scarce food), while the months of November to March will hold the greatest appeal for birders, as resident birds are supplemented by flocks of Palaearctic migrants.

GETTING THERE AND AWAY

✈ BY AIR

Rwanda's new airline Rwandair Express (✆ *Kigali 575757/503687;* f *503689;* e *wb@rwandair.com; www.rwandair.com*) flies directly between Kigali and Entebbe (Uganda), Johannesburg (South Africa), Nairobi (Kenya) and Bujumbura (Burundi).

Other direct flights to Kigali are run by Kenya Airways from Nairobi, SN Brussels Airlines from Brussels, Ethiopian Airlines from Addis Ababa and Bujumbura, and South African Airways from Johannesburg. All of these carriers operate a good network of intra- and intercontinental flights – travellers coming from Europe are best off flying via Brussels, Nairobi and Addis Ababa, those from the Americas and Australasia will do best to aim for Johannesburg or Nairobi.

The international airport lies less than 10km from central Kigali, and taxis are available to/from the city centre. See *Chapter 6*, page 83. The departure tax that used to be payable at the airport is now included in your ticket – but check when you book, in case this changes again.

On no account neglect to **confirm your return flight at least three days in advance**, via an airline office or travel agent in Kigali. Unless you do this, there is – at least with some airlines – a serious risk of being 'bumped' at the last minute.

Air tickets A number of travel companies are good sources of **cut-price tickets**, as well as offering various other services. London is the best place for cheap fares, hence the bias of the list below! It isn't exhaustive but should give you a start. As shown on their websites, most of the companies listed also have offices in other countries.

UK (London)

Africa Travel Centre 4 Medway Court, Leigh St, London WC1H 9QX; ☏ 0845 450 1520; e info@africatravel.co.uk; www.africatravel.co.uk
Flight Centre ☏ (booking) 0870 499 0040; www.flightcentre.com. Flight Centre has several offices in London and elsewhere in UK. It offers cut-price airfares and insurance services. Also in Australia, New Zealand, South Africa, USA.
STA Travel ☏ 0870 1 630026; e enquiries@statravel.co.uk; web (very comprehensive): www.statravel.co.uk. Has 65 branches in UK and over 450 worldwide.

Trailfinders 194 Kensington High St, London W8 7RG (one-stop travel shop); ☏ 0845 058 5858; web (very comprehensive): www.trailfinders.com. Also in Ireland, Australia, etc.
WEXAS 45–49 Brompton Rd, Knightsbridge, London SW3 1DE; ☏ 020 7838 7901; www.wexas.com. There is an annual subscription to WEXAS (for current details e mship@wexas.com or phone 020 7589 3315) but membership gives access to a whole range of useful services (good rates for hotels and airport parking, use of airport lounges, visas...) as well as an excellent travel magazine, Traveller.

OVERLAND Four countries border Rwanda: Burundi to the south, the Democratic Republic of the Congo (DRC) to the west, Uganda to the north and Tanzania to the east. Assuming peaceful conditions, frontier formalities aren't too much of a hassle – but nor are they standardised. Most frontier offices open at 08.00; they may close at 17.00 or 18.00. See page 39 for details of which nationalities don't require visas; for others, to buy a visa at the border costs around US$60. (But, for safety, check with your nearest embassy beforehand that it's still possible.) Don't count on official exchange facilities being available; there are likely to be 'black-market' money-changers around, but you should decide in advance what rate you're prepared to accept.

At the time of writing, although there are still buses running between Kigali and Bujumbura in **Burundi**, it's a volatile area and the route isn't advisable for tourists. Air travel is safer.

The **DRC** seems to be settling down now and travel is becoming safer in the immediate Rwanda border area. Regular minibus services run between Kigali and Goma/Bukavu. Lake transport is starting up again too; see pages 64 and 157. But peace doesn't become widespread overnight; so do check current conditions and follow local advice. On both sides of each border there is accommodation reasonably close by – in the case of Cyangugu and Gisenyi, only a few minutes away, but further for Bukavu. Travelling further into the DRC remains highly risky.

Crossing to and from **Uganda** is simple. Direct buses and minibus-taxis connect Kampala and Kigali, taking 10–12 hours and costing around US$15. One of the best buses on offer is Regional Coach Services (☏ *575963 (Kigali) or +256*

John Osman

When you bring your vehicle into Rwanda you need to buy a *Carte d'Entrée* for Rfr5,000 at customs. Police at checkpoints will often ask to see this slip of paper, so don't lose it!

Compulsory vehicle insurance is also available at the border, just after you go through Rwandan customs. You may be approached by an insurance salesman even while you're still going through the customs registration for the car, but we preferred to go to one of the official offices set up in that area rather than to deal with a guy 'on the street'. The insurance process is quick and easy. Minimum coverage is for three days, then one week, and so on. For one week's coverage we paid Rfr 7,100 for a 2000cc 4-wheel-drive. The procedure is all carried out in English, in case anyone is worried about having to cope with French.

Police at checkpoints on Rwandan roads may ask to see if you have a fire extinguisher and triangles (which you're supposed to set up on the road to warn of an accident) in your car. Luckily we'd been warned of this beforehand, so we'd bought a little Russian-made fire extinguisher in Kampala for around US$6 and a pair of triangles for about US$10. The police were perfectly satisfied with that.

41 256862/3 (Kampala)), which departs Kampala for Kigali at 09.00 daily and has connections on to Nairobi and Dar es Salaam. There are plenty of local minibus-taxis along the roughly 50km road between Kisoro in southwest Uganda and Musanze (formerly Ruhengeri) in northwest Rwanda (an hour's trip, not allowing for changing vehicles and other delays at the Cyanika border post, which might add another hour to the journey). It is also easy to travel by minibus-taxi between Kabale, the largest town in southwest Uganda, and Kigali, though once again you might have to change vehicles at the border – this trip should take about five hours in total. Entering from Uganda in your own vehicle is relatively hassle-free.

Crossing between Rwanda and **Tanzania** is something of a slog, due to the poor state of roads and lack of large towns in northwest Tanzania. The Rusumo border post lies about 160km from Kigali, roughly a four-hour trip by minibus-taxi, with the possibility of staying the night en route at the town of Kibungo (see page 223), 60km from the border. Or there is a restaurant with basic accommodation at Rusumo itself, on the Rwandan side (page 228). The closest Tanzanian town to the border is Ngara, which is connected to Rusumo by occasional minibus-taxis taking about six hours, and has a few small guesthouses. From Ngara, daily buses to Mwanza on Lake Victoria take 12–18 hours depending on the condition of the road. Mwanza is a large port with a full range of accommodation and other facilities, including thrice-weekly rail links to Dar es Salaam on the coast and daily buses to Arusha in northeast Tanzania. A rail link between Rwanda and Tanzania is planned, but don't count on it being up and running in the near future. See also the box *Travelling from Kigali to Mwanza* on page 227.

INTERNATIONAL TOUR OPERATORS All those listed below will arrange gorilla visits plus international travel. Most offer both scheduled tours and tailor-made trips. More will start to cover the rest of Rwanda during the life of this guide. The many operators in neighbouring countries (Uganda etc) are deliberately not all listed, because readers in those countries are less likely to need them. The Rwandan tour operators listed on page 38 can also arrange international travel.

United Kingdom *(national code +44)*

Aardvark Safaris ✎ 01980 849160;
e mail@aardvarksafaris.com; www.aardvarksafaris.com
Abercrombie & Kent ✎ 0845 070 0611;
www.abercrombiekent.co.uk
Absolute Africa ✎ 020 8742 0226;
e absaf@absoluteafrica.com; www.absoluteafrica.com.
Overland truck and camping safaris.
Africa Travel Centre ✎ 0845 450 1541;
e info@africatravel.co.uk; www.africatravel.co.uk
Discovery Initiatives ✎ 01285 643333; f 01285
885888; e enquiry@discoveryinitiatives.com;
www.discoveryinitiatives.com. Part of the Steppes Travel
Group
Exodus ✎ 0870 240 5550; e info@exodus.co.uk;
www.exodus.co.uk
Expert Africa (formerly Sunvil) ✎ 020 8232 9777;
e africa-holidays@sunvil.co.uk; www.sunvil.co.uk
Footprint Adventures ✎ 01522 804929; e sales@
footprint-adventures.co.uk; www.footprint-adventures.co.uk
Imagine Africa ✎ 020 7228 5655; e info@
imagineafrica.co.uk; www.imagineafrica.co.uk
Naturetrek ✎ 01962 733051;
e info@naturetrek.co.uk; www.naturetrek.co.uk

Okavango Tours & Safaris ✎ 020 8343 3283;
e info@okavango.com; www.okavango.com
Rainbow Tours ✎ 020 7226 1004; f 020 7226
2621; e info@rainbowtours.co.uk;
www.rainbowtours.co.uk
Reef & Rainforest Tours ✎ 01803 866965; f 01803
865916; e mail@reefandrainforest.co.uk;
www.reefandrainforest.co.uk
Safari Consultants Ltd ✎ 01787 228494;
e bill@safariconsultantuk.com; www.safari-
consultants.co.uk
Vintage Africa Ltd ✎ 01451 850803;
e vintagelon@vintageafrica.com;
www.vintageafrica.com (offices also in South Africa,
Tanzania, Kenya)
Volcanoes Safaris UK office: ✎ 0870 870 8480;
f 0870 870 8481; e salesuk@volcanoessafaris.com;
www.volcanoessafaris.com (offices in UK, US, Uganda
and Rwanda – also see details on page 23)
Wildlife Worldwide ✎ 0845 130 6982; f 020 8667
1960; e sales@wildlifeworldwide.com;
www.wildlifeworldwide.com

USA *(national code +1)*

Africa Adventure Company ✎ (toll free US & Canada)
1 800 882 9453; e noltingaac@aol.com;
www.africa-adventure.com
Ker & Downey ✎ 281 371 2500, (toll free US &
Canada) 800 423 4236; e safari@kerdowney.com;

www.kerdowney.com
Volcanoes Safaris ✎ 770 730 0960;
e salesus@volcanoessafaris.com;
www.volcanoessafaris.com (also see under UK,
above)

Canada *(national code +1)*

Leisure Connection Tours Ltd ✎ (toll free US &
Canada) 800 364 5104;

e info@lcadventuretravel.com;
www.lcadventuretravel.

Europe

BELGIUM *(national code +32)*
Continents Insolites
✎ 2218 2484; e info@insolites.be; www.insolites.be
GERMANY *(national code +49)*
Globetrotter Select ✎ 8171 997272; e
info@globetrotter-select.de; www.globetrotter-select.de

Top Trail Tours ✎ 221 270 8960;
e info@toptrailtours.de; www.toptrailtours.de
SPAIN *(national code +34)*
Kananga Travel ✎ 93 268 7795; e
info@kananga.com; www.kananga.com

Kenya *(national code +254)* and Uganda *(national code +256)*

Magic Safaris (Uganda) ✎ (+256) 41 342926;
e info@magic-safaris.com; www.magic-safaris.com
The Far Horizon (Uganda) ✎ (+256) 41
343468/235168; e info@thefarhorizons.com;
www.thefarhorizons.com (also have an office in Rwanda)
Origins Safaris (Kenya) ✎ (+254) 20 331191,
222075; e info@originsafaris.info;
www.originsafaris.info

Volcanoes Safaris (Uganda) ✎ (+256) 41 346464;
e salesug@volcanoessafaris.com;
www.volcanoessafaris.com (see also under UK,
above)
Wild Frontiers (Uganda) ✎ (+256) 41 321479;
e info@wildfrontiers.co.ug; www.wildfrontiers.com
(see also under South Africa, opposite)

Rwanda *(national code + 250)*

Kiboko Tours ➲ 083 00502/ 084 26593;
e kiboko@rwanda1.com; www.kibokotravels.org.rw
Bizidanny Safaris ➲ 085 01461;
e bizidanny@yahoo.fr; www.bizidanny.bi.funpic.de
JK Safaris ➲ +254 20 3876629/36; f +254 20
576720; m +254 734 696969;

e info@jksafaris.com; www.jksafaris.com
Rwanda Multi Service Agency ➲ 0830 3068;
e rwandamsagency@yahoo.com
Thousand Hills Expedition ➲ 250 504330 /250
08351000; e info@thousandhills.rw;
www.thousandhills.rw

South Africa *(national code +27)*

Unusual Destinations ➲ 11 706 1991; f 11 463
1469; e info@unusualdestinations.com;
www.unusualdestinations.com

Wild Frontiers ➲ 11 702 2035;
e wildfront@icon.co.za; www.wildfrontiers.com (also
have offices in Uganda and Tanzania)

RED TAPE

Check well in advance that you have a valid **passport**, and that it won't expire within six months of the date you intend to leave Rwanda. Should your passport be lost or stolen, it will generally be easier to get a replacement if you travel with a photocopy of the important pages.

Visas are required by all visitors except for nationals of the UK, Germany, Sweden, Canada, USA, Hong Kong, Burundi, DRC, Kenya, Mauritius, South Africa, Tanzania and Uganda (for stays of less than three months). For all others they cost around US$60, depending on the place of issue. For air travellers, visas are now issued at Kigali airport on arrival, and you can also usually buy visas at overland borders, but do check via an embassy that this is still the case when you travel. Details of Rwandan embassies abroad are given below. Nationals of countries without an embassy can also obtain a visa on arrival by prior arrangement with their hosts, who can arrange a *facilité d'entrée*.

If there is any possibility that you'll want to drive or hire a vehicle while you're in the country, do organise an **international driving licence** (via one of the main motoring associations in a country in which you're licensed to drive), which you may be asked to produce together with your original licence. You may sometimes be asked at borders for an **international health certificate** showing you've had a yellow-fever shot.

For **security** reasons, it's advisable to detail all your important information on one sheet of paper, photocopy it, and distribute a few copies in your luggage, your money-belt, and amongst relatives or friends at home: the sort of things you want to include on this are travellers' cheque numbers and refund information, travel insurance policy details and 24–hour emergency contact number, passport number, details of relatives or friends to be contacted in an emergency, bank and credit card details, camera and lens serial numbers, etc. You might also want to email this information to yourself immediately before you leave, so it is stored in your in-tray throughout your travels. It's also handy to carry a photo of your suitcase or other luggage, to save trying to describe it if it's misplaced by an airline.

ⓔ RWANDAN EMBASSIES AND CONSULATES ABROAD

Belgium 1 Av des Fleurs, 1150 Brussels; ➲ (+32)
02 763 0738; f 02 763 0753; e ambabruxelles@
minaffet.gov.rw
Burundi 24 Av de la République Démocratique du
Congo, BP 400 Bujumbura; ➲ (+257) 228755;
f 223254; e ambuja@minaffet.gov.rw
Canada 153 Gilmour Street. Ottawa, ➲ +1613 722

5835; f +1613 722 4052; e ambaottawa@
minaffet.gov.rw
China Hsieu Shaouei Bei Yie, Beijing; ➲ (+861) 065
321820; f 065 322006; e ambabeijing@
minaffet.gov.rw
Ethiopia Africa Av, H 17k-20 No 001, PO Box 5618
Addis Ababa; ➲ (+251) 161 0300; f 161 0411;

e ambaddis@minaffet.gov.rw
France 12 Rue Jadin, 75017 Paris; tel +33 1 476 65420; **f** +33 1 422 77469;
e ambaparis@minaffet.gov.rw
Germany Beethovenallee 72, 53173 Bonn; ✆ (+49) 228 3670238; **f** 228 351922;
e ambabonn@minaffet.gov.rw
India B 112 Neet Bash, New Delhi 110016; ✆ (+91) 11 656 8083; **f** 11 656 8085;
e ambadelhi@minaffet.gov.rw
Kenya Kilimani, Kahahwe Rd, PO Box 30.619, Nairobi; ✆ (+254) 257 5977; **f** 257 5976;
e ambanairobi@minaffet.gov.rw
South Africa 35 Marais St, Brooklyn, Pretoria; ✆ (+27) 12 460 0709; **f** 12 460 0708;
e ambapretoria@minaffet.gov.rw
Switzerland Rue de la Serviette 93, CH-1202 Geneva; ✆ (+41) 22 919 1000; **f** 22 919 1001;

e ambageneve@minaffet.gov.rw
Tanzania 32 Ali Hassan Mwinyi Rd, PO Box 2918 Dar es Salaam; ✆ (+255) 222 115889; **f** 222 115888;
e ambadsm@minaffet.gov.rw
Uganda 2 Nakaima Rd, PO Box 2446 Kampala; ✆ (+256) 41 344045; **f** 41 258854;
e ambakampala@minaffet.gov.rw
United Kingdom 120–122 Seymour Place, London W1H 1NR; ✆ (+44) 020 7224 9832; **f** 020 7224 8642; e uk@ambarwanda.org.uk; www.ambarwanda.org.uk
United States 124 East 39th St, **New York**, NY 10016; ✆ (+1) 212 679 9010; **f** 212 679 9133; e ambanewyork@minaffet.gov.rw. Also 1724 New Hampshire Av NW, **Washington, DC** 20009; ✆ (+1) 202 462 8495; **f** 202 232 4544; e ambawashington@minaffet.gov.rw; www.rwandemb.org

Details provided by the Ministry of Foreign Affairs, Kigali. For updates and additions, refer to website www.rwandatourism.com.

PACKING

In 1907, when the Duke of Mecklenburg set off on an expedition through Rwanda with a group of scientific researchers, he carried (or rather his team of bearers carried) numerous cases of soap, candles, rope and cigars, as well as such items as salt, wire, beads and woollen blankets to barter with the natives. You could probably cut down on this a little.

In fact Rwanda is a relatively well-stocked little country, in terms of clothing, toiletries, stationery, batteries and so forth. Unless you have particularly exotic tastes (or your schedule is too crowded to allow you time for shopping), you should be able to find most of the everyday items a traveller needs, even if the brands are unfamiliar. Obviously you should bring a supply of any personal medication (and some extra, in case your return home is delayed); also bring a stock of whatever type of film you like to use, as well as enough sunscreen. Otherwise, unless you plan to go way off the beaten track (or you need camping/trekking gear, which is in shorter supply), don't feel that you must fill your bag up with a lot of semi-useful items 'just in case'. Buying things locally helps Rwanda's economy!

The comments below apply as much to any neighbouring African countries you may pass through or visit as they do to Rwanda.

CARRYING YOUR LUGGAGE Visitors who are unlikely to be carrying their luggage for any significant distance will probably want to pack most of it in a conventional suitcase. Make sure it is tough and durable, and that it seals well, so that its contents will survive bumpy drives and boisterous baggage handlers at airports. Travellers carrying a lot of valuable items should look for a bag that can be easily padlocked. A locked bag can, of course, be slashed open, but that would be highly unusual in Rwanda – you are more likely to be exposed to casual theft of the sort to which a lock would be real deterrent.

If you are likely to use public transport, then a backpack is the most practical solution. An internal frame is more flexible than an external one. Again, ensure your pack is durable and that it has several pockets. If you intend doing a lot of hiking, you definitely want a backpack designed for this purpose. On the other hand, if you'll be staying at places where it might be a good idea to shake off the sometimes negative image attached to backpackers, then there would be advantages in using a suitcase that converts into a backpack.

However you travel, a small daypack will be useful for gorilla-tracking and other walks, and to stow any breakable goods on your lap during long drives – anything like an mp3 player or camera will suffer heavily from vibrations on rutted roads.

CAMPING EQUIPMENT There are only a few opportunities for camping in Rwanda, and the financial advantages are limited since affordable accommodation is generally available. Balanced against that, for those without transport the campsite at Nyungwe is a far more convenient base for walks than the resthouse, and a tent is essential for hiking in off-the-beaten-track areas. Also, although there is now accommodation in Akagera Park, camping there gets you closest to the wildlife.

For backpackers who decide to carry camping equipment, the key is to look for the lightest available gear. It is now possible to buy a lightweight tent weighing little more than 2kg, but make sure that the one you choose is mosquito proof. Other essentials for camping include a sleeping bag and a roll-mat, which will serve as both insulation and padding. You might want to carry a stove and Camping Gas cylinders (not readily available in Rwanda). A box of firelighter blocks will get a fire going in the most unpromising conditions. It would also be advisable to carry a pot, plate, cup and cutlery.

CLOTHES Try to keep your clothes to a minimum, especially if you are travelling with everything on your back. Bear in mind that you can easily and cheaply replace worn items in markets. In my opinion, the minimum is one or possibly two pairs of trousers and/or skirts, one pair of shorts, three shirts or T-shirts, one light sweater or similar, one heavy sweater or similar, a waterproof jacket during the rainy season, enough socks and underwear to last five to seven days, one solid pair of shoes or boots for walking, and one pair of sandals, thongs or other light shoes.

It's widely held that jeans are not ideal for African travel, since they are bulky to carry, hot to wear and take ages to dry. In their favour, however, jeans do have the advantages of durability and comfort, and of hiding the dust and dirt that tend to accumulate during public transport rides – and they are excellent for gorilla-tracking and other forest walks A good alternative is light cotton trousers, which dry more quickly and weigh less, but try to avoid light colours, as they show dirt more easily. Skirts are best made of a light natural fabric such as cotton. T-shirts are lighter and less bulky than proper shirts, though the top pocket of a shirt (particularly if it buttons up) is a good place to carry spending money in markets and bus stations, since it's easier to keep an eye on than a trouser pocket. A couple of sweaters or sweatshirts will be necessary in places such as Nyungwe, which get chilly at night.

Socks and underwear *must* be made from natural fabrics. Bear in mind that re-using sweaty undergarments will encourage fungal infections such as athlete's foot, as well as prickly heat in the groin region. Socks and underpants are light and compact enough to make it worth bringing a week's supply. As for footwear, only if you're a serious off-road hiker should you consider genuine hiking boots, since they are very heavy whether on your feet or in your pack. A good pair of walking shoes, preferably made of leather with good ankle support, is a good compromise. For gorilla-tracking, a pair of old gardening gloves can be handy when you're grabbing for handholds in thorny vegetation.

Another factor in selecting your travel wardrobe is local sensibilities. In Rwanda, which is predominantly Christian, this isn't the concern it would be in several other parts of Africa, but travellers are nevertheless advised to dress relatively modestly. For women, the ideal garment is a knee-length skirt, though long trousers – while unconventional female wear in rural Rwanda – are most unlikely to give offence. For men, shorts are not unacceptable, but few local men wear them and it is considered more respectable to wear trousers. Walking around in a public place without a shirt is dodgy.

Many Africans think it is insulting for Westerners to wear scruffy or dirty clothes in their country, reasoning that we wouldn't dress like that at home. It is difficult to explain that at home you also wouldn't spend a morning slithering around the muddy Virungas in your last clean outfit! If you're travelling rough, you're bound to look a mess at times, but it's worth trying to look as spruce as possible, particularly since many Rwandans dress well.

OTHER USEFUL ITEMS Most backpackers, even those with no intention of camping, carry a **sleeping bag**. I've never seen the necessity for this, particularly in Rwanda. You might meet travellers who, when they stay in local lodgings, habitually place their own sleeping bag on top of the bedding provided. Nutters, in my opinion: I'd imagine that a sleeping bag placed on a flea-ridden bed would be unlikely to provide significant protection – it would be more likely to become flea-infested itself.

I wouldn't leave home without **binoculars**, which some might say makes *me* the nutter. Seriously, though, if you're interested in natural history, it's difficult to imagine anything that will give you such value-for-weight entertainment as a pair of light, compact binoculars, which these days needn't be much heavier or bulkier than a pack of cards. Binoculars are essential if you want to get a good look at birds (Africa boasts a remarkably colourful avifauna even if you've no desire to put a name to everything that flaps) or to watch distant mammals in game reserves. For most purposes, 7x21 compact binoculars will be fine, though some might prefer 7x35 traditional binoculars for their larger field of vision. Serious birdwatchers will find a 10x magnification more useful.

Some travellers like to carry their own **padlock**. This is useful if you have a pack that is lockable, and in remote parts of the country might be necessary for rooms where no lock is provided. If you are uneasy about security in a particular guesthouse, you may like to use your own lock instead of, or in addition to, the one provided. Although combination locks are reputedly easier to pick than conventional padlocks, I think you'd be safer with a combination lock in Rwanda, because potential thieves will have far more experience of breaking through locks with keys.

Your **toilet bag** should at the very minimum include soap (secured in a plastic bag or soap holder unless you enjoy a soapy toothbrush!), shampoo, toothbrush and toothpaste. This sort of stuff is easy to replace as you go along, so there's no need to bring family-sized packs. Men will probably want a **razor**. Women should carry enough **tampons** and/or **sanitary pads** to see them through at least one heavy period, since these items may not always be immediately available. If you wear **contact lenses**, be aware that the various fluids are not readily available in Rwanda, and, since many people find the intense sun and dust irritate their eyes, you might consider reverting to glasses. Nobody should forget to bring a **towel**, or to keep handy a roll of **loo paper**, which although widely available at shops and kiosks cannot always be relied upon to be present where it's most urgently needed. A lot of washbasins in Rwanda lack plugs, so one of those 'universal' rubber plugs that fit all sizes of plughole can be useful.

Other essentials include a **torch**, a **penknife** and a compact **alarm clock** for those early morning starts. If you're interested in what's happening in the world, you might also think about taking a **short-wave radio**, though these days the ubiquity of internet access probably makes it redundant. Some travellers carry **games** – most commonly a pack of cards, less often chess or draughts or travel Scrabble.

You should carry a small **medical kit**, the contents of which are discussed in the chapter on health, as are **mosquito nets**. For those who wear **glasses**, it's worth bringing a spare pair, though in an emergency a new pair can be made up cheaply (around US$10) and quickly in most Rwandan towns, provided that you have your prescription available.

$ MONEY

ORGANISING YOUR FINANCES Normally there are three ways of carrying money: hard cash, travellers' cheques and credit cards. However, at the time of writing credit cards are of limited use in Rwanda. Unusually for this part of Africa, MasterCard is far more widely accepted than Visa (the Visa stickers you see outside some hotels refer to cards issued domestically). But even so, the use of MasterCard extends only to certain upmarket hotels in Kigali and a very few places outside the capital. If you are relying on using a card, then best to check what cards your hotel accepts when you make your booking. Worth noting here too that the ORTPN head office in Kigali also accepts MasterCard but not Visa – see box *Booking a gorilla permit* on page 45.

It is also possible to draw up to €2,500 per day (or the equivalent in Rwanda Francs or any other hard currency to hand) against Visa or MasterCard in the Bancor on Ave de la Paix in Kigali. This is a remarkably straightforward procedure but be warned that it does depend on the bank having access to a specific website – if the electricity is down, or the computers or the internet server or the website itself, then this service will be unavailable and you may have to wait a day or two for it to come back online.

As for travellers' cheques (it's best if they're in euros or US dollars) – again, theoretically they can be cashed up to a value of US$200 daily at the Banque Commerciale du Rwanda (BCR) and a few other banks in central Kigali, but in practice this can fall apart, or be quite a slow procedure. You'll get a poorer exchange rate for travellers' cheques than for cash. When cashing them, you must generally show the sales advice slip that you got when you obtained them – that's the slip of paper that one is supposed never to keep in proximity to the cheques!

That leaves cash. The preferred foreign currencies are the dollar or euro, but all main currencies should be exchangeable, whether in banks or in official or private forex bureaux. The official forex bureaux are clearly signed on the street and have standard facilities. The 'private' ones are small offices or rooms where the moneychangers who used to tout their wares on the street now operate since the black market was declared illegal. They may offer a slightly better exchange rate than the official forex bureaux (and it's worth bargaining), which in turn is better than the rate in banks. They generally also give a better rate for larger-denomination notes, which anyway are less bulky for you to carry. Above all, because there is no paperwork involved, they have the advantage of being very quick compared with banks – the transaction should literally take no longer than a minute or two.

Bear in mind that this is a changing scene. Conditions regarding credit cards and travellers' cheques may be different – and better – by the time you travel. But do have enough cash in case of glitches. If you don't want to carry too much, arrange for a friend to send it to you from home when necessary, via Western Union – there are offices in Kigali and all the main towns. It isn't cheap – the cost depends on the amount being transferred – but it's quick and secure. Any Rwandan francs left over at the end of your trip can be changed back into dollars, euros or whatever by banks, forex bureaux or money-changers.

Budget planning Any budget will depend so greatly on how and where you travel that it is almost impossible to give sensible advice in a general travel guide. As a

CHANGING MONEY AT BORDERS

The black markets that once thrived in East Africa were killed off some years ago, but you might still need to exchange money on the street at some international borders, so that you have enough local currency to pay for transport to the next town, for a room when you get there, and – should you expect to arrive outside banking hours or over the weekend – to cover other expenses until the next banking day. As a rule you won't get the greatest rate of exchange at any border, which is fair enough, considering that moneychangers, like banks, profit by offering different rates of exchange in either direction. So there's no sense in exchanging significantly more money than you'll require before you reach a bank or forex bureau. The only exception is when you have a surfeit of cash from the country you're leaving and no intention of returning there – the border may be the last place you can unload it.

Many private moneychangers are incidental con artists, so be prepared. Check the exchange rate in advance and calculate roughly what sum of local currency you should expect. Put whatever bills you intend to change in a pocket discrete from your main stash of foreign currency before you arrive at the border. And don't stress too much if you are offered a slightly lower rate than might be expected, since pushing too hard for a good rate carries the risk of weeding out the honest guys so you end up dealing with a con artist And be wary of a quick-talking moneychanger trying to exploit the mind-boggling decimal shifts involved in many African currency transactions

Should you be surrounded by a mob of yelling moneychangers, pick any one of them and tell him that you will only discuss rates when his pals back off. Having agreed a rate, insist on taking the money and counting it before you hand over, or expose the location of, your own money. Should the amount be incorrect, it is almost certainly phase one of an elaborate con trick, so safest to hand it back and refuse to have anything further to do with that person. Alternatively, if you do decide to continue, then recount the money after it is handed back to you and keep doing so until you have the correct amount counted in your hand – some crooked moneychangers possess such sleight of hand they can seemingly add notes to a wad right in front of your eyes while actually removing a far greater number of notes. Only when you are sure you have the right amount should you hand over your money.

rule, readers who are travelling at the middle to upper end of the price range will have pre-booked most of their trip, which means that they will have a good idea of what the holiday will cost them before they set foot in the country. Pre-booked packages do vary in terms of what is included in the price, and you are advised to check the exact conditions in advance, but generally the price quoted will cover everything but drinks, tips and perhaps some meals.

For budget travellers, Rwanda is not the cheapest country in Africa, but it's damn close to it – and after Ghana it offers the best value for money of any country I've visited in the last couple of years. Throughout the country, a soft drink will cost you around US$0.40 and a 700ml beer less than US$1 in a local bar, more in a hotel or restaurant that caters primarily to Westerners. A meal in a local restaurant will cost US$1–2 while a meal in a proper restaurant might cost US$4 upwards (see page 66). Budget accommodation can average out at about US$5 per head, quite often for a self-contained room (two people) with a hot shower or bath. Public transport is cheap – typically about US$1 per 50km – and distances are relatively small. Taking the above figures into account I think that budget travellers could scrape by in most parts of Rwanda on around US$10–15 per day for one person or US$20 per day for two. Double this amount, and within reason you can eat and stay where you like. The above prices assume an exchange rate of around **500 Rwandan francs per dollar**. They will increase if the franc grows stronger, as may well happen.

The above calculations don't allow for more expensive one-off activities, such as gorilla-tracking or visiting the other national parks (not expensive unless you hire a vehicle). If you want to keep to a particular budget and plan on undertaking such activities, you would be well advised to treat your day-to-day budget separately from one-off expenses.

BOOKING A GORILLA PERMIT

The one thing that almost all tourists to Rwanda want to do is track gorillas in Volcanoes National Park, and – unlike when the first edition of this book was researched, in 2000 – it is no longer the case that you can just pitch up in Kigali and be almost certain of obtaining a permit for the next day, or failing that, the day after. Particularly during the peak season of June to September, and again over the Christmas and New Year holiday period, it is now often the case that all 40 gorilla permits available daily are booked up months in advance for several days running – a scenario that is likely to become increasingly normal as greater volumes of tourists visit Rwanda.

What this means is that any visitors with a tight schedule should book their permits as far in advance as possible. If a tour operator arranges your trip, they will also arrange your gorilla permit and will normally include it in the cost of the trip (or specify it as an extra). But if you are travelling independently, you will need to arrange it yourself. There are two approaches to doing this. The first is to get a reliable local tour operator to act as a go-between and buy the permit on your behalf, which can save a lot of hassle but normally means the operator will add a small service charge – typically around US$25 – to the normal cost of US$375 (inclusive of park fees).

The other option is to book directly through ORTPN, which is normally a fairly straightforward procedure. Booking queries can be emailed to reservation@rwandatourism.com (for other contact details see page 61). In order to secure the booking, you will be required to transfer a deposit of at least US$100 per permit a month prior to your tracking date, with the outstanding balance to be paid upon your arrival in Kigali. The best way to pay this is in US dollars cash, but ORTPN accepts cash in most other hard currencies (including sterling and euros) calculated at the official US$ bank rate for the day, as well as travellers' cheques (but with an additional US$20 levied per activity to cover their bank costs). MasterCard can also be used to pay for your gorilla permit (and other fees) at the head office in Kigali, at an additional charge of 4%. Or you can transfer the full amount upfront and save yourself the hassle of paying in Rwanda. It is possible to book (and if you like pay for) any other activities and park entrance fees associated with Volcanoes National Park at the same time.

If you are prepared to take the risk, it does remain possible to pitch up at the ORTPN office in Kigali until 17.00 on the day before you want to track, and – assuming availability – to buy a permit on the spot. And if you are coming from across the Uganda border and want to skip Kigali altogether, you can also buy a permit at the ORTPN office in Musanze (Ruhengeri) or the Volcanoes National Park headquarters at Kinigi at around 17.00–17.30 (when bookings are radioed through from Kigali) on the day before you want to track, or at Kinigi on the morning of departure. There is of course no guarantee that a permit will be available at such short notice, particularly at busy times when there may well already be a waiting list, and you should be aware that the offices in Kinigi and Musanze take cash only.

Rwanda is so small, and all parts of it are so easily accessible from Kigali, that you needn't engage in any complicated planning. Your first port of call should be Kigali, to gather information and to get your **gorilla-viewing permits** from the ORTPN (see page 45). It's sensible not to rush off to the gorillas immediately; take a few days to get the feel of the country and to acclimatise, because the trek can be quite strenuous and the altitude can catch you unawares.

The best **map** available outside Rwanda is currently *Rwanda and Burundi*, scale 1:400,000, published in Canada by International Travel Maps (*www.itmb.com*). There is also *Tanzania, Rwanda and Burundi*, scale 1:1,500,000, published by Nelles Guides & Maps (*www.nelles-verlag.de*). ORTPN sells a tourist map of Rwanda.

All **GPS** readings in this guide are taken with Map Datum set to 'Cape'.

Bear in mind that some towns have been renamed following the administrative reorganisation of provinces in early 2006. At the time of writing, Butare has become Huye and Ruhengeri has become Musanze; more changes seem likely to follow.

Useful **websites** for information on Rwanda are www.rwandatourism.com, www.rwandemb/org (of the Rwandan Embassy in Washington), and www.ambarwanda.org.uk (of the Rwandan Embassy in London), all of which give relevant addresses and contact details and have numerous links. For all-purpose information there is www.rwandagateway.org; and good sites for current news are www.allafrica.com and www.newtimes.co.rw. Finally, www.rwandaphonebook.com is a kind of condensed Yellow Pages, giving phone numbers for hotels, restaurants, businesses etc. Also see *Appendix 2*, page 249.

The international country telephone code for Rwanda is **250**. There are no area codes.

4

Health and Safety

✚ **HEALTH** *with Dr Jane Wilson-Howarth and Dr Felicity Nicholson*

Rwanda itself isn't a particularly unhealthy country for tourists and you'll never be far from some kind of medical help. The main towns have hospitals (for anything serious you'll be more comfortable in Kigali) and all towns of any size have a pharmacy, although the range of medicines on sale may be limited. In Kigali, the pharmacy in Boulevard de la Révolution is open 24 hours.

Outside of Kigali, Rwanda has 34 district hospitals and over 380 health centres spread around the country. A health centre is generally staffed by one or two nurses, supported by medical assistants. In rural areas traditional medicine is also widely used.

The severe shortage of qualified medical personnel – particularly doctors – caused by the targeting of professionals during the genocide has not yet been remedied: there are around 3,900 inhabitants per nurse and 50,000 per doctor. However, the private medical sector is developing fast around the country (particularly in Kigali), and now includes more than 300 private clinics and dispensaries.

The incidence of HIV/AIDS is approximately 14% but hard to estimate accurately.

The guidelines below relate to tropical Africa in general, since travellers may well want to spend time in more than one country.

BEFORE YOU GO As you should for any trip to a tropical or remote area, visit your doctor about eight weeks before leaving for Rwanda to discuss your plans and requirements. Preparations to ensure a healthy trip to anywhere in Africa should include checks on your immunisation status: it is wise to be up to date on tetanus (ten-yearly), polio (ten-yearly), diphtheria (ten-yearly), hepatitis A and typhoid. For many parts of Africa, immunisations against yellow fever, meningococcal meningitis and rabies are also needed.

In Rwanda, as with some other countries in Africa, yellow fever vaccination is required for all travellers over one year old. You are advised to carry the certificate as proof of vaccination as you may need to show it on arrival. This also applies if you arrive from another country where yellow fever is a risk. The certificate is not valid until ten days after your vaccination, so be sure to have this done in good time. This potentially lethal virus (its mortality rate can be up to 50%) is spread by mosquito bites and is currently on the increase worldwide, so keep your vaccination up to date. If you are unable to have the yellow fever vaccination (eg: if you are immuno-compromised, or are allergic to eggs) then you will need to obtain an exemption certificate. This will usually allow you entry into one country, so if you are planning to visit more than one country you will need to check with each embassy as to whether an exemption certificate will be accepted.

Certain countries in sub-Saharan Africa also require a certificate of vaccination for cholera. There is now a more effective oral cholera vaccine (Dukoral) which can be administered if there is a known outbreak or if you are considered at risk. This would apply to people working in poorer rural areas or those with chronic medical conditions. The vaccine is given as two doses at least one week and no more than six weeks apart and should be taken at least one week before entering the area. The vaccine is considered to be effective for up to two years for those aged six years and above. If vaccination is not considered necessary then certificates of exemption can be acquired from immunisation centres. Currently this is not necessary for Rwanda, but seek up-to-date information before you travel.

It is wise to be immunised against hepatitis A (eg: with Havrix Monodose or Avaxim). One dose of vaccine lasts for one year and can be boosted to give protection for up to 20 years. The course of two injections costs about £100. The vaccine can be used even close to the time of departure. Gamma globulin is no longer used as protection for hepatitis A in travellers, since there is a theoretical risk of CJD (the human form of mad cow disease) with this blood-derived product.

The newer typhoid vaccines last for three years and are about 75% effective. They are advisable unless you are leaving within a few days for a trip of a week or less, when the vaccination would not be effective in time.

Vaccinations for rabies are advised for travellers visiting more remote areas. Ideally three injections should be taken over a minimum of three weeks, at 0, 7 and 21 days. The timing of these doses can be extended if you have allowed more time. (see *Rabies*, page 57).

Hepatitis B vaccination should be considered for longer trips (two months or more), or if you'll be working with children or in situations where contact with blood is increased. Three injections are ideal: they can be given at 0, 4 and 8 weeks prior to travel or, if there is insufficient time, then on days 0, 7–14, then 21–28. At the time of writing, the only vaccine licensed for the latter more rapid course is Engerix B and then only for those aged 18 or over. The longer course is always to be preferred as immunity is likely to be longer lasting. In both cases a booster dose after a year would be advised.

A BCG vaccination against tuberculosis (TB) is also advisable for trips of two months or more. This should be taken at least six weeks before travel.

Malaria prevention Malaria is probably the greatest health risk to travellers in Rwanda, although it is less prevalent there than in some other African countries. There is no vaccine against malaria, but using prophylactic drugs and preventing mosquito bites will considerably reduce the risk of contracting it. Seek professional advice to ascertain the preferred anti-malarial drugs for Rwanda at the time you travel. Mefloquine (Lariam) is still the most effective prophylactic agent for most countries in sub-Saharan Africa. If this drug is suggested then you should start taking it at least two and a half weeks before departure to check that it suits you. Stop immediately if it seems to cause depression or anxiety, visual or hearing disturbances, fits, severe headaches or changes in heart rhythm. Anyone who is pregnant, has been treated for depression or psychiatric problems, has diabetes controlled by oral therapy, or who is epileptic (or has suffered fits in the past) or has a close blood relative who is epileptic should not take mefloquine. Malarone is another very effective alternative if mefloquine is not recommended, but it is quite expensive and therefore is more suited to shorter trips. It is currently licensed in the UK for trips of up to three months. It is taken once a day, starting two days before arriving into a malarial area, whilst you are there and for seven days after leaving (unlike other regimes, which need to be continued for four weeks after leaving). It is well tolerated and, unlike mefloquine, can be used by people with depression and/or epilepsy. There is also a paediatric form of Malarone, which can be used for children weighing more than 11kg. The number of tablets given is calculated by weight so it is helpful to know the weight of any children under 40kg travelling with you.

The antibiotic doxycycline (100mg daily) is almost as effective as mefloquine and Malarone and is much cheaper than the latter so may be more cost-effective for longer trips. Like Malarone, it need only be started one to two days before travel but, like mefloquine, must be taken for four weeks after leaving. It may also be used by travellers with epilepsy, although anti-epileptic therapy may make it less effective. Also there is a possibility of allergic skin reactions developing in sunlight; this can occur in about 1–3% of users. The drug should be stopped if this happens, as there is a risk of more serious allergic reactions. You should then seek medical advice as soon as is practical as to what to do next. Women using the oral contraceptive should use an additional method of protection.

Chloroquine and paludrine should no longer be used for this part of Africa except as a last resort.

Some travellers like to take a treatment for malaria, as well as prophylaxis if they are travelling for more than six months. Whatever you decide, you should take up-to-date advice to find out the most appropriate medication.

There is no malaria transmission above 3,000m; at intermediate altitudes (1,800–3,000m) the risk exists but is low.

In addition to taking anti-malarial medicines, it is important to avoid mosquito bites between dusk and dawn, which is when the *anopheles* (malaria-carrying) mosquito is most active. Pack a DEET-based insect repellent, such as one of the Repel range, and take either a permethrin-impregnated bednet or a permethrin spray so that you can treat bednets in hotels. Permethrin treatment makes even very tatty nets protective and mosquitoes are also unable to bite through the impregnated net when you roll against it. Putting on long clothes (including long-sleeved shirts or blouses) at dusk means you can reduce the amount of repellent needed; but be aware that malaria mosquitoes hunt at ankle level and will penetrate through socks, so apply repellent to your feet and ankles too. Travel clinics usually sell a good range of nets, treatment kits and repellents.

Important While you are away, assume that any high fever lasting more than a few hours is malaria, regardless of any other symptoms. Always seek medical help. And remember that malaria may occur anything from seven days into your trip to up to one year after leaving Africa. If symptoms appear after you have returned home, visit your doctor immediately, and mention that you have been travelling in a malarial area.

Travel clinics and health information A full list of current travel clinic websites worldwide is available from the International Society of Travel Medicine on www.istm.org. For other journey preparation information, consult www.tripprep.com. Information about various medications may be found on www.emedicine.com. For information on malaria prevention, see www.preventingmalaria.info.

UK

Berkeley Travel Clinic 32 Berkeley St, London W1J 8EL (near Green Park tube station); ☏ 020 7629 6233
British Airways Travel Clinic and Immunisation Service 213 Piccadilly, London W1J 9HQ; ☏ 0845 600 2236; www.ba.com/travelclinics. The clinic offers a walk-in service (no appointment necessary), open Mon, Tue, Wed, Fri 08.45–18.15, Thu 08.45–20.00, Sat 09.30–17.00. Apart from providing inoculations and malaria prevention, they sell a variety of health-related goods.

Cambridge Travel Clinic 48a Mill Rd, Cambridge CB1 2AS; ☎ 01223 367362; ✉ enquiries@ cambridgetravelclinic.co.uk; www.cambridgetravelclinic.co.uk. Open Tue–Fri 12.00–19.00, Sat 10.00–16.00.

Edinburgh Travel Clinic Regional Infectious Diseases Unit, Ward 41 OPD, Western General Hospital, Crewe Rd South, Edinburgh EH4 2UX; ☎ 0131 537 2822; www.link.med.ed.ac.uk/ridu. Travel helpline (0906 589 0380) open weekdays 09.00–12.00. Provides inoculations and antimalarial prophylaxis and advises on travel-related health risks.

Fleet Street Travel Clinic 29 Fleet St, London EC4Y 1AA; ☎ 020 7353 5678; www.fleetstreetclinic.com. Vaccinations, travel products and latest advice.

Hospital for Tropical Diseases Travel Clinic Mortimer Market Building, Capper St (off Tottenham Ct Rd), London WC1E 6AU; ☎ 020 7388 9600; www.thehtd.org. Offers consultations and advice, and is able to provide all necessary drugs and vaccines for travellers. Runs a healthline (0906 133 7733) for country-specific information and health hazards. Also stocks nets, water purification equipment and personal protection measures.

Interhealth Worldwide Partnership House, 157 Waterloo Rd, London SE1 8US; ☎ 020 7902 9000; www.interhealth.org.uk. Competitively priced, one-stop travel health service. All profits go to their affiliated company, InterHealth, which provides health care for overseas workers on Christian projects.

MASTA (Medical Advisory Service for Travellers Abroad) London School of Hygiene and Tropical Medicine, Keppel St, London WC1 7HT; ☎ 0906 550 1402; www.masta.org. Individually tailored health briefs available for a fee, with up-to-date information on how to stay healthy, inoculations and what to bring. There are currently 30 MASTA pre-travel clinics in Britain. Call 0870 241 6843 or check online for the nearest. Clinics also sell malaria prophylaxis memory cards, treatment kits, bednets, net treatment kits.

NHS travel website www.fitfortravel.scot.nhs.uk. Provides country-by-country advice on immunisation and malaria, plus details of recent developments, and a list of relevant health organisations.

Nomad Travel Store/Clinic 3–4 Wellington Terrace, Turnpike Lane, London N8 0PX; ☎ 020 8889 7014; travel-health line (office hours only) 0906 863 3414; ✉ sales@nomadtravel.co.uk; www.nomadtravel.co.uk. Also at 40 Bernard St, London WC1N 1LJ; ☎ 020 7833 4114; 52 Grosvenor Gardens, London SW1W 0AG; ☎ 020 7823 5823; and 43 Queens Rd, Bristol BS8 1QH; ☎ 0117 922 6567. For health advice, equipment such as mosquito nets and other anti-bug devices, and an excellent range of adventure travel gear.

Trailfinders Travel Clinic 194 Kensington High St, London W8 7RG; ☎ 020 7938 3999; www.trailfinders.com/clinic.htm

Travelpharm The Travelpharm website, www.travelpharm.com, offers up-to-date guidance on travel-related health and has a range of medications available through their online mini-pharmacy.

Irish Republic

Tropical Medical Bureau Grafton Street Medical Centre, Grafton Buildings, 34 Grafton St, Dublin 2; ☎ 1 671 9200; www.tmb.ie. A useful website specific to tropical destinations. Also check website for other bureaux locations throughout Ireland.

USA

Centers for Disease Control 1600 Clifton Rd, Atlanta, GA 30333; ☎ 800 311 3435; travellers' health hotline 888 232 3299; www.cdc.gov/travel. The central source of travel information in the USA. The invaluable *Health Information for International Travel*, published annually, is available from the Division of Quarantine at this address.

Connaught Laboratories PO Box 187, Swiftwater, PA 18370; ☎ 800 822 2463. They will send a free list of specialist tropical-medicine physicians in your state.

IAMAT (International Association for Medical Assistance to Travelers) 1623 Military Rd, 279, Niagara Falls, NY14304-1745; ☎ 716 754 4883; ✉ info@iamat.org; www.iamat.org. A non-profit organisation that provides lists of English-speaking doctors abroad.

International Medicine Center 920 Frostwood Drive, Suite 670, Houston, TX 77024; ☎ 713 550 2000; www.traveldoc.com

Canada

IAMAT Suite 1, 1287 St Clair Av W, Toronto, Ontario M6E 1B8; ☎ 416 652 0137; www.iamat.org

TMVC Suite 314, 1030 W Georgia St, Vancouver BC V6E 2Y3; ☎ 1 888 288 8682; www.tmvc.com

TMVC ☏ 1300 65 88 44; www.tmvc.com.au. 31 clinics in Australia, New Zealand and Singapore, including: *Auckland* Canterbury Arcade, 170 Queen St, Auckland; ☏ 9 373 3531 *Brisbane* 6th floor, 247 Adelaide St, Brisbane, QLD 4000; ☏ 7 3221 9066

Melbourne 393 Little Bourke St, 2nd floor, Melbourne, VIC 3000; ☏ 3 9602 5788 *Sydney* Dymocks Bldg, 7th floor, 428 George St, Sydney, NSW 2000; ☏ 2 9221 7133 **IAMAT** PO Box 5049, Christchurch 5, New Zealand; www.iamat.org

South Africa and Namibia

SAA-Netcare Travel Clinics P Bag X34, Benmore 2010; www.travelclinic.co.za. Clinics throughout South Africa. **TMVC** 113 D F Malan Drive, Roosevelt Park,

Johannesburg; ☏ 011 888 7488; www.tmvc.com.au. Consult website for details of other clinics in South Africa and Namibia.

Switzerland

IAMAT 57 Chemin des Voirets, 1212 Grand Lancy, Geneva; www.iamat.org

Travel insurance Before you travel, make sure that you have adequate medical insurance – choose a policy with comprehensive cover for hospitalisation as well as for repatriation in an emergency. Nowadays the range of cover available is very wide – choose whatever suits your method of travel. Be aware (if you plan to use motorbike taxis in Rwanda) that not all policies cover you for this form of transport. Remember to take all the details with you, particularly your policy number and the telephone number that you have to contact in the event of a claim.

Personal first-aid kit The more I travel the less I take. My minimal kit contains:

- a good drying antiseptic, eg: iodine or potassium permanganate (don't take antiseptic cream)
- a few small dressings (Band-Aids)
- sunscreen
- insect repellent; malaria tablets; impregnated bednet
- aspirin or paracetamol
- antifungal cream (eg: Canesten)
- Ciprofloxacin antibiotic (take 500mg followed by a second tablet six to twelve hours later for diarrhoea with blood and/or slime and or a fever. Norfloxacin may be prescribed as an alternative in countries outside the UK.
- Tinidazole (2g taken in one dose then repeat seven days later) for amoebic dysentery or giardiasis
- another broad-spectrum antibiotic like amoxycillin (for chest, urine, skin infections, etc) if going to a remote area
- pair of fine-pointed tweezers (to remove hairy-caterpillar hairs, thorns, splinters etc)
- condoms or femidoms
- possibly a malaria treatment kit
- a travel thermometer (not containing mercury; airlines ban these)

COMMON MEDICAL PROBLEMS

Travellers' diarrhoea At least half of those travelling to the tropics/developing world will experience a bout of travellers' diarrhoea during their trip; the newer you are to exotic travel, the more likely you will be to suffer. By taking precautions against travellers' diarrhoea you will also avoid typhoid, cholera, hepatitis, dysentery, worms, etc.

Health and Safety HEALTH

4

Dr Jane Wilson-Howarth

It is dehydration which makes you feel awful during a bout of diarrhoea and the most important part of treatment is drinking lots of clear fluids. Sachets of oral rehydration salts give the perfect biochemical mix to replace all that is pouring out of your bottom but they do not taste nice. Any dilute mixture of sugar and salt in water will do you good, so if you like Coke or orange squash, drink that with a three-finger pinch of salt added to each glass. Otherwise make a solution of a four-finger scoop of sugar with a three-finger pinch of salt in a glass of water. Or add eight level teaspoons of sugar (18g) and one level teaspoon of salt (3g) to one litre (five cups) of safe water. A squeeze of lemon or orange juice improves the taste and adds potassium, which is also lost during a bout of diarrhoea. Drink two large glasses after every bowel action, and more if you are thirsty. If you are not eating, then you need to drink three litres a day plus the equivalent of whatever is pouring into the toilet. If you feel like eating, take a bland, high-carbohydrate diet. Heavy, greasy foods will probably give you cramps.

If the diarrhoea is bad, or you are passing blood or slime, or you have a fever, you will probably need antibiotics in addition to fluid replacement. A three-day course of Ciprofloxacin 500mg twice daily (or Norfloxacin) is appropriate treatment for dysentery and bad diarrhoea. If the diarrhoea is greasy and bulky and is accompanied by 'eggy' burps, the likely cause is giardia. This is best treated with Tinidazole (2g in one dose repeated seven days later if symptoms persist).

From food Travellers' diarrhoea and the other faecal-oral diseases come from getting other peoples' faeces in your mouth. This most often happens from cooks not washing their hands after a trip to the toilet, but even if the restaurant cook does not understand basic hygiene you will be safe if your food has been properly cooked and arrives piping hot. The maxim to remind you what you can safely eat is:

PEEL IT, BOIL IT, COOK IT OR FORGET IT.

This means that fruit you have washed and peeled yourself, and hot foods, should be safe, but raw foods, cold cooked foods, salads, fruit salads prepared by others, ice cream and ice are all risky, as are foods kept lukewarm in restaurant or hotel buffets. Self-service or buffet meals are popular in Rwanda, so try to eat these when the food is hot and freshly cooked – for example a late buffet lunch eaten in mid-afternoon will have been sitting around a long while. If you do get travellers' diarrhoea, see box above for treatment.

From water It is also possible to get sick from drinking contaminated water, so try to drink from safe sources. Tap water is supposedly safe in Kigali but not elsewhere in Rwanda. To make risky water safe it should be brought to the boil (even at altitude it only needs to be brought to the boil), passed through a good bacteriological filter or purified with iodine; chlorine tablets (eg: Puritabs) are also adequate although theoretically less effective, and they taste nastier. Micropur tablets are tasteless but take at least two hours to become effective. If you buy bottled water (which is widely available in Rwanda) make sure the seal is intact. Iodine is not recommended in pregnancy so you should ask a doctor what you should do.

Dengue fever This mosquito-borne disease resembles malaria but there is no prophylactic available to deal with it. The mosquitoes which carry this virus bite during the daytime, so it is worth applying repellent if you see them around.

Symptoms include strong headaches, rashes and excruciating joint and muscle pains with high fever. Dengue fever lasts for only a week or so and is not usually fatal if you have not previously been infected. Complete rest and paracetamol are the usual treatment. Plenty of fluids also help. Some patients are given an intravenous drip to keep them from dehydrating.

Insect bites It is crucial to avoid mosquito bites between dusk and dawn; as the sun is going down, don long clothes and apply repellent on any exposed flesh. This will protect you from malaria, elephantiasis and a range of nasty insect-borne viruses. Malaria **mosquitoes** are voracious, hunt at ankle-level, and can penetrate through socks. Sleep under a permethrin-treated bednet or in an air-conditioned room. During the day it is wise to wear long, loose (preferably 100% cotton) clothes if you are pushing through scrubby country; this will deter **ticks** as well as **tsetse flies** and day-biting *Aedes* mosquitoes which may spread dengue and yellow fever. Tsetse flies hurt when they bite and are attracted to the colour blue; locals will advise on where they are a problem and where they transmit sleeping sickness.

Minute pestilential biting **blackflies** spread river blindness in some parts of Africa between 190°N and 170°S; the disease is caught close to fast-flowing rivers since flies breed there and the larvae live in rapids. The flies bite during the day but long trousers tucked into socks will help keep them off. Citronella-based natural repellents do not work against them.

Tumbu flies or *putsi* are a problem in areas of eastern, western and southern Africa where the climate is hot and humid. The adult fly lays her eggs on the soil or on drying laundry and when the eggs come in contact with human flesh (when you put on clothes or lie on a bed) they hatch and bury themselves under the skin. Here they form a crop of 'boils' each of which hatches a grub after about eight days, when the inflammation will settle down. In *putsi* areas either dry your clothes and sheets within a screened house, or dry them in direct sunshine until they are crisp, or iron them.

Jiggers or **sandfleas** are another kind of flesh-feaster. They latch on if you walk barefoot in contaminated places, and set up home under the skin of the foot, usually at the side of a toenail where they cause a painful, boil-like swelling. These need picking out by a local expert; if the distended flea bursts during eviction the wound should be dowsed in spirit, alcohol or kerosene, otherwise more jiggers will infest you.

QUICK TICK REMOVAL

Dr Jane Wilson-Howarth

African ticks are not the prolific disease transmitters they are in the Americas, but they may occasionally spread disease. Lyme disease, which can have unpleasant after-effects, has now been recorded in Africa, and tick-bite fever also occurs. The latter is a mild, flu-like illness, but still worth avoiding. If you get the tick off whole and promptly the chances of disease transmission are reduced to a minimum.

Manoeuvre your finger and thumb so that you can pinch the tick's mouthparts, as close to your skin as possible, and slowly and steadily pull away at right angles to your skin. This often hurts. Jerking or twisting will increase the chances of damaging the tick which in turn increases the chances of disease transmission, as well as leaving the mouthparts behind.

Once the tick is off, dowse the little wound with alcohol (local spirit, whisky or similar is excellent) or iodine. An area of spreading redness around the bite site, or a rash or fever coming on a few days or more after the bite, should stimulate a trip to a doctor.

Dr Jane Wilson-Howarth

Long-haul air travel increases the risk of deep vein thrombosis. Although recent research has suggested that many of us develop clots when immobilised, most resolve without us ever having been aware of them. In certain susceptible individuals, though, large clots form and these can break away and lodge in the lungs. This is dangerous but happens in a tiny minority of passengers.

Studies have shown that flights of over five-and-a-half-hours are significant, and that people who take lots of shorter flights over a short space of time form clots. People at highest risk are:

- Those who have had a clot before – unless they are now taking warfarin
- People over 80 years of age
- Anyone who has recently undergone a major operation or surgery for varicose veins
- Someone who has had a hip or knee replacement in the last three months
- Cancer sufferers
- Those who have ever had a stroke
- People with heart disease
- Those with a close blood relative who has had a clot

Those with a slightly increased risk:

- People over 40
- Women who are pregnant or have had a baby in the last couple of weeks
- People taking female hormones or other oestrogen therapy
- Heavy smokers
- Those who have very severe varicose veins
- The very obese
- People who are very tall (over 6ft/1.8m) or short (under 5ft/1.5m)

Bilharzia or schistosomiasis

With thanks to Dr Vaughan Southgate of the Natural History Museum, London

Bilharzia or schistosomiasis is a disease that commonly afflicts the rural poor of the tropics who repeatedly acquire more and more of these nasty little worm-lodgers. Infected travellers and expatriates generally suffer fewer problems because symptoms will encourage them to seek prompt treatment and they are also exposed to fewer parasites. However, it is still an unpleasant problem that is worth avoiding.

The parasites digest their way through your skin when you wade, bathe or even shower in infested freshwater. Unfortunately many African lakes, rivers and irrigation canals carry a risk of bilharzia. In Rwanda, the bathing areas of Lake Kivu are currently said to be safe.

The most risky shores will be close to places where infected people use water, where they wash clothes, etc. Winds disperse the cercariae, though, so they can be blown some distance, perhaps up to 200m from where they entered the water. Scuba-diving off a boat into deep offshore water, then, should be a low-risk activity, but showering in lake water or paddling along a reedy lake shore near a village carries a high risk of acquiring bilharzia.

Although absence of early symptoms does not necessarily mean there is no infection, infected people usually notice symptoms two or more weeks after penetration. Travellers and expatriates will probably experience a fever and often a wheezy cough; local residents do not usually have symptoms.

There is now a very good blood test which, if done six weeks or more after likely

A deep vein thrombosis (DVT) is a blood clot that forms in the deep leg veins. This is very different from irritating but harmless superficial phlebitis. DVT causes swelling and redness of one leg, usually with heat and pain in one calf and sometimes the thigh. A DVT is only dangerous if a clot breaks away and travels to the lungs (pulmonary embolus). Symptoms of a pulmonary embolus (PE) include chest pain that is worse on breathing in deeply, shortness of breath, and sometimes coughing up small amounts of blood. The symptoms commonly start three to ten days after a long flight. Anyone who thinks that they might have a DVT needs to see a doctor immediately who will arrange a scan. Warfarin tablets (to thin the blood) are then taken for at least six months.

PREVENTION OF DVT Several conditions make the problem more likely. Immobility is the key, and factors like reduced oxygen in cabin air and dehydration may also contribute. To reduce the risk of thrombosis on a long journey:

- Exercise before and after the flight
- Keep mobile before and during the flight; move around every couple of hours
- During the flight drink plenty of water or juices
- Avoid taking sleeping pills and excessive tea, coffee and alcohol
- Perform exercises that mimic walking and tense the calf muscles
- Consider wearing flight socks or support stockings (see www.legshealth.com)
- Taking a meal of oily fish (mackerel, trout, salmon, sardines, etc) in the 24 hours before departure reduces blood clotability and thus DVT risk
- The jury is still out on whether it is worth taking an aspirin before flying, but this can be discussed with your GP.

If you think you are at increased risk of a clot, ask your doctor if it is safe to travel.

exposure, will determine whether or not parasites are going to cause problems, and then the infection can be treated. While treatment generally remains effective, it does fail in some cases for reasons that are not yet fully understood; retreatment seems to work fine and it is not known if some drug resistance is developing. Since bilharzia can be a nasty illness, avoidance is better than waiting to be cured and it is wise to avoid bathing in high-risk areas. Take local advice about this.

Avoiding bilharzia If you are bathing, swimming, paddling or wading in freshwater which you think may carry a bilharzia risk, try to stay in no longer than ten minutes. Afterwards dry off thoroughly with a towel; rub vigorously. Avoid bathing or paddling on shores within 200m of villages or places where people use the water a great deal, especially reedy shores or where there is lots of water weed. Covering yourself with DEET insect repellent before swimming will help to protect you. If your bathing water comes from a risky source try to ensure that the water is taken from the lake in the early morning and stored snail-free, otherwise it should be filtered or Dettol or Cresol should be added. Bathing early in the morning is safer than bathing in the last half of the day. If you think that you have been exposed to bilharzia parasites, arrange a screening blood test (your GP can do this) *more* than six weeks after your last possible contact with suspect water.

Skin infections Any mosquito bite or small nick in the skin provides an opportunity for bacteria to foil the body's usually excellent defences; it will surprise many travellers how quickly skin infections start in warm humid climates and it is essential to clean and cover even the slightest wound. Creams are not as effective as a good drying antiseptic such as dilute iodine, potassium permanganate (a few crystals in half a cup of water), or crystal (or gentian) violet. One of these should be available in most towns. If the wound starts to throb, or becomes red and the redness starts to spread, or the wound oozes, and especially if you develop a fever, antibiotics will probably be needed; flucloxacillin (250mg four times a day) or cloxacillin (500mg four times a day). For those allergic to penicillin, erythromycin (500mg twice a day) for five days should help. See a doctor if the symptoms do not start to improve in 48 hours.

Fungal infections also get a hold easily in hot moist climates so wear 100% cotton socks and underwear and shower frequently. An itchy rash in the groin or flaking between the toes is likely to be a fungal infection. This needs treatment with an antifungal cream such as Canesten (clotrimazole); if this is not available try Whitfield's ointment (compound enzoic acid ointment) or crystal violet (although this will turn you purple!).

Prickly heat A fine pimply rash on the torso is likely to be heat rash; cool showers, dabbing (not rubbing) dry, and talc will help; if it's bad you may need to check into an air-conditioned hotel room for a while. Slowing down to a relaxed schedule, wearing only loose, baggy 100% cotton clothes and sleeping naked under a fan reduce the problem.

Sun damage The incidence of skin cancer is rocketing as Caucasians are travelling more and spending more time in the sun. Keep out of the sun during the middle of the day and, if you must expose yourself, build up gradually from 20 minutes per day. Be especially careful of sun reflected off water and wear a T-shirt and lots of waterproof SPF 15 suncream when swimming and Bermuda shorts to protect the back of your thighs when snorkelling. Sun exposure ages the skin and causes premature wrinkles; cover up with long loose clothes and wear a hat when you can.

Meningitis This is a particularly nasty disease as it can kill within hours of the first symptoms appearing. The telltale symptoms are a combination of a blinding headache (light sensitivity), a blotchy rash and a high fever. Immunisation with the newer tetravalent vaccine ACWY protects against the most serious bacterial form of meningitis and is usually recommended for longer-stay trips to Rwanda or if you are working closely with the local population – in particular with children. A single injection gives good protection for three years. Other forms of meningitis exist (usually viral) but there are no vaccines for these. Local papers normally report outbreaks. If you show symptoms go immediately to a doctor.

Sexual risks Travel is a time when we may enjoy sexual adventures, especially when alcohol reduces inhibitions. Remember the risks of sexually transmitted infection are high, whether you sleep with fellow travellers or with locals. About 40% of HIV infections in British heterosexuals are acquired abroad and AIDS is a serious problem in Rwanda. Use condoms or femidoms, preferably bearing the British kite mark and ideally bought before travel. If you notice any genital ulcers or discharge get treatment promptly.

EBOLA So far this has never occurred in Rwanda, but it has claimed some lives in Uganda. It is a rare, but deadly, highly contagious, virally induced disease which causes haemorrhagic fever. In the unlikely event of an outbreak, protective measures will be taken and you should follow whatever local advice is given.

USEFUL CONTACTS IN KIGALI

Central Hospital of Kigali ☎ 575555
King Faycal Hospital (Kigali) ☎ 82421
Sun City Pharmacy Bd de la Révolution. Open 24 hours.

Pharmacie Conseil Av des Mille Collines (opposite Belgian School). Open 08.00–21.00 Mon–Sat; 10.00–15.00 Sun.

ANIMALS

Rabies Rabies can be carried by all mammals and is passed on to man through a bite, scratch or a lick of an open wound. You must always assume any animal is rabid (unless personally known to you). The closer the bite is to the face the shorter the incubation time of the disease, but it is always wise to get medical help as soon as possible. In the interim, scrub the wound with soap and bottled/boiled water, then pour on a strong iodine or alcohol solution. This helps stop the rabies virus entering the body and will guard against wound infections including tetanus. If you intend to have contact with animals and/or are likely to be more than 24 hours away from medical help, then pre-exposure vaccination is advised. Ideally three doses should be taken over a minimum of three weeks. Contrary to popular belief these vaccinations are relatively painless! If you are exposed as described, then treatment should be given as soon as possible, but it is never too late to seek help as the incubation period for rabies can be very long.

Those who have not been immunised will need a full course of injections together with rabies immunoglobulin (RIG), but this product is expensive (around US$800) and may be hard to come by – which is a reason why pre-exposure vaccination should be encouraged in travellers who are planning to visit more remote areas. Tell the doctor if you have had pre-exposure vaccine as this will change the treatment you receive. Remember that if you do contract rabies, mortality is 100% and death from rabies is probably one of the worst ways to go!

Snakebite Snakes rarely attack unless provoked and bites to travellers are unusual. You are less likely to get bitten if you wear stout shoes and long trousers when in the bush. Most snakes are harmless and even venomous species will only dispense venom in about half of their bites. If bitten, then, you are unlikely to have received venom; keeping this fact in mind may help you to stay calm. Many so-called first-aid techniques do more harm than good: cutting into the wound is harmful; tourniquets are dangerous; suction and electrical inactivation devices do not work. The only treatment is antivenom. In case of a bite which you fear may have been from a venomous snake:

- Try to keep calm – it is likely that no venom has been dispensed.
- Prevent movement of the bitten limb by applying a splint.
- Keep the bitten limb BELOW heart height to slow the spread of any venom.
- If you have a crepe bandage, bind up as much of the bitten limb as you can, but release the bandage every half hour.
- Evacuate to a hospital which has antivenom.

And remember:

- NEVER give aspirin; you may offer paracetamol, which is safe.
- NEVER cut or suck the wound.
- DO NOT apply ice packs.
- DO NOT apply potassium permanganate.

If the offending snake can be captured without risk of someone else being bitten, take it to show to the doctor – but beware, since even a decapitated head is able to dispense venom in a reflex bite.

Health and Safety **HEALTH**

4

FURTHER READING Self-prescribing has its hazards so, if you are going anywhere remoter than Rwanda, or if you like to have facts at your fingertips, then consider taking a health guide. For adults there is *Bugs, Bites & Bowels: The Cadogan Guide to Healthy Travel* by Jane Wilson-Howarth (1999); if travelling with children look at *Your Child's Health Abroad: A Manual for Travelling Parents* by Jane Wilson-Howarth and Matthew Ellis, published by Bradt Publications in 1998.

SAFETY

THEFT The following security hints are applicable anywhere in Africa:

- Most casual thieves operate in busy markets and bus stations. Keep a close watch on your possessions in such places, and avoid having valuables or large amounts of money loose in your daypack or pocket.
- Keep all your valuables and the bulk of your money in a hidden money belt. Never show this money belt in public. Keep any spare cash you need elsewhere on your person – a button-up pocket on the front of the shirt is a good place as money cannot be snatched from it without the thief coming into your view. It is also advisable to keep a small amount of hard currency (ideally cash) hidden in your luggage in case you lose your money belt.
- Where the choice exists between carrying valuables on your person or leaving them in a locked room I would tend to favour the latter option (thefts from locked hotel rooms are relatively rare in Africa). Obviously you should use your judgement on this and be sure the room is absolutely secure. Bear in mind that some travellers' cheque companies will not refund cheques which were stolen from a room.
- Leave any jewellery of financial or sentimental value at home.

Useful contact
Police ☏ 08311117

OTHER HAZARDS People new to exotic travel often worry about tropical diseases, but it is accidents which are most likely to carry you off. Road travel isn't as dangerous in Rwanda as in some other African countries but still accidents aren't uncommon, and the number of vehicles is increasing; so be aware and do what you can to reduce risks. For example, try to travel during daylight hours and refuse to be driven by anyone who is drunk. Always heed local advice about where you should (or should not) travel, or about areas where you should take particular care. At the time of writing, Rwanda is a relatively safe country – but, sadly, it has been seen elsewhere that an increase in tourism can lead to an increase in opportunistic crime. Be as sensible in Rwanda as (I hope!) you would be in any other strange country about carrying your cash discreetly and not flaunting jewellery, and (particularly in towns) about where you walk after dark. Also be sensible in hotels and guesthouses: don't leave tempting items too readily accessible.

5

Travelling in Rwanda

TOURIST INFORMATION AND SERVICES

The **Office Rwandais du Tourisme et des Parcs Nationaux**, more commonly referred to as ORTPN (*Or-ti-pen),* doubles as both tourist office and national parks authority. The ORTPN offices in the airport arrivals hall and in central Kigali stock a fair range of booklets and maps, and are the best places to seek out current information relating to the national parks and other reserves. The office in central Kigali (Boulevard de la Révolution at its junction with Avenue de l'Armée) handles advance bookings and issues permits for gorilla-tracking and other activities in the Volcanoes National Park (see box *Booking a gorilla permit,* page 45). It's open 07.00–17.00, Monday-Friday; 08.00–14.00 weekends and holidays. Permits can sometimes – depending on availability – also be bought at the ORTPN office in Musanze (formerly Ruhengeri; see *Place names,* page 69), but check in Kigali first.

ORTPN (*BP 905 Kigali;* ✆ *573396, 576514;* f *576515;* e *info@rwandatourism.com, reservation@rwandatourism.com; www.rwandatourism.com*) can also provide details of hotels around the country, as well as lists of car-hire agencies in Kigali, tour operators, public transport and local events. It's best to call in personally.

Two bookshops in central Kigali with a reasonable stock of guidebooks and maps, as well as a wide selection of background reading, are the **Librairie Caritas** near the GPO, and the **Librairie Ikirezi** in Avenue de la Paix. (Remember that in French *librairie* means bookshop; lending library is *bibliothèque*.)

Tour operators and travel agents (see pages 37–9) are also sources of local information.

PUBLIC HOLIDAYS AND EVENTS

In addition to the following fixed public holidays, Rwanda recognises Good Friday and Easter Monday.

1 January	New Year's Day	15 August	Assumption Day
1 February	National Heroes' Day	25 September	Republic Day
7 April	Genocide Memorial Day	1 October	Patriots' Day
1 May	Labour Day	1 November	All Saints' Day
1 July	Independence Day	25 December	Christmas Day
4 July	National Liberation Day		

The week around Genocide Memorial Day is an official week of mourning during which commemorative ceremonies are held and some activities may be reduced.

Two public events may draw crowds large enough to affect the availability of accommodation in some areas: the International Peace Marathon and Fun Run held annually in and around Kigali in May (see www.kigalimarathon.com and page 110), and the Gorilla Naming Ceremony held near the Volcanoes National Park in June (details from the ORTPN and on page 212).

The last Saturday of the month is Public Cleaning Day and some businesses may be closed.

$ MONEY

The unit of currency is the Rwandan franc (Rfr). In 2006, the exchange rate against the dollar was around Rfr550, depending on whether the transaction involved cash or travellers' cheques, and where it took place. In Rwanda more than most African countries, the US dollar is by far the most widely recognised foreign currency, though the euro increasingly runs it a close second. Except in Kigali, US dollars cash is the only foreign currency easily exchangeable outside of banks.

FOREIGN EXCHANGE All Rwandan banks have branches in Kigali and there's at least one bank in each other main town. There are also several private bureaux de change (known locally as forex bureaux) in the capital, which generally offer slightly better rates than banks against cash, not to mention a quicker service, but don't handle travellers' cheques. The street traders who once proliferated around the post office in central Kigali have been illegalised. There are also private forex bureaux in several other large towns, particularly those that lie close to a border crossing (eg: Musanze (Ruhengeri), Gisenyi and Cyangugu) and banks in the likes of Huye (formerly Butare) and Gitarama, but they will generally deal in cash only and rates tend to be poorer than in the capital.

Banking hours are from approximately 08.00 to 12.00 and 14.00 to 17.00 Monday to Friday (some banks stay open longer), and 08.00 to 12.00 Saturday. Private forex bureaux keep slightly longer hours than banks. Both are closed on Sundays and public holidays.

The situation with credit cards is bad at present but may improve (see page 43). Don't be misled by the gleaming ATMs you may see around Kigali – they accept only cards issued by a local bank (the BCDI). If your budgeting has fallen apart and you need a rescue transfer from home, there are Western Union facilities at the Banque Commerciale du Rwanda, and Moneygram facilities (accessed via any branch of Thomas Cook in the UK) at the Banque Continentale Africaine Rwanda, both in Boulevard de la Révolution in Kigali. Western Union has various other offices in Kigali (including at the Novotel) and in all main towns.

PRICES IN THIS BOOK Most services in Rwanda are best paid for in local currency. The exceptions are gorilla-tracking fees and some upmarket hotels, which charge in US dollars. Throughout this guide, prices are quoted in local currency except where the institution in question quotes rates in another currency such as US dollars or euro. Prices were correct as of early 2006, but – as anywhere – may be subject to inflation during the lifespan of this edition.

GETTING AROUND

✈ BY AIR Rwandair Express (see page 35) operates regular thrice-weekly flights between Kigali and Cyangugu. There has been talk of privately run helicopter links from Kigali to Akagera and Musanze (formerly Ruhengeri), but nothing is up and running at the time of writing.

🚗 SELF-DRIVE Several travel agencies in Kigali rent out saloons and 4x4s, with or without drivers. For their contact details see *Chapter 6,* page 111. Further up-to-date listings are given in the tourism section of the Rwanda website www.rwandatourism.com; also you can get details from ORTPN in Kigali. Rates vary according to whether you'll be driving outside Kigali, and whether fuel is included. A 4x4 can cost from US$100 to US$150 per day including driver, depending on its type/size. If the deal excludes fuel, bear in mind that this is not cheap – the equivalent of around US$1 per litre – and that most 4x4s have a heavy consumption.

If you rent a self-drive vehicle, be aware that Rwanda follows the continental custom of driving on the right side of the road. Check the vehicle over carefully and ask to take it for a test drive. Even if you're not knowledgeable about the working of engines, a few minutes on the road should be sufficient to establish whether it has any seriously disturbing creaks, rattles or other noises. Check the condition of the tyres and that there is at least one spare tyre, better two, both in a condition to be used should the need present itself. Ask to be shown the wheel spanner and jack, check that all parts of the latter are present, and ensure that the licence is valid for the duration of your trip. Ask also to be shown filling points for oil, water and petrol and check that all the keys do what they are supposed to do. Once on the road, check oil and water regularly in the early stages of the trip to ensure that there are no existing leaks. See also the box *Driving into Rwanda*, page 37, for further survival tips.

Most trunk roads in Rwanda are surfaced and in reasonable condition, including the main road from Kigali to Cyangugu via Huye (Butare); to Gisenyi via Musanze (Ruhengeri); to Rusumo via Kibungo; to Kibuye via Gitarama; and to the Uganda border via Byumba or Umutara. A big programme of road improvement is under way; meanwhile there are still some pot-holed sections along all these routes which, together with the winding terrain and the tendency for Rwandans to drive at breakneck speeds and particularly to overtake on sharp or blind corners, necessitate a more cautious approach than one might take at home.

The unsurfaced roads most likely to be used by tourists include the long stretch running parallel to Lake Kivu between Gisenyi, Kibuye and Cyangugu; the approach roads to Akagera National Park (and roads within the park); and approach roads to the Volcanoes National Park and Lakes Burera and Ruhondo from Musanze. In all cases, these roads are in fair condition, and should be 'do-able' in a saloon car, though a 4x4 would certainly be preferable. Bear in mind, however, that unsurfaced roads tend to vary seasonally, with conditions most difficult during the rains and least so towards the end of the dry season. Even within this generalisation, an isolated downpour can do major damage to a road that was in perfectly good nick a day earlier, while the arrival of a grader can transform a pot-holed 4x4 track into one navigable by any saloon car.

The main hazard on Rwandan roads, aside from unexpected pot-holes, is the road-hog mentality of most drivers. Minibus-taxis in particular regularly overtake on blind corners, and speed limits (60–80/km per hour) are universally ignored except when enforced by road conditions. On all routes, be alert to banana-laden cyclists swaying from the verge, and livestock and pedestrians wandering blithely into the middle of the road. Putting one's foot to the floor and hooting like a maniac is the customary Rwandan approach to driving through crowded areas; driving rather more defensively than you would at home is the safer one!

A peculiarly African road hazard – one frequently taken to unnecessary extremes in Rwanda – is the giant sleeping policeman, which might be signposted in advance, might be painted in black-and-white strips, or might simply rear up without warning like a 30cm-tall macadamised wave. It's to be assumed that the odd stray bump will exist on any stretch of road that passes through a town or village, so slow down at any looming hint of urbanisation.

Rwandans, like many Africans, display an inexplicable aversion to switching on their headlights except in genuine darkness – switch them on at any other time and

APPROXIMATE DISTANCES BETWEEN MAIN TOWNS

	Kigali	Huye	Byumba	Gitarama	Kibungo	Kibuye	Gisenyi	Gikongoro	Musanze	Cyangugu
Kigali		135	60	53	112	144	187	164	118	293
Huye	135		210	82	247	129	237	29	190	158
Byumba	60	210		128	187	219	173	240	104	349
Gitarama	53	82	128		165	91	177	112	108	221
Kibungo	112	247	187	165		256	299	277	230	386
Kibuye	144	129	219	91	256		108	258	199	130
Gisenyi	187	237	173	177	299	108		366	69	238
Gikongoro	164	29	240	112	277	258	366		220	128
Musanze	118	190	104	108	230	199	69	220		307
Cyangugu	293	158	349	221	386	130	248	128	307	

every passing vehicle will blink its lights back at you in bemusement. In rainy, misty or twilight conditions, it would be optimistic to think that you'll be alerted to oncoming traffic by headlights, or for that matter to expect the more demented element among Rwandan drivers to avoid overtaking or speeding simply because they cannot see more than 10m ahead. It's best to avoid driving at night, since a significant proportion of vehicles lack functional headlights, whilst others go around with their lights permanently on blinding full beam!

MOUNTAIN BIKING OR CYCLING The relatively short distances between tourist centres and the consistently attractive scenery should make Rwanda ideal for travelling by mountain bike. These cannot easily be bought locally, so you would have to bring one with you (some airlines are more flexible than others about carrying bicycles; you should discuss this with them in advance). More and more Rwandans are using cycles now, and if you ask around you should be able to find some for hire – but check the brakes carefully and carry a repair kit. Minibuses will allow you to take your bike on the roof, though expect to be charged extra for this. Minor roads vary in condition, but in the dry season you're unlikely to encounter any problems. Several of the more off-the-beaten-track destinations mentioned in this book would be particularly attractive to cyclists.

HITCHING This is an option on main routes, though you should expect to pay for lifts offered by Rwandans. Some minor roads carry little traffic so you could face a long wait.

PUBLIC TRANSPORT
Boat and rail There are no rail services in Rwanda (although a rail link with Tanzania has been under discussion for some time), nor is there at present a public ferry service on Lake Kivu, although private links operate between Cyangugu, Kibuye, Gisenyi and Goma. This may change in the near future; check with ORTPN (see page 61) for the latest news. It's possible to rent local dugouts for

short excursions on the lake. Motor boats are also available for hire on Lake Kivu – see *Cyangugu* and *Gisenyi* in *Chapter 10*. Small boats can be used to get around the smaller lakes, such as Burera and Ruhondo, by making an informal arrangement with the boat owner.

Road The main mode of road transport is shared **minibuses**, generally known as *taxis* (and referred to in this book as minibus-taxis to distinguish them from cabs). These connect all major centres (and most minor ones) and leave from the town's minibus station (*gare taxi/minibus*) when they are full. No smoking inside is the rule, as it is on all public transport. Departures continue throughout the day but it's best not to wait until too late, in case the last one proves to be full. Fares generally work out at around Rfr500 (US$1) per 50km. Travel times along main surfaced roads typically average about 50km per hour, with frequent pauses to drop off passengers balanced against driving that verges on the manic between the stops. Overloading is not the problem it is in many African countries, nor are tourists routinely overcharged, though the latter does happen from time to time so check the fare with other passengers if it feels too high. You pay just before you alight rather than when you board, so there's the opportunity to see what other people are paying. On some routes **buses** are also available, which leave at fixed times. In and around Kigali there's a network of **urban minibuses**, running on set routes through the capital and its suburbs.

In some larger towns you'll also find normal **taxis** – identifiable by a yellow or orange stripe round the side – known as *taxi-voitures* to distinguish them from taxi-minibuses. The same rules apply as in most African countries – agree a price in advance and haggle if it seems extortionate. Fares in Kigali are fixed according to distance.

PRIVATE MINIBUSES Between Kigali and all main towns, private companies operate minibuses to fixed timetables and with bookable seats. These start and finish at the company's offices rather than at the public minibus stations. The price is generally much the same as for public minibuses. Details appear under the relevant towns in *Part Two*.

There are also privately owned minibuses which operate flexibly throughout the country, in much the same way as taxis, with passengers sharing the fare. If you're hitching, you may well come across these.

TWO-WHEELED TAXIS In and around minibus-taxi stations you may find 'taxis' in the form of motorbikes (*motos*) or bicycles. They're handy for short distances – but be aware that your travel insurance may not cover you for accidents when on either of them, and you certainly won't be offered a safety helmet. Agree a price beforehand, and check with a passer-by if it seems excessive. If you've got a heavy bag, a comfortable alternative is to stick it on the saddle of the bicycle and walk alongside.

ACCOMMODATION

There are hotels of international standard in Kigali, Kinigi, Lake Burera, Akagera and Gisenyi. Elsewhere, accommodation consists of mid-range hotels, geared to local businesspeople as much as to tourists, and cheaper local guesthouses. Where midrange hotels are available – in Musanze, Huye and the Lake Kivu resorts – rates generally work out at under Rfr30,000 (about US$60) for a clean double with en-suite hot bath or shower. Budget accommodation mostly falls into the Rfr5,000–15,000 (US$10–30) price range, and in many cases this will get you a very clean room with en-suite hot shower. In hotels of all standards, if you're staying for more than a few days you may be able to negotiate a lower rate.

Most accommodation establishments are recognisably signposted as a hotel, *logement,* guesthouse or similar, but some local places are signposted as *Amacumbi* (pronounced amachoombi) – which literally means 'Place with Rooms' in Kinyarwanda. Note, too, that in the Swahili language – not indigenous to Rwanda but more widely spoken by locals than any other exotic tongue – a *hoteli* is a restaurant, which can create confusion when asking a non-French speaker for a hotel.

Homestays – the opportunity to stay in a Rwandan home and take part in local activities – are just getting under way on a small scale, with Amahoro Tours (see page 183 in *Chapter 11*) leading the field.

Few formal campsites exist in Rwanda. Some hotels will permit camping in the gardens, but at little saving over the price of a budget room. A new tented camp with both camping sites and fixed safari tents is due to open near Musanze in mid 2007 – see Ikoro Tented Camp on page 179. There are campsites at the Volcanoes and Akagera national parks and in Nyungwe Forest. At Nyungwe, the campsite is far more attractively located than the resthouse for travellers without a vehicle. A tent may also come in handy for travellers backpacking or cycling through relatively non-touristed rural areas, where you are strongly advised to ask permission of the local village official before setting up camp.

✕ EATING AND DRINKING

EATING OUT Kigali boasts a good range of restaurants representing international cuisines such as Indian, Italian, Chinese and French. In most other towns, a couple of hotels or restaurants serve uncomplicated Western meals – chicken, fish or steak with chips or rice. Possibly as a result of the Belgian influence, restaurant standards seem to be far higher than in most East African countries, and Rwandan chips are among the best on the continent. Servings tend to be dauntingly large, and prices very reasonable – around Rfr1,000 (US$2) for a melange (mixed plate) at local eateries and Rfr3,000–5,000 (US$6–10) for a main course at a smarter restaurant.

Buffet or self-service meals are also on offer, often at very inexpensive rates (as little as Rfr1,000 in local restaurants) – and are said to originate from a period in the 1980s when the government decreed that civil servants should have shorter lunch breaks. As a result, enterprising restaurants dreamed up this way of enabling them to eat faster. Smarter restaurants, especially in Kigali, may be closed or take a while to rustle up food outside of normal mealtimes.

Wherever you travel, local restaurants serve Rwandan favourites such as goat kebabs (brochettes), grilled or fried tilapia (a type of lake fish), bean or meat stews. These are normally eaten with one of a few staples: *ugali* (a stiff porridge made with maize meal), *matoke* (cooking banana/plantain), *chapatti* (flat bread), and boiled potatoes (as in Uganda, these are somewhat mysteriously referred to as Irish potatoes) – not to mention rice and the ubiquitous chips. At local restaurants, you should be able to fill yourself adequately for US$2 or less.

Unless you have an insatiable appetite for greasy omelettes or stale *mandazi* (deep-fried dough balls not dissimilar to doughnuts), breakfast outside of Kigali (where good French bread and croissants are available) or the larger hotels can be a problematic meal. One area in which Rwanda is definitely influenced more by its anglophone neighbours than by its former coloniser is baking: in common with the rest of East Africa, the bread is almost always sweetish and goes stale quickly. In such cases a bunch of bananas, supplemented by other fresh fruit, is about the best breakfast option: cheap, nutritious and filling.

CHEDDAR IN RWANDA

Many's the long night I've dreamed of cheese – toasted, mostly.

Treasure Island, Robert Louis Stevenson

I don't know about toasted, but certainly there's more locally made cheese available in Rwanda now, although shortage of refrigerated transport limits its distribution. On supermarket shelves in Kigali you'll see Rwandan 'gouda', Rwandan 'feta' and less ambitiously named 'local goats' cheese'.

For Rwandan 'cheddar' you must head off to Nyabisindu. Take the Nyanza turning from the Gitarama–Huye road and, after 1–2km, take a right turn signed 'Oakdale Demonstration Farm'. Follow a twisty dirt road down into the valley (bearing left at a confusing fork with coffee trees); turn right just before crossing the valley floor. The Lac du Roi Rudahigwa is ahead on your left and you'll come to the 'cheese factory' on your right – a small, new building on the edge of the road. In the spotless interior, four women (widows) prepare the cheeses.

Much is made from the milk of the farm's own cows, but farmers can also bring in their own milk – it is checked for quality and then, if suitable, made into cheese. The cheeses are waxed for storage, so can be transported. Bought at the farm, a 1kg Oakdale cheese costs US$7; bought in Kigali, many times more. (To make four 1kg cheeses takes 38.5 litres of milk.)

To make an appointment beforehand (the manager will show visitors round by request) phone 583139 or 08540565. The farm has pigs and turkeys as well as cows and will soon be digging fishponds; already some fish is farmed in the lake. Even if you don't want to buy cheese, the beautiful and peaceful valley is worth a visit.

COOKING FOR YOURSELF The alternative to eating at restaurants is to put together your own meals at markets and supermarkets. The variety of foodstuffs you can buy varies from season to season and from town to town, but in most major centres you can rely on finding a supermarket that stocks frozen meat, a few tinned goods, biscuits, pasta, rice and chocolate bars. If you're that way inclined, and will be staying in hotels rather than camping, bring a small electric immersion heater for use in your bedroom (sockets take standard continental two-pin plugs), plus some teabags or instant coffee, so you can supplement your picnic with a hot drink.

Fruit and vegetables are best bought at markets, where they are very cheap. Potatoes, sweet potatoes, onions, tomatoes, bananas, sugar cane, avocados, paw-paws, mangoes, coconuts, oranges and pineapples are seasonally available in most towns.

For hikers, about the only dehydrated meals available are packet soups. If you have specialised requirements, you're best doing your shopping in Kigali, where a wider selection of goods (cheese, local yoghurt…) is available in the supermarkets; there are also a handful of excellent bakeries, with mouth-watering goodies hot from the oven.

DRINKS Brand-name soft drinks such as Pepsi, Coca-Cola and Fanta are widely available, and cheap by international standards. Tap water is debatably safe to drink in Kigali, although the smell of chlorine may put you off; bottled mineral water is widely available if you sensibly prefer not to take the risk. Locally bottled fruit juice (passion fruit, orange, pineapple…) isn't bad and comes in concentrated versions too.

The most widely drunk hot beverage is tea (*chai* or *icyayi* in Swahili/Kinyarwanda). In rural areas, the ingredients are often boiled together in a pot: a sticky, sweet, milky concoction that definitely falls into the category of

MARABA BOURBON GOURMET COFFEE

Rwanda's Maraba Bourbon coffee is one of the country's most recent success stories. Beans being grown at Maraba, near Huye (Butare), have excelled in international taste tests – in a US study they were classed as second best worldwide – and are being marketed actively in the UK and US. Maraba is a very special type of Arabica coffee from Bourbon coffee trees, characterised by a smooth, full-bodied, almost fruity flavour with no astringency or after-taste.

The coffee plantation is run by the Abahuzamugambi Co-operative, many of whose members are women widowed in the genocide who were struggling to support their families. The sale of the Maraba coffee has enabled them to pay school fees, rebuild damaged homes and acquire livestock. Membership has grown from an initial 200 in 2001 to around 2,000 in 2006. In the UK, Sainsbury's has been promoting Maraba coffee in several of its stores during annual Comic Relief campaigns and also sells a speciality beer containing Maraba coffee. In the US, the coffee is available from Starbucks as well as from speciality stores whose customers care more for quality than price. Sales in 2005 via the Inter-American Coffee Company (US) and the Union Coffee Roasters of London (UK) raised over US$266,000.

Traditionally, Arabica coffee has been Rwanda's principal export, but quality and quantity declined seriously after the genocide. According to OCIR-Café, the state coffee board, the 19,600 tonnes produced in 2001 were about half the pre-1994 output. With Maraba Bourbon, this is changing fast: almost 70,000kg were produced in 2004, and other plantations around Rwanda are achieving similar success.

Many organisations have contributed to the success story of Maraba Bourbon coffee: USAID, ACDI/VOCA, PEARL, Comic Relief, Union Coffee Roasters... enabling new washing stations to be built and adequate equipment to be installed. The overseas markets are still enthusiastic – at present Sweden is expressing a strong interest, and in 2005 the Co-operative won the prestigious City of Göteborg International Environmental Prize – and Maraba Bourbon is also being promoted in Rwanda by restaurants and hotels. Its growth is self-perpetuating. Watch out for it – whether in the UK, the US or Rwanda – and enjoy!

acquired tastes. Most Westernised restaurants serve tea as we know it, but if you want to be certain, specify that you want black tea. The milk served separately with it is almost always powdered, but of a type that dissolves well and doesn't taste too bad. Coffee is one of Rwanda's main cash crops, but you'd hardly know it judging by the insipid slop that passes for coffee in most restaurants and hotels – unless they are serving Maraba coffee (see box above). You're on safe if unexciting ground with instant coffee (ask for *Nescafé*); after a few days in the country we made a policy of checking whether coffee was of the brewed or instant variety before we ordered – if the former, we settled for tea.

The most popular alcoholic drink is beer, brewed locally near Gisenyi. The cheaper of the two local brands is Primus, which comes in 700ml bottles which cost anything from Rfr350–400 (less than US$1) in local bars to Rfr2,000 (US$4) in Kigali's swankiest hotels. The alternatives are Mutzig, which tastes little different, costs about 30% more, and comes in 700ml or 350ml bottles, and the more expensive premier brand Amstel. There's also the local banana beer, *urwagwa*.

South African and French wines are sold at outrageously inflated prices in a few upmarket bars and restaurants. Far more sensibly priced are the boxes of Spanish or Italian wine sold in some supermarkets. If you want to check out your capacity for locally brewed banana wine (also called *urwagwa*) before ordering it with a meal (at least one of the authors finds it delicious…!) most supermarkets and some small grocers/snack bars have bottles on sale. It comes in many varieties – some have honey added, and I've heard of a kind made in the northeast that contains hibiscus flowers. There's also a banana liqueur.

As for the harder stuff – *waragi*, a millet-based clear alcohol from Uganda, is available everywhere; either knock it back neat or mix it as you would gin. (In its undistilled form it could strip away a few layers of skin!) The illegal Rwandan firewater, *kanyanga*, is also available widely: treat with care.

LANGUAGE

The local language is Kinyarwanda, but almost all Rwandans speak a little of at least one international language. In rural areas, this is most likely to be KiSwahili, a coastal Bantu language with strong Arabic influences which, thanks largely to the 19th-century slave caravans, has come to serve as the lingua franca of East Africa. Most educated Rwandans who were brought up within the country also speak passable to fluent French, but may not speak English. By contrast, many returned long-term exiles were educated in Uganda, Kenya or Tanzania or another Anglophone territory, and don't know any French, but do speak fluent English.

The upshot of this is that French speakers will have no difficulty getting by in the towns, and should always be able to find somebody who can speak French in rural areas. English speakers will struggle more, though particularly in Kigali and Musanze (formerly Ruhengeri) they'll find that a fair number of people speak English. Travellers who know some Swahili will also find this very useful, particularly in rural areas. The potential for chaos is, of course, immense: in Musanze, I regularly tried my faltering Swahili in a bar or hotel to no avail, followed up on this in my even more limited French, only to have the person I was addressing ask me whether perhaps I spoke English!

Both French and English are now taught from primary school onwards, with the aim of making Rwanda a trilingual country; however, *the* national language, spoken by everyone, remains Kinyarwanda, and for the sake of friendliness and courtesy you should try to take on board a few words. At the very least aim for *yégo* (yes), *oya* (no), *murakozé* (thank you), *muraho* (hello, good morning/afternoon), *bitesé*? (how are you?) and *byiza* (good). For me, an essential phrase in any language is 'What's your name?', to be used on children; their faces light up and they start to take you seriously! Then point to yourself and say your own name, and the introduction is complete. In Kinyarwanda it's easy – *Witwandé*? The above words are written phonetically – the value of consonants may change a bit in different parts of the country; for example 'b' may sometimes sound more like 'v' or 'w'. If you're linguistically ambitious, turn to the more comprehensive vocabulary in *Appendix 1*.

PLACE NAMES In Kinyarwanda, as in most African languages, place names are more or less phonetic, so that the town of Base, for instance, is pronounced *Bah-say*. But the transcription of place names in Rwanda displays some other quirks that I've not encountered anywhere, namely the occasional pronunciation of 'g' as 'j' (Kinigi, for instance, is pronounced Kiniji), and of an initial 'k' as 'ch' and 'cy' as 'sh'(Kigali = Chigali, Cyangugu = Shangugu). Further complication is created by the African tendency to treat 'r' and 'l' as interchangeable, and the local custom of distinguishing certain towns from the synonymous region by adding the French word *ville* to the end of the town's name. Hence, when you hear a bus conductor yelling *Chigari-ville* at the top of his voice, he is in fact referring to the city of Kigali!

Janice Booth

The transposition of r and l can be tongue-twisting as well as confusing. I have friends named Hilary and Florence – in Rwanda aka Hiraly and Frolence. The multiple mwamis or kings of Rwanda – les rois – can be called les lois (the laws); while the queen (la reine) can sound like la laine (the wool!). In a recent letter, a young girl asked me to 'play' for her – which, unmusical as I am, would be difficult. She meant 'pray'. And New Year greetings wished me the 'fun and floric of the festive season'. Fortunately I've never heard the transposition applied to gorilla.

Particularly when travelling in off-the-beaten-track areas, it can pay to recognise that the names of communes – the smallest administrative unit in the country – are often used interchangeably with town or village names. This can create confusion where a commune and its principal settlement have the same name, something that happened to us on the east side of Lake Burera, where it took me quite some time to understand why we were in Butaro and not in Butaro at the same time – Butaro is the name of both the commune and its administrative centre. The opposite thing happened to us when we crossed into the next commune: later I grasped that the town people referred to as Cewyu is actually called Kirambo, but is referred to by the name of the commune for which it serves as an administrative centre. There are no hard and fast rules; just be alert to the fact that the names given on maps and in other secondary sources of information – this travel guide included – may not entirely coincide with local conventions.

A further complication here is that **Ruhengeri** (the access town for the Volcanoes National Park) has, as you've probably already gathered, just been renamed **Musanze** as part of an administrative reorganisation. Even more recently, **Butare** has become **Huye**. New road signs etc are being erected at the time of writing; but local people are likely to continue using the old names for quite some while. In this edition of the guide we are using the new names but with frequent reminders of the old ones, for the sake of clarity.

HASSLES

OVERCHARGING AND BARGAINING Tourists may sometimes need to bargain over prices, but this need is often exaggerated by guidebooks and other travellers. Hotels, restaurants and supermarkets generally charge fixed prices, and deliberate overcharging is so rare that it's not worth challenging a price unless it is blatantly ridiculous. In other situations – mostly markets or in the street – you're bound to be asked a higher price than the vendor will expect, and a certain degree of bargaining is considered normal. It is, however, important to keep this in perspective. Some travellers, after a couple of bad experiences, start to haggle with everyone from hotel owners to old women selling fruit by the side of the road, often accompanying their negotiations with aggressive accusations of dishonesty. This may be the easiest way to find out whether you are being overcharged, but it is unfair on the majority of Rwandans who are forthright and honest in their dealings with tourists.

Minibus conductors may occasionally ask tourists for higher fares than normal. The way to counter this is to watch what other people are paying, or to ask a fellow passenger what the fare should be. The main instance where bargaining is essential is when buying handicrafts or curios. However, the fact that a curio seller is open to negotiation does not mean that he or she was initially trying to rip you off. Vendors will generally quote a starting-price knowing full well that you are going to bargain it down – they'd probably be startled if you didn't – and it is not necessary to respond aggressively. It is impossible to say what size of reduction you should expect (some people say that you should offer half the asking price and be prepared to settle at around two-thirds, but my experience is that curio sellers are far more whimsical than such advice allows for). The sensible approach is to ask the price of similar items at a few different stalls before you actually contemplate buying anything.

In fruit and vegetable markets and stalls, bargaining is often the norm, even between Africans, and the most healthy approach to this sort of haggling is to view it as an enjoyable part of the travel experience. There will normally be an accepted price-band for any particular commodity. To find out what it is, listen to what other people pay (it helps if you know some Kinyarwanda) and try a few stalls – a ludicrously inflated price will drop the moment you walk away. When buying fruit and vegetables, a good way to feel out the situation is to ask for a bulk discount or a few extra items thrown in. And bear in mind that the reason why somebody is reluctant to bargain may be that they asked a fair price in the first place.

Above all, don't lose your sense of proportion. No matter how poor you may feel, it is your choice to travel on a tight budget. Most Rwandans are much poorer than you will ever be, and they do not have the luxury of choosing to travel. If you find yourself quibbling with an old lady selling a few piles of fruit by the roadside, stand back and look at the bigger picture. There is nothing wrong with occasionally erring on the side of generosity.

THEFT So far as tourists need be concerned, Rwanda is perhaps the most crime-free of African countries. Kigali is a very safe city, even at night, though it would probably be courting trouble to stumble around dark alleys with all your valuables on your person. Be aware, too, that this sort of thing can change very quickly: as recently as 1995, muggings and petty theft were practically unheard of in Malawi, but today you won't spend long in that country without meeting somebody who has been mugged or pick-pocketed. As tourism increases, so does opportunistic and petty crime. See the *Safety* section of *Chapter 4*, page 58, for a list of tips applicable to anywhere in Africa.

BEGGING To anyone who knows Africa it should come as no surprise to see beggars on the streets; the surprise, in view of Rwanda's recent past, is that they aren't more numerous. Nor are they often aggressive. For a charity (one of several) helping Kigali's street kids, see *rYico* on page 79. The maimed, handicapped and very old tell an obvious story. I can't advise you what to do about them. It's true that if you give to one you risk being surrounded by a dozen – but sometimes it's hard to walk on by. Rwandans themselves often recommend that you give something; they and the country's budget have little enough to spare. I set aside a 'ration' of small notes each day – when they're used up, that's it. If you don't believe in giving cash, see *Becoming involved*, pages 77–80, which lists some charities where your money will be well used.

BRIBERY AND BUREAUCRACY For all you read about the subject, bribery is not the problem to travellers in Africa that it is often made out to be. Those who are most often asked for bribes are the ones with private transport; and even they only have a major problem at some borders and from traffic police in some countries (notably Mozambique and Kenya). If you are travelling in Rwanda on public transport or as part of a tour, or even if you are driving yourself, I doubt whether you need to give the question of bribery serious thought, although if you make a day trip into the DRC you may encounter someone inventively explaining why you should part with a few thousand francs.

Janice Booth

As a lone female traveller, I have experienced far less hassle and anxiety in Rwanda during my several visits than I have in many other countries. I travelled all over the country by public transport feeling completely safe. There was a refreshing absence of 'smart Alecs' trying to engage me in dubious conversation.

In one town, a young man (Congolese, as it turned out) overheard me asking directions to the guesthouse and spontaneously walked with me, chatting occasionally, to make sure I found it safely. Then he shook my hand and went off. Another time I left my unlockable duffel bag with a smiling girl in a small wooden drinks kiosk near a minibus stop while I explored a village; when I returned to collect it, it had been stowed safely in a corner and the girl's baby was gurgling happily on top. I felt a kind of 'sisterhood', particularly with village women – if I smiled it was always reciprocated, although often shyly, and I always asked a woman first if I needed help or directions.

In Kigali I spent a lot of time walking both in and outside the city centre and never felt threatened, although there are some poorer areas which (and a Rwandan woman friend agrees with me) become scarier after dark. This applies to men too, of course, but women are generally seen – rightly or wrongly! – as a target less likely to put up resistance. The rule here is to take the same sensible precautions you'd take in any capital city, and then relax.

As a matter of courtesy, watch what the local women wear and don't expose parts of yourself that they leave covered, particularly in village areas. In business areas people are smartly dressed; I was glad I'd brought a skirt and some crumple-free tops. Be sensitive to the fact that people here have suffered a great deal; if someone is reluctant to talk or to answer questions, don't push it.

You may not be as fortunate as I was. Nor do I suggest that you drop your guard and behave over-confidently. There can be bad apples in any barrel. Would-be Lotharios exist in any country and they tend to home in on female travellers. In fact, one night in Kigali a strange man did knock on my bedroom door at 11pm, but it turned out that he needed money to take a sick street kid to hospital (yes, honestly!).

I place Rwanda very high on the list of relatively hassle-free countries where good manners, honesty and trust are the order of the day – and of course this should be a two-way process.

There is a tendency to portray African bureaucrats as difficult and inefficient in their dealings with tourists. As a rule, this reputation says more about Western prejudices than it does about Africa. Sure, you come across the odd unhelpful official, but then such is the nature of the beast everywhere. The vast majority of officials in the African countries I've visited – Rwanda included – have been courteous and helpful in their dealings with tourists, often to a degree that is almost embarrassing.

A factor in determining the response you receive from African officials – and those in Rwanda are unlikely to be an exception – will be your own attitude. If you walk into every official encounter with an aggressive, paranoid approach, you are quite likely to kindle the feeling held by many Africans that Europeans are arrogant and offhand in their dealings with other races. Instead, try to be friendly and patient, and remember that the person to whom you are talking does not speak English (or French) as a first language and may thus have difficulty understanding you. Treat people with respect rather than disdain, in Rwanda as elsewhere, and they'll tend to treat you in the same way.

● FOREIGN REPRESENTATION IN RWANDA

Foreign embassies and consulates in Kigali (or in other East African countries, if there is none in Rwanda) are given below. International dialling codes are Rwanda 250; Kenya 254; Uganda 256.

Austria (Kenya) City House, Wabera St, PO Box 30560 Nairobi; ☎ (2) 228281/2; f 331792
Belgium Rue de Nyarugenge, BP 81 Kigali; ☎ 575551-4; f 573995
Burundi 4 Rue Ntaruka, BP 714 Kigali; ☎ 517529, 575718, 573465; f 576418
Canada 1534 Rue Akagera, BP 1177 Kigali; ☎ 573210; f 572719
China 44 Bd de la Révolution, BP 1545 Kigali; ☎ 575415; f 510489
Denmark (Uganda) 3 Lumumba Av, PO Box 11234 Kampala; ☎ (41) 256687, 256783, 250938; f 254970; e denmark@emul.com
Egypt Bd de l'Umuganda, BP 6073 Kigali; ☎ 587560; f 587510
France Av Paul VI, BP 53 Kigali; ☎ 575206, 575225; f 576957; e ambafrance@rwanda1.com
Germany 8 Rue de Bugarama, BP 355 Kigali; ☎ 575141, 575222; f 577267; e amball@rwanda1.com
India (Uganda) 11 Kyadondo Rd, PO Box 7040 Kampala; ☎ (41) 257368, 342994; f 254943
Ireland (Uganda) Plot 12, Acacia Av, Kololo, Kampala; ☎ (41) 344348, 344344; f 344353
Japan (Kenya) ICEA Building, Kenyatta Av, PO Box

60202 Nairobi; ☎ (2) 332955/6/7/8/9; f 216530
Libya Libyan People's Bureau, 8 Rue Cyahafi, BP 1152 Kigali; ☎ 572294; f 572347
Netherlands Bd de l'Umuganda, PO Box 2549 Kigali; ☎ 584348/78, 510604; e kig@minbuza.nl
Norway (Uganda) Acacia Av Quarter, Kololo, PO Box 22770 Kampala; ☎ (41) 343621, 346733, 346757, 340848; f 343936
Russian Federation 19 Av de l'Armée, BP 40 Kigali; ☎ 575286; f 574818
South Africa 1370 Bd de l'Umuganda, BP6563, Kigali; ☎ 583185-7; f 511758
Sweden ☎ 586003-6, f 586008
Switzerland 38 Bd de la Révolution, BP 1257 Kigali; ☎ 575534, 575072; f 572461
Tanzania Plot 1253, Kimihurura III, BP 3973 Kigali; ☎ 505400; f 505402
Uganda Plot 9, Av de l'Akagera, BP 656 Kigali; ☎ 576854
United Kingdom Parcelle 1131, Bd de l'Umuganda, BP 576 Kigali; ☎ 585281-7, 586072, 584098, 585771; f 582044; 510588; e Embassy.Kigali@fco.gov.uk; www.britishembassykigali.org.rw
USA 55 Bd de la Révolution, BP28, Kigali; ☎ 505601-3; f 570319; http://kigali.usembassy.gov

For updates and/or additions, either ask ORTPN or check website www.rwanda1.com or www.rwandatourism.com.

MEDIA AND COMMUNICATIONS

NEWSPAPERS AND MAGAZINES Rwanda has two English-language newspapers: *The New Times* (thrice weekly, on Mon, Wed and Fri, with a new Sunday edition launched in 2006; *www.newtimes.co.rw*) which supports the government, and *Rwanda Newsline* (weekly) which works hard at being independent. Imported dailies and weeklies from Uganda are also widely available on the streets of Kigali and Huye. A very limited range of international papers can be bought at the kiosks of upmarket hotels such as the Mille Collines in Kigali. News magazines such as *Time* and *Newsweek* are available from street vendors and some bookshops. The Ikirezi bookshop in Kigali has a good stock, and also sells them at the airport.

● **INTERNET, EMAIL AND FAX** The electronic communications age has fast gained a foothold in Rwanda, with increasing use of email. Outside of Kigali, however, local servers tend to be slow and subject to breakdowns, and there are still a few towns (eg: Kibuye) that have no internet facilities at all. Judging by past developments and those in neighbouring countries, it is simply a matter of time

Ariadne Van Zandbergen

EQUIPMENT Although with some thought and an eye for composition you can take reasonable photos with a 'point-and-shoot' camera, you need an SLR camera if you are at all serious about photography. Modern SLRs tend to be very clever, with automatic programmes for almost every possible situation, but remember that these programmes are limited in the sense that the camera cannot think, but only make calculations. Every starting amateur photographer should read a photographic manual for beginners and get to grips with such basics as the relationship between aperture and shutter speed.

Always buy the best lens you can afford. The lens determines the quality of your photo more than the camera body. Fixed fast lenses are ideal, but very costly. Zoom lenses allow you to change the composition without having to change lenses the whole time. If you carry only one lens, a 28–70mm (digital 17–55mm) or similar zoom should be ideal. For a second lens, a lightweight 80–200mm or 70–300mm (digital 55–200mm) or similar will be excellent for candid shots and varying your composition. Wildlife photography will be very frustrating if you don't have at least a 300mm lens. For a small loss of quality, tele-converters are a cheap and compact way to increase magnification: a 300 lens with a 1.4x converter becomes 420mm, and with a 2x it becomes 600mm. Note, however, that 1.4x and 2x tele-converters reduce the speed of your lens by 1.4 and 2 stops respectively.

For wildlife photography from a safari vehicle, a solid beanbag, which you can make yourself very cheaply, will be necessary to avoid blurred images, and is more useful than a tripod. A clamp with a tripod head screwed on to it can be attached to the vehicle as well. Modern dedicated flash units are easy to use; aside from the obvious need to flash when you photograph at night, you can improve a lot of photos in difficult 'high contrast' or very dull light with some fill-in flash. It pays to have a proper flash unit as opposed to a built-in camera flash.

DIGITAL/FILM Digital photography is now the preference of most amateur and professional photographers, with the resolution of digital cameras improving the whole time. For ordinary prints a 6 megapixel camera is fine. For better results and the possibility to enlarge images and for professional reproduction, higher resolution is available up to 16 megapixels.

Memory space is important. The number of pictures you can fit on a memory card depends on the quality you choose. Calculate in advance how many pictures you can fit on a card and either take enough cards to last for your trip, or take a storage drive on to which you can download the content. A laptop gives the advantage that you can see your pictures properly at the end of each day and edit and delete rejects, but a storage device is lighter and less bulky. These drives come in different capacities up to 80GB.

before internet facilities become more fast and reliable countrywide. Most hotels of mid-range and upwards have email and fax facilities, and in Kigali there's an efficient fax office at the main post office in Avenue de la Paix. Sending faxes here costs under US$2 to Europe and US$2.50 to the US; receiving a fax costs under US$1. If you want someone at home to fax you there, the number is (250) 576574.

***TELEPHONE** Rwanda's telephone system is reasonably efficient. From overseas, it is definitely one of the easier African countries to get through to first time. The international code is 250. Because of the small size of the country, and limited number of phones, no area codes are in use. All fixed lines now comprise a six digit

Bear in mind that digital camera batteries, computers and other storage devices need charging, so make sure you have all the chargers, cables and converters with you. Most hotels have charging points, but do enquire about this in advance. When camping you might have to rely on charging from the car battery; a spare battery is invaluable.

If you are shooting film, 100 to 200 ISO print film and 50 to 100 ISO slide film are ideal. Low ISO film is slow but fine grained and gives the best colour saturation, but will need more light, so support in the form of a tripod or monopod is important. You can also bring a few 'fast' 400 ISO films for low-light situations where a tripod or flash is no option.

DUST AND HEAT Dust and heat are often a problem. Keep your equipment in a sealed bag, stow films in an airtight container (eg: a small cooler bag) and avoid exposing equipment and film to the sun. Digital cameras are prone to collecting dust particles on the sensor which results in spots on the image. The dirt mostly enters the camera when changing lenses, so be careful when doing this. To some extent photos can be 'cleaned' up afterwards in Photoshop, but this is time-consuming. You can have your camera sensor professionally cleaned, or you can do this yourself with special brushes and swabs made for the purpose, but note that touching the sensor might cause damage and should only be done with the greatest care.

LIGHT The most striking outdoor photographs are often taken during the hour or two of 'golden light' after dawn and before sunset. Shooting in low light may enforce the use of very low shutter speeds, in which case a tripod will be required to avoid camera shake.

With careful handling, side lighting and back lighting can produce stunning effects, especially in soft light and at sunrise or sunset. Generally, however, it is best to shoot with the sun behind you. When photographing animals or people in the harsh midday sun, images taken in light but even shade are likely to be more effective than those taken in direct sunlight or patchy shade, since the latter conditions create too much contrast.

PROTOCOL In some countries, it is unacceptable to photograph local people without permission, and many people will refuse to pose or will ask for a donation. In such circumstances, don't try to sneak photographs as you might get yourself into trouble. Even the most willing subject will often pose stiffly when a camera is pointed at them; relax them by making a joke, and take a few shots in quick succession to improve the odds of capturing a natural pose.

Ariadne Van Zandbergen is a professional travel and wildlife photographer specialising in Africa. She runs The Africa Image Library. For photo requests, visit www.africaimagelibrary.co.za or contact her on ariadne@hixnet.co.za.

number starting with '5' – if you come across old numbers (five digits only) just add the '5' prefix and the number should work fine.

In Kigali, international phone calls can be made from the central post office in Avenue de la Paix and from various other shops and kiosks in the city. For calls within Rwanda the street kiosks and shops with public phones work well – calls are metered and you pay when you've finished, so there's no fussing with coins or tokens. Some of these can handle international calls too. To make an international call out of Rwanda, dial 00 then the country code, area code and local number.

Cell phones (mobiles) have caught on in a big way in Rwanda. Cell-phone numbers can be recognised as an eight-digit number starting with '08' (eg 08 123456). Mobile phone owners can buy a local SIM card giving them a local number using the local satellite network for the equivalent of US$1 (as part of an Rfr3,000 'starter pack' with Rfr2,500 of airtime included) – international text messages work out at Rfr100 each and international phone calls are also very cheap from local mobile phones. A new development is satellite phones, which have a 10-digit number starting '0808' (eg 0808 123456).

POST Post from Rwanda is cheap and reasonably reliable, but can be slow. Yellow post-buses with *Iposita* on the side shuttle mail around Rwanda. Letterboxes outside post offices have a variety of appellations – sometimes *Boite aux Lettres*, sometimes (eg: in Huye) *Box of Letters* and sometimes (a Belgian/Flemish relic in Kibuye) *Brievenbus*.

RADIO AND TELEVISION The BBC World Service comes across loud and clear, on different frequencies according to the time of day. Local radio stations broadcast in Kinyarwanda, French, English and Swahili. TV is largely piped in from elsewhere, giving CNN, Sky, BBC News, etc at different times of day: generally more informative for visitors than the local channel, although that does have occasional news bulletins in English. For football fans, the Supersport Channel operated by the South African company DSTV shows most international and English Premiership matches and can be seen at bars all around the country.

SHOPPING

All basic requirements (toiletries, stationery, batteries and so forth) are available in Kigali, and, away from the capital, most towns of any size have a pharmacy as well as a reasonable supermarket or general store. In Kigali, the pharmacy in Boulevard de la Révolution is open 24 hours. Photographic equipment (film etc) is available in Kigali – try the photographic shop in Avenue de la Paix or the well-established Fotolab in Rue Kalisimbi, opposite the Isimbi Hotel – but may be scarcer (or out of date) in smaller places, so it's best to bring whatever you'll need.

For handicrafts you've a very wide range – wood-carvings, weaving, pottery, baskets, clay statues, beadwork, jewellery, masks, musical instruments, banana-leaf products, batik – see *Handicrafts* in the Kigali chapter (pages 107–8) and the Huye (Butare) section (page 131) for more details. CDs or cassettes of Rwandan music make good gifts, as does local honey: buy it in a market and decant it into a screw-top soft-drinks bottle for travelling. (Some countries prohibit the import of foodstuffs, so check local regulations before you take any home.) Some markets stock candles made of local beeswax. Locally made wines, spirits and liqueurs are heavier to carry but generally appreciated! For traditional musical instruments, you need a well-informed local advisor to help you to pick the best and most authentic.

Women can buy lengths of brightly dyed fabric in the market and have street dressmakers make up a garment on the spot; men can similarly kit themselves out with hand-tailored shirts. And just browsing in any large street market will give you dozens more ideas…

ARTS AND ENTERTAINMENT

Concerts (whether pop or classical) and displays of traditional dance are held from time to time in the various stadiums – check for details with the ORTPN (see page 61). The Centre for Franco-Rwandan Cultural Exchanges (see page 104) organises presentations of theatre, music, dance and cinema in its theatre in Kigali – either contact the centre for its current programme or ask at the ORTPN. The cinema in the Kigali Business Centre (see page 104) has daily screenings of international movies.

The National Museum of Rwanda in Huye (Butare) (see pages 132–3) is excellent, and there are plans to open more museums around the country as part of a project to record '500 years of Great Lakes History'. It may or may not happen during the lifetime of this guide.

BECOMING INVOLVED

You may leave Rwanda without a backward glance, or you may find that it has affected you more than you realised. It's an amazing country. If you do want to become further involved with its people and its culture, a few suggestions are given below, to add to those already mentioned. There are many more: ask around when you're in Rwanda, or do an internet search for whatever aspect of development interests you. For gorilla conservation charities, see pages 210–11.

RWANDA UNITED KINGDOM GOODWILL ORGANISATION (RUGO)
Mike Hughes
RUGO (UK Registered Charity No 1074088; www.rugo.org) was formally launched on July 4 1997, coinciding with the third anniversary of the end of genocide in Rwanda. The aim of the organisation is to provide a channel whereby the people of UK can support the people of Rwanda as they rebuild after the 1994 Genocide. RUGO received charity status in February 1999, with Baroness Chalker of Wallasey as its Patron.

Objectives RUGO's stated mission is:
The advancement of education and training of the people of Rwanda, and the relief of poverty, sickness and distress, through the provision and support of community-based projects designed to improve the conditions of life for those in necessitous circumstances.

Vocational training After its launch, RUGO noted that one of the consequences of the genocide was that most of Rwanda's artisans with skills had been lost. With that in mind, two of the institutions it has assisted are a new vocational school at Nyamata and the Amizero Vocational Training Centre at Kayonza. Both of these have training places where young people who do not achieve places at secondary school can acquire important skills, which enable them to make a living for themselves and their families and assist in the reconstruction of their country.

RUGO collected about £120,000 worth of tools and equipment for ETO Nyamata where courses include masonry & construction, carpentry, plumbing & appropriate technology, information technology, and tailoring. Nyamata is in the Bugesera, a region of Rwanda previously undeveloped because the presence of tsetse fly makes it unsuitable for pastoralists and its dry climate does not favour cultivation. Nyamata was also one of the areas worst affected by the 1994 Genocide.

At Amizero VTC, where RUGO has donated computers for use in its computer courses, many students come from disadvantaged backgrounds; for example they may be genocide survivors, demobilised soldiers, released prisoners or young people from extremely poor families.

Additional activities RUGO has also:

- Issued newsletters to inform people about the situation in Rwanda
- Received donations of computers and books for the National University of Rwanda and other educational establishments in Rwanda
- Held social events to fundraise and promote Rwandan culture

- Supported centres such as Kigali Junior Academy; Kigali Parents' School; Village of Hope (part of the Rwanda Women's Network); Village d'Orphelins (orphanage in Kibuye) and Uyisenga N'Imanzi (which supports child-headed households)
- Held memorial services in remembrance of the victims of genocide
- Facilitated and raised funds for the construction of a Parish Community Centre in Kayonza in partnership with St Andrew's parish in Harrow.

Income RUGO's income derives from members' subscriptions, donations and fundraising. The organisation employs no-one and is administered by volunteers; thus almost every penny goes towards RUGO's objectives. The annual membership subscription is currently £20 for an individual, £30 for a family and £100 for corporate bodies.

Further information *For further information, contact either Mike Hughes (Chairman) on 01252 861059, e mikehughesuk@yahoo.com; or Alex Morton (Acting Secretary) on 0797 0119793, e alegisi2004@yahoo.co.uk. Or write to Alex Morton, RUGO Acting Secretary, 86 Dover Road, London E12 5EA. RUGO's website is www.rugo.org.*

LIVESTOCK FOR LIFE The UK-based charity **Send a Cow** (*Registered Charity No 299717;* ✎ *01225 874222;* e *info@sendacow.org.uk; www.sendacow.org.uk*) works with the people of Africa to overcome poverty and malnutrition through the sustainable development of livestock farming systems and self-reliant local groups. Current programmes are in Lesotho, Kenya, Tanzania, Uganda, Zambia and Ethiopia – as well as Rwanda, where Send a Cow mainly provides livestock plus training in animal care and natural manure/compost-based organic farming. The beneficiaries are as many as their backgrounds are varied.

The Ihururiro Group This group was set up in 2004 with the encouragement of Console Musabyimana, the HIV/AIDS counsellor at the Masaka Health Clinic. When she first started her job, she realised that most HIV positive people were living lives of shame and secrecy, too scared even to ask for the anti-retroviral drugs that would prolong their lives.

By encouraging the group to come together, and provide support to each other, she has helped them to overcome much of the stigma associated with the disease in their communities. As a result of the new openness created by the group, the number of people coming forward to take the drugs has trebled and infection rates have nearly halved in the past two years.

'When our association formed we were determined to get involved in advocacy,' says Moses Twagiramungu, the Ihururiro Group's treasurer. 'We did this by going out into the community. People started waking up to the fact that there is AIDS in their community, and the fear associated with talking openly about it started to subside.'

'However,' he continues, 'we are still weak. We do not have access to enough food to really benefit from the drugs. We need good nutrition to complement the treatment. So when we heard that a charity called Send a Cow was helping vulnerable people we applied for help.'

In discussions between Send a Cow and the Ihururiro Group, everyone agreed that cows would be too much for the weakest group members to manage, so Send a Cow agreed to give 60 dairy goats to group members, two per recipient, to be handed over in June 2006.

Goat milk is particularly good for people weakened by malnutrition, and the new owners can also sell some of the milk, bringing in extra income for more food.

The goats' manure enables them to increase their vegetable and cassava crops. And when the first kids are born, the female offspring are passed on to other group members, who will repeat the process.

'We all know farmers who have already received livestock from Send a Cow,' says Perpetual Kantamage, 'so we know the benefits that they can bring to a family.'

'We were lucky to have a little help from another organisation who helped us supplement our diets while we waited for our livestock,' says Moses, 'but that was only a short-term solution. Send a Cow is a long-term solution.'

RWANDAN YOUTH INFORMATION COMMUNITY ORGANISATION (RYICO) The
Rwandan Youth Information Community Organisation, known as rYico *(UK Registered Charity No 1004274; Brighton (UK) office (+44) 01273 234836;* e *info@rYico.org; www.rYico.org)*, is a small NGO based in both Rwanda and the UK.

Activities In Kigali, rYico runs the **Centre Marembo** (↘ *+250 588140*), a youth centre that provides a space for young people from all backgrounds to meet and to access information and education. Further afield, rYico has started an exchange programme in which the vibrancy of Rwandan culture is brought to the UK through arts and commemorative events, while seeking partnerships and support for Centre Marembo.

Centre Marembo Centre Marembo offers young people free access to its library, computing facilities and team of dedicated volunteers that counsel, train, educate, supervise and care for them. Since opening in September 2005, the centre has offered food and shelter to 18 boys aged 10–22 who previously lived and worked on the street. It opens its gates weekly to a further 80 street kids for showering and washing their clothes, sharing lunch together, and a programme of training and educational games.

Vulnerable young people also have the opportunity to follow a transitional programme that encourages them to give up their street habits for the classroom. The centre has welcomed the help and involvement of volunteers from the Kigali Institute of Education, Kigali Health Institute, secondary schools and local businesses, all offering their skills and time to support and challenge the youngsters at the centre. Marembo recently started an informal school offering the chance to study at the centre three days a week. Furthermore there are now a variety of activities on offer such as an AIDS awareness club, a youth journal, mechanic's training and crafts workshops; plus, every weekend, the centre welcomes many young people to come and join the volunteers for study groups.

Gradually the centre is reaching out to more and more young people – mostly boys at present, but more activities will be developed to encourage girls to join. The centre also aims to work with organisations that can support its residents' families, providing the required holistic approach to reintegrate the young people into their families and the community.

At the end of your visit, if you've any clothing or other practical items that you don't want to take back home with you, do contact the Marembo Centre to see whether they can make use of them.

SURVIVORS FUND (SURF) For more than nine years, UK-based Survivors Fund has
helped survivors of the Rwandan genocide deal with and recover from the tragedies of 1994, supporting a wide range of services for victims in Rwanda and assisting survivors in the UK. Funded by a variety of public and private organisations and individuals, SURF acts as a channel to distribute financial assistance to groups, individuals and charitable organisations in the day-to-day

operations of bringing the people of Rwanda hope, safety, and a decent standard of living.

Current activities are focused on: HIV/AIDS, psychosocial support projects, education/vocational training, income-generating activities, shelter, and legal assistance/advocacy.

SURF, 10 Rickett Street, West Brompton, London SW6 1RU; ↘ *020 7610 2589;* e *info@survivors-fund.org.uk; www.survivors-fund.org.uk.*

ENGALYNX This is a small UK charity operating from Manningtree in Essex and set up after the genocide to help Rwanda rebuild. Its name, Engalynx, meaning 'England links with…', was chosen by the children of a local school which also became involved. Since then, with the help of local friends and businesses and even a football club, Engalynx has sent not only funds but also packages and a container with computers, tools, clothes, shoes, stationery, sewing machines, hairdressing equipment, photocopiers, cycles, seeds, etc. It is helping to support a school in a particularly poor area of Gitarama, and is providing support and equipment to Kibuye Hospital. It has given microscopes to students, goats to child-headed families, handicrafts outlets (in the UK) to craftspeople – and is opening a small home for Kigali's street kids and other vulnerable young people. It is trying to organise health insurance (including AIDS treatment) for families (costing about £8 per family per year) and school fees for children (about £55). Wherever Engalynx sees a need and a possibility, it steps in!

Engalynx, 35 Birch Drive, Brantham, Suffolk, CO11 1TG; ↘ *01206 393022;* e *lantern@cpwpost.com. Founder and director: Maralyn Bambridge.*

INVESTING IN RWANDA

The ultimate involvement in Rwanda is to invest in one of the many opportunities that the country's rapid development has created. The **Rwanda Investment and Export Promotion Agency** (*Avenue du Lac Muhazi; PO Box 6239 Kigali;* ↘ *(250) 510248, 585221/3,* f *510249;* e *info@rwandainvest.com; www.rwandainvest.com*) can provide full information, including the generous incentives and concessions available. The mechanisms are straightforward and investor-friendly, with a minimum of red tape.

Openings exist in many sectors; for example food processing (tea, coffee, fruit, vegetables…), flower production, tourism (hotels, restaurants, watersports, training, hospitality services, handicrafts, transport…), livestock, solar installations, medical services, telecommunications, power, ICT, construction, transportation and finance. It's an Aladdin's cave of opportunity.

If any of the above raises even a tiny flicker of interest, do check it out. The website is very comprehensive. If you don't, you may miss a life-changing opportunity. And Rwanda needs you!

Cards from Africa (↘ *08300844/08543276;* e *info@cardsfromafrica.com; www.cardsfromafrica.com*) is a small business that was started in November 2004 to provide employment to vulnerable orphaned youths, who are responsible for their younger brothers and sisters. They make paper by hand (from office waste), and then use that to make greeting cards, etc. CfA practices fair-trade principles, ensuring a fair wage to the card makers. They are 10-minute bumpy-road drive from Remera, near the airport. *Call to arrange a visit. Open Mon–Fri 9.00–16.00.*

Part Two

THE GUIDE

6

Kigali

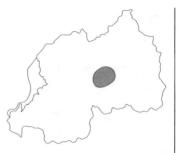

Rwanda's attractive capital, Kigali, straggles over several hills, with the city centre on one and the government/administrative quarter on another. When Ruanda-Urundi (the capital of which was Usumbura, now Bujumbura) split into Rwanda and Burundi at the time of independence in 1962, the strongest contender to become Rwanda's new capital seemed to be Butare, which had been used by the Belgians as Rwanda's administrative capital during colonisation.

However, Kigali's central position and good road links to the rest of the country won out. As a result, while Butare (recently renamed Huye) has avoided capital-city brashness and remains relatively calm, Kigali has grown dramatically, its population rising from a mere 25,000 at independence to 240,000 in 1991 and an estimated 800,000 today. Empty spaces on the hillsides are filling with new housing, and pollution in the valleys (from the increasing volume of traffic) could soon be a problem.

The centre of Kigali is bustling, colourful and noisy, but (for an African city) surprisingly clean and safe. Its occupants, from smart-suited business-persons to scruffy kids hawking newspapers or pirated cassettes, go purposefully about their activities, only lessening tempo briefly in the middle of the day. Occasional traffic lights, roundabouts, a strictly enforced one-way road system and a cacophony of car horns manage (more or less) to regulate the traffic, although it's heavy and congested at peak times. Peaceful, tree-lined residential streets stretch outwards and generally downwards from the city's heart, and give visitors scope for strolling.

The government and administrative area, in Kacyiru quarter on a neighbouring hill, is newer and quieter, with wide streets and some striking modern architecture. Kigali was the centre of much fighting during the genocide and offices were ransacked; when workers returned after the end of the war they had virtually no usable typewriters, phones, stationery or furniture and had to start again from scratch. Also files, archives and other documentation had been destroyed.

There aren't many tourist attractions in Kigali itself and you're unlikely to want to spend many full days there, but there are some good hotels, the services (shops, banks, etc) are plentiful and the ambience is pleasant, making it an excellent base for exploring the rest of Rwanda, all parts of which are easily accessible by road in less than a day. Car-hire is easily arranged via one of the many tour operators and travel agencies – see page 111.

GETTING THERE AND AWAY

BY AIR See pages 35–6 for details of flights to and from Rwanda – which means to and from Kigali, since the country's only international airport is situated about 5km from the city centre. There are plans to relocate the airport to Nyamata, about 30km south of Kigali, which would free the land for further development and

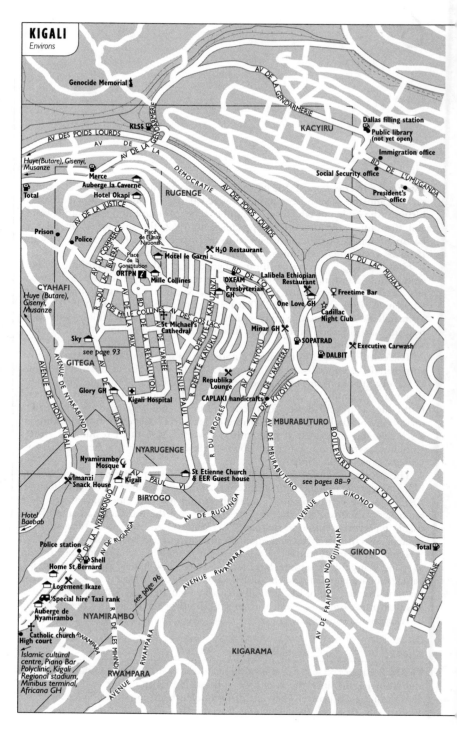

KIGALI
Environs

Genocide Memorial

Huye(Butare), Gisenyi, Musanze

Total

Merce
Auberge la Caverne
Hotel Okapi

KLSS

AV DE LA GENDARMERIE

AV DES POIDS LOURDS
AV DE LA

KACYIRU

Dallas filling station
Public library (not yet open)

Immigration office

BD DE L'UMUGANDA

Social Security office

President's office

RUGENGE

DEMOCRATIE
AV DES POIDS LOURDS

Prison
Police

Place de l'Unité National

Place de la Constitution

ORTPN

Mille Collines

H2O Restaurant

Motel le Garni

BD DE L'OUA

AV DU LAC MUHAZI

Lalibela Ethiopian Restaurant

OXFAM

Presbyterian GH

One Love GH

Freetime Bar

Cadillac Night Club

CYAHAFI

Huye (Butare), Gisenyi, Musanze

Sky

St Michael's Cathedral

Minar GH

SOPATRAD

Executive Carwash

DALBIT

GITEGA

see page 93

Glory GH
Kigali Hospital

Republika Lounge

CAPLAKI handicrafts

AV DE L'AKAGERA

R DE KIYOVU

MBURABUTURO

NYARUGENGE

AVENUE DE MONT KIGALI

R DU PROGRES

AV DE MBURABUTURO

see pages 88–9

BOULEVARD DE L'OUA

Nyamirambo Mosque

Imanzi Snack House

Kigali

St Etienne Church & EER Guest house

BIROGYO

AVENUE DE GIKONDO

Hotel Baobab

AV DE RUGUNGA

Police station

Shell

Home St Bernard

Logement Ikaze

'Special hire' Taxi rank

Auberge de Nyamirambo

Catholic church
High court

NYAMIRAMBO

Islamic cultural centre, Piano Bar
Polyclinic, Kigali
Regional stadium,
Minibus terminal,
Africana GH

AV RWAMPARA

AVENUE RWAMPARA

RWAMPARA

GIKONDO

Total

R DE LA DOUANE

AVENUE DE FRAIPOND NDAGIJIMANA

KIGARAMA

see page 96

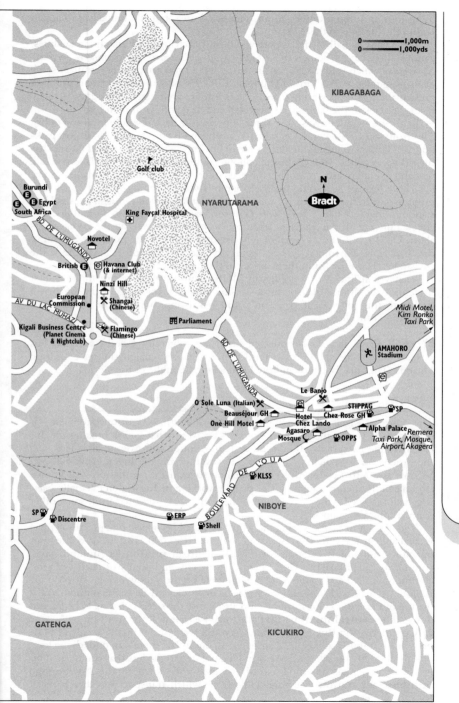

bring jobs and opportunities to an underused area, but it's unlikely to happen within the lifetime of this edition.

In the arrivals hall of the airport you'll find exchange and telephone facilities, various shops and a branch of ORTPN (*Office Rwandais du Tourisme et des Parcs Nationaux*) which is Rwanda's tourist office, where you can get a preliminary stock of maps, guides and so forth. (The main ORTPN office is in the city centre.) At present there is no pestering from porters – there aren't any – just grab a trolley from the stack in the baggage reclaim area and deal with your own bags.

To get into Kigali town you've three options. (Or four, if you're prepared to beg a lift from some fellow traveller who has a vehicle.) If your hotel does airport pick-ups, you'll have arranged this at the time of booking; give them a ring if no-one has turned up to collect you. (At the telephone counter, calls are metered, so you talk first and pay afterwards, removing the need to have coins or phone cards.) If you've very little luggage and some small change in Rwandan francs, you can pick up a minibus-taxi in the road outside the airport and it'll take you to Kigali's central bus station. Otherwise take a *taxi-voiture* (a normal taxi, as opposed to a minibus-taxi). Agree a price with the driver in advance. At the time of writing the going rate is about US$15, but rates do legitimately rise over time. (If the exchange bureau in the airport is closed, taxi-drivers generally accept US dollars, but check the exchange rate on the list in the window of the bureau.)

Whatever airline you've used, you MUST confirm your return flight at least three days in advance of departure – airline offices or travel agents in Kigali will deal with this for you. If you don't, you risk being 'bumped' or having your reservation cancelled.

BY ROAD Kigali is a well-connected little city – literally. Good roads and bus services link it to all the main border crossings with neighbouring countries: Uganda, Tanzania, Burundi and the Democratic Republic of the Congo.

GETTING AROUND

The centre of Kigali – for shopping, banks, airline offices, tour operators, etc – is tiny, so once you're there, you'll never be far from what you're looking for. It's based around two streets, Boulevard de la Révolution and Avenue de la Paix, and the various roads branching off them. However, if you ask directions you'll soon become aware that people don't go much on street names, rather on well-known landmarks. Remember that a lot of people working in Kigali don't actually *know* Kigali all that well – they'd never been there until they returned from some other country after the genocide.

A good foldout map covering the whole of Kigali (as opposed to just the centre) is available from ORTPN (see page 61) for Rfr7,000, also from some tour operators and hotels. There's a network of urban **minibuses** (minibus-taxis, commonly called taxis) serving all areas of the city, and plenty of **taxis** (saloons, commonly called *taxi-voitures* and recognisable by the yellow/orange stripe along the side) – they park, among other places, in Boulevard de la Révolution and at the top of Place de la Constitution, and also cruise the streets waiting to be flagged down. The **central minibus-taxi station** in Kigali is at the junction of Avenue de Commerce and Rue Mont Kabuye – you'll recognise it by the gaggle of beat-up white minibuses and general air of chaos, but in fact there's an underlying level of sanity and, if you ask someone, you'll be pointed to the bus that you need. This is where you pick up minibus-taxis to take you down to the **Nyabugogo minibus-taxi station** (see page 113), from which transport to other parts of Rwanda leaves.

Virtually all of the Kigali hotels in the 'Luxury' to 'Middle' categories can arrange airport pick-ups – just ask (and check the cost, if any) at the time of booking. Unless otherwise specified, bedrooms in all of the Kigali hotels listed here have en-suite facilities with either bath or shower. Hotels in Remera suburb are closer to the airport than are those in the centre.

LUXURY *(above US$115 double)*
Four hotels in Kigali match up to international standards, of which all but one are typical city hotels: large, bland and impersonal, catering primarily to business travellers, with the sort of facilities one would expect of any four-to-five-star address in an African capital. The new InterContinental is the smartest hotel anywhere in Rwanda, approaching five-star in standard and priced accordingly, but the more established Novotel Umubano and Mille Collines (the latter of Hotel Rwanda fame) don't lag far behind in quality, and are significantly cheaper. Altogether different is the owner-managed Motel le Garni du Centre, a homely and relatively affordable option on the edge of the city centre.

⌂ **Hotel InterContinental Kigali** (104 rooms)
↘ 597100; f 597101; e reservations@ickigali.co.rw or contactus@southernsun.com;
www.southernsun.com or www.intercontinental.com. This top-notch hotel opened in late 2003 on the site of the former Diplomates in the tree-lined Boulevard de la Révolution, a flat 10-min stroll from the city centre. It's part of the South African Southern Sun group (website as above) and has the full works: comfortable bedrooms and suites with DSTV, mini-bar and tea/coffee facilities, 550-seat conference centre, boutiques, top-class cuisine at 2 restaurants, 24-hour business services, 24-hour room service, free air-conditioned airport shuttle, and friendly staff. The compact green grounds are centred on a large swimming pool and the relaxed poolside Banana Jam Café. Credit cards are accepted. Food and other items (linen, staff uniform, candles...) are sourced locally where possible, to benefit the local economy. *US$248/278 sgl/dbl; US$268/298 superior; US$318 upwards for suites; all rates b&b.*

⌂ **Kigali Novotel Umubano** (98 rooms) ↘ 585816; f 582957; e umubano@rwanda1.com; www.novotel.com. This spacious hotel is quietly situated on a pretty 4ha stand in the administrative quarter of Kacyiru, which lies between central Kigali and the airport, and is linked to both by plenty of transport, whether minibus-taxis or taxi-voitures. It's an efficient but relaxed place, very popular with local people for functions, and the personnel are friendly. There's a post office near by and banking facilities (with Western Union) in the hotel, which also has a good restaurant and bar, swimming pool, mini-golf, tennis courts, conference facilities, fitness centre, internet access, and various boutiques inc an irresistible patisserie in the foyer. Credit cards are accepted. *US$145/160 en-suite sgl/dbl with AC, DSTV, safe; suites US$185-230.*

⌂ **Hotel des Mille Collines** (112 rooms) ↘ 576530/3; f 576541; e millecollines@millecollines.net; www.millecollines.net. This Kigali institution gained recent international fame as the subject of the 2005 film *Hotel Rwanda*. Despite its convenient location a 5-min moderately sloping walk from the city centre, it lies in attractive grounds dominated by a large swimming pool area and a massive fig tree (which looks as if it has been there since time began, but is only 40 years old) that offers some enjoyable urban birdwatching. The hotel has a good restaurant, pricey bar, tennis court, conference and business facilities inc internet access, and various boutiques. Credit cards are accepted. Some renovation/refurbishment is due to start around October 2006. *€110/125 en-suite sgl/dbl with AC, DSTV; suites from €201; add €12 pp for b/fast.*

⌂ **Motel le Garni du Centre** (11 rooms) ↘/f 572654; e garni@rwanda1.com; www.garni.co.rw. This likeable little hotel is tucked away down a side street close to the centre of town, near the Centre Culturel d'Echanges Franco-Rwandaises. The quiet, comfortable rooms, which come with TV, phone and mini-bar, are simply but stylishly decorated, and overlook the garden and small swimming pool. Lunch and dinner are available by request; the Restaurant Chez Robert and the Hotel des Mille Collines are only a few mins' walk

Kigali **WHERE TO STAY**

6

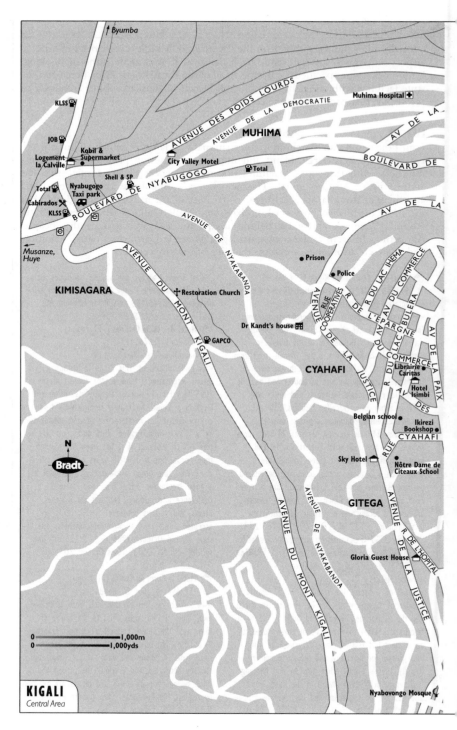

↑ Byumba

KLSS

JOB
Logement
la Calville
Kobil &
Supermarket
City Valley Motel

AVENUE DES POIDS LOURDS
AVENUE DE LA DEMOCRATIE
MUHIMA
Muhima Hospital
BOULEVARD DE

AV DE LA

Shell & SP
Total
Nyabugogo
Taxi park
Cabirados
KLSS

BOULEVARD DE NYABUGOGO
Total

AV DE LA

Musanze,
Huye

AVENUE DE NYAKABANDA

Prison
Police

KIMISAGARA

AVENUE DU MONT KIGALI

✝ Restoration Church

Dr Kandt's house

AVENUE DE LA JUSTICE
RUE COOPERATIVES
R DU LAC IHEMA
R DU LAC BULERA
R DE L'EPAYON DU COMMERCE
AV DU COMMERCE
R DU LAC DES
AV DES
RUE DE LA JUSTICE
AV DE LA PAIX

GAPCO

CYAHAFI

Librairie
Caritas
Hotel
Isimbi

Belgian school
Ikirezi
Bookshop
CYAHAFI

Sky Hotel
Nôtre Dame de
Citeaux School

GITEGA

AVENUE DE NYAKABANDA

AVENUE DE L'HÔPITAL

Gloria Guest House

AVENUE DU MONT KIGALI

N

Bradt

0 — 1,000m
0 — 1,000yds

Nyabovongo Mosque

KIGALI
Central Area

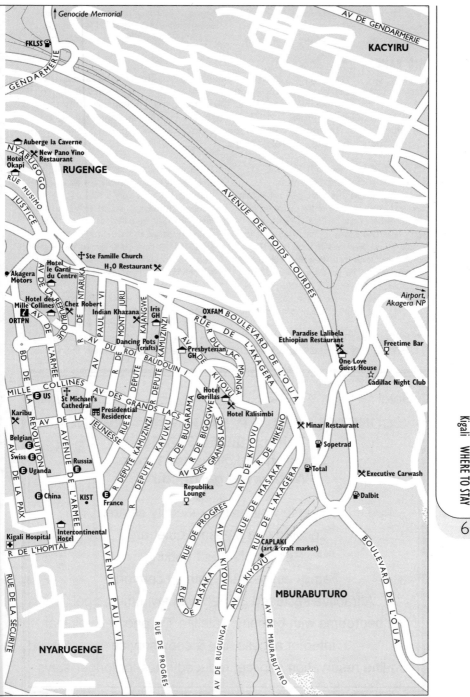

Genocide Memorial ↑

FKLSS

AV DE GENDARMERIE

KACYIRU

GENDARMERIE

NYABUGOGO

Auberge la Caverne
New Pano Vino Restaurant
Hotel Okapi

RUGENGE

RUE MUSIMO

JUSTICE

AVENUE DES POIDS LOURDES

Ste Famille Church
Hotel le Garni du Centre
H₂O Restaurant
Akagera Motors
Hotel des Mille Collines
Chez Robert
ORTPN
Indian Khazana
Dancing Pots (crafts)
Iris GH
OXFAM
Presbyterian GH

Airport,
Akagera NP

Paradise Lalibela
Ethiopian Restaurant

Freetime Bar

One Love
Guest House

Cadillac Night Club

BOULEVARD DE L'OUA

RUE DU LAC MPANGA

AV DE NTARUKA
AV DE LA REPUBLIQUE
AV PAUL VI
R DE MONT JURU
R DE ROI
KAJANGWE
AV DE KAMUZINZI
AV DU KIYOVU

Hotel Gorillas
Hotel Kalisimbi

BAUDOUIN I

MILLE COLLINES
US
St Michael's Cathedral
Presidential Residence
Karibu
Belgian
Swiss
Uganda
China
Russia
France
KIST
Intercontinental Hotel
Kigali Hospital

BD DE L'ARMEE
AV DE LA REVOLUTION
AV DE LA PAIX
AVENUE DE L'ARMEE
AV DES GRANDS LACS
DEPUTE KAMUZINZI
DEPUTE KAMUZINZI
DEPUTE KAYUKU
AVENUE JEUNESSE
R DE BUGARAMA
R DE BIGOGWE
AV DES GRANDS LACS

Minar Restaurant
Sopetrad
Total
Executive Carwash
Dalbit

R DE L'HOPITAL

AVENUE PAUL VI

Republika Lounge

CAPLAKI
(art & craft market)

RUE DE PROGRES
AV DE KIYOVU
RUE DE MASAKA
R DE L'AKAGERA
R DE MIKENO

BOULEVARD DE L'OUA

MBURABUTURO

RUE DE LA SECURITE

AV DE RUGUNGA
AV DE MBURABUTURO

RUE DE PROGRES

NYARUGENGE

away. There's a log fire in the lounge for chilly evenings, and the Swiss owner-manager – who lives on the premises – is very obliging. It's deservedly popular so book in advance (this can be done online). *From US$98/118 sgl/dbl for 1 night, inc a superb buffet b/fast, with discounts for longer stays.*

MID-RANGE *(US$50–80 double)*

This header covers a wide variety of smaller and less impersonal hotels offering decent tourist-oriented accommodation at rates that are more likely to be affordable to non-business travellers. Difficult to pick favourites, but the Iris Guesthouse, Gorillas Hotel and Chez Lando are popular and their guests return for repeat visits. Dropping considerably in price, a good option is the centrally located and well organised Hotel Okapi.

Hotel Gorillas (31 rooms) 501717/8; f 501716; e gorillashotel@rwanda1.com; www.gorillashotel.com. This smart, calm and efficient new hotel, about 1km east of the city centre, has very comfortable rooms and one of Kigali's most highly rated (and priciest...) restaurants. Facilities include internet access and TV in all rooms. The downhill walk to the hotel from the centre of town is manageable but the upward walk into town is quite steep; however plenty of *taxi-voitures* ply the route and minibus-taxis run nearby. *US$50/70 standard sgl/dbl, US$60/80 deluxe rooms, excluding b/fast.*

Iris Guesthouse (18 rooms) 501172, 501181; f 576929; e iris1@rwanda1.com. Situated almost around the corner from the Gorillas Hotel in Rue Député Kajangwe, this relatively new place – it opened in 2001 – is more a hotel than a guesthouse. It stands in pleasant grounds in a shady street away from the traffic, and the very good continental restaurant has meals in the Rfr3,000–4,000 range (10% discount for guesthouse residents). *Rfr25,000/35,000 for a clean en-suite sgl/dbl; Rfr50,000 apt; all rates b&b.*

Hotel Okapi (39 rooms) 571667; m 08 745389; f 574413; e okapi@hotmail.com. This popular and reasonably priced multi-storey hotel in central Kigali has a back terrace with a panoramic view across the Kigali landscape. Unfortunately it's in a side street (Rue Musima), between Boulevard de

Nyabugogo and Avenue de la Justice, which is unsurfaced and a bit tatty — guests might not feel safe walking back there at night, though this may improve as the area is reconstructed. The restaurant offers a limited but acceptable range of international meals and snacks. *En-suite dbls Rfr15,000/25,000 without/with TV; rooms with a view Rfr35,000 and suites Rfr55,000.*

🏠 **Ninzi Hill Hotel** (15 rooms) ☎ 587711–5; f 587716; e ninzihill@yahoo.fr or ninzi@rwanda1.com. Set in the administrative quarter not far from the Novotel, this is a quiet, comfortable place well away from city bustle, and it has a pleasantly laidback feel. The spacious tiled rooms are close to luxury in standard, with queen-size bed, DSTV and balcony, and those at the back overlook gardens and greenery. There's a BCDI branch on the ground floor offering foreign exchange facilities 7 days a week from 08.00 to 20.00, and a good mid-price restaurant. Nearby is the Shangai Chinese Restaurant, with swings for the children and a family shopping centre — and it's an easy 10-min walk to the Kigali Business Centre, with its cinema, bar-restaurant and shops. *US$56/86 sgl/dbl inc 'tropical' b/fast – ie: continental plus fruit!*

🏠 **Hotel Chez Lando** (52 rooms) ☎ 582050, 584328, 84394; f 84380; e lando@rwandatel1.rwanda1.com; www.hotelchezlando.com. This well-established place with a quiet garden lies just off the main road through the suburb of Remera, an easy taxi or minibus-taxi ride from town, and is popular with locals and visitors alike. All the en-suite rooms are spacious, with satellite TV, international direct dialling and internet access for guests with their own laptop. The Zoom nightclub/disco is popular at weekends. The indoor, upstairs restaurant does a good buffet b/fast but can be slow and cheerless for other meals; for these the outdoor, downstairs restaurant is brisker and livelier. Several good restaurants and shops lie within easy walking distance of the hotel, as does a fast internet café and a sauna/massage centre. *US$50/60 sgl/dbl in the old building; US$60/70 bungalow; US$80/100 in the newest extension.*

🏠 **Alpha Palace Hotel** (38 rooms) ☎ 582981; m 08 535981; f 584134; e alphapalace@rwanda1.com; www.alphapalace.com. Also in Remera, about 1km from the airport and 4km from the centre of town, this is a comfortable, modern hotel with a swimming pool, a 24-hour restaurant with French, African and oriental cuisine, a snack-bar for grills, and a nightclub on Friday/Saturday. The tiled rooms are very comfortable and spacious, and come

with king-size beds, DSTV, balcony and en-suite bath and shower. *Rfr28,500/34,000/37,000 sgl/dbl/twin, inc continental b/fast.*

🏠 **Presbyterian Auberge d'Accueil** (30 rooms) \ 578915; f 578919; e epr@rwandatel1.rwanda1.com. Close to the

Gorillas Hotel, a 10-min walk downhill from the city centre, this church hostel is a clean, relaxing place with cheerful rooms and a good-value dining room. It can get busy with church guests so book in advance. Good monthly rates are available. *Rfr15,000/20,000 sgl/dbl or 30,000/40,000 suite, all rates b&b.*

BUDGET *(US$20–40 double)*

The hotels listed below are more basic and in some cases a little seedy by comparison with those placed in the mid-range bracket, but will still meet the requirements of less demanding or more cost-conscious tourists. Top picks include the central Isimbi, Castel and Sky Hotels, and the suburban Hotel Baobab and Auberge Beau Séjour.

🏠 **Hotel Isimbi** (20 rooms) \ 572578/81; f 575109; e isimbi@hotmail.com or isimbi@rwanda1.com; www.hotelisimbi.co.rw. The most central hotel in this range, situated on Rue Kalisimbi just a few mins' walk from the market, post office and shops, this is an efficient, clean, business-type hotel. The unpretentious en-suite rooms with hot water are good value (the back ones are quietest), and there's a non-smoking snack-bar and restaurant for main meals (up to around Rfr3,500), as well as room service. *Rfr15,000/18,000 sgl/dbl.*

🏠 **Sky Hotel** (25 rooms) \ 516690/2/3, m 08 300323/513343; f 516690; e skyhotel1@yahoo.fr. This multi-storey hotel on Avenue de la Justice at the southern verge of the city centre has comfortable albeit rather tired-looking en-suite rooms with TV, queen-size bed, balcony, hot water, 24-hour internet access, and a lovely view over the valley from the back. The room rates are very reasonable, as is the restaurant, and there's an affordable night-club at weekends, as well as a few other bars and restaurants within 5 mins' walk. If you don't fancy the short but steep walk into the town centre, *taxi-voitures* cruise along the main road past the hotel and there's a minibus-taxi stop directly opposite. *Rfr14,000/18,000 sgl/dbl b&b.*

🏠 **Castel Hotel** (23 rooms) \ 576377, 578491/501687; f 587456; e hotelcastel2002@yahoo.fr; www.castelhotel.com. Also in Avenue de la Justice, but at the other end as it approaches the Place de l'Unité Nationale, this relatively new hotel offers clean accommodation with TV, phone and small fridge. The hotel is built on a steep hillside so the restaurant at the back (service can be slow) has dramatic views across the valley. It's spotlessly clean, and the en-suite rooms are good value – but be warned (if it bothers you) that no alcohol is served. *Rfr16,000/18,000 sgl/dbl.*

🏠 **Hotel Baobab** (9 rooms) \ 575633, 516616;

f 571048; e baobab@inbox.rw. This great place is full of character but some distance from the city centre, down in Nyakabanda suburb in the southwest near Mount Kigali and the Stadium Regional de Kigali. If you have your own transport (or don't mind taking taxis), do consider it. The area is peaceful, with widespread views across the valley and to Mount Kigali, and the possibility of quite rural walks. The restaurant (mostly outdoor) has a good reputation locally. Rooms are en-suite with hot water, phone and TV. *Rfr14,000 dbl; b/fast not included.*

🏠 **Agasaro Motel** (15 rooms) \ 583293; f 582226; e agasaromotel@yahoo.fr; www.agasaromotel.itgo.com. A few mins from the Alpha Palace, on the opposite side of the same road, this small hotel offers good-value accommodation in simple but bright en-suite rooms with queen-size bed, TV and hot water. If you're arriving late by air and just want a straightforward night's sleep near the airport before moving on the next day, give it a try – reception is open 24 hours and it seems a well-cared-for place. *Rfr15,000/18,000 sgl/dbl b&b.*

🏠 **Auberge Beau Séjour** (19 rooms) \ 582527; \/f 582601; e beausejourhotel@yahoo.com. This homely lodge lies just off the main road to the airport and has a good reputation locally. The rooms are very pleasant, and come with TV and hot bath. Dinner is served by request. The owner supervises personally and takes a pride in the place – there are thoughtful touches like drinking-water in the bedrooms, and all rooms lead out to the well-cared-for garden. *Rfr15,000/17,000 sgl/dbl b&b.*

🏠 **One Love Guesthouse** (10 rooms) \ 575412, 513154; e onelove@rwanda1.com. This welcoming place is run by an NGO (the Mulindi Japan One Love Project) that supports the disabled and works practically to help them – all profits are ploughed back into the NGO. There are simple but spacious

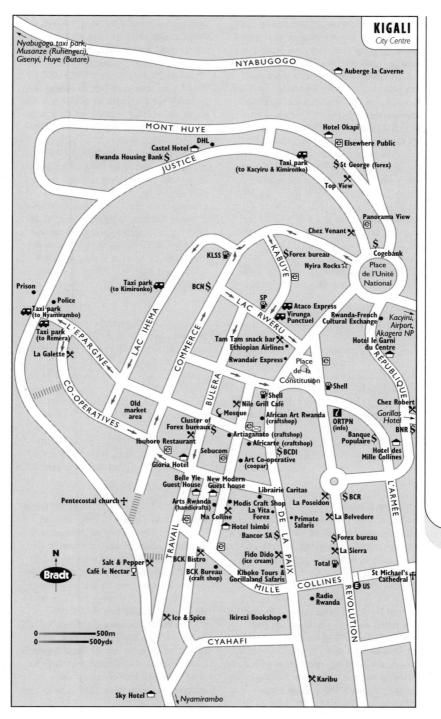

KIGALI
City Centre

Nyabugogo taxi park,
Musanze (Ruhengeri),
Gisenyi, Huye (Butare)

NYABUGOGO

Auberge la Caverne

MONT HUYE

Hotel Okapi

Elsewhere Public

Castel Hotel

DHL

JUSTICE

Rwanda Housing Bank

Taxi park
(to Kacyiru & Kimironko)

St George (forex)

Top View

Panorama View

Chez Venant

Cogebank

KLSS

KABUYE

Forex bureau

Place
de l'Unité
National

Nyira Rocks

BCN

LAC RWERU

SP

Ataco Express

Taxi park
(to Kimironko)

Virunga
Punctuel

Prison

Police

Taxi park
(to Nyamirambo)

Taxi park
(to Remera)

L'EPARGNE

LAC IHEMA

COMMERCE

Rwanda-French
Cultural Exchange

Kacyiru,
Airport,
Akagera NP

Hotel le Garni
du Centre

Tam Tam snack bar
Ethiopian Airlines

Rwandair Express

Place
de la
Constitution

La Galette

CO-OPERATIVES

BULERA

Shell

Shell

Old market
area

Nile Grill Café

Mosque

Shell

African Art Rwanda
(craftshop)

Chez Robert

Gorillas
Hotel

BNR

Cluster of
Forex bureaux

Artiaganato (craftshop)

Africarte (craftshop)

ORTPN
(info)

Banque
Populaire

Ibuhoro Restaurant

Sebucom

Art Co-operative
(coopar)

BCDI

Hotel des
Mille Collines

Gloria Hotel

Belle Vie
Guest House

New Modern
Guest house

Librairie Caritas

BCR

Pentecostal church

Arts Rwanda
(handicrafts)

Modis Craft Shop

La Poseidon

La Belvedere

Ma Colline

La Vita
Forex

Primate
Safaris

Hotel Isimbi

Bancor SA

Forex bureau

La Sierra

N

Salt & Pepper

Café le Nectar

BCK Bistro

Fido Dido
(ice cream)

Kiboko Tours &
Gorillaland Safaris

Total

St Michael's
Cathedral

BCK Bureau
(craft shop)

MILLE

COLLINES

US

Radio
Rwanda

REVOLUTION

DE LA PAIX

L'ARMEE

REPUBLIQUE

TRAVAIL

Ice & Spice

Ikirezi Bookshop

0 ——— 500m
0 ——— 500yds

Bradt

CYAHAFI

Karibu

Sky Hotel

Nyamirambo

Kigali WHERE TO STAY

6

93

twin rooms with balconies and some cooking facilities, and you may also be permitted to pitch a tent in the garden. Young people and backpackers would feel comfortable here. There's also a restaurant with a range of snacks/meals. It's a secure place, with good parking, in the valley between Kiyovu and Kacyiru next to the Lalibela Ethiopian Restaurant. There are minibus-taxis and taxi-voitures nearby. Rfr15,000 per day or 250,000 per month.

🏠 **City Valley Motel** (10 rooms) ☎ 08 558173. Situated on Av des Poids Lourds a few hundred metres from Nyabugogo Taxi Park, this is a pleasant hotel with a decent-looking garden bar and restaurant attached, and a nightclub due to open in late 2006. The location, on a road used by heavy trucks, is potentially noisy, so best to ask for a room facing away from the traffic. The large rooms all have fan, net, TV and a balcony. Rfr10,000 dbl using common showers; Rfr15,000 en-suite with hot water.

🏠 **Chez Rose Guest House** (20 rooms) ☎ 584086, ☎ 08 574800; e ncuro@yahoo.com. This is

another homely set-up along the airport road, with cheerful en-suite rooms set round a courtyard, again with thoughtful touches; US$20 inc a good b/fast with fruit, other meals by request.

🏠 **One Hill Motel** (10 rooms) ☎ 08 628888. Situated a few doors down from the Auberge Beau Séjour, this isn't great value: the location feels rather isolated (no meals are available) and the tiled or carpeted en-suite rooms with TV are rather gloomy. Rfr16,000/18,000 sgl/dbl.

🏠 **Glory Guesthouse** (8 rooms) ☎ 08 867863. Situated to the south of the city centre not far from the Sky Hotel, this prominently signposted new place offers adequate but seriously overpriced accommodation in drab en-suite rooms. Rfr20,000 dbl.

🏠 **Solace Ministries** ☎ 585005/585153; ☎ 08 305094; e mucyo@rwanda1.com. Situated near the Novotel, this lodge has clean, bright, en-suite rooms (with hot water) in a newly built block. US$25 pp per night, or US$40 inc 3 enormous meals per day.

SHOESTRING (below US$20 double)

The lodgings listed below are all on the basic side, with rooms using common showers or cold water only – or both! Most cater primarily to the local market, though they are also suitable to backpackers and other travellers on a tight budget. In terms of quality, the pick in this range is the Auberge la Caverne, while the cheapest option for those on a rock-bottom budget is the Motel Centre d'Accueil Nyakabanda. Probably the best overall compromise between price and quality, however, is the Auberge de Nyamirambo, which also has the advantage of being close to a cluster of similarly-priced options you could fall back on if it's full.

City centre

There are surprisingly few budget hotels in the city centre, of which only the pleasant Auberge la Caverne and adequate Gloria Hotel can be recommended without reservations.

🏠 **Auberge la Caverne** (11 rooms) ☎ 574549. Top of the budget list for central Kigali is this pleasant, and clean lodge whose spacious and mostly en-suite rooms with hot water are set away from the traffic around a central courtyard in Boulevard de Nyabugogo. Back windows have a good view out over the valley. The restaurant does a standard range of meals. It's a steepish but short walk up into the town centre, but the hotel lies along the main road used by minibus-taxis to/from the intercity Nyabugogo Taxi Park. Rfr5,000/7,000/10,000 sgl/twin/dbl.

🏠 **Gloria Hotel** (15 rooms) ☎ 571957. Comfortably the best of a trio of very central budget hotels in the commercial area near to the market, this long-serving but poorly signposted hotel is on the first floor of a building at the traffic-light junction in Rue du Lac

Burera (aka Bulera, aka Rue du Travail) just downhill from the Caritas bookshop. It's basic, safe, clean, functional and friendly. There's no restaurant, not even for b/fast, but there are plenty of eateries in the area. En-suite rooms have cold water only, but the staff will bring you a bucket of hot on request. Being near the old market area, this is a less glamorous part of Kigali – it's safe enough, but do be sensible if you come and go after dark. Rfr6,000 dbl.

🏠 **New Modern Guesthouse** (10 rooms) ☎ 574708. Tucked away on a small, unnamed road on the right as you go uphill from the Gloria towards the Caritas Bookshop, this functional and friendly but rather seedy local hotel offers very basic accommodation using common cold showers. Rfr3,000/4,000 sgl/dbl.

🏠 **Belle Vie Restaurant** (4 rooms) 📞 570158. Situated directly opposite the New Modern, this busy local restaurant has 4 plain and overpriced rooms with washbasins sharing a common cold separate shower. *Rfr5,000 dbl.*

🏠 **Logement la Calville** (20 rooms) The only clear virtue of this scruffy and rather overpriced multi-storey block is its proximity to the Nyabugogo Taxi Park, 2km northwest of the city centre — convenient for a very early start or if you arrive in town after dark. *Rfr3,000 sgl using common shower; Rfr6,000 en-suite dbl.*

Nyamirambo and Nyakabanda

The lively, characterful quarter of Nyamirambo, which lies to the south of the city centre between the mosque and Islamic Centre, was one of the first parts of Kigali to be settled. It offers the city's best selection of budget options, including the isolated Kigali Hotel near the mosque and a cluster of cheaper lodges centred upon the Auberge de Nyamirambo about 1km further south. To reach it on foot (if you're energetic), continue walking southwards and downhill from the Sky Hotel. *Taxi-voitures* to the centre cost around Rfr1,000–1,500 depending on where you're going. The steady stream of minibus-taxis that run along the main road between the city centre and Islamic Centre, passing within 100m of all these hotels, cost Rfr100 per person.

🏠 **Kigali Hotel** (16 rooms) 📞 571384/574542. Situated a block past the mosque on a one-way stretch of Avenue de la Justice, this is a good-value hotel, offering accommodation in small en-suite rooms with hot water, phone and TV. There's no restaurant or bar, so it's pretty quiet — if you can ignore the passing traffic and early morning mosque calls! There are plenty of other eateries and bars in the area. Minibus-taxis from central Kigali stop right opposite — ask for 'Chez Mayaka' or the mosque. *Rfr6,500/8,000 sgl/dbl.*

🏠 **Auberge de Nyamirambo** (10 rooms) 📞 572879. This homely and secure 2-storey lodge is one of the best value options in Kigali, with clean en-suite rooms and a convenient location on the main road out of town towards the Islamic Centre. There's no restaurant or bar, but you can eat nearby — try the excellent brochettes and grilled chicken or fish at the anonymous brick-walled bar with the Amstel sign on the opposite side of the road a block back towards central Kigali. There's a good internet café next door. *Rfr4,000/6,000 sgl/dbl.*

🏠 **Logement la Vedette** (6 rooms) 📞 573575. Situated around the corner from the Auberge de Nyamirambo, this unpretentious guesthouse has comfortable large rooms with sinks and clean common showers — nothing special but fine at the price. *Rfr4,000/5,000 sgl/dbl.*

🏠 **Home St Bernard** (8 rooms) 📞 573575. Across the road from the Logement la Vedette and under the same management, this slightly smarter double-storey lodge might not offer the warmest of welcomes, but the clean and rather garishly decorated en-suite rooms (cold water only) seem fair value. *Rfr8,000 dbl.*

🏠 **Logement Ikaze** (8 rooms) 📞 573655. The least inviting of the lodges in Nyamirambo, this place has spacious rooms, but the overall feel is rather dingy. *Rfr3,000 sgl using common shower; Rfr6,000 en-suite dbl.*

🏠 **Motel Centre d'Accueil Nyakabanda** (30 rooms) 📱 08 484860. With a rather isolated location in the suburb of Nyakabanda, a short distance west of Nyamirambo, this place consists of a row of simple and rather rundown en-suite sgls with running cold water. The green gardens offer good views across suburbia to Mount Kigali, and inexpensive drinks and meals are available nearby at the popular Green Corner Bar. Minibus-taxis from Nyabugogo to Nyakabanda run within 50m of it. *Rfr2,500 sgl.*

🏠 **Episcopal Church Resthouse** (13 rooms) 📞 576340; 📠 573213. Part of the St Etienne Church on Avenue Paul VI in Biryogo (aka Bilyogo) district some 500m east of Nyamirambo Mosque, this church guesthouse is not that convenient and the clean but rundown rooms with nets are indifferent value. Inexpensive meals are available. *Rfr6,000 twin or Rfr1,800 per dorm bed.*

APARTMENTS For a longer stay you may want to consider a self-catering apartment; one agency that can help with this is the **Multi Service Agency** in rue des Coopératives, whose full advertisement is on page 97.

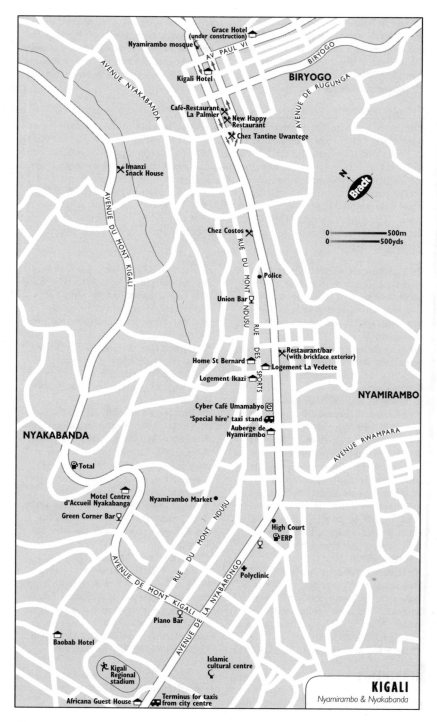

Grace Hotel
(under construction)

Nyamirambo mosque

AV PAUL VI

Kigali Hotel

BIRYOGO

Café-Restaurant
La Palmier

New Happy
Restaurant

Chez Tantine Uwantege

AVENUE NYAKABANDA

BIRYOGO

AVENUE DE RUGUNGA

Imanzi
Snack House

N

Bradt

AVENUE DU MONT KIGALI

Chez Costos

RUE DU MONT NDUSU

0   500m
0   500yds

Police

Union Bar

RUE DES SPORTS

Restaurant/bar
(with brickface exterior)

Home St Bernard

Logement La Vedette

Logement Ikazi

NYAMIRAMBO

Cyber Café Umamabyo

'Special hire' taxi stand

Auberge de
Nyamirambo

AVENUE RWAMPARA

NYAKABANDA

Total

Motel Centre
d'Accueil Nyakabanga

Green Corner Bar

Nyamirambo Market

High Court

ERP

RUE DU MONT NDUSU

Polyclinic

AVENUE DE LA NYABARONGO

AVENUE DE MONT KIGALI

Piano Bar

Baobab Hotel

Islamic
cultural centre

Kigali
Regional
stadium

Africana Guest House

Terminus for taxis
from city centre

KIGALI

Nyamirambo & Nyakabanda

For this section we are indebted to the author of the guide *75 Restaurants à Kigali*, André Verbruggen, who has lived and worked in Kigali for well over a decade. If you're a serious foodie, look for the forthcoming (2006) new edition of this book – '*Guide André*' – in ORTPN offices and the Ikirezi Bookshop, or contact André on e avak2000@hotmail.com. Meanwhile, because you probably won't have time to sample them all, here is just a small selection to get you started. The hotel restaurants listed below are included because they're particularly good, but all of Kigali's hotels offer acceptable food so, if you prefer to eat wherever you're staying, you won't necessarily miss out.

Expensive

✖ **Panorama Restaurant** ☎ 576530. On the top floor of the Hotel des Mille Collines, this exclusive place has an appropriately panoramic view over the city. Official dinners and banquets are held here and there are regular 'themed evenings'. The 'suggestion of the day' plus dessert is around Rfr8,000 but it's easy to spend more. The wine list is comprehensive.

✖ **Diplomat Restaurant** ☎ 597100. This highly rated restaurant in the new InterContinental Hotel serves a good selection of mostly continental-style dishes at similar prices to the above.

✖ **Restaurant Le Dos Argenté** ☎ 501717. On the ground floor of the Hotel Gorillas, this smaller

restaurant – whose name translates as silverback – is a member of the *Chaine des Rotisseurs* and the food usually lives up to its reputation. Main dishes (French cuisine) go up to around Rfr10,000, desserts to Rfr4,000. Service is relaxed.

✖ **Restaurant Hellenique** ☎ 583731. Slightly less expensive than the two above, this is tucked away in a residential part of Kimihurura not far from the Cadillac Club, in the valley between Kiyovu and Kacyiru – taxi-drivers will know it and it's signposted. The food is Greek/International with a good wine-list, the ambience is relaxed and there's a pleasant terrace. Service is attentive but may be slow. Government VIPs and ambassadors come here.

✖ **Kigali Novotel Umubano** ☎ 583361. The poolside restaurant here has a good and varied midday and evening buffet (sizzling main dishes, salads, calorific desserts …) as well as the type of general menu you'd expect from a hotel of this standard and special menus for functions or celebrations. Service is attentive and the atmosphere is relaxed. It's deservedly one of Kigali's most popular meeting places.

Medium

✖ **Restaurant Chez Robert** ☎ 575573. This relatively central restaurant, formerly called Caprices du Palais, is situated on Avenue de la République opposite the Hotel des Mille Collines and close to the Motel Garni du Centre, where it is easily distinguished by the two elephants marking its walk-in entrance (though the drive-in entrance is actually a block east, on Rue de Ntaruka). It serves a good selection of continental dishes for around Rfr5,000, as well as a popular lunchtime buffet at Rfr4,000 pp, and brochettes and other snacks for around Rfr1,500 upwards.

✖ **Republika Lounge** ☎ 504051. Tucked away along a dirt side road branching downhill from Avenue des Grand Lacs about 15 mins' walk from the city centre, this is probably the most good-looking eatery in Kigali, and the earthy adobe architecture makes it blissfully cool inside on a humid day. The funky décor contrasts attractively with the more stolid appearance of most other Kigali restaurants, and there's a large wooden deck with views across to a eucalyptus-clad hill. It's mainly a drinking hole, and popular with expatriates, but a selection of grills and brochettes are served in the Rfr3,000–4,500 range.

✖ **Indian Khāzana Restaurant** ☏ 08 499599/600. Situated on Kajangwe Avenue about 10 mins' walk downhill from the Mille Collines and the city centre, this new place is probably the top Indian Restaurant in Kigali, and good value with most main courses in the Rfr4,000–5,000 range and excellent Indian bread.

✖ **La Belvédère** ☏ 08 562226. Situated on Boulevard de la Révolution, this is perhaps the only reasonably smart restaurant in the city centre, and one of the few central eateries in any category to open for lunch and dinner 7 days a week. Continental dishes and grills are in the Rfr4,000–5,000 range.

✖ **Flamingo Chinese Restaurant** ☎ 501944; ☏ 08 300333. Generally rated to be the best Chinese in Kigali, this is now installed on the top floor of Telecom House, on the same traffic circle as the Kigali Business Centre near the Novotel. Mains are in the Rfr4,000–6,000 range.

✖ **New Cactus Restaurant** ☎ 575572; ☏ 08 678798. Situated in Rue Député Kayuku (near the Hotel Gorillas) this is a super place, particularly for pizza-lovers – it's very welcoming, with a pleasant outdoor terrace giving a beautiful view over Kigali, and good food (French cuisine as well as pizzas). Steak and fish main dishes up to Rfr5,000. There's also a take-away pizza service – phone beforehand and it'll be ready for you to collect. Open 12.00–14.00 and 18.00–22.30. Closed Tuesdays.

✖ **O Sole Luna** ☎ 583062. Slightly cheaper than most of the above, out along the airport road at the edge of Remera, this Italian restaurant has a good range of pizzas and pasta, well presented – and a beautiful view over the city from its terraces. Service is friendly and reasonably brisk.

✖ **Minar Restaurant** ☎ 573121. Situated next to the Uganda Embassy, this is a branch of the well-known Kenyan chain of Indian eateries, and the smart décor, relaxed service, tasty dishes and reasonable prices (main courses Rfr3,500–5,000) are unlikely to disappoint.

✖ **Iris Restaurant** ☎ 501172. Situated in the same part of town as the Indian Khāzana, the popular terrace restaurant at this upmarket guesthouse has a good choice of (mostly) continental dishes and grills in the Rfr3,000–4,000 range, as well as brochettes and other lower-priced snacks.

✖ **H₂O Restaurant** This promising new 2-storey open-sided restaurant lies within walking distance of the city centre and has a pleasantly organic feel to the décor. Grills and Indian dishes are mostly around Rfr4,000, and there's a big buffet on Friday and Saturday nights for Rfr3,000 pp.

✖ **Kigali Paradise Lalibela Ethiopian Restaurant** ☏ 08 505293. Situated off Avenue des Poids Lourds in the valley dividing the city centre from Kacyiru, this snappily-named Ethiopian restaurant lies in attractive gardens and serves a good selection of Rwanda-style brochettes and other grills for around Rfr1,000, as well as spicy Ethiopian fare for Rfr3,000 per main course. The best time to eat here is Saturday evening, when a large Ethiopian buffet (Rfr4,500 pp) is complemented by a traditional 'coffee ceremony'.

Budget and snack (main dishes below US$8)

✖ **Ice & Spice** ☎ 570608. This little Indian restaurant in Rue du Lac Bulera is one of the more interesting options in the city centre, though it's not as cheap as it used to be and the food is rather variable in quality. Still, it has an extensive menu, with all dishes available mild, medium and hot, and most main courses work out at less than Rfr4,000. The 'ice' part means just that – a colourful range of ices. The English-speaking staff is attentive and service is relatively quick.

✖ **Karibu Restaurant** ➘ 501793. At the edge of the city centre on Avenue de la Paix, this is a shady place to stop for a cool drink or snack if you're in central Kigali, and it also has a convenient and varied lunchtime buffet (Rfr1,500); this is deservedly popular, so try to get there before 13.00 when it tends to fill up with business people. It closes in the evening.

✖ **Shangai Restaurant** ➘ 08 503111. Near the Ninzi Hill Hotel and within walking distance of the Novotel, this popular Chinese restaurant is friendly and good value; if you have children you can let them loose on the swings and other play equipment. The name board had vanished at the time of writing but it's easy to spot.

✖ **Planet Cinéma** Situated in the Kigali Business Centre or KBC and, you've guessed it, right at the door of Kigali's cinema, this café-bar serves sandwiches, snacks, salads etc, so is a convenient place to get food if you're going to a movie.

✖ **Havana Club** ➘ 510440/1. Beside the Novotel, this rather misleadingly named place isn't the sleazy cigar-stained bar you might expect, but a bright and modern pizzeria and general restaurant, serving good takeaways as well as sit-down meals.

✖ **Chez John** ➘ 571678. Situated in Kiyovu, in Rue de Masaka but poorly signposted, this rather rustic local restaurant stands opposite a school. It has recently been extended and improved; the food is good, and it offers a popular local buffet (midday and evening) for around Rfr1,000 with meat, cheaper without.

✖ **Le Banjo Resto-Bar** This is a smart local eatery in Remera, diagonally opposite the nearby Hotel Chez Lando, and it also serves a good and inexpensive African buffet.

✖ **Amy's** ➘ 517004. For fast food in the city centre you could try either branch of this cheap and cheerful mini-chain: one is on the corner of Rue de la Préfecture on Place de la Constitution and the other is beside the petrol station just after the traffic lights on Boulevard de l'OUA as you approach the centre from Kimihurura. These are new, clean, brisk places based on the US model, with genuinely 'fast' food (and no alcohol).

✖ **Tam-Tam Snack Bar** Situated close to the central bus station, this is a convenient place for a bite if you are just passing through – snacks are mostly around Rfr500–1,500 while full meals cost up to Rfr3,000.

✖ **Addis Restaurant** ➘ 574175. This simple but good Ethiopian restaurant, offering something very different from standard Rwandan or international fare, closed down in 2005 but may be reopening. It's reached via a steepish but short mud track going down behind the petrol station just after the traffic lights on Boulevard de l'OUA.

✖ **La Galette** ➘ 757434. To combine sustenance with shopping, try the snack-bar attached to this excellent supermarket (sometimes still remembered by its old name of Baguette), which is located towards the bottom of Rue du Marché just after it turns sharply to join Rue de l'Epargne. This is a popular meeting place for ex-pats and aid workers, and there are notice boards listing various items (cars, dogs, homes, motorbikes, TVs, garden hoses...) wanted or for sale. The supermarket has a good (not cheap) range of groceries and household items; the snack-bar does b/fasts, sandwiches, salads, light meals, pastries (inc croissants) and good coffee – b/fast nirvana!

✖ **La Sierra** ➘ 575486. Founded in 1968, this is a more low-key and central equivalent to La Galette, combining a good supermarket with a pleasant terrace snack-bar on Boulevard de la Révolution – in addition to the expected burgers, sandwiches, and light meals, it serves pancakes and waffles, and is a good spot for b/fast (open from 07.30).

✖ **Le Poseidon** ➘ 501564. Also on Boulevard de la Révolution, this is a good spot for a buffet lunch in the city centre – just Rfr1,000 for a plateful inc a small serving of meat.

✖ **La Palmier** One of several good local eateries dotted around the one way roads around Nyamirambo Mosque – also worth trying, should you be staying in this area, are the New Happy Restaurant, Chez Costos and Chez Tantine Uwantege, all of which serve buffets and meals for around Rfr1,000.

NIGHTLIFE

For a capital city, Kigali isn't over-rich in nightclubs and discos. The biggest and best known is the **New Cadillac** in Kimihurura, of which there are two parts: one for VIPs and the smart set and one for more relaxed and younger people. The VIP part, which charges a rather steep entrance fee, consists of a good Thai restaurant (the Bran Thaï), piano bar, live band and disco, and opens 11.00–15.00 and 18.00–midnight Tuesday to Sunday. Drinks aren't exorbitant, with beer at around US$2–3. If a group of visitors wants traditional music or dancers, this can be arranged. For young people, the New Cadillac Night Club functions Wednesday to Sunday, 21.00 to dawn. For a more chilled outdoor drink, the rather oddly named **Executive Carwash** around the corner is recommended.

Smaller than the New Cadillac but the same price is the **Planète Club** – a smart place – in the Kigali Business Centre complex. The most expensive in Kigali, but still very popular, is **Memories**, close to the Havana Club pizzeria in the Kubaho Plaza near the Novotel: entrance US$10 and drinks US$4 upwards. Smoking is allowed.

Kigali's oddest nocturnal haunt is surely the **Nyira Rock Café**, which lies in the city centre just off Boulevard de l'OUA. This relaxed but boozy dive is centred on a semi-professional karaoke set-up, which features among others a wholly improbable and surprisingly accomplished trio of Beyonce-ified drag artists miming in bootylicious splendour. There's no entrance fee, the drinks aren't unreasonably priced, and the mostly young crowd appears to contain an overtly (though perhaps not universally welcome) gay element – a first in East Africa?

Other hotel nightclubs are at the **Hotel Chez Lando** and the **Sky Hotel**. Finally, the **Alpha Palace Hotel** also has one on Fridays/Saturdays: US$2 entry and a mixture of traditional/modern music. A popular out-of-town drinking hole is the **Green Corner Bar**, a lofty outdoor set-up in Nyakabanda offering cheap chilled beers and great views towards Mount Kigali.

PRACTICALITIES

MONEY The four most accessible **banks** in central Kigali are the Banque Commerciale du Rwanda (BCR) and the Banque Continentale Africaine Rwanda (BACAR) in Boulevard de la Révolution, and the Banque de Kigali and Bancor in Avenue de la Paix. Queues are slow but orderly and there's generally no hassle. The BACAR has a Moneygram service and the BCR a Western Union service via which funds can be transferred quickly from abroad. Bancor is your best bet for drawing money against Visa or MasterCard – up to €2,500 daily (or the Rfr or USD equivalent) assuming that the computers aren't down! In fact Western Union has hit Rwanda in a big way – there are several other offices in Kigali, and at least one in each of the other main towns. See also *Chapter 3*, pages 43–5, for what transactions are possible.

The **money-changers** who used to hang out around the main post office and in other areas of Kigali have been declared illegal and gone under cover. Now they operate from **foreign exchange (forex) bureaux** near their old pitches and still tout for custom! Exchange rates are generally chalked on blackboards; but bargain if you're changing large amounts, and keep your wits about you. High-denomination notes may get a better rate. The main cluster of forex bureaux is opposite the central post office, but there are others opposite the BCR in Boulevard de la Révolution and in Avenue de la Paix near its junction with Avenue des Mille Collines.

Another option outside banking hours is the **BCDI** on the ground floor of the Ninzi Hill Hotel in Kacyiru. This stays open from 08.00 to 20.00 seven days a week, and it can exchange cash in most hard currencies but doesn't deal with travellers' cheques or credit cards.

COMMUNICATIONS The main **post office** in Avenue de la Paix has a counter for international phone calls and an efficient fax office; faxes to Europe cost US$2 per page, to the US $2.50. If you want someone to send a fax to you there, the number is (250) 576574. Receiving a fax costs under US$1. This is where you can collect post restante. There's also a philatelic counter.

Cyber cafés are springing up fast and you'll see them (or internet facilities without the café) all over the city. One hour online typically costs around Rfr600. The main hotels (and some smaller ones) also offer internet access. Public business facilities generally close on Sundays.

Public telephones are found in shops and kiosks all over Kigali – they are metered, so you pay when you've finished and don't need handfuls of small change. Calls to mobile phones from these are more expensive than those to normal phones, although calls from mobile to mobile are cheaper. Rwanda is now said to have one of the most modern telephone systems in East Africa. You can get a 'starter pack' to convert most imported **mobiles** for use in Rwanda; these cost around Rfr3,000 inclusive of Rfr2,500 airtime and are available from MTN (Mobile Telephone Networks) shops – there's one in Avenue des Mille Collines opposite the Belgian School, another in Boulevard de la Révolution near the Sierra Restaurant, and various others around the city. Then it's a pay-as-you-go system: you buy cards to top up the balance in your account.

SHOPPING Before you set off for the shops, be aware that in 2005 plastic bags were banned in Rwanda, following a city clean-up in which almost a million old bags or remnants were discovered, and this ban is being enforced; so it's best to carry your own (non-plastic!) shopping bag if you plan to make many purchases.

Apart from the market area (see pages 108–9), the shops you're likely to use are in the 'square' formed by Boulevard de la Révolution, Avenue de Commerce, Avenue des Mille Collines and Rue de l'Epargne. Outside this area there's a good supermarket on the eastern side of Place de la Constitution, next to the petrol station that is opposite the ORTPN office; and the very good Ikirezi Bookshop is on Avenue de la Paix but just westward of the 'square'.

In **Boulevard de la Révolution**, the large Banque Commerciale du Rwanda is on the eastern side, almost on Place de l'Indépendance (where the fountain is). Looking across the road from the bank you have, among other small shops/offices: the Poseidon Restaurant, a small supermarket, the Belvedere Restaurant, internet facilities, Sun City Pharmacy (open 24 hours), an MTN phone shop, an archway leading to Top Travel & Tours, the Sierra Restaurant, the Banque Continentale Africaine Rwanda and a petrol station. Roughly opposite the petrol station and well barricaded is the US Embassy, which however may move to a new location during the lifetime of this guide.

Turn right at the petrol station into Avenue des Mille Collines, then right again into **Avenue de la Paix**. On the opposite side of Avenue de la Paix before it reaches Avenue de Commerce you have (not necessarily in order) a florist, a bank, a forex bureau, various clothing and stationery shops, phone/internet facilities, various tour operators and travel agents, Fidodido ice creams, Café de la Fontaine and Dates Café-Resto.

Turn downwards into **Avenue de Commerce** (the Banque de Kigali is on the opposite corner); and on the left a little way down is the Caritas bookshop. Take the first left turn after it, into **Rue Kalisimbi** – on your right (opposite the Isimbi Hotel) is a good photographic shop (*Fotolab; BP 155 Kigali;* ☏ *76508; www.aw7.com/fotolab*), with a small dairy/milk bar and internet facilities just before it.

Continue along Rue Kalisimbi passing the Isimbi Hotel and you come to the T-junction with **Avenue des Mille Collines**; there's a good supermarket opposite and to the right which has a useful range of groceries, fresh bread and pastries and (sometimes) good local honey. Turn left up Mille Collines; the Belgian School is on your right, with Changa Travel, Kenya Airways, other travel agencies, the Pharmacie Conseil (open seven days including 10.00–15.00 Sunday), an MTN phone shop and a florist opposite them on your left.

To complete your city-centre tour: go back to the junction of Avenue de la Paix and Avenue de Commerce. Go downhill but, instead of turning left into Rue Kalisimbi, turn right (also into Kalisimbi). On your right you'll come to the ASAR craft shop (see page 107). The next junction is with **Rue de l'Epargne**. Turn right (uphill) and you return to Avenue de la Paix, with the post office on your left. Opposite the post office is a kiosk with a public phone; just beyond the kiosk is a craft shop/workshop which has some traditional musical instruments (bargain hard).

If you're ready for a snack or drink after your stroll, stay on the same side as the post office (keeping it on your left) and continue downhill to the Place de la Constitution – you'll see Amy's snack-bar ahead on your left.

FURTHER INFORMATION If there's anything else you want to know, try ORTPN (below). They should have – or be able to get – most information you may need.

WHAT TO SEE AND DO IN KIGALI

Your first stop in Kigali should be ORTPN (Office Rwandais du Tourisme et des Parcs Nationaux), which is the Rwandan Tourist Office. For details see page 61. They have information about all current events and can advise you. Also they have street maps of Kigali and information about transport – minibus-taxis, car-hire and so forth.

The ORTPN office is where you buy permits to visit the national parks – you MUST do this before setting off for the park (or at the very least check with ORTPN whether you can do it on arrival at the park office), otherwise you risk being refused entry.

For a capital city, Kigali doesn't offer a great deal in terms of buildings, museums and historical/cultural sites – but it is a pleasant place for strolling and people-watching.

KIGALI CITY TOUR The Tourist Board now offers visitors guided bus tours of Kigali, Monday to Saturday. Cost: US$20 per person, minimum of four persons. Bookings can be made through ORTPN (see page 61). Major sights include, among others:

- the **historic house of Richard Kandt** (soon to be the **Museum of Natural History**). Kandt came to Africa in 1898 seeking the source of the Nile and later (1907–13) was the first and only *Kaiserliche Resident* during German colonisation. The Nile source that he discovered in 1898 was unchallenged until the *Ascend the Nile* expedition in 2006 (of which details are on page 151)
- **Nyamirambo**, the oldest quarter of Kigali, called 'the city that never sleeps' (see page 109); the new, modern residential quarter of **Nyarutarama**
- the **Kigali Institute of Science and Technology** (see www.kist.ac.rw)
- **Caplaki Handicrafts Co-operative** (a gathering of craftspeople selling all types of traditional and new handicrafts: irresistible to shoppers! – see page 107)
- **Gisozi Genocide Memorial** (see box opposite) and the **Heroes' Cemetery**
- **Parliament Building**
- the **Geological Museum**

- **Dancing Pots** (with the chance to learn more about the Batwa people and participate in a traditional pottery workshop and a display of lively dancing – see pages 30 and 107).

KIGALI GENOCIDE MEMORIAL This dignified memorial (*www.kigalimemorialcentre.org*) has been constructed in the Gisozi area of Kigali and opened fully for the tenth anniversary of the genocide in April 2004. You can see it across the valley – a large, white, modern building with terraces in front – on the right as you go downhill on Boulevard de Nyabugogo. To drive there is easy as it's in sight for much of the way – take a right turn halfway down Boulevard de Nyabugogo, continue downwards into the valley, when you're a little way past the memorial take a left turn across the valley, then (at a T-junction) go sharp left along a short dirt road and you'll come to the gate.

A rose garden has been planted around the outside of the centre, in memory of the dead, and there's an open view out across Kigali. Inside, among other exhibits, is a Children's Memorial dedicated to the many thousands of children who lost their lives; each of its 14 windows details the life and death of a single child. There's also a Wall of Names under construction, which will eventually display the names of thousands of victims.

A guide takes visitors around the memorial, telling the story and showing the skulls and bones of victims, as well as graves. The idea behind displaying bones in

---

GISOZI GENOCIDE MEMORIAL AND EDUCATION CENTRE

There will be no humanity without forgiveness, there will be no forgiveness without justice, but justice will be impossible without humanity.

Yolande Mukagasana

Gisozi, in Kigali, is the burial site of over 250,000 people killed in a three-month period during Rwanda's 1994 genocide. Nine years later, victims are still being located in and around Kigali as new evidence emerges from trials of those accused of genocide. They are taken to Gisozi as their final resting place.

Founded by the mayor of Kigali, the memorial building at Gisozi was designed by a local architect. So far, the construction undertaken here has been financed largely from Kigali City Council Revenue. This means that the citizens of one of the world's poorest countries pay through their taxes to give dignity to their murdered families, whom the rest of the world abandoned.

The international community failed Rwanda. It could have prevented the loss of a million men, women and children, but the United Nations viewed the killings as an internal matter and pulled out. Now that a million people have been murdered, we need to learn how and why such tragedies happen, so we can prevent them in the future.

The UK Holocaust Centre was invited by the Kigali City Council to work with its sister organisation Aegis, and survivors, to help complete the site by telling the story of the genocide in this building. It will assist Gisozi to function as an education centre.

The challenge facing Rwanda and the Great Lakes region is how to build a society free from the threat of dangerous ideology. Building stability starts by acknowledging the truth. Providing survivors with a place where their voice can be heard strengthens efforts towards unity. Schoolchildren can come to Gisozi and learn about the consequences of hatred and division. The environment of Gisozi will not accuse, but rather challenge.

Adapted from a leaflet produced by Aegis Rwanda, PO Box 7251 Kigali; ✆ *08567289.*

this and other genocide memorials is to prevent anyone, ever, from claiming 'there was no genocide in Rwanda'. There are photos and information panels. The description in the box on page 103 is taken from an information leaflet currently available at the Memorial. The 'Aegis' mentioned in the box is the Aegis Trust (*www.aegistrust.org*), a non-sectarian, non-governmental organisation based in the Holocaust Centre, Nottingham, United Kingdom.

ARTS AND ENTERTAINMENT The new Planet Cinema is in the Kigali Business Centre in Avenue du Lac Muhazi. There are afternoon performances and evening performances of international movies (often in English with French sub-titles), children's performances, special screenings, etc. Tickets are inexpensive and with the Planet Cinéma snack-bar and club in the same block, a long and full evening of entertainment is possible! The rather more downmarket Cine El May opposite the Kigali Hotel in Nyamirambo shows somewhat more dated Western films as well as screening live international and Premiership football fixtures.

Performances of traditional dancing and music take place from time to time in various venues around the city – these are publicised on local radio and in the local press. ORTPN should also have a list.

Dancing Pots (see pages 30 and 107) will arrange performances of traditional Batwa dances and participation in pottery workshops. The dance is a lively affair lasting over two hours, full of colour and energy, in a covered marquee – a donation is appropriate. Your tour operator should be able to include this in your programme by request.

The Centre Culturel d'Echanges Franco-Rwandaises (↘ 576223), not far from the Hotel des Mille Collines, has a small theatre and presents a variety of cultural events – theatre, films, music, dance and so on. Call in to ask them for their current monthly programme or else check with ORTPN. The Centre Culturel can be a useful source of other information too, as they have a comprehensive library (see page 106).

SPORT Kigali caters for both golfers and cricketers! For **cricket**, see the box below. The 18-hole **Nyarutarama Golf Club** is in an attractively green corner of northeastern Kigali; a round costs US$15 for non-members. For details phone 08524619 (or contact the club at PO Box 4762 Kigali). See also www.rwanda-golf.com. (If you want to play your way around Rwanda, the Mountain Gorilla's Nest in Kinigi (see page 188) also has a golf course.)The **Cercle Sportif** in Lower Kiyovu has facilities for tennis, table tennis, basketball, volleyball, badminton, darts, swimming, etc. Also check out the current **football** fixtures – enthusiast Chris Frean explains how:

Going to a football match in Kigali is simple as long as you know that it's on. Matches generally take place at the Amahoro Stadium on Sunday afternoons at 4pm, sometimes preceded by each side's reserves' match on the same pitch. Fixtures are generally advertised in the New Times during the week beforehand. It is, however, pretty simple to find out if something is about to happen at Amahoro. Just go up to Kisimenti crossroads – the one by Chez Lando – and check the activity. If you see matatus with fans, and police on the crossroads holding up ordinary traffic for dignitaries, then something is on. Domestically the Kigali teams APR, Kiyovu and Rayon continue to dominate. You can tell by the colours who is playing. Black and white means APR; blue and white Rayon; green and white Kiyovu.

Inside the ground, you shouldn't expect anything like a programme or team info; although during 2005, with the league sponsored by Primus (the brewers), you could actually buy a drink in the ground. For the World Cup qualifiers, tents were set up outside the stands, and a barbeque too.

International match tickets are easy enough to come by too. Just go up to the main

CRICKET IN RWANDA

Chris Frean

Cricket continues to flourish in Kigali. In 2005, matches of 40 overs a side were being played on Sundays almost throughout the year, several tournaments were held, and the national side travelled abroad to participate in International Cricket Council competitions.

The enthusiasm was there, but there was still too much red tape and too little money.

Four sides existed in Kigali in 2005: the long-running Kigali Cricket Club, led by the Jasat brothers and based around the city's moslem traders; Asian-dominated Indorwa, started by the then employees of the Indorwa petrol company and led by local businessman Kalpin Patel of Medirwa Pharmacy; Challengers Cricket Club, led by businessman and national team captain Srinath of the MFI company; and the Right Guards team, led by captain Henry Zizinga of Sekanyolya, made up from the Rwandan and British communities.

Cricket has actually been played for several years in Rwanda. In Butare, the University boys, under Professor Singh, had been playing for quite some time. There was a match on a volcanic field in Gisenyi in the 1990s, which finally received appropriate recognition in *Wisden Cricketers' Almanack 2004*. A further report was recorded in the *Cricket Round the World* section of *Wisden 2005*.

By 2003 the RCA managed to get the ground at the Ecole Technique Officielle in the Kicukiro district of Kigali into a good enough condition for regular matches. The ground is the school's sports field, so is not exclusive to the Rwanda Cricket Association. Games are subject to regular interruptions, some of the more unusual having been unannounced athletics meetings and the 2004 filming of the BBC feature film 'Shooting Dogs' with John Hurt, which was a dramatisation based on events which happened at the school in 1994. The BBC wanted to film on the site to add authenticity.

These days, weekend matches are interrupted by local residents who continue to stroll or cycle across the outfield, oblivious to the game. Was it ever like this on Broadhalfpenny Down, I wonder.

On the bureaucratic front, early attempts to bring in kit proved a headache. The Rwanda Revenue Authority, anxious to squeeze whatever they could from persons perceived to have money to burn, decided that a rubber matting pitch supplied free of charge by the ICC was in fact a carpet, and should be subject to duty. Months of wrangling and negotiation failed to convince them. We could only assume a member of RRA staff wanted it to carpet her home.

Sponsors continue to play a key role as there is no state funding; so businesses like FedEx, Akagera Motors, Sulfo, Faruki and the Minar Restaurant keep the game alive financially. A committee meets every Wednesday. Anyone interested in getting involved could contact the RCA President, Mr Charles Haba, at the BHR on Avenue de la Justice; or Mr Mukri at Faruki near the bus park.

Amahoro stadium in the hours before kick-off. The main stand price will usually be no more than Rfr5,000, the terraces much cheaper. But beware: you're not allowed to take a mobile phone into the main stand for an international. For the Angola match in late 2005, I had to submit to a metal detector and was told my phone was not allowed. This, the police later told me, was because people might use phones in the ground to contact hooligans outside and cause problems. However, this policy is only in place when the President is likely to attend a match.

There's more on football (and rugby) in *Chapter 2*, pages 32–4.

LIBRARIES AND BOOKSHOPS Depending on how soon you visit, Kigali may have its own, brand-new, specially designed public library, built with funds raised both nationally and internationally in an initiative by the Rotary Club of Kigali-Virunga. See below for more details. The Centre Culturel d'Echanges Franco-Rwandaises (see page 104) also has three lending libraries: for adults, for children and for scientific research. Much of the material is in French at present. There's also a reading room.

Two good bookshops in Kigali, both of them stocking a wide range of books on the history and culture of Rwanda, the background to the genocide and an assortment of other relevant themes, are the Librairie Caritas (⏷ *576503;* e *librcar@rwanda1.com*) in Rue de Commerce just downhill from its junction with Avenue de la Paix, and the Ikirezi Bookshop (⏷ *570298;* ⏷f *571314;* e *ikirezi@rwanda1.com; www.ikirezi.biz*) in Avenue de la Paix. The Ikirezi, which sometimes holds book signings and other events, is open 09.00–12.30 and 14.00–18.00 (closes at 13.00 on Saturday) as well as 10.30–13.00 on Sunday; while Caritas keeps normal shop hours.

The saddest casualty of the energetic clean-up operation carried out recently in Kigali is the wonderful old secondhand bookshop that was at the end of Avenue de

---

KIGALI PUBLIC LIBRARY

In 1999, the Rotary Club of Kigali-Virunga decided to build a public library, its first major project as a chartered Rotary Club, to counter the serious shortage of books in Rwanda and the consequent lack of a culture of reading. Also, a key path to ending violence and preventing another genocide is to make knowledge and ideas – from books – freely available to all Rwandans, regardless of social and economic status.

Rwanda's first public library is not just for adults. Its young people's section will play a major role in opening children's minds, helping to transport them from the commonplace to the extraordinary. Finally, it will help to build a sense of community, and will preserve the past, with special collections on subjects such as Rwandan history and literature.

This is no daydream! The library has received generous financial support both from overseas and from local Rwandan companies. It is supported by the American Friends of the Kigali Public Library (AFKPL) – via whom the international literary association, PEN, pledged US$45,000 in April 2002. The Government of Rwanda has pledged US$500,000 of which US$100,000 was released in July 2003. Construction work started on the foundations in 2002. Funds are still urgently needed and fundraising has taken place at all levels, in and outside Rwanda, from large companies to small schools and individuals. Secondhand book sales (another 'first' for Kigali) have been held.

In 2002, a young Rwandan boy named Sam called into the office of the Chairman of the Kigali Public Library Project – who initially thought he had come to ask for school fees, a common practice among Rwanda's youth who struggle every year to find the necessary amount. However, what Sam wanted was to donate 200 Rwandan francs (less than 50 US cents, but for him a large sum). He'd discovered the project through one of the secondhand book sales, and wanted to contribute in order to make sure the library would be completed.

At the time of writing, the buildings are coming on well and it's just a matter of time before they can be used and filled with books, so that Sam and his friends can read to their hearts' content.

Check out the progress of the library on its website, www.kigalilibrary.com

Commerce by the Place de l'Unité Nationale. Quite, quite gone! I used to browse so happily there and picked up some real gems. If you come across another good source of secondhand books, please let us know for the next edition.

HANDICRAFTS A wide range of handicrafts are sold in Kigali and there's great scope for browsing.

For pottery, visit **Dancing Pots**, the Batwa pottery workshop-cum-showroom (see pages 30). It's next to the Iris Guesthouse – walk down Avenue Roi Baudouin (Ave Rusumo) from the Hotel des Mille Collines; then about halfway down turn left into Rue Député Kajangwe. (Look out for fruit bats; they sometimes roost in the trees in Ave Rusumo.) There's a huge range of pottery, with some attractive new designs among the traditional ones.

Also a selection of their pots, some with plants inside, are laid out on the pavement near the bottom of Avenue Rusumo – keep walking downhill past the Kajangwe turning. (Taxis generally cruise this area if you don't want to walk back up the steepish hill.)

A successful newcomer on the handicrafts scene is the **Caplaki** handicrafts co-operative, near the Cercle Sportif. As part of the recent Kigali clean-up, the clutter of craft stalls and pavement vendors in the city centre (for example along the edge of Avenue de l'Armée) had to move. A group of about 35 craftspeople approached the Kigali City Council asking for a piece of land where they could relocate. In line with the government's policy of encouraging small-scale income-generating projects, land was allocated. The craftspeople contributed by building the 30-odd wooden huts and stalls.

The complex isn't too far from the city centre, on the Gikondo/Nyenyeri minibus-taxi route. There's parking space inside and outside for a few cars. The stallholders, men and women of all ages, between them sell a huge variety of goods. Carvings, weaving, sculpture, batik, pottery, metalwork, semi-precious stones, palm-fibre items, musical instruments, leather, fabrics, toys, stationery, small furniture, novelties ... there's every chance you'll find it at Caplaki. You can visit as part of the Kigali City Tour (see page 102), catch a minibus-taxi or take a *taxi-voiture*.

Weaving is one of the specialities of Rwanda – baskets, mats, hangings and pots appear in a variety of shapes and sizes, with carefully interwoven traditional patterns. They are sold by some street vendors, and there's a good selection (including woven hammocks) in the craft shop called ASAR (Association des Artistes Rwandais; Rue Karisimbi; BP 939 Kigali; ℡ *571139*). This is an excellent little shop, combining the work of several craft-making co-ops; some items are very touristy but others are traditional and all make good gifts. As well as the weaving there are carvings, musical instruments, pottery, beadwork, palm-leaf

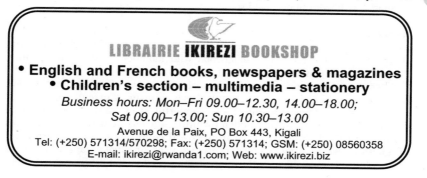

Patrick S

The prospects for tourism in Rwanda lie mainly in the safe haven offered to the remaining mountain gorillas in our Volcanoes National Park, other various flora and fauna in the Akagera National Park and Nyungwe Forest, and physical features like the volcanoes on our border with the DRC, the Rusumo Falls in southern Rwanda, etc.

But the Rwandan people also have an important part to play. Among other talents, we are skilled at carving, sculpture and weaving. Most of this is done by the ordinary Rwandan. Weaving is particular to women and girls while wood-carving is done mostly by men.

Most importantly, the work is created according to various themes: mother nature, beauty, achievement and virtues such as valour etc, as well as everyday scenes. A woman carrying a baby on her back, a pot of milk on her head and a bundle of firewood under her arm is a common sight around here. An old man sitting on a traditional stool with a long straw dipped in a pot is also familiar.

However, it is sad when in some cases such talent is wasted through poor sales, bad storage and poor preservation. Many pieces are sold on roadsides where they gather so much dust, washed away by rains, that even an occasional tourist who passes by can hardly notice their beauty!

A lot can be done to keep this heritage alive through publicity abroad: Rwandan embassies setting up sales-points for such goods, modest though they may be, and interested individuals taking it upon themselves to sell Rwandan handicrafts for the good of it. But most of all, local government can help by giving assistance to these craftspeople and tourists can help by purchasing their products.

The price of such items is quite small and affordable. The Caplaki centre near the Cercle Sportif in Kigali is one place to find them on display. Even at the Kigali International Airport there is a stall, and another near the Rwanda Revenue Authority offices. Also independent vendors display and sell their wares in the street.

Come and buy 'at your eye's pleasure'! And help to promote traditional craftsmanship in Rwanda as you explore the beauties of our Republic of a Thousand Hills.

crafts (including decorated notepaper and cards) and even stuffed toys. Prices are marked, so you needn't worry about bargaining – but a reduction for quantity would be legitimate.

You'll also find street vendors selling most kinds of small handicrafts – carvings, jewellery, woven baskets, masks, musical instruments, notepaper and postcards decorated with palm fibres – and so on.

MARKETS In all market areas, TAKE CARE – crowds are popular with pickpockets and opportunistic thieves, and there have been instances of crime. Also be tactful about taking photos; for every dozen people who don't object to being in a picture, there'll be someone who does. Respect their privacy.

The main market area, shown on the map on page 93, off and around the Ave de Commerce, is a victim of the recent Kigali clean-up. Currently it's boarded off and awaiting redevelopment. It was wonderful: stacks of mattresses in floral cotton covers; roughly made wooden furniture; ancient, dented kitchen utensils being recycled; clothing imported from far-off countries; cassettes blaring out of ghetto-blasters; eggs teetering precariously on shaky tables; rows of multicoloured vegetables with their damp, earthy smell; footwear; shiny watches; creamy candles made of local beeswax; chunky farm cheeses; tools, cushions, mirrors...

Ah well. You can still find good markets elsewhere in Rwanda. The little stalls and pavement vendors around the central minibus station have been cleared away too – but the frenetic market across the road from the Nyabugogo bus station still exists, at the bottom of Rue du Lac Hago. It's like a human kaleidoscope – a changing, shifting mass of colours and noise. A few minutes being jostled by these brisk crowds, determinedly going about their own business, may be enough for you – but it's a typical and non-touristy experience which it would be a pity to miss completely. See the *To Nyabugogo market* below.

STROLLING ROUND KIGALI If you don't mind the unavoidable hills, Kigali offers some good strolls. There are plenty of places where you can stop for a snack or a drink if you need to cool off. Two walks which could each fill up a morning, depending on how often you stop en route, are given below; but just look at a map of the whole city and you'll see that there are plenty more.

To the mosque and Nyamirambo district

One way of getting to the big mosque in the Muslim quarter is to walk southwards along Avenue de la Justice, with views out across the valley to your right; the mosque is at the junction where Rue de la Sécurité joins from the left. Continue for a few minutes and you're in a lively, busy district (Nyamirambo) of small streets and colourful little local shops. The atmosphere has a touch of London's Soho about it. This is said to be the part of the present-day city where people first settled, long ago. There's a lot of small-scale activity going on here, and small bar/cafés where you can stop for a drink.

To return to the centre, you can either catch a minibus-taxi (they serve Avenue de la Justice; look out for the yellow signs indicating bus stops) or flag down a taxi. (A short stretch of Avenue de la Justice is one-way and minibuses only travel outward from the centre; to get one going back you'll need to be in the two-way part.) Or else retrace your steps towards the mosque and look out for Avenue Paul VI on your right – follow this upwards and it'll bring you on to the area covered by the map on page 93. Or – be adventurous and find your own variations!

To Nyabugogo market

This takes you through an area of many small shops and market stalls, finishing at the busy market opposite Nyabugogo minibus-taxi stand. If you can cope with seething crowds and a lot of jostling, try it (but don't take photos without the permission of the subjects).

Walk down Rue de l'Epargne or along Avenue de la Justice until you come to the prison. As you face it from the road, the first road beside it to your right, turning off at a sharp angle, is Rue du Mont Huye, an unsurfaced road running downhill. Take this and follow it – you'll pass homes, small shops, an enclosed market area off it to your right, and then you arrive at the bottom – and the chaos of Nyabugogo market. Just look at the variety of people here – you'll see so many different bone structures, shades of colour, styles of clothing...

If you cross over into the minibus-taxi station (which is a 'market area' all of its own, with vendors offering everything from leather shoes and hi-fi equipment to – improbably – plastic hair curlers and freshly baked bread) you can get a minibus-taxi back to the central minibus station or else take a normal taxi; they park just inside the main gate. Or turn right up the main road as you leave the market; this upward hill is Boulevard de Nyabugogo and will take you back to Place de l'Unité Nationale and the centre of town.

INTERNATIONAL PEACE MARATHON

This colourful and energetic event is an initiative of the European Federation of Soroptimists (*www.soroptimisteurope.org*), aimed at giving people from other countries the chance to run shoulder to shoulder with Rwandans in the name of peace. After long and careful preparations by the Soroptimists and Rwanda's Ministry of Youth, Sports and Culture, the first International Peace Marathon took place in Kigali on 15 May 2005. On that bright, hot Sunday morning, 2,000 runners from 20 different nations flocked into the Amahoro Stadium. Among them were 500 children, who set off with the less athletic participants on the accompanying 5km Fun Run.

As you might expect in the 'Land of a Thousand Hills', the marathon itself was, inevitably, hilly! And Kigali's altitude of 1,500m caused breathlessness among some runners from lower countries. It was a day of huge good humour, energy, enthusiasm and fellowship.

The 2006 Peace Marathon, Half Marathon and Fun Run will take place on 14 May, too late for us to give you the results here. Participants are expected from the USA, UK, Italy, France, Finland, Belgium, Germany, Austria, Netherlands, Greece, Luxembourg, Malta, Morocco, Kenya, Ethiopia and other African countries. Again there will be many children – 1,000 of them, aged around 11–12 years old, selected from schools all over Rwanda to take part in the fun run. Many are from underprivileged backgrounds, and the Soroptimists have raised funds to provide each with a commemorative T-shirt, a contribution to his/her school fees for a year, and a backpack with some school equipment. The Ministry of Sport looks after their transport and accommodation.

The Peace Marathon has become now an annual event, to be held in May each year. Check out the details on www.kigalimarathon.com. And start training now...!

EXCURSIONS FROM KIGALI

VIA TOUR OPERATORS All of the tour operators listed below can organise excursions for you and/or arrange vehicle hire. All have some English-speaking staff, and can book accommodation for you, collect you from the airport, arrange permits for gorilla-viewing, and so forth. In addition there are several more travel agents, who can deal with national and international travel but don't necessarily obtain gorilla permits (which are issued by ORTPN).

It is claimed that there are over 230 sites of historic or cultural interest in Rwanda (no-one has yet listed them all to me!) so you shouldn't be stuck for choice. If you're phoning from abroad, remember that the international code for Rwanda is 250. There are no regional codes in Rwanda.

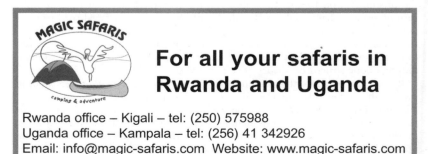

Some tour operators in Kigali A recommended first stop is **Volcanoes Safaris** (*office at Hotel des Mille Collines;* ☎ *502452, 576530;* e *salesrw@volcanoessafaris.com; www.volcanoessafaris.com*), a well-established and highly regarded company specialised in Rwanda and Uganda (also included under international operators on pages 37–9). Volcanoes runs regular gorilla trips (including fly-in visits) as well as tours to most other corners of the country, and their new Virunga Lodge near the Volcanoes National Park is one of the most beautifully located and best run in Rwanda. See their advertisement on page 23.

Another very reliable operator is **Thousand Hills Expeditions** (*office at Hotel des Mille Collines;* ☎ *504330;* e *jacqui@thousandhills.rw; www.thousandhills.rw*), whose manager worked with the highly rated Kenya-based safari operator Abercrombie & Kent for several years, and now handles their Rwanda tours as well as all general tourism. See advertisement on page 248.

In Avenue de la Paix, you will find **Primate Safaris** (*roughly opposite Nord-Sud Travel; BP 158 Kigali;* ☎ *511718;* m *08520106, 08520103;* e *primate_safaris@yahoo.com; www.primatesafaris.com*) ; **Kiboko Tours & Travel** (*BP 6628 Kigali;* ☎ *520118, 520119;* f *501741;* e *kiboko@rwanda1.com; www.kibokotravels.org.rw – see advertisement below*) who also operate a speed-boat on Lake Kivu; and **Nord-Sud International Travel & Tours** (☎ *575310;* f *575349;* e *nordsudinternational@yahoo.fr*).

In the SORAS building, on the left side of Boulevard de la Révolution as you walk along from the town centre towards the InterContinental Hotel, you'll find **Concord Rwanda** (☎ *575988;* e *info@magic-safaris.com; www.magic-safaris.com; knowledgeable about trekking in the Virungas; see advertisement below*); and **International Tours & Travel** (☎ *574057, 578831/2;* f *575582;* e *itt@rwanda1.com; www.itt.co.rw*).

A new operator offering small-scale tailor-made trips is **Bizidanny Tours & Safaris** (*rue des Coopératives near La Galette; BP 395 Kigali;* ☎ *08501461;* e *infobizidanny@yahoo.fr; www.bizidanny.com & http://bizidanny.over-blog.com – see advertisement on page 112*); as well as all the standard trips he offers visits to schools, orphanages, women's cooperatives, local development projects etc. In a similar context see the Musanze/Ruhengeri-based operator **Amahoro Tours** on page 185.

There are several others around the city – too many to list here – and more are opening at the time of writing. Check the current position on www.rwandatourism.com. Their non-inclusion in this guide doesn't mean there's anything wrong with them, so by all means give them a go – and send in recommendations for the next edition!

INDEPENDENT VISITS

Public minibus-taxis Most places in Rwanda are easily accessible by public minibus-taxi, leaving from the Nyabugogo minibus-taxi station (*gare routière Nyabugogo*) about 2km from the centre of Kigali. It's a huge place and they are lined up in ranks – some

signposted with destinations and others not – but just ask someone and you'll be shown the right place to wait. The minibuses leave as soon as they've a full complement of passengers – and that does mean *full* as in can of sardines – but everyone gets a seat. There's a non-smoking policy on board. Fares are collected just before you alight rather than when you board; you'll see other passengers getting their money ready as their destinations approach. If you're not sure of the fare (it's helpful to offer the correct money) ask anyone what you should be paying. Fares are much the same as those of the Taxis de la Poste, shown below. If you're carrying luggage, either (if it's small enough) keep it on your lap or else ask for it to be stuffed in at the back or put on the roof. If you have anything fragile, keep it with you.

If you're returning to Kigali the same day, don't leave it too late, as there's no set schedule; it's sensible to ask the driver for an estimate of the time of the last minibus, and to be there well before it's due to depart.

While you're waiting for your minibus to leave, vendors of all sorts will be trying to catch your eye and sell you something – including bottled drinks and fruit, as well as fresh bread and cakes, which are handy if you've a long journey ahead. You can even buy hard-boiled eggs, and season them from the salt and pepper pots conveniently provided!

Minibus-taxis to the Nyabugogo station leave from the central minibus station at the junction of Avenue de Commerce and Rue Mont Kabuye. Or take a *taxi-voiture*.

Private minibus-taxis Many companies run these – Okapicar, Volcano Express, T2000, de la Poste, Rwanda Express, Stella, etc – and they come and go, so there'll be new names by the time you read this. Some have offices near the central minibus station, others in Place de la Constitution. Ask around. Recommended are the Taxis de la Poste, which start from the central post office. The representative costs below relate to Ataco, a centrally located company (office and departures on Kabuye Road) that runs several departures daily to most destinations countrywide including hourly minibuses to Byumba, Nyagatare Ruhengeri and Gisenyi (all on the hour from 06.00 to 16.00 or 17.00), Kibuye (quarter past the hour from 06.15 to 13.15), Nyanza (ten past the hour from 06.10 to 17.10), Kibungo (quarter to the hour from 06.45 to 17.45) and Huye (on the hour from 07.00 to 17.00) as well as regular departures to Kayonza via Rwamagana (18 daily from 06.10 to 18.00), Gitarama (20 daily between 06.00 and 17.30) and Cyangugu (four daily from 06.30 to 13.30).

- Nyanza, Ruhengeri: Rfr1,000
- Kibungo, Huye, Nyagatare, Kibuye: Rfr1,200–1,400
- Gisenyi, Rusumo: Rfr1,800–2,000
- Cyangugu: Rfr3,000

Government-run buses These rather smart vehicles – previously yellow but now being replaced by brand-new white ones – come under the government department Onatracom. They rattle about to all parts of Rwanda, including some rough roads which must tax their springs severely. You may see them parked in Nyamirambo, near the mosque, but that's not where you catch them; they leave from the Nyabugogo minibus station, which is where you can get current details of their timetable and destinations.

NATIONAL PARKS Akagera Park (see *Chapter 14*) can be visited from Kigali in a day but you'll need your own transport for a very early start and would get a lot more from the exercise by overnighting in or near the park. The mountain gorillas in the **Volcanoes Park** (*Chapter 12*) can also be visited as a day trip – but again you'll need your own transport (which any of the tour operators listed above can organise) in order to get to the park headquarters by 07.00, otherwise you should spend the previous night in either Ruhengeri or Kinigi and arrange transport from there. ORTPN may be able to advise you on this when you buy your permit. The **Nyungwe Forest** (*Chapter 9*) is too far for a day trip, but minibus-taxis running between Huye and Cyangugu can drop you off nearby and you can either camp or stay overnight in the ORTPN Guesthouse.

HUYE (FORMERLY BUTARE) Huye and the National Museum (see *Chapter 8*) are an easy day trip from Kigali, by either public or private minibus-taxi. A private operator with smart new vehicles is Volcano Express, whose office is near the central minibus station. If you go by public minibus-taxi, you can ask to be dropped at either the museum or the centre of town; to return to Kigali, you must start from the minibus-taxi station on the northern edge of town (see map on page 93). The private companies stop and start in the centre of Huye but should drop you off at the museum if you ask.

KIBUYE If you leave early and check the return times, you should be able to visit the attractive little lakeside town of Kibuye (see pages 161–5) and get back the same day, now that the very good road from Kigali has been completed. If you do, then be sure to visit the memorial church there – a beautiful, peaceful place very different from the two genocide memorials listed below.

GENOCIDE MEMORIALS There are two memorials to the south of Kigali, both accessible as a day trip. The church at **Nyamata**, about 30km from Kigali, was the scene of a horrific massacre. The interior has been cleared and left empty; there are still some bloodstains on the walls; and, in the courtyard outside, an underground chamber has been dug in which are stored – and displayed – the skulls and bones of many hundreds of victims. Visitors can see them and be reminded of the enormity of the crime. A guide will take you round and explain the background – and ask you to sign the visitors' book, in which you may spot some internationally known names.

Ntarama church, about 5km down a right-hand fork which branches off the Nyamata road roughly 20km outside Kigali (so you can visit both of them on the same drive), has been left empty and just as it was after the bodies had been removed – there are scraps of cloth and personal items still on the floor. Beside it is another building where more people, seeking safety, were slaughtered. It's a silent place, surrounded by trees: very evocative, very poignant. The guide (French-speaking) recounts the events precisely – and powerfully. A sign outside the gate records that around 5,000 victims died there.

Both memorials are grim, Nyamata more so than Ntarama because of the bones and skulls, and both convey the appalling scale of the tragedy. There's no charge for entry to the sites and the guides do their job with dignity – a tip is expected and deserved.

7

The Road to Huye (Butare)

The surfaced 136km road between Kigali and Butare (recently renamed Huye – see page 127) can usually be covered in about two hours, depending to some extent on how often you get stuck behind trucks on the steeper slopes, and how aggressively your driver attempts to overtake such obstacles. The largest town en route, Gitarama sprawls alongside the main road for several kilometres either side of the junction westward to Kibuye, while nearby tourist attractions include the Kabgayi Cathedral and an associated museum, as well as the former royal compound at Nyanza, either of which can be visited as a day trip out of Kigali or en route to Huye.

GITARAMA

This somewhat scattered and unmemorable settlement comes across as an improbable contender for the honour of second-largest town in Rwanda, yet that is exactly what it is, with a population of 85,000 in the 2002 census now likely to be approaching the 100,000 mark. Despite its unassuming appearance, Gitarama has also often been involved in Rwanda's recent history. It is famous as the location of the historic gathering on 28 January 1961 at which the people first declared Rwanda a republic, and it was the probable starting point for the violence that led to the imposition of martial law under Colonel Guy Logiest in November 1959. Gitarama was the birthplace of Rwanda's first president Grégoire Kayibanda, whose modest tomb now stands in the town centre alongside a disused open-air auditorium built during his rule.

Thanks to its strategic location at the junction of the roads running southward to Huye and westward to Lake Kivu, Gitarama is passed through by a great many tourists, but explored by few. And, with the exception of the cathedral and associated museum at nearby Kabgayi (more details below), there really is very little to do or see in this workaday town, though the everyday hustle and bustle of ordinary Rwandans going about their lives can be a change from more intensive tourism.

If you do opt to explore Gitarama, helpfully a Banque de Kigali stands opposite the main taxi-minibus park in the town centre, as do a handful of small shops, and the bar/restaurants Tranquillité and Le Palmier. The post office is about 1km away: turn right as you leave the minibus stand and keep straight on; you'll come to it on the left just after the Rwanda Revenue Authority. There are motorbike-taxis at the minibus stand – but you won't be given a helmet, so be sure that your insurance includes this form of transport.

GETTING THERE AND AWAY Gitarama lies about 50km south of Kigali, a drive that shouldn't take longer than an hour except in very heavy traffic. Regular minibus-taxis connect the centrally located taxi park to Kigali, Kibuye, Butare and smaller towns en route.

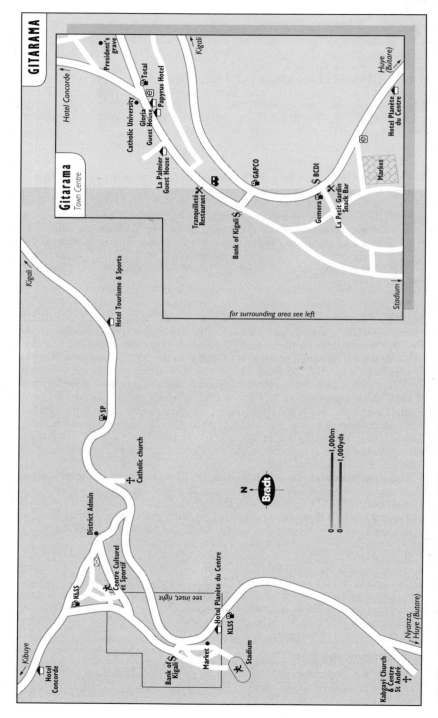

GITARAMA

Gitarama
Town Centre

for surrounding area see left

President's grave

Hotel Concorde

Kigali

Catholic University

Gloria
Guest House

Total

Papyrus Hotel

La Palmier
Guest House

Tranquilleté
Restaurant

Bank of Kigali

GAPCO

Gemera

La Petit Gardin
Snack Bar

BCDI

Market

Hotel Planète
du Centre

Huye
(Butare)

Stadium

Kigali

Hotel Tourisme & Sports

SP

Catholic church

District Admin

Centre Culturel
et Sportif

KLSS

Hotel
Concorde

Kibuye

Bank of
Kigali

Market

Hotel Planète du Centre

see inset, right

KLSS

Stadium

Kabgayi Church
& Centre
St André

Nyanza,
Huye (Butare)

N

Brad

1,000m
1,000yds

0
0

116

WHERE TO STAY

Centre St André (84 rooms) ☏ 562812/2450; m 08 421378/478563; e saintandrekabgayi@yahoo.fr; ✪ S 02°05.896, E 029°45.147, 1,867m. Situated alongside Kabgayi Cathedral about 3km south of central Gitarama and some 200m or so off the Huye road, this large and reasonably priced church-run guesthouse is undoubtedly the best place to stay in the area, assuming that you don't mind the non-central location. Rooms range from basic dbls using common showers to comfortable mini-suites, while facilities include a restaurant, a bar (serving beer as well as soft drinks), an internet café, and a well-equipped business centre. It can fill up if there's a religious convocation, so you might want to book in advance. *Rfr2,000 pp using common showers; Rfr3,000/5,000 en-suite sgl/dbl; Rfr10,000–12,000 mini-suite, b/fast an additional Rfr1,000 pp, other meals Rfr2,000.*

Hotel Tourisme et Sports (14 rooms) ☏ 562269; ✪ S 02°04.551, E 029°46.1679, 1,880m. Situated about 3km from the town centre alongside the main road to Kigali, this is a newish hotel, and probably the best secular option in Gitarama, the outlying location notwithstanding. It's a pleasant, peaceful place with large rooms and concrete-dominated grounds, and serves evening meals by request. *En-suite rooms with net and hot water Rfr6,500/7,500 sgl (³/₄ bed)/twin.*

La Planète du Centre (20 rooms) ☏ 562905; ✪ S 02°05.111, E 029°45.246, 1,891m. This quirky 3-storey building is clearly signposted alongside the main Huye road just outside central Gitarama. The rooms are large but rather rundown and the location is potentially noisy, making it rather poor value at the asking price. *Rfr8,000 en-suite dbl, Rfr4,000 sgl using common showers, Rfr2,000 for a bed in a 4-berth dorm.*

Le Palmier (7 rooms) ☏ 562183; ✪ S 02°04.788, E 029°45.123, 1,884m. This is the pick of 3 small guesthouses in Gitarama, and very conveniently located more-or-less opposite the main taxi park. The clean spacious rooms are centred around a pleasant courtyard, shaded by the namesake palm tree, and basic meals and drinks are served. The entrance is rather poorly signposted and well-hidden behind a photo studio. *Dbl with common shower Rfr3,000; en-suite dbls Rfr5,000.*

Hotel Concorde (6 rooms) ☏ 562720. Rather seedy and not madly convenient, this small hotel along the Kibuye road consists of a few basic and arguably overpriced rooms using common showers scattered around a tired-looking garden. It has no restaurant, but there is a bar, and it will do b/fast. *Rfr4,000/5,000 sgl/twin.*

WHERE TO EAT Most of the hotels offer meals of a sort, and there are several other eateries dotted around the market and bus station area, of which the **Restaurant Tranquilleté** stands out as a super little place. It consists of a cheerful courtyard, with assorted shapes and sizes of tables, a handful of energetic waitresses serving customers really briskly, and a blackboard with the dishes of the day chalked on it. The food is simple (meat, fish or chicken with chips/salad, fresh fruit for dessert) but good, and cheap, for which reason it does get busy at lunchtime.

EXCURSIONS

Kabgayi Cathedral & Museum The massive cathedral of Kabgayi, which lies a couple of hundred metres from the Huye road just 3km from Gitarama (see Centre St André under *Where to Stay*), is the oldest in the country, dating from 1925; missionaries were already installed in Kabgayi by 1906 and it became the seat of the first Catholic bishop. The cathedral, with its huge and tranquil interior, is worth a visit, and there's a small museum nearby. Children may spot you and come to sell handicrafts. During colonisation various training schools were set up in Kabgayi – for midwives, artisans, printers, carpenters and blacksmiths, among others.

The little museum beside the cathedral opens Monday to Friday 08.00 to 17.00. Saturday and Sunday visits are also possible if booked in advance. Entry costs around U$2.50. Within the very small interior are many historically and culturally interesting items such as:

* Ancient hand tools and weapons: knives, hoes, spears, arrows, etc
* Tools and implements connected with the iron industry

With its distinctive tall green stem topped by a luxuriant clump of thick, wide leaves, the banana (or plantain, known locally as *insina*) is an integral feature of the Rwandan landscape, occupying a full 35% of the country's cultivated land. Grown at a wide range of altitudes – from as low as 800m to above 2,000m – the banana thrives in Rwanda's characteristically moist climate, and is unquestionably the most important cash crop countrywide, accounting for 60–80% of the income of most subsistence-level households.

So it might come as a surprise to many visitors to learn that the banana is not indigenous to Rwanda – or anywhere else in Africa for that matter. One Ugandan legend has it that the first banana plant was brought to the region by Kintu, whose shrine lies on a hill called Magonga (almost certainly a derivative of a local Ugandan name for the banana) alongside a tree said to have grown from the root of the plant he originally imported. If this legend is true, it would place the banana's arrival in east-central Africa in perhaps the 13–15th century, probably from the Ethiopian highlands. Most botanists argue, however, that the immense number of distinct varieties grown in the region could not have been cultivated within so short a period – a time span of at least 1,000 years would be required.

Only one species of banana, *Musa ensete*, is indigenous to Africa, and it doesn't bear edible fruit. The more familiar cultivated varieties have all been propagated from two wild Asian species, *M. acuminata* and *M. balbisiana* and hybrids thereof. Wild bananas are almost inedible and riddled with hard pits, and it is thought that the first edible variety was cultivated from a rare mutant of one of the above species about 10,000 years ago – making the banana one of the oldest cultivated plants in existence. Edible bananas were most likely cultivated in Egypt before the time of Christ, presumably having arrived there via Arabia or the Indian Ocean. The Greek sailor and explorer Cosmas Indicopleustes recorded that edible bananas grew around the port of Adulis, in present-day Eritrea, circa AD525 – describing them as 'moza, the wild-date of India'.

The route via which the banana reached modern-day Rwanda is open to conjecture. The most obvious point of origin is Ethiopia, the source of several southward migrations in the past two millennia. But it is intriguing that while the banana is known by a name approximating the generic Latin *Musa* throughout Asia, Arabia and northeast Africa – 'moz' in Arabic and Persian, for instance, or 'mus' or 'musa' in various Ethiopian languages and Somali – no such linguistic resemblance occurs in East Africa, where it is known variously as 'ndizi', 'gonja', 'matoke', 'insina' et al. This peculiarity has been cited to support a hypothesis that the banana travelled between Asia and the East African coast either as a result of direct trade or else via Madagascar, and that it was entrenched there before regular trade was established with Arabia. A third possibility is that the banana reached east-central Africa via the Congolese Basin, possibly in association with the arrival of Bantu-speakers from West Africa.

However it arrived, the banana has certainly flourished there, forming the main subsistence crop for most people in the region – indeed, Rwanda's mean banana consumption of almost 2kg per person per week ranks among the highest in the world. Some 50 varieties are grown in the region, divided into four broad categories based on their primary use – most familiar are sweet bananas, eaten raw as a snack or dessert,

- Ancient examples of clothing: bark cloth etc
- Musical instruments
- Methods of transportation used for chiefs, high-born women and the sick
- Clay pots and pipes
- Baskets – ornamental and for domestic use

while other more floury varieties are used especially for boiling (like potatoes), roasting, or distillation into banana beer or wine.

The banana's uses are not restricted to feeding bellies. The juice from the stem is traditionally regarded to have several medicinal applications, for instance as a cure for snakebite and for childish behaviour. Pulped or scraped sections from the stem also form very effective cloths for cleaning. The outer stem can be plaited to make a strong rope, while the cleaned central rib of the leaf is used to weave fish traps and other items of basketry. The leaf itself forms a useful makeshift umbrella, and was traditionally worn by young girls as an apron. The dried leaf is a popular bedding and roofing material, and is also used to manufacture the head pads on which Rwandan women generally carry their loads.

The banana as we know it is a cultigen – modified by humans to their own ends and totally dependent on them for its propagation. The domestic fruit is the result of a freak mutation that gives the cells an extra copy of each chromosome, preventing the normal development of seeds, thereby rendering the plant edible but also sterile. Every cultivated banana tree on the planet is effectively a clone, propagated by the planting of suckers or corms cut from 'parent' plants. This means that, unlike sexually reproductive crops, which experience new genetic configurations in every generation, the banana is unable to evolve mechanisms to fight off new diseases.

In early 2003, a report in the *New Scientist* warned that cultivated bananas are threatened with extinction within the next decade, due to their lack of defence against a pair of fungal diseases rampant in most of the world's banana-producing countries. These are *black sigatoka*, an airborne disease first identified in Fiji in 1963, and the soil-borne *Panama Disease*, also known as Fusarium Wilt. Black sigatoka can be kept at bay by regular spraying – every ten days or so – but it is swiftly developing resistance to all known fungicides, which in any case are not affordable to the average subsistence farmers. There is no known cure for Panama Disease.

So far as can be ascertained, Panama Disease does not affect any banana variety indigenous to Rwanda or neighbouring countries, but it has already resulted in the disappearance of several introduced varieties. Black sigatoka, by contrast, poses a threat to every banana variety in the world. It has been present throughout Uganda for some years, where a progressive reduction exceeding 50% has been experienced in the annual yield of the most seriously affected areas, and recent reports suggest it is rapidly spreading into parts of Rwanda and the DRC. In addition to reducing the yield of a single plant by up to 75%, black sigatoka can also cut its fruit-bearing life from more than 30 years to less than five.

International attempts to clone a banana tree resistant to both diseases have met with one limited success – agricultural researchers in Honduras have managed to produce one such variety, but it reputedly doesn't taste much like a banana. Another area of solution is genetic engineering – introducing a gene from a wild species to create a disease-resistant edible banana. Although ecologists are generally opposed to the genetic modification of crops, the domestic banana should perhaps be considered an exception, given its inability to spread its genes to related species – not to mention its pivotal importance to the subsistence economies of some of world's poorest countries, Rwanda among them.

- The prestigious Milk Bar and jugs from the palace of the last queen mother (1961)
- Old indoor games such as igisoro, which are still popular in Rwanda and neighbouring countries
- Ancient military officers' costumes and pips

- A national drum captured from Ijwi Island (Kivu) in 1875, thereby effectively annexing it to Rwanda
- Information about traditional medicines, and tokens (kwe) formerly used as currency
- Modern clothing and historical photographs

RUHANGO

Straddling the Huye road about 25km south of Gitarama, and connected to it by regular public transport, Ruhango is another nondescript but well-equipped and surprisingly substantial town, with a population of 43,750 in 2002 making it the twelfth largest in the country. It is of limited interest to tourists except on Friday mornings, when it hosts one of the largest markets in the country. Vendors trek in for the occasion from far afield, carrying their wares, and an astonishing range of merchandise is on sale, from livestock and vegetables to hi-fi equipment, household goods and swathes of brightly coloured cotton fabric. You could consider spending a Thursday night here and then watching activities unfold the next morning. Otherwise, the area is notable primarily for *Uratare rwa Kamageri* (Kamageri's Rock – see box opposite), which is signposted by the roadside ten minutes' walk south of the town centre.

🏠 WHERE TO STAY AND EAT

🏠 **Hotel Umuco** (12 rooms) ☎ 560017; m 08 464553. Centrally located, and arranged around a pleasant courtyard, this sensibly priced hotel provides travellers with basic but clean accommodation close to the taxi park, as well as inexpensive meals such as goat brochette and chips or beef stew and rice. *Sgl using common shower Rfr2,000; en-suite dbl Rfr5,000; meals Rfr800–1,000.*

🏠 **Pacis Hotel** (6 rooms) ☎ 560121, m 09 597483. Set alongside the Kigali Road about 1km from the town centre, this reasonably pleasant hotel, though inferior to the Umuco, also offers en-suite accommodation and adequate meals. *Rfr5,000 dbl.*

🏠 **Restaurant-Bar Ituzi** (6 rooms) Situated right alongside the Umuco and probably only worth considering if its smarter neighbour is full, this new lodge has basic sgls using a common shower only, but the outdoor bar looks to be a pleasant spot for a drink or meal. *Rfr2,000 sgl.*

NYANZA

In 1899, Mwami Musinga Yuhi V, his sense of absolute authority undermined by the growing colonial presence in Rwanda, decided to break with the royal tradition of mobility that had led to his predecessor having had an estimated 50–60 residences scattered through the kingdom. The recently enthroned Musinga selected Nyanza Hill, some 30km north of modern-day Butare (now Huye), as the site of the first permanent royal capital, a role it would retain throughout both his reign and that of his son Rudahigwa Mutara III, who built two large houses on the site, until 1961, when the traditional monarchy was abolished. Today, the partially restored capital is a (highly worthwhile) museum.

The town of Nyanza, also sometimes known as Nyabisindu, lies a short distance north of the former capital along a surfaced 2km road leading westward from the main Huye–Kigali road at Kubijega (literally, 'Place of Storage', in reference to a trio of nearby metal warehouses). With its wide, dusty streets, Nyanza has something of a Wild West feel, and it boasts few tourist facilities – just one formal hotel at Kubijega, a small internet café, a handful of restaurants, and that's about it. But it's a reasonably substantial town all the same (in fact, a population of 56,000 makes it the eighth largest in the country) and the museum is well worth the minor diversion from the Huye road, whether you use private or public transport.

It happened during the reign of Mwami Mibambwe II Sekarongoro II Gisanura, who ruled Rwanda almost four centuries ago. He was a fair and just ruler. Among other innovations, he required his chiefs to bring jars of milk from their own cows to the court – and these were then distributed to the poor and needy, three times a day: morning, noon and evening.

One day, so the story goes, a man was convicted of stealing from the Mwami, who then asked two of his chiefs to devise a suitable punishment. It seems that they saw this as an opportunity to impress the Mwami with their thoroughness.

The chief named Mikoranya suggested an instrument of torture based on a shaft of wood extending from a hut; while the chief named Kamageri proposed to the Mwami that a large, flat rock near Gitarama be heated until red-hot and the criminal be spread-eagled across it.

The Mwami asked the chiefs to demonstrate their ideas, so that he could understand what they proposed. Eagerly they set to work.

When the rock was glowing red-hot (it took a week of brushwood fires to achieve this) and the torture implement was prepared, the Mwami arrived with his retinue. 'Is everything ready?' he asked Kamageri and Mikoranya, and they nodded proudly, expecting praise and possibly some reward.

The Mwami called forward his guards, to whom he had already explained what would happen. 'Take them,' he ordered. 'And subject them to their own punishments! Let Kamageri roast on his rock and Mikoranya suffer his own torture. They were too cruel. There is no place for these men in my kingdom.'

The rock where Kamageri supposedly roasted to death can still be seen, at Ruhango on the Gitarama–Huye road. Tourists stop to photograph it and guides recount various versions of the story.

GETTING THERE AND AWAY Nyanza lies 2km west of Kubijega junction (✛ S 02°20.749, E 029°46.001; 1,811m) on the main Kigali-Huye road less than two hours' drive from Kigali and just 45 minutes' drive from Huye. A good surfaced road (culminating in a one-way loop) leads all the way to the hilltop museum. Direct minibus-taxis to/from Huye, Gitarama and Kigali leave from the town centre, adjacent to the market, but it is also pretty easy to pick up passing traffic at Kubijega – minibus-taxis in either direction stop alongside the JOB filling station at the junction.

WHERE TO STAY AND EAT

🏠 **Nyanza Guesthouse** (10 rooms) ☎ 533121; ▥ 08 422263. Situated alongside the Kigali Road some 200m from the Nyanza junction, right next to the metal eyesores that gave Kubijega its name (see opposite), this newish hotel offers comfortable accommodation in clean, tiled en-suite rooms set around a small, rather untidy garden. No food is served but a bar immediately opposite sells cold drinks, brochettes, chips and other typical local snacks. *Rfr5,000 sgl or dbl, Rfr8,000 twin.*

🏠 **CNFDJ Guesthouse** ☎ 533238. This unsignposted institution close to the stadium currently offers clean en-suite accommodation, but do phone in advance – the rooms are sometimes filled by conference groups, and it may well close down completely during the lifespan of this edition. *Rfr5,000/6,000 sgl/dbl.*

🏠 **Olivier's House** (3 rooms) ▥ 08 539379. This private house between the stadium and the town centre consists of 3 dbl bedrooms and a shared bathroom and sitting room. *Rfr8,000 per bedroom per night, long-stay rates negotiable.*

🏠 **Club Tropicana** Mainly a bar, but a relatively upmarket one, this newish and conspicuous white building on the road towards the palace also serves a selection of tasty snacks and light meals. It has a public phone and may well develop other services.

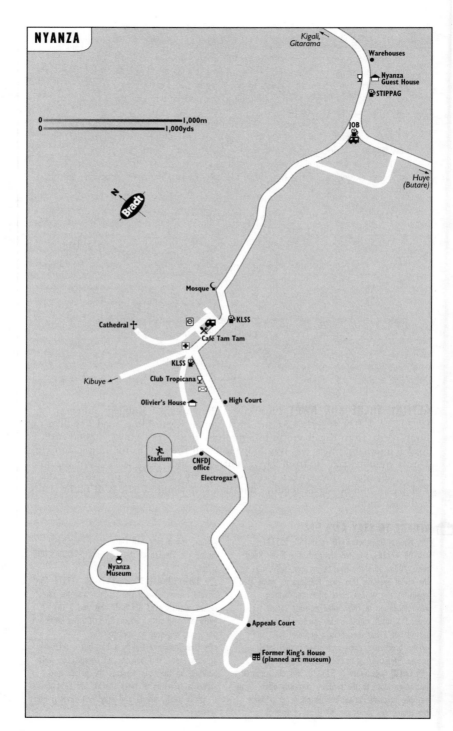

In 1862, when Speke prepared for his first audience with King Mutesa of Buganda (part of modern-day Uganda), he put on his finest clothes, but admitted that he 'cut a poor figure in comparison with the dressy Baganda [who] wore neat bark cloaks resembling the best yellow corduroy cloth, crimp and well set, as if stiffened with starch'.

Known as *impuzu* in Rwanda, the stiff, neat bark-cloth cloak described by Speke was then the conventional form of attire in this part of Africa. Exactly how and when the craft arose is unknown. One tradition has it that King Wamala of Bacwezi Kingdom (legendary precursor to both Rwanda and Buganda) discovered bark cloth by accident on a hunting expedition, when he hammered a piece of bark to break it up and instead found that it expanded laterally to form a durable material.

Bark cloth can be made from the inner bark lining of about at least 20 tree species. The best-quality cloth derives from four species of the genus *Ficus* known locally as *umutaba, umuhororo, umurama* and *umugombe*, all of which were extensively cultivated in pre-colonial times. Different species of tree yielded different textures and colours, from yellow to sandy brown to dark red-brown.

The common bark-cloth tree can be propagated simply by cutting a branch from a grown one and planting it in the ground – after about five years the new tree will be large enough to be used for making cloth. The bark will be stripped from any one given tree only once a year, when it is in full leaf. After the bark has been removed, the trunk is wrapped in green banana leaves for several days, then plastered with wet cow dung and dry banana leaves to help it heal. If a tree is looked after this way, it may survive 30 years of annual use.

The bark is removed from the tree in one long strip. A circular incision is made near the ground, another one below the lowest branches, then a long line is cut from base to top, before finally a knife is worked underneath the bark to ease it carefully away from the trunk. The peeled bark is left out overnight before the hard outer layer is scraped off, then it is soaked. It is then folded into two equal halves and laid out on a log to be beaten with a wooden mallet on alternating sides to become thinner. When it has spread sufficiently, the cloth is folded in four and the beating continues. The cloth is then unfolded before being left to dry in the sun.

There are several local variations in the preparation process, but the finest cloth reputedly results when the freshly stripped bark, instead of being soaked, is steamed for about an hour above a pot of boiling water, then beaten for an hour or so daily over the course of a week. The steaming and extended process of beating are said to improve the texture of the cloth and to enrich the natural red-brown or yellow colour of the bark. Although it is used mostly for clothing, bark cloth can also serve as a blanket or a shroud, and is rare but valued as bookbinding.

Oral tradition has it that the cloth was originally worn only by the king and members of his court. Ironically, however, this historical association between bark cloth and social prestige was reversed during the early decades of colonial rule, when clothing made from cotton and other fabrics became a status symbol. By the 1950s, bark cloth had practically disappeared from everyday use.

WHAT TO SEE

The King's Palace This is the top touristic reason for visiting Nyanza, situated on a hilltop about 2km from the centre, and signposted (⊕ S 02°21.468, E 029°44.395; 1,805m). The traditional ancient palace of the Mwami has been reconstructed, together with some other buildings, 3–4km away from its original site, beside the newer Western-style palace built for Mwami Rudahigwa Mutara III in 1932. In olden times, Nyanza was the heart of Rwanda and seat of its monarchy, background to the oral tradition of battles and conquests, power struggles and royal intrigues. It is where the German colonisers came, at the end of the 19th century, to visit the *mwami* – and contemporary reports tell of the great pomp and ceremony these visits occasioned, as well as the impressive size of the *mwami's* court.

> The capital of the kingdom was composed of a group of huts, an ephemeral town of some 2,000 inhabitants, well organised as far as the administration of the country and the comfort of the nobility were concerned... At his court the Mwami maintained the following retinue: the 'Ntore', adolescent sons of chiefs and notables, who formed the corps de ballet; the 'Bakoma', soothsayers, magicians and historians; the 'Abashashi', keepers of the arsenal, the wardrobe and the furniture; the 'Abasisi' and 'Abacurabgenge', mimes, musicians and cooks; the 'Abanyabyumba', palanquin bearers and night watchmen; the 'Nitalindwa', huntsmen and runners; the 'Intumwa', artisans working for the Mwami; and finally the hangmen, attentive servants of jurists, ever ready to respond to the brief order to fetch and kill.

> *Traveller's Guide to the Belgian Congo and Ruanda-Urundi*,
> Tourist Bureau for the Belgian Congo and Ruanda-Urundi, Brussels, 1951

The traditional palace has been carefully reconstructed and maintained, and contains the king's massive bed as well as various utensils. English- and French-speaking guides are available to relate the history and traditions of the royal court – there is even significance attached to some of the poles supporting the roof; for example, the one at the entrance to the king's bed is named 'do not speak of what happens here' and another conferred sanctuary on anyone touching it.

The newer palace is a typical colonial-era building with its spacious rooms and wide balcony. The *Travellers' Guide* above also states: 'In certain circumstances, and with the permission of the local authorities, he [the Mwami] may be visited at his palace which is built on modern lines, furnished in good taste and richly decorated with trophies in an oriental manner.' In more recent times, the rundown palace served for several years as the part-time home of Rwanda's National Ballet (the Intore dancers, see pages 29), but it has recently been restored to something approaching its former beauty. Several original items of royal furniture decorate the interior, and by the time you read this the walls should also be adorned with monochrome photographs and other displays depicting the palace when it was in use. For its history and its peaceful, attractive location, it is worth seeing. Entry to the palaces costs Rfr1,000, but a further photography fee of Rfr1,000 and video fee of Rfr5,000 are charged to happy (or should that be unhappy?) snappers. There is some talk locally of converting a more modern former palace on a hilltop, visible from the existing museum (✪ S 02°22.050, E 029°44.452; 1,834m), into an art museum.

Other places of interest En route to the palaces you'll pass the **Ikivuguto National Dairy**, started during Belgian colonisation and still going strong. In theory you can just turn up and ask for a free tour, but in practice it would be courteous to ask about this on your way out to the palaces and then have your tour (if convenient) on the way back.

As you return towards the main Huye road from Nyanza, there's a left-hand turn about 2km from the junction with a sign to the Oakdale Demonstration Farm. If you fancy following this mud road to the source of some Cheddar cheese, see the box on page 67!

Continuing to Huye there's a sign on the right to the Gatagara Pottery. Turn off on to the mud road and after about 3km you reach a home for the handicapped;

Rosamond Halsey Carr

My introduction to the Mwami and his royal court was in 1956, when the Hollywood film King Solomon's Mines was shown to the king and queen and the royal courtiers. The movie, which was partially filmed on location in Ruanda and starred Stewart Granger and Deborah Kerr, contains some of the most authentic African dance sequences on film, including a dazzling depiction of the dance of the Intore.

The showing had been arranged by the American consulate in Léopoldville and took place in the royal city of Nyanza. Many of the European residents of Ruanda were invited, myself included. The Mwami and his queen, their courtiers, and the Tutsi nobles who took part in the film were all present. It was a mild, clear night, charged with an air of excitement and wonder. A large screen was erected in the middle of a wide dirt road. On one side of the screen, chairs had been set up for the invited guests. On the other side (the back side), a huge crowd of Banyaruanda sat with expectant faces waiting for the movie to begin.

The king and his entourage made a ceremonial entrance. One would be hard-pressed to find a more majestic figure than this giant of a monarch who could trace his family dynasty back more than four hundred years. Rudahigwa and his courtiers were dressed in traditional white robes with flowing togas knotted at their shoulders, and his queen, Rosalie Gicanda, was wrapped in billowing layers of pale pink...

...The soundtrack for the film was in English and, as a result, the Africans were unable to understand the dialogue. Restlessness and murmurs of disappointment rippled through the crowd until the action sequences progressed to the familiar landscape of Ruanda. From that point on, the spectators provided their own soundtrack with cheers and improvised dialogue, as they followed the safari adventure across the desert to the royal city of Nyanza, shouting with glee each time they recognised friends – and in some instances themselves – on the big movie screen.

The city of Nyanza was almost entirely devoid of Western influence, as the Belgian administration had refrained from intruding upon the royal seat of the Tutsi monarchy. There were no hotels, and outside visitors were discouraged. When the movie ended, the Mwami and his entourage and most of the invited guests assembled at the one small restaurant in town for sandwiches and drinks.

From: *Land of a Thousand Hills: My Life in Rwanda* by Rosamond Halsey Carr with Ann Howard Halsey. Viking, 1999. See *Appendix 3*, page 252.

the pottery is on the left at the entrance. You can watch potters (they are Batwa, see page 30 in *Chapter 2*) at work and see the clay in all its stages – also there's a small shop with a good range of finished pots, plates, animals, etc. Marcell Claassen, who is setting up a new luxury Tented Camp near Musanze (Ruhengeri), has made purchases here and comments: 'The quality is one of the best of the various potters we've visited.'

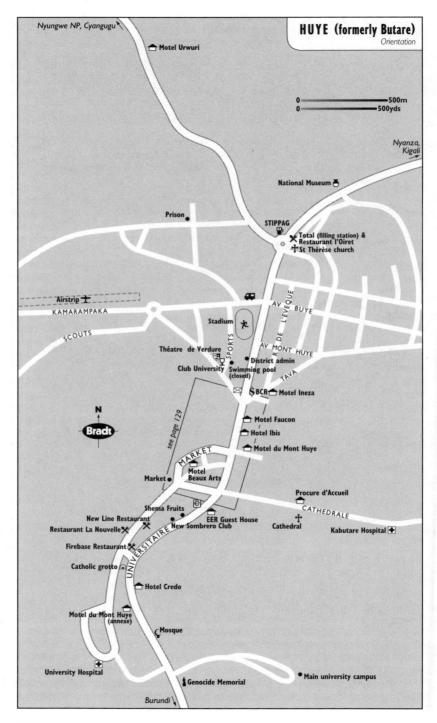

HUYE (formerly Butare)
Orientation

0 ————— 500m
0 ————— 500yds

Nyungwe NP, Cyangugu

Motel Urwuri

Nyanza, Kigali

National Museum

Prison

STIPPAG

Total (filling station) & Restaurant l'Oiret
St Thérèse church

Airstrip
KAMARAMPAKA

AV DE L'EVEQUE
AV BUYE

Stadium

SCOUTS

AV DE MONT HUYE

Théatre de Verdure

SPORTS

District admin

Club University

Swimming pool (closed)

TAVA

N

Bradt

see page 129

BCR   Motel Ineza

Motel Faucon

Hotel Ibis

Motel du Mont Huye

MARKET

Motel Beaux Arts

Market

Procure d'Accueil

CATHEDRALE

Shema Fruits

New Line Restaurant

Restaurant La Nouvelle

EER Guest House

New Sombrero Club

Cathedral

Kabutare Hospital

Firebase Restaurant

UNIVERSITAIRE

Catholic grotto

Hotel Credo

Motel du Mont Huye (annexe)

Mosque

University Hospital

Genocide Memorial

Main university campus

Burundi

126

8

Huye (Butare)

The town of Butare has been renamed Huye following an administrative reorganisation in 2006 which also incorporated the former Butare Province into the new South Province. Set at an altitude of 1,755m, this pleasant, businesslike town is often called the country's 'intellectual centre': the first secondary school in what is now Rwanda opened here in 1928, and it has been the site of the national university since 1963. During the colonial era, Butare served as the administrative centre of the northern half of Ruanda-Urundi and it was the largest town in the joint territory after the capital Bujumbura (in modern-day Burundi). Popular with colonial settlers, Butare was renamed Astrida in 1935, in tribute to Queen Astrid, the 29-year-old Swedish wife of Belgium's King Leopold III, who died in a car accident, but it reverted to its original name in 1962.

At the time of independence it seemed almost inevitable that Huye would become the capital city of Rwanda. In the end, however, Kigali was favoured for its more central location. So while Kigali has mushroomed, Huye remains peaceful and compact – though it is still the third-largest town in Rwanda, with a population estimated at 95,000 in 2006, and its neatly laid out centre still displays strong architectural evidence of its favoured status during the colonial era. During term-time Huye has probably the country's greatest concentration of students, in relation to its size – not only at the university but also at other technical and training schools and colleges. It's something of a religious centre, too, with its massive cathedral and other churches.

GETTING THERE AND AWAY

Huye lies 136km south of Kigali (⊕ of Hotel Ibis S 02°35.993; E 29°44.508), a two-hour drive along good tarred roads. Most public minibus-taxis from Kigali to Huye leave from Nyabugogo taxi park, and will drop you either at the minibus station on the northern edge of town or opposite the market in the centre. The fare is Rfr1,300. Some companies offer regular departures between the city centres – Ataco Express, for instance, operates an hourly service leaving from its office on Rue du Kabuye in central Kigali on the hour from 07.00 to 17.00 (✆ 08 531978). There are also direct minibuses to Huye from Cyangugu and Gitarama.

When you are ready to leave Huye, most minibus-taxis depart from the main taxi park opposite the stadium about 500m north of the town centre. There are also several private operators running services out of the town centre – Okapi Cars and Ataco Express (✆ 08 841512) on the main road both run regular departures to Kigali (every hour on the hour from 06.00 to 18.00), and the latter also runs a twice-daily service to Cyangugu, leaving at 08.00 and 14.00.

GETTING AROUND

The National Museum and the University are no more than about 5km apart, so theoretically everything is manageable on foot. If you should get weary or want to go further afield, however, a few beat-up taxis wait by the turning from the main street leading to the market. The prices asked seem to be standard, but, if you feel you're being overcharged, either bargain or ask to see the official tariff. In any case, agree on a price in advance. Rates may well have increased by the time you read this, but at the time of writing it costs about Rfr1,000–1,500 from the town centre to the museum, Rfr10,000–12,000 to Nyanza and Rfr12,000–15,000 to Kibeho (see page 134). Waiting time costs extra.

WHERE TO STAY

Moderate

Credo Hotel (30 rooms) ☎ 530505/530855; f 530201; m 08 302216/504176; e credohotel@yahoo.fr. Generally regarded to be the smartest option in Huye, this relatively new (it opened in 1999) and rather characterless hotel is situated 500m from the town centre along the road to the university. All rooms are en-suite, with impeccably clean WC and showers, and most also have a TV, telephone and balcony. There's a peaceful view across fields at the back, while facilities include a swimming pool, restaurant and outdoor poolside restaurant-bar. With a bit of notice, car-hire can be arranged here for trips to Nyungwe Forest. It's sometimes used by tour groups or for conferences, so you'd do well to book in advance. *Rfr10,000/13,000 b&b for a sgl/dbl without TV; Rfr15,000/18,000 with TV; 23,000/26,000 suite.*

Hotel Ibis (14 rooms) ☎ 530005/0335; m 08 323000; e campionibis@hotmail.com; www.hotel-ibis-rwanda.com. Established in 1942, this centrally located, family-run hotel is something of a local institution, and it certainly wins out over the upstart competition when it comes to character. The cosy en-suite rooms all come with satellite TV, internet connection and phone, and the bedside lights are a welcome touch. It is also one of the few Rwandan hotels outside of Kigali to offer an online booking service. The main restaurant is good (quite pricey) and there's a pleasant terrace snack-bar. *Rates range from Rfr15,000/18,000 sgl/dbl b&b to Rfr23,000/26,000 depending on the room size.*

Budget

Hotel Faucon (11 rooms) ☎ 531126; e faucon@yahoo.fr. Presumably of similar vintage to the nearby Ibis, but somewhat more run down, this remains an attractive old building with its thick walls, high ceilings and faint colonial-era echoes! The en-suite rooms and suites, though rather sparsely furnished, are very spacious and some come with TV. Rooms are set round a large courtyard, away from the street, and the back windows have a peaceful view of greenery. There's a good main restaurant, also a bar/snack-bar, and the substantial b/fast is possibly the best value in town. *Rfr5,000/8,000 sgl/dbl, or Rfr20,000 for a 2-bedroom apt, with b/fast an additional Rfr1,500 pp.*

Motel du Mont Huye (18 rooms) ☎ 530765; m 08 561005. Arguably the best value of all the budget places is this centrally located but peaceful spot, which lies along a small side road away from the main street and its traffic. The clean, comfortable en-suite rooms with ³/₄ bed all have hot water and a small balcony opening on to a central garden, and there's an adequate restaurant. It's popular with Catholic Relief Services, NGOs, etc, so it's best to book in advance, though extra rooms are now available at an annexe on the university road about 100m past the Hotel Credo. *Rfr5,000/7,500 sgl/dbl; Rfr12,000–15,000 for a 2-bedroom apt at the annexe.*

Motel Ineza (12 rooms) ☎ 530387. Situated along a side road opposite the post office on the north side of town, this popular and pleasant hotel — with friendly English-speaking staff — is most notable for its secluded garden, where you can sit out and eat, write or just enjoy the peace and quiet. Unfortunately the en-suite rooms, though very clean and equipped with mosquito netting (a rarity in Huye), are rather cramped, and the so-called dbls have a ³/₄ bed only. B/fast aside, it no longer serves any meals, though it's so close to the town centre that's not a major drawback. *Rfr4,000/7,000 sgl/dbl occupancy.*

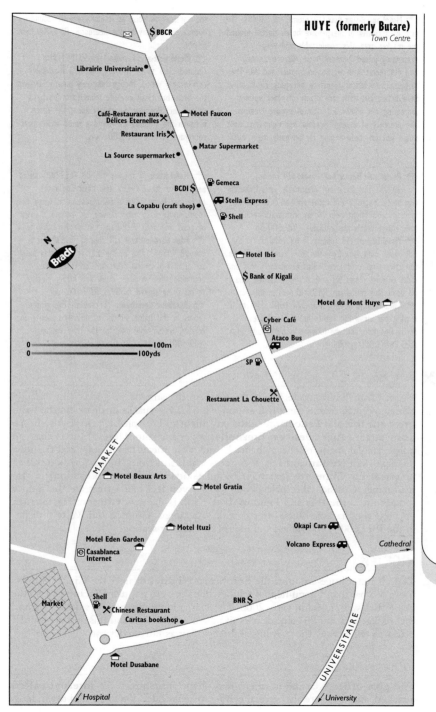

HUYE (formerly Butare)
Town Centre

⊠
$ BBCR

Librairie Universitaire ●

Café-Restaurant aux ✗● 🏠 Motel Faucon
Délices Eternelles
Restaurant Iris ✗
● Matar Supermarket
La Source supermarket ●

BCDI $ 🚌 Gemeca
🚐 Stella Express
La Copabu (craft shop) ●
🚌 Shell

🏠 Hotel Ibis

$ Bank of Kigali

Motel du Mont Huye 🏠

Cyber Café
ⓔ
🚌 Ataco Bus

SP 🚌

Restaurant La Chouette ✗

N
Bract

0 ——————100m
0 ——————100yds

M
A
R
K
E
T

🏠 Motel Beaux Arts

🏠 Motel Gratia

🏠 Motel Ituzi

Okapi Cars 🚐

Motel Eden Garden
ⓔ Casablanca
Internet
🏠

Volcano Express 🚐

Cathedral →

Shell
🚌 ✗ Chinese Restaurant
Market
Caritas bookshop ●

BNR $

U
N
I
V
E
R
S
I
T
A
I
R
E

🏠 Motel Dusabane

↙ Hospital

↙ University

Motel aux Beaux Arts (10 rooms) ☎ 530037. The pick of a cluster of inexpensive hotels dotted around the market area, this comfortable and very reasonably priced 2-storey hotel offers clean twin and dbl rooms with washbasin, shower and WC. The restaurant no longer seems to offer any meals other than b/fast, but there are plenty of other options for eating out within a couple of hundred metres. The presence of a large outdoor bar right next door might put off those hoping for an early night, but the bar isn't as noisy as it looks and the sound doesn't really carry to the bedrooms. *Rfr4,000 twin or dbl.*

Motel Gratia (11 rooms) ☎ 531044. Also situated close to the market, this is a reasonably comfortable set-up, though relatively poor value, with the basic but clean en-suite twins (adorned by a solitary net dangling pointlessly above the space between the 2 beds) set round a small, well-watered courtyard garden. *Rfr5,000 twin.*

Shoestring

Procure de Butare Guesthouse (20 rooms) ☎ 530993) This basic but reasonably priced church-run hostel opposite the cathedral has clean shared facilities and bright twin rooms with wash-basins. Inexpensive meals are available. *Rfr2,000 pp.*

Motel Urwuri (13 rooms) ☎ 08 740873. On the Gikongoro road 2km from the town centre, this is an attractive semi-rustic lodge with reasonably priced and clean en-suite rooms set around pretty gardens and an acceptable restaurant. *Rfr3,000 twin or dbl.*

Chez Mimi (6 rooms) This new hotel close to the market has clean but rather cell-like en-suite accommodation, and the location is potentially noisy. *Rfr3,500/5,000 sgl/dbl.*

Motel Ituze (8 rooms) m 08 466229. Situated next to the Motel Gratia, this basic and rather overpriced lodge offers accommodation in dingy twin rooms using a common shower, set around a patch of grass and with deckchairs outside. *Rfr4,000 twin.*

Eden Garden Hotel (13 rooms) ☎ 530446; m 08 409083. Also in the market area, this hotel, set around a central courtyard, offers adequate accommodation in plain, clean and rather gloomy rooms using shared facilities. *Rfr3,500 twin.*

Dusabane Guesthouse (11 rooms) The grotty rooms at this lodge, which lies directly opposite the market, are suitable only for the truly desperate. *Rfr2,500 sgl.*

WHERE TO EAT AND DRINK

Plenty of small restaurants round the market offer snacks and good-value *mélanges* of rice, vegetables and meat/fish at under US$2. For snacks or drinks in the main street, the **Ibis** and **Faucon** are both convenient and reasonably priced. Also in the main street, **Aux Délices Eternelles** opposite the Hotel Faucon has an unspectacular menu of cheapish snacks and main meals but is quiet and friendly; the next-door **Restaurant Iris** does a reasonable lunchtime buffet for about US$3 upwards. **La Chouette** (between Motel Gratia and the petrol station) is also reasonable. Considerably pricier but good if you feel like a treat are the indoor restaurants at the **Ibis** and **Faucon**. Better still is the new **Chinese Restaurant** opposite the market, which offers a wide selection of Chinese and Western dishes in the Rfr3,000–5,000 range, and indoor or outdoor seating.

NIGHTLIFE

There's not a huge amount: the **Sombrero Nightclub** near the Credo Hotel is more of a bar than a genuine nightclub, while the once popular **Piscine** behind the post office was closed in early 2006. There are plenty of small bars dotted around the market area, and the terrace bars and the hotels Faucon and Ibis remain popular places to while away the evening in the open air as Huye goes by.

PRACTICALITIES

The **post office** is at the northern end of the main street. An **internet café** is attached, and there are also several private internet cafés dotted around town, most offering reasonably fast services (but slower than Kigali) at around Rfr100 per 10 minutes – try Casablanca Cyber Café opposite the market or the anonymous cyber café a few doors down from the Hotel Ibis.

The **Banque Commerciale du Rwanda** opposite the post office and the **Banque de Kigali** midway down the main street offer normal services, but there are no private forex bureaux, so you are generally better off changing money in Kigali or (if you're heading that way) Cyangugu. The BCR has Western Union.

There are two **bookshops**: the Librairie Universitaire at the northern end of the main street has a fair range of books and student stationery, as well as some dusty but original handicrafts. Librairie Caritas at the other end of the main street has a few more touristy books and items of stationery, as well as some international magazines and games.

For **self-caterers**, the central market is a good place to buy local produce such as fruit and vegetables, and there's a good bakery nearby, alongside the Chinese Restaurant. For imported goods, try the Matar and La Source Supermarkets, which stand more-or-less opposite each other on the main road. Locally made fruit juice and jams can be bought at Shema Fruits on the university road next to the Sombrero Nightclub.

For **handicrafts**, there's an excellent shop opposite the Ibis Hotel, selling products made by the *Co-opérative des Producteurs Artisanaux de Butare* (COPABU). The items are priced, but a little gentle bargaining will do no harm, particularly if you're buying more than one. The co-op was set up in 1997 with 47 members, working in banana-leaf products, wood-carving and reed baskets. Three years later it had 954 members (99 individuals and 35 associations) of which 66% were women. Handicrafts in the Huye area have been well organised, with the help of German aid; see www.copabu.co.rw. For more details, e gtzpab@rwanda1.com.

SECURITY For all its laid-back atmosphere, Huye is a busy town with a mixed population, so take normal precautions such as not carrying conspicuous wealth. The larger street kids can be a bit pushy, but treat them understandingly and they're manageable. In the evenings some may gather to sniff solvents around the petrol stations. See box *After the genocide* on page 19. If you go out to eat at night it's wise to take a torch/flashlight. Yes, the streets are well lit, but if there's a power cut (rare, but it happens) they become very black indeed, and finding your way back to your hotel might not be easy.

WHAT TO SEE AND DO

NATIONAL UNIVERSITY OF RWANDA Although not really a tourist 'sight', the National University (*BP 56 Butare;* 530122; f 530121; e *nurcc@nur.ac.rw; www.nur.ac.rw*) is by far Huye's most important institution. Created in 1963, and with only 51 students and 16 lecturers when it opened, it now has over 4,500 students and 275 lecturers. The university lost many of its students and personnel during the genocide and suffered considerable damage, but managed to reopen in 1995. It is now a vibrant and forward-looking institution, comprising faculties of agronomy, law, arts & human sciences, medicine, science & technology, economics, social sciences & management, and education, as well as schools of journalism & communication and modern languages. You may run across visiting professors in any of Huye's hotels and guesthouses.

Out by the university is the **Ruhande Arboretum**, started in 1934. Its objective at the outset was to study the behaviour of imported and indigenous species, to determine what silvicultural methods were most suitable, to evaluate the trees' productivity and timber quality, and to develop the best of them. Now, it is of interest for the range and variety of its species – and it's a peaceful, shady place. Get permission from the university if you'd like to visit. If you have an interest in the arts, you might want to check out whether any student productions are running at the **Théâtre de Verdure**, part of the Centre Universitaire des Arts, which lies along a back road behind the post office (☏ *530215;* e *cua_centre@yahoo.com*).

THE NATIONAL MUSEUM OF RWANDA If you're in Huye – indeed even if you're in some other part of Rwanda – you should allow time to visit this beautifully presented collection of exhibits on Rwandan history and culture. The museum is exceptional. Opened in 1988, and presented to Rwanda as a gift from Belgium's King Baudouin I, its seven spacious rooms illustrate the country and its people from earliest times until the present day.

Room 1 (the entrance hall) has space for temporary displays as well as numerous shelves of traditional handicrafts for sale. **Room 2** presents a comprehensive view of Rwanda's geological and geographical background and the development of its terrain and population. In **Room 3** the occupations of its early inhabitants (hunter-gathering, farming and stock raising) are illustrated, together with the later development of tools and methods of transport. The social importance of cattle is explained and there are even detailed instructions for the brewing of traditional banana beer (see box below). **Room 4** displays a variety of handicrafts and the making of traditional household items: pottery, mats, baskets, leatherwork and the wooden shields of the Intore dancers. **Room 5** illustrates traditional styles and methods of architecture – and a full-scale royal hut has been reconstructed. In **Room 6** traditional games and sports are displayed and more space is given to the costumes and equipment of the Intore dancers. Finally, **Room 7** contains exhibits relating to traditional customs and beliefs, history, culture, poetry, oral tradition and the supernatural.

At the reception desk, various pamphlets and books are on sale. Until recently, no descriptions or background material were available in English, but booklets containing English translations of the Kinyarwanda and French labels are now available for loan – one booklet for each of the seven rooms.

At present the museum (☏ *530586, 530207;* f *530211;* e *museumrwanda@yahoo.fr; www.museum.gov.rw*) is open daily, 07.00–17.00. The entrance fee for non-resident

THE PREPARATION OF BANANA BEER

(Free translation)
- When the bunches of fruit are ready, cut them.
- Cover the bunches with banana leaves and leave them in the courtyard to ripen for two to three days.
- Clean out the pit in which the fruit ripened.
- Lay banana branches across the top of the pit.
- Place the bananas on top of the branches.
- Wrap the bananas in fresh banana leaves and then scatter a layer of earth on top.
- Put leaves in the ditch under the bananas and set the leaves alight. Leave for three days.
- Peel the fruit, then crush it, then mix a little water into the pulp.
- Press the pulp and filter the juice.
- Grind up a small amount of sorghum.
- Pour the juice into a large jar and add the sorghum to it.
- Leave to ferment for three days.
- The beer is ready to drink.

The intellectual and cultural spirit of Butare – as it was then – was so strong that initially it seemed that it could resist the madness of slaughter that erupted elsewhere in the country on 6 April 1994. For decades Hutus and Tutsis had lived and studied peacefully together there. When the killing started, people flocked to Butare from outlying areas believing that they would find safety – as indeed they did, for a while. The prefect of Butare, Jean-Baptiste Habyarimana (no relation to the late president), was the only Tutsi prefect in Rwanda at the time of the genocide. He took charge, welcoming the refugees, reassuring parishioners, and demonstrating such authority that, for two weeks while the killing raged elsewhere, relative calm prevailed in Butare, punctuated by isolated instances of violence.

It couldn't last. Because of his defiance, Habyarimana was sacked from his post and murdered, to be replaced by a hardline military officer, Colonel Tharcisse Muvunyi, and an equally hardline civilian administrator. Under their orchestration, paramilitary units from Kigali were airlifted to Butare, and the killing started immediately. Ultimately, the massacres in and around Butare proved to be some of the worst of the genocide, and the death tally of 220,000 was the highest of any prefecture. Tharcisse Muvunyi later fled to Britain, where he was tracked down and arrested in Lewisham (London) in February 2000.

adults is Rfr1,000. If you want to go somewhere for a drink and snack after your visit, a short walk Huye-wards along the main road brings you to the Bar-Restaurant l'Oiret which is open 07.00–23.00. There's a lunchtime buffet.

If you don't fancy the walk from Huye (about 1.5km from the centre), then a taxi to the museum will cost about Rfr1,000–1,500, more if you ask it to wait. If you're coming by minibus-taxi from Kigali you can ask to be dropped off there; and, if you want to go straight back to Kigali afterwards, you could try flagging down a minibus that has come from Huye – if it has spare seats inside, it will probably stop. Or to be sure of getting one you can walk to the minibus-taxi stand, which is less than 1km away.

OTHER POINTS OF INTEREST The huge, red-brick, Roman Catholic **cathedral**, built in memory of Belgium's Princess Astrid in the late 1930s, is the largest in the country and worth a visit. Its interior is fairly plain, but the atmosphere is tranquil and the size impressive. A service there can be a moving experience.

There is some attractive **architecture** and the tranquil, tree-lined residential streets away from the centre are good territory for strolling. It's possible to take a turning to the right a short distance east of the Motel Ineza and then to cross twisty tracks through the green and cultivated valley until you reach the cathedral, but ask for directions and advice. A clear heritage of Belgian colonisation (in Belgium even the motorways are lit) is the generous amount of street lighting in Huye.

Spectacular displays of **traditional dance** (*Intore*) take place in Huye and can be arranged on request (and for a fee); ask at the museum (opposite) about this.

EXCURSIONS FROM HUYE

VIAKI CRAFTS VILLAGE Start this trip at the handicrafts shop (COPABU, see page 131) opposite the Ibis Hotel – they will give you a leaflet about this project. Three associations of woodcarvers have set up a workshop, a shop (selling their products) and a small snack-bar. Finance came from the Rhineland Palatinate and the German Embassy in Kigali. You can watch them at work and see carvings progress from a chunk of rough wood to the finished article. Prices at the Viaki shop are slightly lower than those in Huye.

There's a map in the leaflet – but follow the main Burundi road south for 13km and you'll see the sign. It's a lovely area and there are walks. Linked to the same project, but closed at present because it's up for sale, is the Kigembe Fish Farm in the Rwabisemanyi valley. Continue for a further 8km along the Burundi road and then follow the sign (on the left) to 'Etangs Piscicoles'. When functioning, this place should have a small restaurant serving fish fresh from the farm – and it's a beautiful valley, so do check with either COPABU or Viaki to see whether it has reopened. Also see www.pab-faab.org.rw.

The same leaflet gives details of the drive up Mount Makwaza, 40km from Huye – there's a tremendous view from the summit. A 4x4 is advisable. All of these areas are likely to see more tourist development within the next few years.

KIBEHO Before the genocide, Kibeho hit the headlines because of the visions of the Virgin Mary allegedly seen there by young girls from 1981 onwards, starting with that of teenager Alphonsine Mumureke in November 1981. The phenomena were reported both nationally and internationally, and the small, remote community became a centre of pilgrimage and faith, as believers travelled from all over Rwanda and further afield to witness the miracles. During the genocide Kibeho suffered appallingly: hospital, primary school, college and church were all attacked. The church was badly burned while still sheltering survivors; a genocide memorial site stands beside it.

You pick up the Kibeho road by driving through the minibus park just north of Huye. Minibuses also make the trip, but not very frequently. It's a beautiful drive through a mixture of wooded valleys and farmland, on an unmade road. There's not a great deal to see at Kibeho, but developments are planned in order to attract tourists.

GIKONGORO There's not a lot to see around here except for a few shops and some beautiful, dramatically hilly landscapes; if the area appeals to you and you feel like some steepish strolling, there's simple, good-value accommodation available in Gikongoro at the **Gikongoro Guesthouse** (✆ 535060) near the Provincial Office: nine en-suite rooms at around Rfr6,000 each. To find it when you're coming from Huye: at the start of Gikongoro there's a hill going down with shops (including the Restaurant Dallas) on the right. At the bottom of this hill, turn right then left – then ask. An alternative is the **Hibiscus Guesthouse**, by the petrol station.

The genocide memorial at **Murambi**, about 2km north of Gikongoro, is one of Rwanda's starkest: over 1,800 bodies, of the 27,000-odd exhumed from mass graves here, have been placed on display to the public in the old technical school. They people the bare rooms, mingling horror with poignancy, as a mute but chillingly eloquent reminder that such events must never, ever, be allowed to recur. During the genocide, under orders from the prefect and with the support of the church authorities, between 40,000 and 60,000 inhabitants were assembled together in and around the school on Murambi hill, supposedly for protection; there were 64 rooms crammed full with people. Then the *interahamwe* attacked, throwing grenades through the windows. Within four days, most of those on the premises had been slaughtered. Later, French soldiers were installed on the site as part of *Opération Turquoise,* and a volleyball pitch was built over one of the mass graves.

9

Nyungwe Forest National Park

If the mountain gorillas of Volcanoes National Park form the single best reason to visit Rwanda, then the less-publicised Nyungwe Forest is probably the best reason to prolong your stay. Extending for 970km² over the mountainous southwest of Rwanda, Nyungwe protects one of the largest tracts of montane forest remaining anywhere in East or Central Africa, forming a contiguous forest block with the 370km² Kibira National Park in neighbouring Burundi. Nyungwe is the most important catchment area in Rwanda, providing water to some 70% of the country, and its central ridges form the watershed between Africa's two largest drainage systems, the Nile and the Congo – indeed, a spring on the slopes of the 2,950m Mount Bigugu is currently claimed as the most remote source of the Nile (see *Ascend the Nile* box on page 151).

As with other Albertine Rift forests, Nyungwe is a remarkably rich centre of biodiversity. More than 1,050 plant species are known to occur in the national park, including about 200 orchids and 250 Albertine Rift endemics. The vertebrate fauna includes 85 mammal, 278 bird, 32 amphibian and 38 reptile species (of which a full 62 are endemic to the Albertine Rift) while a total of 120 butterfly species have been recorded. Primates are particularly well represented, with 13 species resident, including a population of at least 500 chimpanzees, some of which are semi-habituated to tourist visits.

Statistics aside, Nyungwe is, in a word, magnificent. The forest takes on a liberatingly primal presence even before you enter it. One moment the road is winding through a characteristic rural Rwandan landscape of rolling tea plantations and artificially terraced hills, the next a dense tangle of trees rises imperiously from the fringing cultivation. For a full 50km the road clings improbably to steep forested slopes, offering grandstand views over densely swathed hills that tumble like monstrous green waves towards the distant Burundi border. One normally thinks of rainforest as the most intimate and confining of environments. Nyungwe is that, but, as viewed from the main road, it is also gloriously expansive.

Vast though it may be, Nyungwe today is but a fragment of what was once an uninterrupted forest belt covering the length of the Albertine Rift (the stretch of the western Rift Valley running from the Ruwenzori Mountains south to Burundi). The fragmentation of this forest started some 2,000 years ago, at the dawn of the Iron Age, when the first patches were cut down to make way for agriculture – it is thought, for instance, that the isolation of Uganda's Bwindi Forest from similar habitats on the Virunga Mountains occurred as recently as 500 years ago.

It is over the past 100 years that the forests of the Albertine Rift have suffered most heavily. Take northwestern Rwanda's Gishwati Forest, which extended over a comparable area to Nyungwe as recently as the 1930s, but had been reduced to two separate blocks covering a combined 280km² by 1989, and now covers little more than 6km². Nyungwe has fared well by comparison, bearing in mind that it

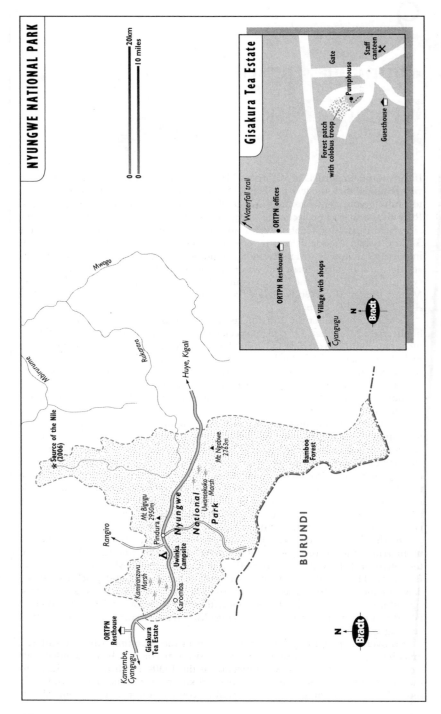

NYUNGWE NATIONAL PARK

0 _____ 20km
0 _____ 10 miles

Gisakura Tea Estate

Waterfall trail

ORTPN Resthouse

● ORTPN offices

Gate

Forest patch with colobus troop

● Pumphouse

Staff canteen

Guesthouse

Village with shops ●

Cyangugu

N Bradt

Mwogo

Mbirurume

Rukarara

Huye, Kigali

✳ Source of the Nile (2006)

Mt Bigugu 2950m

Pindura ▲

Rangiro

Nyungwe

National

Park

Uwasenkoko Marsh

Mt Ngabwe 2763m

Kamiranzovu Marsh

○ Karomba

Uwinka Campsite ▲

ORTPN Resthouse

Gisakura Tea Estate

Kamembe, Cyangugu

BURUNDI

Bamboo Forest

N Bradt

Most of Rwanda's forest inhabitants have a wide distribution in the DRC and/or West Africa, while a smaller proportion is comprised of eastern species that might as easily be observed in forested habitats in Kenya, Tanzania and in some instances Ethiopia. A significant number, however, are endemic to the Albertine Rift: in other words their range is more or less confined to montane habitats associated with the Rift Valley escarpment running between Lake Albert and the north of Lake Tanganyika. The most celebrated of these regional endemics is of course the mountain gorilla, confined to the Virunga and Bwindi Mountains near the eastern Rift Valley escarpment. Other primates endemic to the Albertine Rift include several taxa of smaller primates, for instance the golden monkey and Ruwenzori colobus, while eight endemic butterflies are regarded as flagship species for the many hundreds of invertebrate taxa that occur nowhere else.

Of the remarkable tally of 37 range-restricted bird species listed as Albertine Rift endemics, roughly half are considered to be of global conservation concern. All 37 of these species have been recorded in the DRC, and nine are endemic to that country, since their range is confined to the western escarpment forests. More than 20 Albertine Rift endemics are resident in each of Uganda, Rwanda and Burundi, while two extend their range southward into western Tanzania.

All but one of the 29 endemics that occur on the eastern escarpment have been recorded in Rwanda's Nyungwe Forest. Inaccessible to tourists at the time of writing, the Itombwe Mountains, which rise from the Congolese shore of northern Lake Tanganyika, support the largest contiguous block of montane forest in East Africa. This range is also regarded as the most important site for montane forest birds in the region, with a checklist of 565 species including 31 Albertine Rift endemics, three of which are known from nowhere else in the world. The most elusive of these birds is the enigmatic Congo bay owl, first collected in 1952, and yet to be seen again, though its presence is suspected in Rwanda's Nyungwe Forest.

Several Albertine Rift forest endemics share stronger affinities with extant or extinct Asian genera than they do with any other living African species, affirming the great age of these forests, which are thought to have flourished during prehistoric climatic changes that caused temporary deforestation in lower-lying areas such as the Congo Basin. The Congo bay owl, African green broadbill and Grauer's cuckoo-shrike, for instance, might all be classed as living fossils – isolated relics of a migrant Asian stock that has been superseded elsewhere on the continent by indigenous genera evolved from a common ancestor.

Among the mammals endemic to the Albertine Rift, the dwarf otter-shrew of the Ruwenzoris is one of three highly localised African mainland species belonging to a family of aquatic insectivores that flourished some 50 million years ago and is elsewhere survived only by the related tenrecs of Madagascar. A relict horseshoe bat species restricted to the Ruwenzoris and Lake Kivu is anatomically closer to extant Asian forms of horseshoe bat and to ancient migrant stock than it is to any of the 20-odd more modern and widespread African horseshoe bat species, while a shrew specimen collected only once in the Itombwe Mountains is probably the most primitive and ancient of all 150 described African species.

is now the only substantial tract of forest left in Rwanda. First protected as a 1,140km² forest reserve in 1933, Nyungwe was reduced in area by about 15% between 1958 and 1979 thanks to encroachment by local subsistence farmers, who also harvested it as a source of honey, bush meat, firewood and alluvial gold (an estimated 3,000 goldpanners worked the Nyungwe watershed in the mid-1950s).

Fortunately, Nyungwe's extent has remained reasonably stable since 1984, when a co-ordinated forest protection plan was implemented. This in turn led to the establishment of research projects by the likes of Amy Vedder (Angola colobus) and Beth Kaplin (L'Hoest's and blue monkeys), the creation of a network of tourist trails in the late 1980s, and the first reasonably comprehensive biodiversity survey as undertaken by Dowsett in 1990. The tragic events of 1994 had little long-term effect on Nyungwe, which was formally accorded national park status in 2004.

The main attraction of Nyungwe Forest is its primates. Chimp-tracking can be arranged at short notice. Several other monkeys are readily seen, including the acrobatic Ruwenzori colobus in troops of up to 400 strong (the largest arboreal primate troops in Africa) and the beautiful and highly localised L'Hoest's monkey. Nyungwe is also highly alluring to birders, botanists and keen walkers. One of the joys of Nyungwe is its accessibility. Not only is the forest bisected by the surfaced trunk road between Huye (Butare) and Cyangugu, but it is serviced by a well-organised and moderately priced resthouse and campsite, and easily explored along a well-maintained network of walking trails.

NATURAL HISTORY

Nyungwe is a true rainforest, typically receiving in excess of 2,000mm of precipitation annually. It is also one of the oldest forests in Africa, which is one reason why it boasts such a high level of biodiversity. Scientific opinion is that Nyungwe, along with the other forests of the Albertine Rift, was largely unaffected by the drying up of lowland areas during the last ice age, and thus became a refuge for forest plants and animals which have subsequently recolonised areas such as the Congo Basin. Nyungwe's faunal and floral diversity is not a function only of its antiquity, but also of the wide variation in elevation (between 1,600m and 2,950m above sea level), since many forest plants and animals live within very specific altitudinal bands.

FLORA The forest comprises at least 200 tree species. The upper canopy in some areas reaches 50–60m in height, dominated by slow-growing hardwoods such as *Entandrophragma excelsum* (African mahogany), *Syzygium parvifolium* (water-berry), *Podocarpus milanjianus* (Mulanje cedar), *Newtonia buchananii* (forest newtonia) and *Albizia gummifera* (smooth-barked albizia). A much larger variety of trees makes up the mid-storey canopy, of which one of the most conspicuous is *Dichaetanthera corymbosa*, whose bright purple blooms break up the rich green textures of the forest.

Of the smaller trees, one of the most striking is the giant tree-fern *Cyathea mannania*, which grows to 5m tall, and is seen in large numbers along the ravines of the Waterfall Trail. Also very distinctive are the 2–3m-tall giant lobelias, more normally associated with montane moorland than forest, but common in Nyungwe, particularly along the roadside. Bamboo plants, a large type of grass, are dominant at higher altitudes in the rather inaccessible southeast of the forest, where their shoots are favoured by the rare and elusive owl-faced monkey. Nyungwe also harbours a huge variety of small flowering plants, including around 200 varieties of orchid and the wild begonia.

Within Nyungwe lie several swampy areas whose biology is quite distinct from that of the surrounding forest. The largest of these is the 13km² Kamiranzovu Marsh, sweeping views of which are offered along the main road between the campsite and the resthouse – and which can also now be explored on the guided Kamiranzovu Trail. Formerly a favoured haunt of elephants, this open area is also rich in epiphytic orchids and harbours localised animals such as the Congo clawless otter and Grauer's rush warbler. The higher-altitude Uwasenkoko Marsh, bisected by the main road towards Huye, is dominated by the Ethiopian hagenia and protects a community of heather-like plants sharing unexpected affinities with the Nyika Plateau in distant Malawi.

MAMMALS The most prominent mammals in Nyungwe are primates, of which 13 species are present, including the common chimpanzee (see box, pages 148–9) and eight types of monkey (see pages 140–1). In total, however, an estimated 86 different mammal species have been recorded in Nyungwe, including several rare forest inhabitants.

Of the so-called 'Big Five', elephant, buffalo and leopard were all common in pre-colonial times. Buffalo are now extinct – the last one was shot in 1976 – and elephant have evidently gone the same way in recent years. In 1990, it was estimated that at least six and perhaps as many as 20 elephants lived in the forest. For several years after the civil war, no elephant were seen in Nyungwe. In mid-1999, elephant spoor was observed during a forest inventory, but in November of that year an elephant corpse was found (cause of death unknown) and no spoor has been seen since. Leopard, by contrast, are still present in small numbers, and regularly seen by local villagers, but as a tourist you'd be very lucky to encounter one.

A number of smaller predators occur in Nyungwe, including golden cat, wild cat, serval cat, side-striped jackal, three types of mongoose, Congo clawless otter, common and servaline genet, and common and palm civet. Most of these are highly secretive nocturnal creatures which are infrequently observed.

The largest antelope found in Nyungwe is the bushbuck. Three types of duiker also occur in the forest: black-fronted, yellow-backed and an endemic race of Wein's duiker. Formerly common, all the forest's antelope have suffered from intensive poaching as bush meat. Other large mammals include giant forest hog, bushpig, several types of squirrel (including the monkey-sized giant forest squirrel), Derby's anomalure (a large squirrel-like forest animal which has large underarm flaps enabling it to glide between trees) and the tree hyrax (a rarely seen guinea-pig-like animal whose blood-curdling nocturnal screeching is one of the characteristic sounds of the African forest).

BIRDS Nyungwe is probably the single most important birdwatching destination in Rwanda, with more than 280 bird species recorded, of which the majority are forest specialists and 26 are regional endemics whose range is restricted to a few forests along the Albertine Rift. Birdwatching in Nyungwe can be rather frustrating, since the vegetation is thick and many birds tend to stick to the canopy, but almost everything you do see ranks as a good sighting.

You don't have to be an ardent birdwatcher to appreciate some of Nyungwe's birds. Most people, for instance, will do a double-take when they first spot a great blue turaco, a chicken-sized bird with garish blue, green and yellow feathers, often seen gliding between the trees along the main road. Another real gem is the paradise flycatcher, a long-tailed blue, orange and (sometimes) white bird often seen around the resthouse. Other birds impress with their bizarre appearance – the gigantic forest hornbills, for instance, whose wailing vocalisations are almost as comical as their ungainly bills and heavy-winged flight. And, when tracking through the forest undergrowth, watch out for the red-throated alethe, a very localised bird with a distinctive blue-white eyebrow. The alethe habitually follows colobus troops to eat the insects they disturb, and based on our experience it sees humans as merely another large mammal, often perching within a few inches!

The priorities of more serious birdwatchers will depend to some extent on their experience elsewhere in Africa. It is difficult to imagine, for instance, that a first-time visitor to the continent will get as excited about a drab Chubb's cisticola as they will when they first see a paradise flycatcher or green pigeon. For somebody

The 13 primate species which occur in Nyungwe represent something like 20–25% of the total number in Africa, a phenomenal figure which in East Africa is comparable only to Uganda's Kibale Forest. Furthermore, several of these primates are listed as vulnerable or endangered on the IUCN red list, and Nyungwe is almost certainly the main stronghold for at least two of them.

Disregarding the chimpanzee (see box on pages 148–9), the most celebrated of Nyungwe's primates is the **Ruwenzori colobus** *Colobus angolensis ruwenzori*, a race of the more widespread Angola colobus which is restricted to the Albertine Rift. The Ruwenzori colobus is a highly arboreal and acrobatic leaf-eater, easily distinguished from any other primate found in Nyungwe by its contrasting black overall colour and snow-white whiskers, shoulders and tail tip. Although all colobus monkeys are very sociable, the ones in Nyungwe are unique in so far as they typically move in troops of several hundred animals. A semi-habituated troop of 400, resident in the forest around the campsite, is thought to be the largest troop of arboreal primates anywhere in Africa – elsewhere in the world, only the Chinese golden monkey moves in groups of a comparable number.

Most of the other monkeys in Nyungwe are guenons, the collective name for the taxonomically confusing Cercopithecus genus. Most guenons are arboreal forest-dwelling omnivores, noted for their colourful coats and the male's bright red or blue genitals. The most striking of Nyungwe's guenons is **L'Hoest's monkey** *Cercopithecus l'hoesti*, a large and unusually terrestrial monkey, whose cryptic grey and red coat is offset by a bold white 'beard' which renders it unmistakable. As with the Ruwenzori colobus, L'Hoest's monkey is more or less confined to the Albertine Rift, and is very scarce elsewhere in its restricted range. In Nyungwe, it is the most frequently encountered monkey, with troops of 5–15 animals often seen along the roadside, within the forest, and even in the campsite.

One race of blue monkey – the most widespread of African forest primates – occurs in Nyungwe. Likely to be encountered along the road and around the campsite, the **silver monkey** *C. (mitis) doggetti* is similar in build and general appearance to L'Hoest's monkey, but lacks the diagnostic white beard. The silver monkey typically lives in small family parties, though solitary males are also often encountered in Nyungwe. Some sources list the closely related **golden monkey** *C. (mitis) kandti* for Nyungwe, but this appears to be an error – though it is not impossible that a small population of this Albertine Rift endemic inhabits the remote bamboo forests close to the Burundi border.

These southerly bamboo forests definitely provide refuge to the rare and secretive **owl-faced monkey** *C. hamlyni*, another Albertine Rift endemic whose modern range is restricted to a handful of montane forests. This thickset, plain grey, pug-faced monkey was first recorded in Nyungwe as recently as 1992, and it remains the least-known of the monkeys in the reserve – the 1999 WCS survey was unable to locate a single individual,

coming from southern Africa, at least half of what they see will be new to them, with a total of about 60 relatively widespread East African forest specials headed by the likes of great blue turaco, Ross's turaco, red-breasted sparrowhawk and white-headed wood-hoopoe.

From an East African perspective, however, it is the 26 Albertine Rift endemics that are the most alluring. Depending on your level of expertise, you could reasonably hope to tick off half of these over a few days in the forest. The more common regional endemics are handsome francolin, Ruwenzori turaco (a stunner!), stripe-breasted tit, red-collared babbler, red-throated alethe, Archer's ground robin, but researchers monitoring the population close to the Burundi border reckon they encounter the monkeys at most twice a week.

Another guenon whose status within Nyungwe is uncertain is the **red-tailed monkey** *C. ascanius*, a small and highly active arboreal monkey most easily distinguished by its bright white nose. Generally associated with low-elevation forest, the red-faced monkey now faces extinction within Nyungwe owing to much of its habitat having been cleared for cultivation over recent decades. The solitary individual that hangs out with a colobus troop on the tea estate is presumably unlikely ever to find a breeding partner, though we have been told that a small but viable population of red-tailed monkeys survives on the fringes of the forest reserve near Banda.

Dent's mona monkey *C. mona denti* is widespread within Nyungwe, and occurs at all elevations, but it is infrequently seen by tourists. Another typical forest guenon, Dent's mona is distinguished from other monkeys in the forest by its contrasting black back and white belly, blue-white forehead, and yellowish ear tufts. It often moves with other guenons, and is mostly likely to be seen in the forest patch in the Gisakura Tea Estate or at Karamba, along the road to Uwinka not far from the ORTPN Resthouse. Some sources incorrectly list the **crowned monkey** *C. pogonias* for Nyungwe, but this is a West African lowland species, regarded by some to be a race of mona monkey.

Unlikely to be seen within the forest proper, the **vervet monkey** *C. aethiops* is a grizzled grey guenon of savanna and open woodland, with a distinctive black face mask. Probably the most numerous monkey in the world, the vervet is occasionally encountered on the forest verge and around the ORTPN Resthouse, where it is often quite tame and regularly raids crops.

Another savanna monkey occasionally seen along the road through Nyungwe is the **olive baboon** *Papio anubis*, a predominantly terrestrial primate which lives in large troops. After the chimpanzee, this is by far the largest and most stocky of the forest's primates, with a uniform dark olive coat and the canine snout and large teeth characteristic of all baboons. The olive baboon is very aggressive and, like the vervet monkey, it frequently raids crops.

Intermediate in size between the olive baboon and the various guenons, the **grey-cheeked mangabey** *Cercocebus albigena* is an arboreal monkey of the forest interior. Rather more spindly than any guenon, the grey-cheeked mangabey has a uniform dark-brown coat and grey-brown cape, and is renowned for its loud gobbling call. It lives in small troops, typically around ten animals, and is localised in Nyungwe because of its preference for lower altitudes.

In addition to chimpanzees and monkeys, Nyungwe harbours four types of prosimian, small nocturnal primates more closely related to the lemurs of Madagascar than to any other primates of the African mainland. These are three species of **bushbaby** or galago (a group of tiny, hyperactive wide-eyed insectivores) and the sloth-like **potto**. All are very unlikely to be encountered by tourists.

Kivu ground thrush, Grauer's rush warbler (confined to high-altitude marshy areas), red-faced woodland warbler, Kungwe apalis, Grauer's warbler, yellow-eyed black flycatcher, Ruwenzori batis, blue-headed sunbird, regal sunbird and strange weaver.

The guides at Nyungwe are improving and some are excellent, but others have only limited knowledge. For this reason, you will be highly dependent on a field guide, and without a great amount of advance research you are bound to struggle to identify every bird that you glimpse. Given the above, relict forest patches and the road verge are often more productive than the forest interior, since you'll get clearer views of what you do see.

Common and widespread in Rwanda, but not easily seen unless they are actively searched for, chameleons are arguably the most intriguing of African reptiles. True chameleons of the family Chamaeleontidae are confined to the Old World, with the most important centre of speciation being the island of Madagascar, to which about half of the world's 130 described species are endemic. Another two species of chameleon occur in each of Asia and Europe, while the remainder are distributed across mainland Africa, with at least eight species recorded from Rwanda, most of which are forest species associated with Nyungwe National Park.

Chameleons are best known for their capacity to change colour, a trait that is often exaggerated in popular literature, and which is generally influenced by mood more than the colour of the background. Some chameleons are more adept at changing colour than others, the most variable being the common chameleon *Chamaeleo chamaeleon* of the Mediterranean region, with more than 100 colour and pattern variations recorded. Many African chameleons are typically green in colour but will gradually take on a browner hue when they descend from the foliage in more exposed terrain, for instance while crossing a road. Several change colour and pattern far more dramatically when they feel threatened or are confronted by a rival of the same species. Different chameleon species also vary greatly in size, with the largest being Oustalet's chameleon of Madagascar, known to reach a length of almost 80cm.

A remarkable physiological feature common to all true chameleons is their protuberant round eyes, which offer a potential 180° degree vision on both sides and are able to swivel around independently of each other. Only when one of them isolates a suitably juicy-looking insect will the two eyes focus in the same direction as the chameleon stalks slowly forward until it is close enough to use the other unique weapon in its armoury. This is its sticky-tipped tongue, which is typically about the same length as

OTHER CREATURES While monkeys and to a lesser extent birds tend to attract the most attention, Nyungwe's fauna also includes a large number of smaller animals. With only 12 species recorded, snakes are relatively poorly represented, due to the chilly climate – probably good news for most visitors – but colourful lizards are often seen on the rocks, and at least five species of chameleon occur in the forest. Nyungwe also harbours more than 100 different types of colourful butterfly, including 40 regional endemics. Look out, too, for the outsized beetles and bugs that are characteristic of all tropical forests. Equally remarkable, but only to be admired at a distance of a metre or so, are the vast columns of army ants that move across the forest trails – step on one of these columns, and you'll know all about it, as these guys can bite!

FURTHER INFORMATION A basic fact-sheet about the forest is available from the ORTPN tourist office in Kigali. An excellent booklet entitled *Nyungwe National Park* is sold for Rfr7,000 at ORTPN offices countrywide (including Uwinka).

Keen birdwatchers should try to lay their hands on the out-of-print checklist of the forest's birds, which gives Latin, English and French names as well as a good indication of each species' habitat and relative abundance within the reserve.

A more esoteric publication, of interest primarily to researchers and to a lesser extent birdwatchers, is the WCS Working Paper ed 19 *Biodiversity Surveys of the Nyungwe Forest Reserve in Southwest Rwanda* (Plumptre, Andrew, 2002), which includes detailed results of a mammal and bird inventory that took place in 1999. It can be downloaded from the website www.wcs.org/science.

its body and remains coiled up within its mouth most of the time, to be unleashed in a sudden, blink-and-you'll-miss-it lunge to zap a selected item of prey. In addition to their unique eyes and tongues, many chameleons are adorned with an array of facial casques, flaps, horns and crests that enhance their already somewhat fearsome prehistoric appearance.

In Rwanda, you're most likely to come across a chameleon by chance when it is crossing a road, in which case it should be easy to take a closer look at it, since most chameleons move painfully slowly and deliberately. Chameleons are also often seen on night game drives, when their ghostly nocturnal colouring shows up clearly under a spotlight – as well as making it pretty clear why these strange creatures are regarded with both fear and awe in many local African cultures. More actively, you could ask your guide if they know where to find a chameleon – a few individuals will be resident in most lodge grounds.

The flap-necked chameleon *Chamaeleo delepis* is probably the most regularly observed species of savanna and woodland habitats in East Africa. Often seen crossing roads, the flap-necked chameleon is generally around 15cm long and bright green in colour with few distinctive markings, but individuals might be up to 30cm in length and will turn tan or brown under the right conditions.

Characteristic of East African montane forests, the horned chameleons form a closely allied species cluster of some taxonomic uncertainty. They are typically darker than the savanna chameleons and, significantly, the males of all taxa within this cluster are distinguished by up to three nasal horns that project forward from their face. In Rwanda, the cluster is represented by the Rwenzori three-horned chameleon *C. Johnstoni*, a range-restricted Albertine Rift endemic that can grow up to 30cm long and is reasonably common in Nyungwe National Park, where it supplements a diet of insects with more substantial fare such as small lizards.

GETTING THERE AND AWAY

Nyungwe Forest Reserve is bisected by the main surfaced road between Huye and Cyangugu. The Uwinka Reception Centre and Campsite lies alongside the main road, and is well signposted 90km from Huye and 54km from Cyangugu. The ORTPN Resthouse is also on the main road, 18km closer to Cyangugu, on the right side of the road and about 2km after you exit the western boundary of the forest reserve coming from Huye.

WHERE TO STAY AND EAT

⌂ Uwinka Reception Centre and Campsite
(S 02°26.576; E 029°12.043; 2,442m) Set in the heart of the forest, yet only a couple of hundred metres from the main road, this is the best option provided you have a tent and are reasonably self-sufficient. For bookings and information contact ORTPN (see page 61). The campsite has a perfect (albeit rather chilly) location on a high ridge, with individual sites scattered over a wide area of forest. There's a small orchid nursery near by. A semi-habituated troop of L'Hoest's monkey passes through every morning and most afternoons, as does the occasional troop of silver monkey and a variety of forest birds. The Coloured Trails start from here; so it's the most convenient base, particularly if you have no vehicle, from which to explore the forest and track the 400-strong troop of colobus. The main road adjacent to the campsite is also worth exploring, for the great views and variety of birds. Drinks are available at reasonable prices, and firewood can be arranged, but campers must bring all food and should have sufficient warm clothing to offset the chilly night temperatures at high altitude. There's also a small 2-roomed bungalow available at Uwinka. It's basic – lanterns rather than electricity, hot water is provided in the mornings and a fire at night, but guests must bring their own food. *US$20 pp per night for non-residents, US$10 for residents, and Rfr2,000 for citizens.*

ORTPN Resthouse (S 02°26.281; E 029°05.548; 1,931m) Bookings via ORTPN's Kigali office — see page 61. The alternative for non-campers is this small cosy guesthouse, which lies 2km outside the forest close to the Gisakura Tea Estate. The accommodation here is clean and comfortable. The communal showers and toilets are also clean, and good meals can be prepared with a couple of hours' notice. The main drawback to the resthouse — particularly for travellers dependent on public transport — is that it is outside the forest and 18km from Uwinka, the trailhead for most of the trails. The resthouse does, however, offer good access to the Waterfall Trail and the colobus troop on the Gisakura Tea Estate. Vervet monkeys occasionally pass through the resthouse grounds, a fair variety of birds are present in the small patch of forest in front of the resthouse, while several sunbird species (inc Ruwenzori double-collared sunbird, an Albertine Rift endemic) are likely to be seen when the garden is in bloom. A number of nearby relict forest patches offer good birdwatching, as well as a chance of encountering forest monkeys. *Twin rooms using common hot showers Rfr15,000 b&b; dbls in a large self-contained chalet Rfr20,000; cooked meals Rfr4,800 pp.*

Gisakura Guesthouse (S 02°27.102; E 029°05.194; 1,953m) Situated on the Gisakura Tea Estate, about 1km back towards the forest boundary, this private guesthouse forms a more affordable alternative to the ORTPN Guesthouse, though gaining access to a room is not always as straightforward as it might be — it's impossible to book ahead and the man with the key isn't always present! In addition to dorm-style accommodation, there is a communal lounge, beers and sodas are available at the nearby estate canteen, and meals can be arranged with a few hours' notice. The guesthouse lies less than 500m from the forest patch where colobus are resident, and the area offers good birding. Other trails can be arranged at the ORTPN office next to the ORTPN Resthouse, a 20-min walk away. To reach the tea estate's guesthouse, follow the dirt road into the tea estate (signposted *Usine à thé Gisakura*) for about 500m until you reach a large traffic circle, then follow the central road branching from this circle (at roughly 2 o' clock) for about 200m. *Negotiable rates start at Rfr10,000 for a 4-bed dormitory.*

ACTIVITIES

A large selection of walking possibilities and other excursions is available within Nyungwe. Visitors with a vehicle and sufficient interest could easily keep themselves busy for three or four days without significantly retracing their steps. The options for travellers without private transport are more limited, and depend on whether they base themselves at Uwinka Campsite (where the main attraction is the network of Coloured Trails, a good place for colobus and seasonally for chimps) or at the resthouse (the best base for the Waterfall Trail and for visiting the colobus in Gisakura Tea Estate). In the dry season, you need a private vehicle to go chimp-tracking wherever you are based, and at all times of year you need a vehicle to visit the habituated grey-cheeked mangabey troop and to explore the road to Rangiro.

The forest trails are steep and often very slippery. Dress accordingly; jeans, a thick shirt and good walking shoes are the ideal outfit, and a waterproof jacket will be useful during the rainy season.

PARK FEES Costs can mount up at Nyungwe, with all the possibilities, so plan carefully and check beforehand in case of increases. An entrance fee of US$20 per person per day is charged to non-residents and foreign residents. Chimpanzee tracking costs US$50 for non-residents or US$30 for resident foreigners, while other guided walks cost US$30 per person for non-residents or US$15 for resident foreigners (with substantial discounts available to children under the age of 15). Citizens of Rwanda pay an entrance fee of Rfr1,000 and Rfr2,000–4,000 per person for the various guided walks. It's normal to tip the guides if you feel they've done a good job.

UWINKA AND THE COLOURED TRAILS A relic of an early attempt to develop Nyungwe for tourism, back in the late 1980s, a network of seven walking trails, each designated by a particular colour, leads downhill from the Uwinka Campsite into the surrounding forested hills. Ranging in length from the 1km Grey Trail to the 10km Red Trail, the footpaths are all well maintained and clearly marked, but don't underestimate the steepness of the slopes or – after rain – the muddy conditions, which can be fairly tough going at this high altitude. The Coloured Trails pass through the territory of a habituated troop of 400 colobus monkeys. During the rainy season, a troop of chimpanzees often moves into this area as well, and it is up to you to decide whether to pay extra to track them.

You can reasonably expect to see some primates along any of the Coloured Trails, as well as a good variety of forest birds – though the latter require patience and regular stops where there are open views into the canopy. Unless you opt for a specific primate visit, chance will be the decisive factor in what you see, though the 2.5km Blue Trail is regarded as especially good for primates and birds, while the 10km Red Trail is good for chimpanzees and passes four waterfalls.

Birdwatchers in particular are advised to explore the main road close to the campsite, as they will probably see a wider variety of birds than from within the forest. About 500m east of the campsite, the road offers some stunning views over the forested valleys, and passes a stand of giant lobelias.

THE WATERFALL TRAIL This superb trail starts at the ORTPN Resthouse and takes between three and six hours to cover as a round trip, depending on how often you stop and whether you drive or walk from the resthouse to the car park about 3km from the resthouse. The first part of the trail – in essence following the road to the car park – passes through rolling tea plantations dotted with relict forest patches which are worth scanning closely for silver and other monkeys. These small stands of forest can also be rewarding for birds; keen ornithologists might well want to take them slowly, and could perhaps view this section of the trail as a worthy birdwatching excursion in its own right.

The trail then descends into the forest proper, following flat contour paths through a succession of tree-fern-covered ravines, and crossing several streams, before a sharp descent to the base of a pretty but small waterfall. Monkeys are often seen along the way (the Angola colobus seems to be particularly common) and the steep slopes allow good views into the canopy. This trail can be very rewarding for true forest interior birds, with a good chance of spotting Albertine Rift endemics such as Ruwenzori turaco and yellow-eyed black flycatcher.

GISAKURA TEA ESTATE A relict forest patch in this tea estate, only 20 minutes' walk from the ORTPN Resthouse, supports a resident troop of around 40 Ruwenzori colobus monkeys. This troop is very habituated, far more so than the larger troop at Uwinka, and the relatively small territory the monkeys occupy makes them very easy to locate and to see clearly. Oddly, a solitary red-tailed monkey moves with the colobus, and has done so for at least six years (it was observed during the research trip for both the first and third edition of this book!) – some of the guides say that it is treated as the leader.

Other guides may tell you the odd monkey out at Gisakura is not a red-tailed but a mona (also known as Dent's monkey, and unlikely to be observed elsewhere in East Africa) or a hybrid red-tailed/mona. The apparent cause of this confusion is that a solitary mona monkey does spend some of its time in the same forest patch, and the guides are unable to distinguish it from its red-tailed cousin. In January 2006, this writer saw a red-tailed and a mona monkey concurrently from

Based partially on text kindly supplied by Laura Sserunjogi, of the 'Source of the Nile Gardens' in Jinja, Uganda.

The Nile is the world's longest river, flowing for more than 6,650km (4,130 miles) from its most remote headwaters in Burundi and Rwanda to the delta formed as it enters the Mediterranean in Egypt. Its vast drainage basin occupies more than 10% of the African mainland and includes portions of nine countries: Tanzania, Burundi, Rwanda, the DRC, Kenya, Uganda, Ethiopia, Sudan and Egypt. While passing through southern Sudan, the Nile also feeds the 5.5 million hectare Sudd or Bar-el-Jebel, the world's most expansive wetland system.

A feature of the Nile Basin is a marked decrease in precipitation as it runs further northward. In the East African lakes region and Ethiopian Highlands, mean annual rainfall figures are typically in excess of 1,000mm. Rainfall in south and central Sudan varies from 250-500mm annually, except in the Sudd (900mm), while in the deserts north of Khartoum the annual rainfall is little more than 100mm, dropping to 25mm in the south of Egypt, then increasing to around 200mm closer to the Mediterranean.

The Nile has served as the lifeblood of Egyptian agriculture for millennia, carrying not only water, but also silt, from the fertile tropics into the sandy expanses of the Sahara. Indeed, it is widely believed that the very first agricultural societies arose on the floodplain of the Egyptian Nile, and so, certainly, did the earliest and most enduring of all human civilisations. The antiquity of the name Nile, which simply means river valley, is reflected in the ancient Greek (Nelios), Semetic (Nahal) and Latin (Nilus).

Over the past 50 years, several hydroelectric dams have been built along the Nile, notably the Aswan Dam in Egypt and the Owen Falls Dam in Uganda. The Aswan Dam doesn't merely provide hydroelectric power, it also supplies water for various irrigation schemes, and protects crops downriver from destruction by heavy flooding. Built in 1963, the dam wall rises 110m above the River and is almost 4km long, producing up to 2,100 megawatts and forming the 450km-long Lake Nasser. The construction of the Aswan Dam enforced the resettlement of 90,000 Nubians, whilst the Temple of Abu Simbel, built 3,200 ago for the Pharaoh Rameses II, had to be relocated 65m higher.

The waterway plays a major role in transportation, especially in parts of the Sudan between May and November, when transportation of goods and people is not possible by road due to the floods. Like other rivers and lakes, the Nile provides a variety of fish as food. And its importance for conservation is difficult to overstate. The Sudd alone supports more than half the global populations of Nile lechwe and shoebill (more than 6,000), together with astonishing numbers of other water-associated birds – aerial

the rim, but several hundred metres apart, the former with the main colobus troop, the latter on its own. The two are easy to tell apart – the mona, though it has some white on its face, lacks the almost artificial-looking white beacon of a nose that distinguishes the red-tailed monkey!

Particularly in the early morning, the relict forest patch is also an excellent birdwatching site, since it lies in a ravine and is encircled by a road, making it easy to see deep into the canopy. Most of what you see are forest fringe or woodland species (as opposed to forest interior birds), but numerically this proved to be the most rewarding spot in Nyungwe, with some 40 species identified in an hour, notably black-throated apalis, paradise and white-tailed crested flycatcher, Chubb's cisticola, African golden oriole, green pigeon, olive-green cameroptera, three types of sunbird, two greenbuls and two crimson-wings.

Note that a visit to this forest patch is treated as a primate walk by the ORTPN office and a corresponding fee is charged.

surveys undertaken between 1979 and 1982 counted an estimated 1.7 million glossy ibis, 370,000 marabou stork, 350,000 open-billed stork, 175,000 cattle egret and 150,000 spur-winged goose.

The Nile has two major sources, often referred to as the White and Blue Nile, which flow respectively from Lake Victoria near Jinja and from Lake Tana in Ethiopia. The stretch of the White Nile that flows through southern Uganda is today known as the Victoria Nile (it was formerly called Kiira locally). From Jinja, it runs northward through the swampy Lake Kyoga, before veering west to descend into the Rift Valley over Murchison Falls and empty into Lake Albert. The Albert Nile flows from the northern tip of Lake Albert to enter the Sudan at Nimule, passing through the Sudd before it merges with the Blue Nile at the Sudanese capital of Khartoum, more than 3,000km from Lake Victoria.

The discovery of the source of the Blue Nile on Lake Tana is often accredited to the 18th-century Scots explorer James Bruce. In fact, its approximate (if not exact) location was almost certainly known to the ancients. The Old Testament mentions that the Ghion (Nile) 'compasseth the whole land of Ethiopia', evidently in reference to the arcing course followed by the river along the approximate southern boundary of Ethiopia's ancient Axumite Empire. There are, too, strong similarities in the design of the papyrus 'tankwa' used on Lake Tana to this day and the papyrus boats depicted in Ancient Egyptian paintings. Furthermore, the main river feeding Lake Tana rises at a spring known locally as Abay Minch (literally 'Nile Fountain'), a site held sacred by Ethiopian Christians, whose links with the Egyptian Coptic Church date to the 4th century ad Bruce's claim is further undermined by the Portuguese stone bridge, built circa 1620, which crosses the Nile a few hundred metres downstream of the Blue Nile Falls and only 30km from the Lake Tana outlet.

By contrast, the source of the White Nile was for centuries one of the world's great unsolved mysteries. The Roman Emperor Nero once sent an expedition south from Khartoum to search for it, but it was forced to turn back at the edge of the Sudd. In 1862, Speke correctly identified Ripon Falls as the source of the Nile, a theory that would be confirmed by Stanley in 1875. Only as recently as 1937, however, did the German explorer Burkhart Waldecker locate the most remote of the Nile's headwaters in Burundi: a hillside spring known as Kasumo which forms the source of the Ruvyironza River, a tributary of the 690km long Kagera, the most important river to flow into Lake Victoria. Remarkably, however, the absolute location of the most remote source of the Nile still remains up for grabs in the early 21st century – as you can see in the box *Ascend the Nile* on page 151.

OTHER TRAILS For those spending a bit of time in the forest, the 4km, three-hour **Kamiranzovu Trail** leads to a quite different ecosystem, a relatively low-lying marshy area rich in orchids (particularly during the rainy season) and localised swamp-associated bird species. This used to be the best place to see Nyungwe's elephants, but none has been sighted here in recent years. The trail starts with a steep descent from the main tar road about 12km from Uwinka and 6km from Gisakura.

Aimed squarely at the 'because it's there' fraternity, the steep and slippery 7km **Bigugu Trail** leads to the 2,950m Bigugu Peak, which is the highest point in Nyungwe National Park. Suitable only for reasonably fit walkers, the trail starts about 4km from Uwinka along the Huye Road (the trailhead is clearly marked) and it usually takes at least six hours to complete. For geographers, a freshwater spring on Mt Bigugu has a further significance as possibly the most remote source of the world's longest river (see *Ascend the Nile* box on page 151), the other main

You'll hear them before you see them: from somewhere deep in the forest, an excited hooting, just one voice at first, then several, rising in volume and tempo and pitch to a frenzied unified crescendo, before stopping abruptly or fading away. Jane Goodall called it the 'pant-hoot' call, a kind of bonding ritual that allows any chimpanzees within earshot of each other to identify exactly who is around at any given moment, through the individual's unique vocal stylisation. To the human listener, this eruptive crescendo is one of the most spine chilling and exciting sounds of the rainforest, and a strong indicator that visual contact with man's closest genetic relative is imminent.

It is, in large part, our close evolutionary kinship with chimpanzees that makes these sociable black-coated apes of the forest so enduringly fascinating. Humans, chimpanzees and bonobos (also known as pygmy chimpanzees) share more than 95% of their genetic code, and the three species are far more closely related to each other than they are to any other living creature, even gorillas. Superficial differences notwithstanding, the similarities between humans and chimps are consistently striking, not only in the skeletal structure and skull, but also in the nervous system, the immune system, and in many behavioural aspects – bonobos, for instance, are the only animals other than humans to copulate in the missionary position.

Unlike most other primates, chimpanzees don't live in troops, but instead form extended communities of up to 100 individuals, which roam the forest in small socially mobile subgroups that often revolve around a few close family members such as brothers or a mother and daughter. Male chimps normally spend their entire life within the community into which they were born, whereas females are likely to migrate into a neighbouring community at some point after reaching adolescence. A highly ranking male will occasionally attempt to monopolise a female in oestrus, but the more normal state of sexual affairs in chimp society is non-hierarchical promiscuity. A young female in oestrus will generally mate with any male that takes her fancy, while older females tend to form close bonds with a few specific males, sometimes allowing themselves to be monopolised by a favoured suitor for a period, but never pairing off exclusively in the long term.

Within each community, one alpha male is normally recognised – though coalitions between two males, often a dominant and a submissive sibling – have often been recorded. The role of the alpha male, not fully understood, is evidently quite benevolent – chairman of the board rather than crusty tyrant. This is probably influenced by the alpha male's relatively limited reproductive advantages over his potential rivals, most of whom he will have known for his entire life. Other males in the community are generally supportive rather than competitive towards the alpha male, except for when a rival consciously contests the alpha position, which is far from being an everyday occurrence. One male in Tanzania's Mahale Mountains maintained an alpha status within his community for more than 15 years between 1979 and 1995!

Prior to the 1960s, it was always assumed that chimps were strict vegetarians. This notion was rocked when Jane Goodall, during her pioneering chimpanzee study in Tanzania's Gombe Stream, witnessed them hunting down a red colobus monkey, something that has since been discovered to be common behaviour, particularly during the dry season when other food sources are depleted. Over subsequent years, an average of 20 kills has been recorded in Gombe annually, with red colobus being the

contender being a spring on Burundi's Mount Kikizi, which lies some 6,675km (shortest route by river and lake) from where the Nile empties into the Mediterranean!

One monkey, the **grey-cheeked mangabey**, can only be seen by those who make a special excursion, on a trip which requires a private vehicle. A mangabey prey on more than half of these occasions, though young bushbuck, young bushpig and even infant chimps have also been victimised and eaten. The normal modus operandi is for four or five adult chimps to slowly encircle a colobus troop, then for another chimp to act as a decoy, creating deliberate confusion in the hope that it will drive the monkeys into the trap, or cause a mother to drop her baby.

Although chimp communities appear by-and-large to be stable and peaceful entities, intensive warfare has been known to erupt once each within the habituated communities of Mahale and Gombe. In Mahale, one of the two communities originally habituated by researchers in 1967 had exterminated the other by 1982. A similar thing happened in Gombe Stream in the 1970s, when the Kasekela community as originally habituated by Goodall divided into two discrete communities. The Kasekela and breakaway Kahama community co-existed alongside each other for some years. Then in 1974, Goodall returned to Gombe Stream after a break to discover that the Kasekela males were methodically persecuting their former community mates, isolating the Kahama males one by one, and tearing into them until they were dead or terminally wounded. By 1977, the Kahama community had vanished entirely.

Chimpanzees are essentially inhabitants of the western rainforest, but their range does extend into the extreme west of Tanzania, Rwanda and Uganda, whose combined population of perhaps 7,000 individuals is assigned to the race *P. t. schweinfurthii*. The Rwandan chimp population of at least 500 individuals is now thought to be confined to Nyungwe National Park (including a small community in the Cyamudongo Forest), but it remains faintly possible that a small population recorded in the early 1990s in the more northerly and badly degraded Gishwati Forest still persists. Although East Africa's chimps represent less than 3% of the global population, much of what is known about wild chimpanzee society and behaviour stems from the region, in particular the ongoing research projects initiated in Tanzania's Gombe Stream and Mahale Mountain National Parks back in the 1960s.

An interesting pattern that emerged from the parallel research projects in these two reserves, situated little more than 100km apart along the shore of Lake Tanganyika, is a variety of social and behavioural differences between their chimp populations. Of the plant species common to both national parks, for instance, as many as 40% of those utilised as a food source by chimps in the one reserve are not eaten by chimps in the other. In Gombe Stream, chimps appear to regard the palmnut as something of a delicacy, but while the same plants grow profusely in Mahale, the chimps there have yet to be recorded eating them. Likewise, the 'termite-fishing' behaviour first recorded by Jane Goodall at Gombe Stream in the 1960s has a parallel in Mahale, where the chimps are often seen 'fishing' for carpenter ants in the trees. But the Mahale chimps have never been recorded fishing for termites, while the Gombe chimps are not known to fish for carpenter ants. Mahale's chimps routinely groom each other with one hand while holding their other hands together above their heads – once again, behaviour that has never been noted at Gombe. More than any structural similarity, more even than any single quirk of chimpanzee behaviour, it is such striking cultural differences – the influence of nurture over nature if you like – that bring home our close genetic kinship with chimpanzees.

troop, resident in a patch of forest along the Banda road, has been habituated by researchers, who normally spend every Monday and Friday with it (consequently, these are the best days to visit the monkeys, as they will already have been tracked down when you arrive). The turn-off to Banda, 800m from the Uwinka Campsite towards Huye, is signposted *Eclise Episcopa de Rwanda*. The monkeys are usually found between 5km and 10km along the turn-off. Tracking the mangabeys is regarded as a formal primate visit, and must be done in the company of a guide. L'Hoest's, silver and colobus monkeys are also often seen in this area.

During the rainy season, chimpanzees are often present in the vicinity of the coloured trails, and **chimp tracking** can be undertaken on foot from the campsite. During the dry season, however, the chimps tend to move to higher elevations, and tracking them normally entails a drive followed by a hike of up to four hours in either direction. The chimps are not fully habituated, but they are reasonably approachable. You'll have to check the current situation with the guides.

There are no habituated **mona monkeys** in Nyungwe, but a troop is resident in the vicinity of Karamba, the site of former gold-digging and – immediately before the civil war – a campsite which might yet be reopened. Karamba lies between the campsite and resthouse, but the area can only be explored on foot accompanied by a guide. The troop at Karamba is very large, and reportedly sometimes keeps company with red-tailed monkeys.

The dirt road to **Rangiro**, which leaves the main tar road about 1.5km east of Uwinka, is regarded as the best excursion for birdwatchers. This is because the road passes through both high- and low-elevation forest within a relatively short distance, and affords good views into the canopy in several places. A 4x4 vehicle is essential, and a guide recommended. In addition to birdwatching, the Rangiro road offers some stunning views over the mountains, and is a good place to see mangabeys, silver monkeys, and a variety of butterflies.

CYAMUDONGO FOREST Covering an area of about 6km², this patch of montane forest, situated about 45 minutes' drive south of the Shagasha Tea Estate on the main road between Gisakura and Cyangugu, is now protected as an isolated annexe to Nyungwe National Park. Despite its small size, Cyamudongo still harbours a community of perhaps 20 chimpanzees, and, while these are not properly habituated, they are often easier to locate than the chimps in the main forest block in the dry season (July, August, December), when the chimps tend to range more widely in search of food. Once located, the chimps here are surprisingly approachable (to within about 5m) and walking conditions are slightly flatter. Other mammals present include L'Hoest's monkey, and – as one of the few true high-altitude forests left in Rwanda – Cyamudongo may well still harbour a few rare forest species that are no longer found in the main forest at Nyungwe. Chimp tracking (and other guided walks) can be arranged at Uwinka or the Nyungwe park headquarters at the same price as other forest trails; the staff will advise you when it is better to try to look for chimps in Cyamudongo than the main forest. You will need your own transport and a national park guide, and the drive from Gisakura takes about one hour, branching south from the main road to Cyangugu at the Shagasha Tea Estate. Either way, there are several forks along the road between the tea estate and the forest, so you may need to ask directions (bearing in mind that the forest is known locally as Nyirandakunze after a deceased queen).

Cyamudongo can also be approached from the south, as an extension of a drive to the hot springs at Bugarama. The closest town is Nyakabuye, a sprawl of traditional homesteads and a few tall concrete buildings centred around a bustling marketplace. Nyakabuye lies about 20km from Bugarama town, and 5km past the hot springs, in an area of plantation and bamboo forest. From the town, a steep road leads uphill for 8km, past traditional homesteads (evidently totally unused to tourists), before it winds through the indigenous forest for 2km. The forest ends at a T-junction in front of a large pine plantation, where a left turn along a 15km road, through rolling hills planted with tea, emerges on the surfaced Huye–Cyangugu road at the Shagasha Tea Estate.

With Tracey Clarke

On 19 September 2005, three men set out to make a complete ascent of the Nile from the sea to the source.

Known as the *Ascend the Nile* Expedition, Neil McGrigor, Cam McLeay and Garth McIntyre took to the water in Rashid in Egypt and travelled in tiny inflatable boats ('Zap Cats'), just 4m long and with outboard engines, for the entire length of the river, over 6,700km. Their journey took them through five challenging countries: Egypt, Sudan, Uganda, Tanzania and finally Rwanda.

The expedition was self-sufficient but did receive some support from Fortnum & Mason, the famous store based in London's Piccadilly, which had previously supplied Stanley's 1875 expedition with goodies such as thick-cut marmalade, humbugs and sardines. Hampers were delivered to the team throughout their journey.

En route they faced enormous difficulties, not least ascending the many river rapids, facing crocodiles head on and avoiding numerous pods of hippos. The weather ranged from searing heat to continuous rain, while the river changed from a wide blue delta in Egypt to a muddy puddle at its source in Rwanda.

Apprehension and frustration turned to real fear and sorrow when, in November 2005, the men came under attack from rebels in Uganda. A close friend of the team was killed and the remaining members were injured. The expedition's future was in doubt. But the team decided to continue to their goal.

On 3 March 2006 they resumed, crossing Lake Victoria and reaching the border of Tanzania and Rwanda. It was this part of the journey that offered unexpected challenges: larger-than-predicted rapids, cold nights and achingly slow progress on foot through the Nyungwe Forest as the team edged ever closer to the Nile's new source that they were so determined to find.

Finally, on 31 March 2006, they reached their goal at the headwater of the Rukarara River, a tributary of the Akagera which in turn drains into Lake Victoria. With their patient guides, the team planted a flag to mark the spot on the slopes of Mount Bigugu and the celebrations began. News of the expedition and its findings made its way across the world, reaching as far as China and Russia.

Using research and modern navigation equipment, they have been able to demonstrate that they discovered another, longer source than that pinpointed by Dr Kandt in 1898. Kandt had not had the benefit of either the maps drawn by the Belgians in 1937 or the Global Positioning System from which the team had re-measured the entire length of the Nile – which turns out to be some 107 km longer than previously recorded! The next step is authentication by the Royal Geographical Society of their claim.

The co-ordinates of the new longest source, deep in Rwanda's Nyungwe Forest, are: Latitude S 02 Degrees 16'055.962"; Longitude E 29 Degrees 19'052.470"; Elevation 2428m/ 7966ft. For more details of the expedition, see www.ascendthenile.com.

It isn't easy to reach Cyamudongo Forest without private transport. With patience, it should be possible to catch a lift as far as Nyakabuye on the back of a truck from Bugarama. According to locals, Nyakabuye is also serviced by some sort of public transport direct from Kamembe (Cyangugu) on Wednesdays and Fridays. You'll almost certainly have to walk the 8km from town to the forest boundary, a steep but attractive trail, along which you are bound to attract a lot of friendly attention from curious children (and adults, for that matter). No formal accommodation exists in the area, but it is difficult to imagine that anybody would refuse permission to pitch a tent at one of the homesteads which line the road up to the forest, or that any significant risk would be attached to doing so. But the reality, as with any truly off-the-beaten-track travel, is that this trip should only be attempted by adventurous, flexible travellers who are prepared to deal with a total absence of tourist facilities.

10

Lake Kivu

Running for almost 100km along the Congolese border, Kivu is one of the string of 'inland seas' that submerge much of the Albertine Rift floor north of Zambia and south of the Sudan. With a surface area of 2,200km², Kivu is not comparable in extent to the most expansive of the Albertine Rift lakes, Tanganyika and Albert, but a maximum depth of 480m and total water content of 333km³ place it among the 20 deepest and 20 most voluminous freshwater bodies in the world. It is also very beautiful, with its deep blue water hemmed in by steeply terraced escarpments containing several peaks of 2,800m or higher, and the northern shore overlooked by the smoking outline of volcanic Nyiragongo.

A shallower incarnation of Kivu probably formed about two million years ago as a result of the same tectonic activity that created the Albertine Rift and other associated lakes. Back then, Kivu was probably contiguous with the much lower-lying Lake Edward on the Uganda-DRC border, and it would have been part of the Nile watershed (as Lake Edward still is today). About 20,000 years ago, however, lava from the Virungas created a natural dam at what is now the northern end of Kivu, isolating it from Lake Edward and causing its surface to rise dramatically to a present-day altitude of 1,470m. As a result, the Rusizi River, which formerly drained out of Lake Tanganyika and into Kivu, reversed its flow. Today, the Rusizi flows out of its southern tip at Cyangugu, then follows the Burundi-DRC border southward before emptying into Lake Tanganyika and the Congo Basin.

Kivu supports a somewhat impoverished fauna by comparison with other Rift Valley lakes of similar size. This is thought to be due to the unusually high level of local volcanic activity. The geological record suggests that the release of methane trapped below the lake's surface has resulted in regular mass extinctions every few thousand years. As a result, fewer than 30 fish species are known from the lake, and while this does include 16 endemics, it pales by comparison with the many hundreds of species recorded from Lakes Victoria and Tanganyika. Volcanic activity and/or high methane levels probably also explain the complete absence of hippo and croc from the lake. Unconfirmed rumour has it that bilharzia is also absent from Kivu.

With its attractively irregular shoreline lined by verdant slopes and sandy beaches, Kivu has long served as a popular weekend getaway for residents of this otherwise landlocked country. There are three main resort towns on the Rwandan lakeshore, of which Gisenyi, the most northerly, has far and away the best and most varied tourist facilities, thanks partly to its proximity to the popular Volcanoes National Park. Further south, Kibuye has the advantage of being far closer to Kigali, while Cyangugu can easily be visited in conjunction with Nyungwe National Park and Huye (Butare), but neither has any accommodation approaching international standards.

Shortly before midnight on 15 August 1984, villagers living around Cameroon's Lake Monoun recall being awoken by an explosive noise emanating from within the lake. Come dawn the next morning, 37 residents of a nearby low-lying valley lay mysteriously dead, their skin damaged and discoloured, the surrounding air overhung with the remnants of a pungent smoky cloud; bizarre circumstances that gave rise to any number of macabre and implausible theories: a vicious terrorist attack, a chemical weapon test gone horribly wrong, the malicious work of an angry lake spirit...

The truth was somewhat more prosaic, yet no less frightening. And even before scientific investigators were able to release their tentative findings, it happened again, only 100km further northwest, when an acrid cloud of gas erupted from beneath the surface of a 200m-deep crater lake called Nyos on 22 August 1986. Within the space of hours, 1,750 local villagers living in the surrounding valleys had suffocated to death, together with thousands of animals, with the furthest casualty occurring a full 27km from the lakeshore.

In March 1987, a UNESCO Conference was held at Yaounde to discuss the previously unknown phenomenon, unique to very deep lakes, which investigators called a limnic eruption. What seemed to have happened, in simplistic terms, is that carbon dioxide of volcanic origin seeps continuously into the lower strata of a deep lake, where its high solubility allows it to accumulate in volumes up to five times heavier than normal water, becoming increasingly volatile as it approaches saturation point – the carbonated pressure at the bottom of the lake might be three times greater than that of a sparkling wine or soda! By now, the time bomb is ticking. All it takes is a seemingly innocuous external trigger – a light landslide, a heavy storm, an otherwise inconsequential subterranean volcanic activity – to upset the lake's stratification. Then, suddenly, a cloud of noxious carbon dioxide will belch out from the lake surface, diffusing into lower-lying areas and effectively suffocating all oxygen-dependent creatures in its path until finally it dissipates.

CYANGUGU

The most southerly of Rwanda's Lake Kivu ports, Cyangugu (pronounced *Shangugu*) is also the most amorphous, sprawling along a 5km road through the green hills that run down to the lake shore. It consists of discrete upper and lower towns whose combined population of 59,500 make it the seventh-largest settlement in the country according to the 2002 census. Known as Kamembe, the upper town, which stands high above the lakeshore at a breezy altitude of about 1,620m, is a lively business centre, and the site of the main taxi stand, market, banks and supermarkets, as well as a clutch of local guesthouses and restaurants. Aside from the views of the lake, and a couple of flaking colonial-era buildings, Kamembe is all energy and no character – bustling it may be, but in truth you could be in pretty much any small undistinguished African town anywhere on the continent.

Far more intriguing is the lower town – Cyangugu proper – which has an almost cinematic quality, coming across rather like an abandoned film set used years ago to make a movie about some colonial West African trading backwater. Cyangugu is situated on the lake shore, alongside a bridge across the Rusizi River where it flows out of the lake, which is also the main border crossing between southern Rwanda and the DRC. The town consists of little more than one pot-hole-scored main road, yet within its abrupt confines it does have a decidedly built-up feel, and must once have been rather grand and prosperous. Today, however, many of the old multi-storey buildings have been reduced to shells – victims of one or other war, perhaps, or just decades of neglect – generating an aura of dilapidation underscored

Over the next few years, a French research team travelled around Africa trying to establish whether any other very deep lakes might be at similar risk to Monoun and Nyos. And as it turned out, the only contender for this unwanted distinction is Kivu, whose lower strata are infused with methane and carbon dioxide, a mix made doubly unstable by the high level of volcanic activity around the northern lakeshore. Indeed, it seems more than likely that the periodic faunal extinctions punctuating Kivu's fossil record can be attributed to prehistoric limnic eruptions, and experts regard another such incident as inevitable. Of course, it may not happen for hundreds or thousands of years – but were it to happen tomorrow, the consequences for the two million human inhabitants of the Kivu Basin would be devastating!

At the time of writing, the Cameroonian lakes are in the process of being 'degassed' – a procedure that involves laying a pipe to the lowest strata of the lake and pumping the pressurised water so that it shoots out from the lake surface in a spectacular 50m-high fountain to release the carbon-dioxide safely into the atmosphere. Some fear that the degassing process might itself trigger another disaster, others reckon that it is simply not happening fast enough, but so far things have gone smoothly enough, and optimists believe the two lakes will be degassed to the point of benignity by 2010. Whether a similar procedure might be a realistic prospect for the much vaster Kivu is an open question, but certainly the risk of disaster would be reduced were the lake's practically inexhaustible reserves of methane to be extracted as a source of fuel and energy for local and possibly international consumption – something that currently only takes place on a small scale to fuel the Bralirwa brewery at Gisenyi.

For further information about the phenomenon of limnic eruptions and the methane reserves at Lake Kivu, check out the website perso.wanadoo.fr/mhalb/nyos.

---

by the anomalous Hotel du Lac Kivu, with its freshly painted modern exterior, and the neatly cropped lawn of the Home St François. The outmoded façades of Cyangugu speak of better times past, and while the town's aura of tropical ennui is less than invigorating, it is also somehow rather affecting.

Between and eastward of the two of them (off the map) is Cyangugu's current residential area. Former Bishop of Cyangugu Kenneth Barham, who owns and runs the Peace Guesthouse (see page 157), describes it:

> From the top of the High Street you look across at Mont Cyangugu with the 'mudugudu' of 50 'shelter-housing' properties and the high court at the top of the hill. This hill is designated the Prefecture of the future. The Medical HQ for the Province is there, the Education Centre is now built there, three law courts are there and the space for the Prefecture is there. I have built a Dispensary, which I am expanding into a specialist unit for dentistry and eye work. Our St Matthew's Primary School is there. It is the residential heart of Cyangugu, as opposed to the commercial centre on the other hill. You get to it by turning left on the tarmac as you enter the town, passing our cathedral and turning up a gravel road just after the river.

While the prefecture of Kibuye has the sad distinction of being the site of the most extensive extermination of Tutsis during the genocide, the prefecture of Cyangugu comes second. Before the French set up their 'safe zone', it was estimated that 85–90% of Tutsis here had died. Many communities were completely wiped out.

Unless you are thinking of crossing into the DRC, Cyangugu has to be classed as something of a dead end in travel terms. It is, however, the closest town to Nyungwe, with a few slightly smarter accommodation options than the forest

10

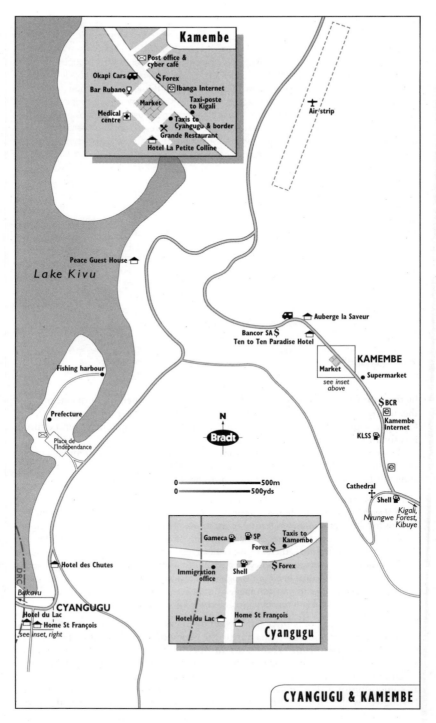

Kamembe

Post office & cyber café

Okapi Cars
Bar Rubano
$ Forex
Ibanga Internet
Market
Taxi-poste to Kigali
Medical centre
Taxis to Cyangugu & border
Grande Restaurant
Hotel La Petite Colline

Air strip

Peace Guest House

Lake Kivu

Auberge la Saveur

Bancor SA $
Ten to Ten Paradise Hotel

KAMEMBE

Market
see inset above
Supermarket

$ BCR
Kamembe Internet

KLSS

Fishing harbour

Prefecture

Place de l'Indépendance

N

Bradt

0 — 500m
0 — 500yds

Cathedral

Shell

Kigali, Nyungwe Forest, Kibuye

Gameca
SP
Taxis to Kamembe
Forex $

Immigration office
Shell
$ Forex

Hotel du Lac
Home St François

Cyangugu

DRC

Bukavu

Hotel des Chutes

CYANGUGU

Hotel du Lac
Home St François
See inset, right

CYANGUGU & KAMEMBE

resthouses, and might therefore make an attractive alternative base for self-drive visitors to Nyungwe. The lakeshore setting is lovely, too, and this atmospheric old town forms a good base from which to explore more off-the-beaten-track destinations such as the Bugarama Hot Springs and Cyamudongo Forest.

GETTING THERE AND AWAY

By air Rwandair Express (see advertisement on page 24) runs thrice-weekly flights between Kigali and Cyangugu.

By road Regular minibus-taxis connect Kigali and Huye to Cyangugu – or more accurately to Kamembe, which is where the main minibus stand for Cyangugu is situated. The fare from Kigali is around Rfr3,000 and from Huye around Rfr1,700.

A steady stream of minibus-taxis run back and forth between Kamembe and the border post at Cyangugu, at a cost equivalent to US$0.25 for the 5km trip. The Peace Guesthouse and Hotel des Chutes both lie within 50m of the taxi route, as does the main harbour and port.

Direct transport between Kamembe and Kibuye is restricted to one bus daily. This costs Rfr1,200, takes 5–6 hours, and leaves the bus park between 07.00 and 7.30 (sit on the left for the best views of the lake). Be warned that there are no minibus taxis from the border post to Kamembe at this time in the morning.

GPS reading for Cyangugu (Hotel du Lac) is S 02°29.390, E 028°53.596 (1,473m) and for Kamembe (Ten to Ten Hotel) ⊕ S 02°28.410, E 028°54.513 (1,613m).

By boat Public lake transport may restart one day; check the current position with ORTPN. Meanwhile the Hotel Centre Béthanie has boats for hire linking Cyangugu to Kibuye and thence to Gisenyi (see page 165). In Cyangugu, the Hotel des Chutes can sometimes arrange lake transport.

WHERE TO STAY

Moderate

Ten to Ten Hotel (30 rooms) ☎ 537796; m 06 645390/778785; e aimbiflx@yahoo.fr. Situated in the heart of Kamembe, a location that has little going for it aside from its proximity to the bus station, this modern 3-storey block, ostensibly the smartest option available in and around Cyangugu, does suffer from something of a character deficit. The large tiled en-suite rooms, though a little frayed at the edges, come with nets, TV, fan, private balcony and hot water. Other facilities include a good restaurant, a rooftop bar, room service and a massage and sauna, and a swimming pool is planned. The echoing passages might make you vulnerable to noise from other guests, and things can get very noisy on Friday/Saturday when the nightclub continues until the early hours. *Rfr12,000 for an ordinary dbl, Rfr15,000 for a dbl with a lake view, or Rfr20,000 for a suite.*

Peace Guesthouse (22 rooms) BP 52 Cyangugu; ☎ 537799; m 08 522727; sat 0808 849334; e info@peaceguesthouse.org; www.peaceguesthouse.org) Overlooking the lake about 1km from Kamembe along the scenic road towards Cyangugu proper, this friendly and justifiably popular guesthouse was constructed by the Anglican Church in 1998 and offers a wide selection of accommodation, ranging from en-suite apts to simple rooms using common hot showers. Several Rwandan VIPs – inc the president – have stayed here! Good-value meals (but no alcohol) are available in the restaurant, and there are internet facilities. See advertisement on page 157. *Sgl using common shower Rfr3,000; en-suite dbl Rfr6,000; apt with 2 dbl bedrooms and en-suite hot bath Rfr20,000–30,000*

Hotel des Chutes (17 rooms) ☎ 537405/537015; m 08 323555/778785. Set on a rise about 500m back from the border post, this pleasant and good value hotel has an attractive location overlooking the lake, and the shady balcony is fun for a drink or snack. Following recent renovations, the rooms are also now among the best on offer in Cyangugu, with clean

tiled floors, comfortable beds and crisp, fresh linen, TV, netting, hot bath, and in some instances a lake-facing private balcony. The restaurant serves good meals and snacks. You may be able to fix lake transport to Kibuye at reception. *Rfr8,000/10,000 en-suite twin/dbl.*

Hotel du Lac (20 rooms) ☎ 537172; m 08 582756. Formerly the smartest option in Cyangugu, this wonderfully located hotel remains a beacon of relative prosperity amidst the row of semi-dilapidated buildings that runs along the river immediately south of the border post with the DRC. Unfortunately, the rooms are starting to look a bit shabby and seem poor value by comparison with other hotels in this range. The hotel's best feature is the open-air riverfront bar and restaurant, which serves excellent brochettes and grilled chicken, as well as more substantial meals. There's also a large – but on last inspection empty – swimming pool! *Rfr12,000 en-suite dbl with hot water and fan, Rfr15,000 for a larger room with TV, Rfr18,000 for a suite with a barren volleyball court of a spare room, whose role is difficult to discern.*

Budget

Home St François (24 rooms) ☎ 537915. Situated directly opposite the Hotel du Lac, this church-run lodge is easily the best budget option in Cyangugu – in fact as good a deal as you'll find anywhere in Rwanda. The rooms are spacious, clean and secure, some with en-suite hot shower, others with access to a common hot bath. Meals are cheap at Rfr700 for b/fast or Rfr1,200 for dinner, but otherwise they're nothing to shout about, so you are probably better off eating at the nearby Hotel du Lac or Hotel des Chutes. The atmosphere is very homely, if not exactly full of cheer, and reception no longer seems to refuse accommodation to unmarried couples. *Rfr2,000/4,000 sgl/dbl.*

La Petite Colline (10 rooms) Sat: 0808 666550. Situated in Kamembe more-or-less opposite the

market, this very local hotel has lots of character and the semi-outdoor bar with banana-leaf roof is full of inventive decorations (flower holders made from old car parts...) alongside more traditional African art. There's a nice feel about the place, and it is very close to the bus station, but the en-suite rooms are a little basic at the asking price. *Rfr10,000 en-suite dbl.*

Auberge la Saveur (12 rooms) ☎ 08 623617. Situated right next to the bus station, this pleasant little local hotel offers unpretentious but comfortable accommodation in twins or dbls with nets and en-suite cold shower. The rooms are round a quiet courtyard, set away from the lively restaurant and bar. Camping may be possible in the garden – negotiate with the owner. *All rooms cost Rfr5,000.*

Self-catering houses The owner of the Peace Guesthouse also has four houses to rent. He describes them: 'I have built four good-quality homes on Mont Cyangugu; they would suit an NGO or other person working in the area. Three have four bedrooms, good-sized sitting room and dining room, two bathrooms, kitchen and store. One is bigger, with five bedrooms, three bathrooms and built-in garage. All are within a 2m-high brick wall and accessible via the stadium road. Details from the Administrator, Box 52 Cyangugu; tel 08 755357.'

✗ WHERE TO EAT AND DRINK The best food overall is probably at the **Hotel du Lac** and the surroundings are so pleasant; its open-air bar is relaxing, as is the terrace at **Hotel des Chutes** which also has a reasonable menu. Up in Kamembe the **Ten**

To Ten restaurant is correct but a bit boring; the **Auberge la Saveur** is good value, organises barbecues by request and has a lively bar. There are also plenty of small places around the market area; and the restaurant at the **Petite Colline** serves a good plateful.

PRACTICALITIES The banks provide the usual **foreign exchange** services at the usual snail's pace. The Banque Commerciale du Rwanda will change travellers' cheques but commission charges are very high. There are now quite a number of forex bureaux dotted around the border post and market area, offering an instant service for cash, generally at better rates than the banks – but do keep your wits about you. The Bank of Kigali has Western Union.

There are several internet cafés in Kamembe. If you are heading on to Kibuye and need to check email, best to do so in Kamembe as no internet facilities are available in Kibuye.

EXCURSIONS Cyangugu forms the obvious base from which to explore the far southwest of Rwanda, a region which sees very few tourists. The southwest boasts a couple of points of interest in the form of the Bugarama Hot Springs and Cyamudongo Forest, though you could argue that these landmarks provide a good pretext to explore a remote corner of Rwanda as much as they rank as worthwhile goals in their own right. With access to a private vehicle, this area could be explored as a day trip out of Cyangugu. Using what limited public transport exists, you're definitely in for an adventure: you should probably plan on spending at least one night out of Cyangugu, and should be prepared for long waits at the roadside, or a lot of walking.

Note that several travel guides refer to the **Rusizi Falls** (*Les Chutes de Rusizi*) on the Rusizi River along the border with the DRC. We spent a morning searching in vain for this, following a variety of confusing directions, only to conclude that whatever waterfall may once have existed is now submerged beneath the waters of the Mururu Dam, which was built in 1958 about 10km south of Cyangugu as a source of hydroelectric power and also serves as an obscure border crossing into the DRC.

Another possible excursion from Cyangugu is to the town of **Bukavu** across the border in the DRC. If you do go into DRC, and if you're of a nationality that needs a visa for Rwanda, then unless you have a multiple-entry (rather than a single-entry) Rwandan visa you'll have to pay again – US$60 – to re-enter Rwanda.

Bugarama Hot Springs Situated slightly less than 60km from Cyangugu by road, the Bugarama Hot Springs lie at the base of a limestone quarry, 5km from the Cimerwa Cement Factory, in a lightly wooded area dotted by large sinkholes. The springs bubble up into a large green pool which, as viewed from the roadward side, is initially somewhat disappointing. You can, however, follow a path around the edge of the pool, past a large sinkhole to your left, then leap over the outlet stream to the base of the cliff. Here you are right next to the main springs, which bubble into the pool like a freshly shaken and opened fizzy-drink bottle, and are sizzling hot to the touch.

In a private vehicle the springs can be reached in about 90 minutes from Cyangugu, but they are rather more inaccessible using public transport. The first part of the trip involves following the partially surfaced road that connects Cyangugu to Ruha (a border post with Burundi) for approximately 40km to the junction town of Bugarama. You need to turn left at this junction, along a dirt road that passes through Bugarama and a series of small villages, until after 11km you reach the strip of tar outside the Cimerwa Cement Factory. Here you must turn

THE CREATION OF LAKE KIVU

A NEW VERSION OF AN ANCIENT TALE Long, long ago, before the beginning of what we now remember, there was nothing but a dry, grassy plain covering the area where Lake Kivu lies today. It was a hard, hot place, whose people had to work ceaselessly to scrape a living from the land. One of these people was a man whose heart was kind; he helped his older neighbours to till their ground and to gather in their crops. His wife scolded him for this, saying: 'Why do you spend so much time filling their grain-stores when our own lies empty?' But Imana had seen his good deeds and was pleased, and wanted to reward the man, so he gave him a cow whose udders yielded milk, millet, beans and peas. Imana warned the man that he must not speak of his special cow to others, lest they envy him and try to steal it, so the man milked his cow in secret and carried home the produce to his wife who began to scold him a little less.

A day came when the man was called away to work at the Mwami's court. Anxiously, he asked Imana what he should do about his cow. Imana said that his wife might be told, and might milk it in the meantime, but that she must not pass on the secret of the cow to others.

With her husband away from home, the woman invited a young man to her house. He dined off the milk and the millet and the beans and the peas, and he wondered how her poor land could produce so much. He searched all round her homestead for an extra storeroom or piece of land but he found nothing, and the cow looked just like an ordinary cow. Insistently the young man questioned the woman, using all kinds of persuasion to discover her secret, and eventually she weakened. She milked the cow in front of him and he was so amazed that he ran to the neighbours, crying: 'Here is an animal that will feed us all – we need work on the land no more!'

Imana heard this, and he frowned deeply, and that night he prepared a punishment. Before going to bed, the woman went out into her field to empty her bladder as usual, thinking to take only a few moments. But the flow was unstoppable. On and on it went, flooding her house and her fields and the land around about. Deeper and deeper it became, until the woman herself was drowned in it and even the trees were covered. Her household utensils – her wooden bowl and her woven mat and the gourd which held her grain – floated away into the distance, broke into bits and became islands. And as the morning sun rose into the sky it lit the new and shining surface of Lake Kivu as it is today.

When the man returned from working at the Mwami's court he found a lake of sweet water lapping at the edge of his fields. The land had become soft and fertile. Fish swam in the lake, and waterbirds bobbed on the wavelets. Of the cow there was no sign, but she had left behind a big heap of millet and peas and beans which he then planted, and his crop and all those after it grew richly on the irrigated land.

And Imana smiled.

right, passing the factory gate. After another 5km, immediately past a signpost reading *Secteur Nyamaranko*, you'll see a hillside quarry and three-way fork to your left. Follow the leftmost fork for about 100m, then turn right on to a small dirt track, and after 100m or so you'll see the pool in front of you. If in doubt, ask for directions to the *Amashyuza* (aka *Amahyuza*). From here, it would be possible to continue on the Cyamudongo Forest (see page 150).

Using public transport, one (very slow) bus and several minibus-taxes cover the Ruha road daily, leaving from Kamembe rather than Cyangugu proper, and taking up to two hours to reach Bugarama town. Bugarama itself isn't much to shout about – a hot, dusty small town ringed by plantations of plantains and pines – but basic accommodation may still be available at the **Tripartite Bar**, 50m from the main junction in the direction of the cement factory. There is no regular public transport along the 16km road between the town and the springs, but we noticed quite a few pick-up trucks, so finding a lift – at least as far as the cement factory – shouldn't present a major problem. From there, the 5km walk is along flat terrain, and shouldn't take longer than an hour in either direction.

KIBUYE

The most conventionally pretty of the lake ports, this modestly sized town of almost 50,000 residents sprawls across a series of hills interwoven with the lagoon-like arms of the lake. Now that the new road from Kigali has been completed, Kibuye is the lakeside town most quickly accessible from the capital, though – partially due to a paucity of tourist-class facilities – it has not caught on with foreign tourists and Rwandan holidaymakers the way Gisenyi has. That said, at weekends you'll often find families from elsewhere in Rwanda enjoying the small beaches and the swimming, some of them former exiles who returned after the genocide and are rediscovering their country. Hills planted with pines and eucalyptus give the locale a pristine, almost Alpine appearance, in contrast to the atmosphere of fading tropical languor which to some extent afflicts the other ports. It's a green, peaceful and appealing place, whose sudden views of the lake sparkling amid overhanging trees are true picture-postcard material.

It's hard to believe, amid today's sunlight and tranquillity, that during the genocide the prefecture of Kibuye experienced the most comprehensive slaughter of Tutsis anywhere in Rwanda. Previously there had been around 60,000 in the prefecture, an unusually high proportion of about 20%. When the French troops arrived afterwards they estimated that up to nine out of every ten had been killed. Whole communities were annihilated, leaving no witnesses to the crime. Near the sports stadium you will see just one of the mass graves, with a sign announcing: 'More than 10,000 people were inhumated here. Official ceremony was presided over by H E Pasteur Bizimungu, President of the Republic of Rwanda. April 26th 1995.' Now birds chirp on the surrounding wall and the laughter of children in the nearby primary school echoes across the enclosure. Here and throughout Rwanda, memories of the genocide remain acute but daily life carries on determinedly around them. As does tourism.

GETTING THERE AND AWAY

By road The main access is by an excellent road from Kigali via Gitarama, started by the Chinese in 1990. On some stretches it's a considerable feat of engineering, cutting through hillsides and teetering around steep valleys. The drive takes at least two hours in a private vehicle. Minibus-taxis are available from Nyabugogo bus station as well as from certain private operators in central Kigali (Ataco departs for Kibuye at 06.15, 08.15, 10.15, 12.15 and 13.15) and costs Rfr1,400. GPS (Hotel Golfe Eden Rock) is S 02°03.559, E 029°20.893.

Travelling from elsewhere on the lakeshore, the drives are mostly on dirt roads. The trip from Cyangugu or Nyungwe National Park takes about four hours in a private vehicle (the junction of the Cyangugu-Nyungwe Road and dirt road to Kibuye is at S 02°25.355, E 029°04.196) and the trip to Gisenyi about three. Note that the trip to Gisenyi involves following the Kigali road east for 17km as far as Rubengera (⊕ S 02°02.916, E 029°24.849), then turning left on to a clearly marked dirt road. There are two minibus-taxis daily from Gisenyi, charging around Rfr1,500. No minibus-taxis run regularly between Cyangugu and Kibuye, but

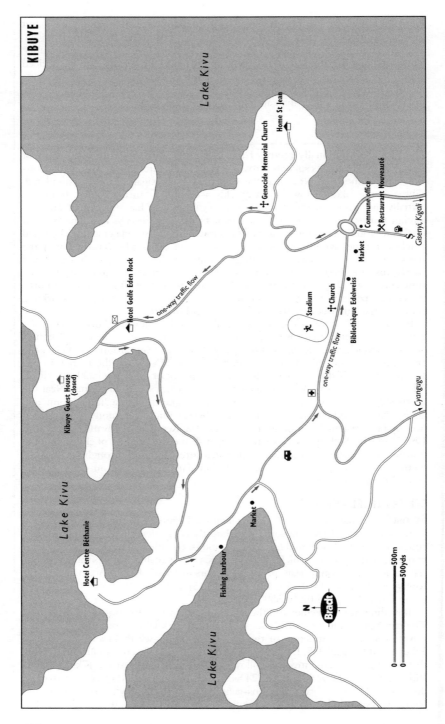

KIBUYE

Lake Kivu

Home St Jean

✝ Genocide Memorial Church

Restaurant Nouveauté

✕ Commune office

Market

Gisenyi, Kigali

Hotel Golfe Eden Rock

one-way traffic flow

✈ Stadium

✝ Church

Bibliothèque Edelweiss

Kibuye Guest House
(closed)

Lake Kivu

one-way traffic flow

Cyangugu

Hotel Centre Béthanie

Lake Kivu

Market

Fishing harbour

N

Bradt

0   500m
0   500yds

there's one bus daily in either direction, leaving at 08.00 and taking about an hour longer than a private vehicle would.

When you arrive in Kibuye by minibus-taxi, alight at the crossroads at the entry to town if you want the Hotel Golfe Eden Rock or the Home St Jean; continue to the final stop by the sports stadium for the Béthanie. There are sometimes some bicycle-taxis around if your bags are heavy. If you are driving in Kibuye, note that the main surfaced loop road around the sprawling town is one-way in an anti-clockwise direction.

By boat Public lake transport should eventually restart now that the situation with the DRC is calmer. In the meantime, the Hotel Centre Béthanie has two boats for hire linking Kibuye to Cyangugu and Gisenyi. The smaller boat holds up to four passengers and takes about one hour to get between Kibuye and either Gisenyi or Cyangugu, while the larger boat, which holds up to 20 passengers, takes about 2–3 hours for each leg. Whichever boat you charter, the cost for the Kibuye–Gisenyi leg is Rfr150,000 and for the Kibuye–Cyangugu leg Rfr220,000. Bookings can be made through the hotel reception.

WHERE TO STAY

Hotel Centre Béthanie (42 rooms)
568235; f 568509. This lively, friendly place is definitely the best option in Kibuye, with a beautiful lakeshore position on a well-wooded peninsula, though it seems a shame that most of that wood consists of eucalyptus, pine and other exotic trees. The brick chalet-style rooms are a bit cramped together, but very clean, and they come with hot showers, netting and a view of the lake. There is also a decent restaurant overlooking the lake. Normally there is plenty of space but it can fill up if there's a religious gathering or seminar, so it's safer to book in advance. *Rfr8,000/10,000/12,000 dbl/twin/suite excluding b/fast.*

Hotel Golfe Eden Rock (60 rooms) 568524, m 08 847675/863131; sat: 0808 309584; e hgolfedenrock@yahoo.fr. Situated near to the (currently closed) Kibuye Guesthouse and roughly opposite the post office, this large hotel re-opened to the public after a lengthy stint serving as a hostel for Chinese road-construction personnel. The location is great, with excellent views over the lake, and there's nothing wrong with the en-suite rooms (dbl bed, netting, polished floor, ask for one that

leads on to the lower balcony), but the dopey staff can become rather exhausting. *Rfr14,000 dbl or twin inc 1 b/fast (a second person pays an additional Rfr2,000).*

Home St Jean (21 rooms) 568526/568193. The cheapest accommodation option in Kibuye, this is tucked away down a lane to the right-hand side of the large church that you'll see on a hill as you enter Kibuye from the east. It is signposted from near the church but rather indistinctly. It took a battering during the genocide but reopened in 1996 and is now very comfortable and good value. The views over the lake are lovely and meals are available by advance order. *Rooms using common showers Rfr3,000 pp; en-suite apts Rfr6,000 pp.*

Kibuye Guesthouse (22 rooms) 568554/568555; www.kibuyeguesthouse.co.rw. Formerly the pick of the accommodation in Kibuye, this state-owned guesthouse has an idyllic location beside a small beach on the grassy lake shore, with great views and Technicolor sunsets. It is closed at the time of writing but likely to reopen under private management in the not too distant future. Contact details may change but you can check via ORTPN or on www.rwandatourism.com.

WHERE TO EAT/DRINK

The pick is probably the **Golfe Eden Rock**, which serves a good selection of snacks and meals in the Rfr1,000–3,000 range, but be warned that service is on the slow side, and nobody seems overly concerned about serving the meal you actually order. The restaurant at the **Béthanie** is also good, with a standard menu, and a lot more efficient. If it ever re-opens, the restaurant at the **Kibuye Guesthouse** should still be excellent, either for a full meal or just for a drink sitting out at a lakeside table admiring the view. In town, two small restaurants near the hospital serve traditional *mélanges* of rice, meat and vegetables, as does the fancifully named **Restaurant Nouveauté** (also good for a snack or drink) at the northern end of town. There are plenty of places for a quick beer or fruit juice when you're strolling.

PRACTICALITIES The **post office** down near the Kibuye Guesthouse has international telephone and fax facilities and the staff are endlessly helpful. At the time of writing, no **internet** facilities are available in Kibuye, and there is no forex bureau, but the **Banque Continentale Africaine Rwanda** should be able to change cash – US dollars and euros will be easier than other currencies. There's a **pharmacy** down a side road to the right of the market as you face it; follow the sign to it and you'll pass the **Bibliothèque Edelweiss**, a tiny lending library with a stock of children's and adults' literature in French.

WHAT TO SEE AND DO Kibuye is such a relaxed, pleasant town that it's enjoyable just strolling and watching life unfold. There's a big **market** on Fridays, in an open area just beyond the hospital, when people come in from outlying villages and across the lake from Idjwi Island. The week-long market in the centre of town hasn't a huge range but is still worth a browse. You'll come across work parties of prisoners quite often in Kibuye, as elsewhere in Rwanda, in their silly pink uniforms and Bermuda shorts – without them, far less reconstruction would have been completed.

As the sketch map shows, you can do a **circular walk** along the main one-way road around Kibuye. This offers some beautiful views across the lake and can be stretched to fill a couple of hours or so, depending on how often you stop to photograph, watch birds, or just enjoy the surroundings. Views are slightly better going clockwise rather than anticlockwise – with the added advantage that you'll be facing any oncoming traffic, so can take evasive action more quickly! Once you've passed the hospital on your way up to the Béthanie there's nowhere to get a drink until you're back down by the Kibuye Guesthouse, so you may want to carry some water.

Boat trips from Kibuye Apart from longer trips to Cyangugu and Gisenyi (see page 165) there are possibilities for trips on Lake Kivu and to nearby islands: Napoleon's Island (it's shaped like his hat) which has a colony of fruit bats, and Amahoro (Peace) Island where there is a restaurant, volleyball and camping (bring your own tent as the ones offered are rather tatty). The Hotel Centre Béthanie (see under hotel listing, above) has two boats that can take you to the islands, at a charge of Rfr26,000 per hour for the four-seat vessel or Rfr32,000 for the 20-seat vessel. Because the charge is per hour, you'll pay a lot more if the boat waits for you at one of the islands than if you are dropped and arrange to be collected later. An independent operator, Jean-Baptiste (✆ 08482315; e rugijean2003@yahoo.fr), has two 30-seater boats;. One of the Kigali tour operators, Kiboko Tours & Travel (see page 111), has a speedboat on Lake Kivu; contact them to arrange water-based activities in advance.

The genocide memorial church As you enter Kibuye from the east, you'll see a large church perched on a hill above the town. During the genocide, over 4,000 died there. Lindsey Hilsum catches the stark horror of it in an article in *Granta* issue 51:

> The church stands among trees on a promontory above the calm blue of Lake Kivu. The Tutsis were sheltering inside when a mob, drunk on banana beer, threw grenades through the doors and windows and then ran in to club and stab to death the people who remained alive. It took about three hours.

In the hills high above Kibuye, often shrouded in mountain mist, Bisesero is a place of great sadness and great heroism. Of the estimated 800,000 or so people who lost their lives throughout the whole country during the genocide, more than 6% were slaughtered here in this one area; but the resistance they mounted against the killers – and maintained for almost three months – was the strongest and most courageous in all of Rwanda.

When the genocide began on 7 April 1994, Tutsis from the whole surrounding region converged on Bisesero for refuge, numbering around 50,000 at their height. Then the killers came, an assortment of military, trained *interahamwe* and villagers, heavily armed and equipped with vehicles. The people of Bisesero had machetes and other rudimentary weapons and managed to survive relatively well until mid-May, killing a number of their attackers and repulsing others. But it was bitterly cold in the hills and raining heavily, and they were short of food.

On 13 May the attackers returned in full force, including many militia and soldiers and with weapons that the refugees in Bisesero could not match, although they did their best to group themselves effectively and fought fiercely hand-to-hand. The battle raged for eight hours and resumed the next day. By the end, around half of the refugees had died. The exhausted survivors had little choice but to hide in the forest and put up what sporadic resistance they could. The attacks continued relentlessly. By the time the French arrived at the end of June, only around 1,300 of the 50,000 were still alive. But – they had survived.

There is a memorial at Bisesero now, and local tour operators (for example Bizidanny Tours & Safaris, whose advertisement is on page 112) will take you there. It's a sad, moving and evocative place, where the sense of history is very strong.

For some time the church remained empty and scarred. Then gradually work started – new mosaics were sketched out and then completed, and new stained glass filled the broken windows. New hangings adorned the altar. A memorial has been built outside by the relatives of those who died there and nearby. During the week it is still empty, for anyone who wants to go to reflect peacefully on the past, but on Sundays now it is filled with worshippers and their singing wafts out across Lake Kivu. Sometimes commemorative services are held. For me, a memorial of this kind is far more evocative and far more moving than the skulls of Nyamata or the corpses of Murambi. Here there is an echoing beauty, which is no bad accompaniment to thoughts of death. Try to find time for a few reflective minutes in this deeply memorable place.

Ndaba Falls On your way back by minibus-taxi along the road to Gitarama, look out for this waterfall some distance away on your right about 20km out from Kibuye. Passengers will point it out to you if you warn them beforehand – in French it's the *Chutes de Ndaba*. In the rainy season it's an impressive 100m cascade, in the dry season a fairly unimpressive straggle. You can ask for the minibus to drop you at the viewpoint. Going in the other direction it's harder to spot.

GISENYI

The most important tourist centre and largest port on the Rwandan shore of Lake Kivu is Gisenyi, an attractively faded resort town situated about 110km north of Kibuye by road, and 60km west of the gorilla-tracking base of Musanze (formerly Ruhengeri). The fifth-largest town in Rwanda, with a population of 67,000 according to the 2002 census, Gisenyi is better equipped for upmarket tourism than any urban centre outside of the capital. It thus forms a good alternative base from which self-drive tourists can visit the gorillas, while also possessing a seductive tropical ambience that makes it a great place to settle into for a few days.

Good roads connect Musanze and Gisenyi to Kigali and southern Uganda, and the region as a whole has an agreeably moderate year-round climate and consistently attractive mountain scenery. Its location close to the Uganda and DRC borders made it an unsettled area both before and for some time after the genocide, because of army and guerrilla activity. From a tourist's perspective, security is no longer a serious concern, but it would still be a good idea to seek local advice before heading off the beaten track.

Gisenyi is split into an upper and lower town, of which the former consists of an undistinguished grid of busy roads centred around a small market, with a northern skyline dominated by the distinctive volcanic outline of Nyiragongo, whose active crater belches out smoke by day and glows ominously at night. The lower town is a more spacious and atmospheric conglomeration of banks, government buildings, old colonial homesteads and hotels, beside a shore lapped by the waters of Lake Kivu. The waterfront, with its red sandy beaches, pleasing mismatch of architectural styles, and shady palm-lined avenues, has the captivating air of a slightly down-at-heel tropical beach resort. Indeed, Gisenyi could easily be mistaken for a sweaty West African or Indian Ocean backwater, except that the relatively high altitude of 1,500m means it has a refreshing climate at odds with its tropical appearance.

In 1907, the Duke of Mecklenburg wrote:

Kissenji possesses an excellent climate, for by virtue of its 1,500 metres above sea level all enervating heat is banished. The natural coolness prevalent in consequence makes a visit there a very agreeable experience. The man who has this place allotted to him for his sphere of activity draws a prize. In front are the swirling breakers of the most beautiful of all the Central African lakes, framed in by banks which fall back steeply from the rugged masses of rock; at the rear the stately summits of the eight Virunga volcanoes.

Gisenyi today offers little in the way of formal sightseeing, but its singular atmosphere, combined with an excellent range of affordable accommodation, makes it the sort of town that you could easily settle into for a few days. It's an interesting place to wander around, too, whether your interest lies in the prolific birds that line the lakeshore, the fantastic old colonial buildings that dot the leafy suburban avenues, lazing around on the beach, or mixing in to the hustle and bustle of the market area. Further afield, the 6km walk or *matatu* drive to Rubona port offers some lovely lake views and, a little further on, some hot springs; while at Rubona itself you can easily arrange to explore the immediate vicinity in a dugout canoe or pirogue. It's also possible to visit the engaging Imbabazi Orphanage nearby (see details and box on pages 172–4).

GETTING THERE AND AWAY All buses and minibus-taxis leave from the bus station next to the market in the old town centre. The main port for Gisenyi is at Rubona, about 6km south of town; the two are connected by regular minibuses. The GPS (Kivu Sun) is ✪ S 01°42.077, E 029°15.605.

To/from Kigali and Musanze Gisenyi lies approximately 60km from Musanze by road, and 160km from Kigali. The road is sealed and mostly in good condition, though there are some pot-holed stretches. The direct drive from Kigali should take no longer than three hours. Regular minibus-taxis connect the three towns: the fare from Gisenyi to Musanze is around Rfr800 and to Kigali Rfr1,800.

Catherine Simmons

My day usually begins with an early wake-up call from the local mosque at around 04.30. Not to be outdone, the church across the road starts early morning mass, complete with drumming and joyful singing, at 05.30. Just as I am drifting off to sleep again, my alarm goes off at 06.00. So I stagger into the bathroom where I am soon wide awake due to the effects of a vigorous cold shower. At least I'm out quickly, which is good for my two flatmates! Coffee is a must so I pop the kerosene stove on in the kitchen. It's accompanied by the BBC World Service if reception is good (BBC is on short-wave only in Gisenyi), or some rousing Rwandan music and the news in French on Radio Rwanda if not.

The school bus arrives at 07.20 and we all pile in, along with some other teachers who live locally. We then drive around Gisenyi, picking up teachers and other staff members as we go. Those who miss the bus get picked up second time around, as with nearly 50 teachers we can't all fit in. These bus rides are a lively mix of gossip, jokes and chat between the teachers in Kinyarwanda and Swahili. We usually screech into school about 10–15 minutes before lessons start, just enough time to straighten up and double-check the staff room notice board for any last-minute meetings. I teach nearly 500 students so every day something unexpected happens and life in the classroom is never boring.

Any hours when I'm not teaching I spend in the English club room preparing lessons or doing marking. When I've finished for the day I catch the local minibus back into the centre of Gisenyi. These bus rides give me a chance to practise my Kinyarwanda: everyone wants to know who I am and what I am doing on the bus.

In town I may do some shopping in the market, go to the bank or use the internet. Being able to speak even basic Kinyarwanda really helps, as does taking the time to stop and talk to people. I also check out the newest bootleg tapes and explain to the tape man that I still don't want to buy that special Greatest Hits of Don Williams (although I did succumb to the Kenny Rogers Christmas Album). A bit of retail therapy!

As I walk on home, people always greet me or ask my name or where I'm going, or ask for sweets or biscuits. It's not unusual for someone to walk home with me just for the conversation and because they are interested.

Evenings in Gisenyi are quite low key. Doing dinner can take longer than you would imagine, especially if the electricity goes off or if the stove runs out of kerosene. We spend the time chatting to each other and talking about our days at school. We might listen to some music, or read a bit. At the weekend we often make a pizza in our special home-made 'oven', scoff home-made cake, go swimming in beautiful Lake Kivu and sunbathe. Sometimes we even treat ourselves to the occasional dinner out!

Cat wrote this when she was teaching in Gisenyi for Voluntary Service Overseas.

To/from Kibuye and Cyangugu To drive from Gisenyi to Kibuye, you first need to head out along the Musanze road for about 5km to Pfunda, before turning right at a poorly signposted junction on to the dirt road that leads to Rubengera on the surfaced road between Kigali and Kibuye. It's a drive of about 110km in all, and the dirt stretch is in variable condition, so three to four hours should be allowed. Although the dirt road runs parallel to Lake Kivu, it offers disappointingly few glimpses of the lake, though this is compensated for by some spectacular mountain scenery and relic patches of Gishwati Forest (see *Gishwati Forest* pages 174–6). From Kibuye, it's another 100km to Cyangugu, a three-to-four-hour drive, mostly along dirt roads.

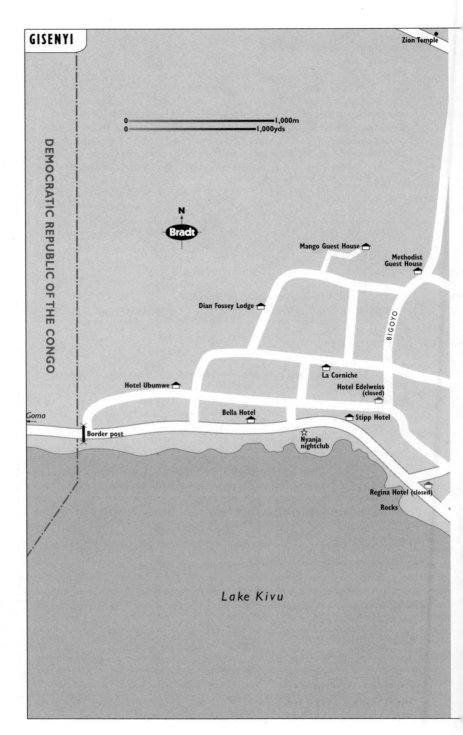

GISENYI

Zion Temple

DEMOCRATIC REPUBLIC OF THE CONGO

0 —————————— 1,000m
0 —————————— 1,000yds

N
Bradt

Mango Guest House

Methodist
Guest House

Dian Fossey Lodge

B I G O Y O

La Corniche

Hotel Ubumwe

Hotel Edelweiss
(closed)

Bella Hotel

Goma

Stipp Hotel

Border post

Nyanja
nightclub

Regina Hotel (closed)

Rocks

Lake Kivu

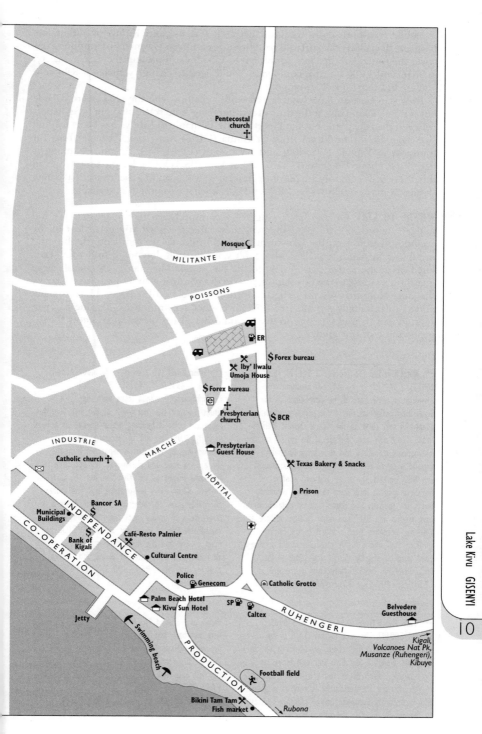

Pentecostal church

Mosque

MILITANTE

POISSONS

ER

Forex bureau

Iby' Ilwalu
Umoja House

Forex bureau

Presbyterian
church

BCR

INDUSTRIE

Catholic church

MARCHÉ

Presbyterian
Guest House

Texas Bakery & Snacks

HÔPITAL

Prison

Bancor SA

Municipal
Buildings

Café-Resto Palmier

Bank of
Kigali

Cultural Centre

INDEPENDANCE

CO-OPERATION

Police

Genecom

Catholic Grotto

Palm Beach Hotel

Kivu Sun Hotel

SP

Caltex

RUHENGERI

Belvedere
Guesthouse

Jetty

Swimming beach

PRODUCTION

Football field

Bikini Tam Tam

Fish market

Rubona

Kigali,
Volcanoes Nat Pk,
Musanze (Ruhengeri),
Kibuye

Public transport along the road between Gisenyi and Kibuye is rather less frequent than along the surfaced road heading east from Gisenyi, but minibus-taxis cover the route daily at a fare equivalent to US$2.50. At present they leave Gisenyi at 06.00 and 14.00 but this could vary. You'll need to change vehicles at Kibuye if you are heading on to Cyangugu.

Boat transport on Lake Kivu lapsed while relations with the DRC were volatile but is now picking up. At the time of writing there is no scheduled public transport between the lake ports, but the Hotel Centre Béthanie in Kibuye has boats for hire (see page 163). The Hotel Ihusi in Goma (DRC) has a fast, 22-seater boat for transport to Kibuye (US$400) and Cyangugu (US$1,000). Advance booking is necessary: phone Vincent (08 5137736) or Vani (08 313108). By the time you read this there will certainly be more operators, so ask around – be aware that safety standards may not always be 100% and check what equipment is available.

WHERE TO STAY Gisenyi has a range of accommodation to suit most tastes and budgets, and prices are generally very reasonable for what you get. Most of the accommodation is on the lake-front, about 15 minutes on foot from the bus and minibus-taxi stand; travellers who don't want to walk down will find a few taxis lined up at the petrol station next to the bus stand. There are a couple of cheap guesthouses close to the bus station, but on the whole it is more pleasant to stay by the lake. Note that several signposts for the long-closed Edelweiss Hotel are still dotted misleadingly around town. More budget accommodation is due to open soon in and around Gisenyi, so if you find other places please let us know for the next edition of this guide.

Upmarket

Hotel Kivu Sun (66 rooms) ☎ 541111; m 08 200123; f 541102; e frontoffice@kivusun.co.rw; www.kivusun.co.rw. Part of the same chain as the Kigali InterContinental, this 4-star property, which opened in mid 2004 on the site of the old Meridien Izubu, is the only hotel outside of the capital to meet international standards, and it forms a justifiably popular weekend retreat for Kigali-based expatriates and NGO workers. The green and well-wooded lakeshore grounds lead down to a sandy swimming beach, the spacious and comfortable en-suite rooms all have air-con and DSTV, and other facilities include a sparkling swimming pool, a fitness centre, English-speaking staff, and a highly rated restaurant serving a good selection of grills, curries and salads in the Rfr3,000–4,000 bracket. MasterCard is accepted. US$102/124/154 sgl/dbl/suite b&b.

Stipp Hotel (10 rooms) ☎ 540450/540060; m 08 304335/6; f 540335; e stipphotels@rwanda1.com; www.stippag.co.rw. Situated about 1km northwest of the Kivu Sun, this renovated colonial building, which opened as a hotel in early 2005, also lies in attractive grounds overlooking the lake, but is separated from the shore by a road and a tall wall. It's not quite in the same league as the Kivu Sun, but the smart modern décor, more personalised feel, and more affordable rates all count in its favour. There is a large, clean swimming pool, the restaurant serves a varied selection of meals for around Rfr5,000 per main course, and the large carpeted en-suite rooms all come with DSTV, internet access and (in most cases) a lake view. Rfr33,600/39,200/44,800 sgl/dbl/suite.

Moderate

Palm Beach Hotel (15 rooms) ☎ 540765; m 08 500407. The pick in this range is this somewhat idiosyncratic set-up, which stands on the lakeshore alongside the Kivu Sun, and boasts an art-deco façade, stylish décor and a light airy ambience to the interiors. The restaurant is very atmospheric, with a distinctly European feel in pleasing contrast to the equally likeable beachfront bar, and most

meals cost around Rfr4,000. Rooms are all en-suite with hot bath, but, typically for an old house, they are quite variable in size and ambience, so ask to look at the room before you check in. Rfr30,000 dbl with lake view, Rfr25,000 dbl without lake view, Rfr15,000 twin, all b&b.

Motel La Bella (3 rooms) ☎ 08 510714. Formerly the Café du Lac, this characterful and affordable gem, which lies about 300m further out of town than the Stipp, consists of a well-maintained old colonial house, with wooden floors, slatted windows and whitewashed exterior, set on a large, attractive lawn sloping down to the lakeshore. The spacious rooms are all on the first floor; 2 have a view of the lake and they share a common hot bath and toilet. Meals and drinks are served in the stylish ground-floor restaurant or on the large lawn — this is one of the best places to eat in Gisenyi, with a good selection of African, Asian and European dishes in the Rfr2,000–3,500 range. *Rfr15,000 dbl.*

🏠 **Paradis Malahide** (4 rooms, more under construction) ☎ 08 648650/756204. Situated in Rubona, 6km south of the town centre, this highly recommended new lodge combines a rustically beautiful lakeshore setting with very comfortable en-suite accommodation in rondawels with stone floors, nets and hot water. A good restaurant/bar is attached, serving meals in the Rfr2,000–4,000 range, and it's ideally sited to enjoy sunsets over the lake while kamikaze pied kingfishers dive into the water and local fishermen cruise past in their distinctive boats (consisting of 3 dugouts held together by long poles). There is also a motorboat for hire if you want to explore the surrounding lakeshore. To get there, follow the road towards Rubona for about 5km; when you can see the brewery ahead of you, turn sharp right, continue

along the lake shore and you'll come to it on your left. A winner at *Rfr15,000 dbl b&b.*

🏠 **Hotel Ubumwe** (12 rooms) ☎ 540267. By comparison with all the above, this is a bit of a non-starter. The reasonably comfortable but otherwise undistinguished rooms with en-suite hot showers and toilets feel rather overpriced and its location is less than ideal: a good 20-min walk from the town centre, and set back a block from the lake. *Rfr18,000 dbl without view; Rfr22,000 with view.*

🏠 **Dian Fossey Lodge** (12 rooms) 08 517591. The only thing that really places this nondescript and decidedly non-central lodge in the moderate category is the inflated room rates. Otherwise, the rooms are quite rundown and the mosquito-infested grounds possess all the character of a building site. *Rfr8,000 sgl using common showers; Rfr10,000/12,000 en-suite dbl/twin.*

🏠 **Hotel Regina** Situated on the beachfront between the Kivu Sun and Stipp Hotel, this former government hotel dates to the colonial era, and exudes a sense of tropical languor befitting Gisenyi. The wide veranda overlooks a tangled garden and the lake, while the bar and restaurant, with their high ceilings and wooden floor, could be a movie set. Closed for renovation and extension at the time of writing, the Regina will re-open soon under the same management as the Gorillas Hotel in Kigali (see pages 90–1), with prices in the moderate bracket.

Budget

🏠 **Presbyterian Church Centre d'Accueil** (11 rooms) ☎ 540397. Situated close to the market and the main taxi park, this pleasant church-run lodge is probably the best deal in this range, despite its distance (about 10 mins' walk) from the lake, with bright and fresh rooms set in spaciously laid out grounds that also contain a basic but good-value restaurant. *Rfr6,000 en-suite dbl with nets and hot water; Rfr1,500 for a bed in a 6- or 8-berth dorm.*

🏠 **Methodist Church Centre d'Accueil** (6 rooms) Set in pleasant grounds to the north of the town centre, this good-value and friendly but rather isolated lodge offers accommodation in clean private rooms with ³/₄ bed, washbasin and shared shower/toilet, as well as in 3-bed dorms. Meals are prepared by request and there's a (very distant) view of the lake. The downhill walk to the beach takes 10–15 mins. *Rfr3,500 private room; Rfr2,000 pp in a dorm.*

🏠 **Mango Guesthouse** (8 rooms) Probably not worth considering unless you have a car, this new and likeably unpretentious hillside lodge is most notable for its large balcony, which offers a grandstand view across the town to the lake. *The large rooms with nets are also quite nice, but not en-suite, and meals are available for around Rfr3,500. Rfr5,000 sgl; Rfr6,000–8,000 dbl.*

🏠 **La Corniche** (8 rooms) 08 322234. Set alongside a pleasant garden bar and restaurant a short walk north of the lakeshore, this is an adequate lodge, but the basic en-suite rooms seem a little overpriced. *Rfr10,000 dbl.*

🏠 **Auberge de Gisenyi** Situated close to the taxi park and market, this is a standard local guesthouse and bar/restaurant with small en-suite rooms (cold water, hot buckets by request). *Rfr4,000/5,000 sgl/dbl.*

✖ **WHERE TO EAT AND DRINK** The best places to eat are generally the hotels. The restaurant at the **Palm Beach Hotel** has attractive decor and good Belgian cuisine in the US$5–7 range, and the beachfront bar is a great place to indulge in the

Since Rosamond Halsey Carr founded the Imbabazi Orphanage in 1994, she and her staff have cared for more than 400 orphans. The orphanage is currently home to some 120 children, aged from two years upwards.

As a young fashion illustrator in New York City, Rosamond Halsey married an adventurous hunter-explorer, Kenneth Carr, and journeyed with him to the Congo in 1949. After their eventual divorce, Kenneth left; Rosamond stayed on. In 1955 she moved to northwest Rwanda to manage a flower plantation, Mugongo; and later bought it. For the next 50 years she witnessed the end of colonialism, celebrated Rwanda's independence and became one of Dian Fossey's closest friends. (In the film *Gorillas in the Mist*, her role is played by Julie Harris.)

During periods of violence and upheaval, Mrs Carr always stayed fast at her home in Mugongo while others fled. But when the genocide began in April 1994 the American Embassy finally insisted that she leave. After several months in the US, she received word that Sembagare, her friend and plantation manager of 50 years, had survived what turned out to be three attempts on his life. In August 1994, aged 82, she returned in a cargo plane, to find her home in ruins and 50 years' worth of possessions either stolen or destroyed. At Mugongo, she and Sembagare did the only thing that made sense to them: they converted an old pyrethrum drying-house and set up the Imbabazi Orphanage, to care for the genocide orphans.

In 1997 the orphanage was forced to move from Mugongo for security reasons, and, having changed locations four times, settled in Gisenyi for several years. At the end of 2005 it moved 'back home' to Mugongo. From time to time some children are traced and reclaimed by family members – while others arrive and are taken in. Now aged 94, Mrs Carr is officially Rwanda's oldest resident; she lives in a house on Gisenyi's lake shore and visits the orphanage several times a week, still managing its affairs. The Mugongo farm continues to provide the orphanage with fresh vegetables and many Rwandan businesses (and weddings!) with fresh flowers, and is the sole source of income for the families who work there.

tradition of sundowners. However, it is now seriously rivalled by the upmarket restaurants – with their stunning views of the lake – in the new **Kivu Sun** and **Stipp Hotels**. You can also eat well in the pretty gardens of the **Motel La Bella**. About 6km from the centre, in the direction of the Bralirwa Brewery, the **Paradis Malahide** serves wonderfully fresh fish and the view across the bay is superb.

Another good spot for sundowners – indeed for a drink at any time of day – is the **Bar-Restaurant Bikini Tam-Tam**, which has a perfect lakefront position marred only slightly by the smell from the fish market next door. A limited selection of snacks and grills is available in the US$2–5 range. There are plenty of budget eateries around the market area, of which the new Texas Bakery is recommended for fresh bread and pastries, pizza, fruit juice and snacks including, um, 'poulet kentaki'!

If you're looking for nocturnal action, the place to head for is the Nyanja Nightclub near the Stipp Hotel. The main club is only open on Friday and Saturday, but the lively bar is open every night. Another good but more subdued spot for a drink is the beachfront bar attached to the Palm Beach Hotel.

PRACTICALITIES For **foreign exchange**, most of the banks marked on the map will change US dollars cash, but you'll get better rates and more efficient service at any of several forex bureaux dotted around the market area. The Banque de Kigali also has Western Union. **Internet** facilities are surprisingly few and far between, but a couple of (often rather slow) cafés can be found in the market

Imbabazi receives funds from various friends and organisations, many of them in the US. (Search 'Imbabazi Orphanage' on the internet and you'll find links to some.) Visitors to Mugongo can meet the children and decide on the spot – as often happens – to sponsor one or more of them, whether for small general needs or for secondary school education. A novel fundraising scheme, 'Through the Eyes of Children', began in 2000, originally as a photographic workshop conceived by photographer David Jiranek. Using disposable cameras, the children at the orphanage took photos of themselves and their surroundings, exploring their community and finding beauty as Rwanda struggled to rebuild after the genocide.

At first the photos were developed locally, displayed on the orphanage walls and put into albums by the children. A year later, the children were invited by the US Embassy to exhibit their work in Kigali, with all proceeds going towards their education. In the 2001 Camera Arts Magazine Photo Contest, eight-year-old Jacqueline won First Prize for portraiture; and the project has won Honourable Mention in an international competition featuring professional and non-professional photographers from around the world.

Unicef invited the Imbabazi children to participate in its 2003 *State of the World's Children* Report. As a result the report's cover photograph was of Murakete, taken by her friend Umuhoza at the orphanage. Also published inside are other photos of the children using their disposable cameras. In addition, New York University invited the project to exhibit at the Gulf & Western Gallery at the NYU Tisch School for the Arts in New York City in December 2002 and January 2003. The photos were also shown at the premiere of the Human Rights Watch International Film Festival in New York in June 2003. For more information, check the comprehensive website www.rwandaproject.org.

Rosamond Carr is the author of *Land of a Thousand Hills: my life in Rwanda* (she wrote the book with her niece, Ann Howard Halsey), chronicling her love affair with Rwanda and describing the country in all its variety and beauty; see *Further Reading*, page 252.

area. Situated next to the Motel La Bella, the **Traser Travel Agency** (\ *540773;* m *08 490521*) can confirm and book international air tickets, as well as making other travel arrangements.

WHAT TO SEE AND DO
Boat trips and watersports Ask at your accommodation for details of local operators offering these, as new ones are starting up. Kiboko Tours & Travel in Kigali (see page 111) have a speedboat on Lake Kivu and can fit various water-based activities into your itinerary.

RUBONA Set on an attractive peninsula 6km from the town centre, Rubona is the main harbour for Gisenyi and the site of Rwanda's largest brewery, Bralirwa. It is connected to the town centre by a surfaced road and regular minibus-taxis, a scenic route which would make for a pleasant stroll in one or other direction. Rubona is a bustling little satellite town, and fun to stroll around, but it is mainly of interest to travellers looking for lake transport, or photographers attracted by the hundreds of small fishing pirogues or dugout canoes that dot the harbour (look out for the distinctive catamaran-style boats consisting of three dugouts held together by poles). The fish in this bay have an unusual diet, as dregs from the brewing process at Bralirwa Brewery are thrown into the water regularly!

Another compelling reason to visit Rubona is the presence of the Paradis Malahide, which offers some of the best value accommodation in the area, and –

even if you don't want to spend the night – makes an excellent spot for a sundowner drink or al fresco lunch.

Hot springs A little beyond Bralirwa are some hot springs, claimed by the local people living nearby to have a curative effect. Allegedly bathing in the waters relieves fatigue, cures skin rashes and even helps to mend simple fractures. More prosaically, in some places the springs are hot enough – and are used by the villagers – to boil potatoes and cassava. It's an attractive spot, but not yet on the tourist circuit, so please don't take photos of people without their permission – and, if you've been there, do let us know your impressions for the next edition of this guide.

EXCURSIONS FROM GISENYI

Imbabazi Orphanage Not far from Gisenyi is the Imbabazi orphanage ($\searrow$ 540740), a positive and heart-warming project started in December 1994 by Rosamond Halsey Carr at her plantation in nearby Mugongo to shelter some of the many genocide orphans and displaced children. After moving to Gisenyi in the 1990s and spending some years there, it returned to new and purpose-built premises in Mugongo at the end of 2005. See box on page 172.

Visitors are welcome, but do phone beforehand to check that it's convenient and you're not interrupting school. You're likely to find yourself being sung and danced to by the smiling, lively bunch of children; they're used to visitors so not at all overawed. Mugongo is up in the hills to the northwest of Gisenyi, only 36km from the town but around 1,000m higher – so the road is steep and offers some beautiful views. Local *taxi-voitures* will take you there.

Goma An interesting half-day trip is across into Goma (DRC) to see the lava flow from the 2002 volcanic eruption. Although much has been cleared and rebuilt, the seas of craggy lava still lie beside the road with truncated buildings arising from them. Now that the situation with DRC is more stable, operators in Gisenyi will surely start to organise day trips to Goma (there are also walks and scenic drives there) so do ask around. Until that happens, the député at Okapi Cars can organise a taxi and a guide to take you across the border for around US$30. At the time of writing, if you're heading into the countryside around the town, it's advisable to do so in the company of a local person – for reasons not of safety but of hassle.

If you feel like an adventure, see the box opposite – but for this you must have proper equipment and be accompanied by a competent guide. Ask around locally, starting in hotels and guesthouses.

You don't need a visa as such but a fee of US$30 is levied at the border. If you're of one of the nationalities that needs a visa to enter Rwanda, then make sure that you have a multiple- rather than a single-entry one otherwise you'll have to pay extra (US$60) to return into Rwanda from DRC. The frontier post normally opens at 08.00 and closes at 18.00 sharp. Goma has taken a beating but was a gracious and attractive town and is well worth a stroll.

Gishwati Forest In the early 20th century, Gishwati was the second-largest tract of indigenous forest in Rwanda, extending over roughly 1,000km^2 along the Albertine Rift escarpment from the base of the Virungas halfway down Lake Kivu. By 1989, when Rwanda's last forest-dwelling Batwa hunter-gatherers were evicted from Gishwati, it consisted of two main forest blocks which together covered less a quarter of its former extent. More forest was cleared in the early 1990s to make way for a forestry plantation and dairy project, and most of what remained was cut down in 1998-9, to accommodate the land needs of returned refugees.

CLIMBING NYIRAGONGO (DRC)

Katot Meyer

We were eight people in total, ranging in age from a 12-year-old boy to about 45 years. On Saturday morning we were at the Rwanda–DRC border in Gisenyi at 08.00. After all the custom procedures to enter DRC, we met up with one of the volcanologists and our guide. They accompanied us to the foot of the volcano where we negotiated a price of US$30 per person and US$20 for the guide. Some of the people hired a porter for US$10.

We left the base office at exactly 10.00. The first bit of the trail goes through beautiful rainforest. It is amazing to see all the indigenous trees and hear the different bird songs. After a while we left the forest to walk on old lava from the 2002 eruption. We followed the lava to our lunch spot, which was about halfway up the volcano. When the volcano erupted in 2002 the lava came out of the side of the mountain and not the top. We saw the place where it emerged and there was still some smoke coming out. The lava flowed down the path we had come up, then stopped before it reached the town. But it then found another way under the volcano and came out of the side of the mountain at another place, near the airport, from where it went through the town and ended up in Lake Kivu.

After lunch we went through rainforest again. The path was now much steeper and we also had some rain. We reached the 'huts' at about 16:30. There used to be three metal huts – one is now down completely, half of the second one is still standing and the third one is still OK. We pitched one tent inside hut number 2 and the other two tents outside.

The guide, guard and porter slept in hut number 3. They also carried up a bag of charcoal and we could warm ourselves up and get our clothes dry. We also used this hut for doing all our cooking. Outside it was quite chilly but the amazing view over the other volcanoes, lake and town made up for it.

After a rest and dinner we climbed for a final 30 minutes to the summit. It was dark so we used torches and head lamps. We could only see a red glowing mist in the big volcano pot. We could hear the lava bubble down under. It sounded like the waves of the sea. We could see the lights of the two towns and all the fishing boats down on the lake.

We were back on the summit the next morning just after sunrise. We traversed for about half an hour around the volcano rim. All the mist lifted out of the huge pot and we could see the lava down at the bottom. What an amazing sight. We were standing on top of a live volcano!

On the way down we investigated the crater at our lunch spot more closely and then followed the lava back to the base. It was an amazing weekend!

This short-sighted decision not only resulted in immense biodiversity loss, but also has led to several landslides that have killed many people, as well as the drying up of streams that once provided water to communities outside the forest. Today, a mere 6km² of true forest remains at Gishwati. Chimpanzees, still known to occur in the reserve in the late 1980s, are almost certainly now locally extinct. Outside of the Virungas, Gishwati was also the only confirmed haunt of the golden monkey, but it seems unlikely that a viable population of this endangered species remains. There has been no recent bird inventory, but it is possible that Albertine Rift endemics such as regal sunbird and strange weaver are still present.

The most substantial remnant of Gishwati can be visited from the road between Gisenyi and Kibuye. Katot Meyer writes:

The road passes a small patch of indigenous forest to the east exactly 40km from Gisenyi. I went for a walk there. Very few people were on the road and luckily I could slip into the forest without any kids following me. There are a lot of trails, most of them with cattle tracks on, but I saw not a soul. Peace and quiet in Rwanda? I thought it to be impossible. There were birds singing in the trees, frogs at the river crossing, an absolute feast. At some places the undergrowth is very thick but as long as you stay on the paths this is an incredible hiking area. I could see the forest stretching over quite a few hills but in some places on the horizon cultivators had already invaded it. I would have thought that the areas closest to the main road would be in the greatest danger, yet I found many trees that had fallen from natural causes and were just left to rot. As in all Rwandan Forest areas, wear long trousers for walking.

11

Musanze and the Virunga Foothills

The big change in this area is that the familiar town of **Ruhengeri**, gateway to the Volcanoes National Park and the mountain gorillas, was renamed **Musanze** as part of an administrative reorganisation in early 2006. For more details see the *History* section of *Chapter 1*, page 6. Throughout this guide we are using the new name but with occasional reminders of the old one, to help readers over the transition. Local people are likely to continue using the old name for quite some time, but new road-signs and other indicators have already been erected and changes will be made to maps.

Location, they say, is everything, and on this score Musanze, the fourth-largest town in Rwanda with a population estimated at 93,000, is privileged indeed. As the closest town to the Volcanoes National Park, it is the most convenient urban base from which to track mountain gorillas, as well as boasting a memorably stirring backdrop in the form of the distinctive volcanic outlines of the three most easterly mountains in the Virunga chain.

Despite its strategic importance as a tourist hub, Musanze is an unremarkable town, sprawling amorphously from the tight grid of pot-holed roads that surround the central market. But as travel bases go, it's difficult to fault: the mood is friendly and free of hassle, and – at an altitude of 1,850m – the temperate climate is most agreeable. The market is lively and worth a visit, and there are some pleasant strolls around town, as well as the possibility of excursions further afield to Lakes Burera, Ruhondo and Karago.

GETTING THERE AND AWAY

The main taxi park recently relocated from Avenue de la Nutrition to a patch of open ground which lies on the edge of the compact town centre, a short distance south of the central market past the Urumuli Hotel. The GPS for the Hotel Muhabura is S 01°29.883, E 029°37.954.

TO/FROM KIGALI Kigali and Musanze are linked by a 96km surfaced road. It's in fair condition, though the combination of outrageous bends, the occasional pot-hole, and some seriously manic local drivers requires caution. Even so, you should cover the distance in 90 minutes.

Regular minibus-taxis connect Kigali (Nyabugogo bus station) and Musanze, leaving in either direction when they have a full complement of passengers. Tickets cost Rfr1,200 and the trip takes around 90 minutes.

About 35km out of Kigali, on your left, you'll see a small but ornate cemetery, very different in style from those elsewhere in Rwanda. The graves there are those of Chinese workers who died during the building of this road and others in Rwanda – the excellent Kigali–Kibuye road is also one of theirs.

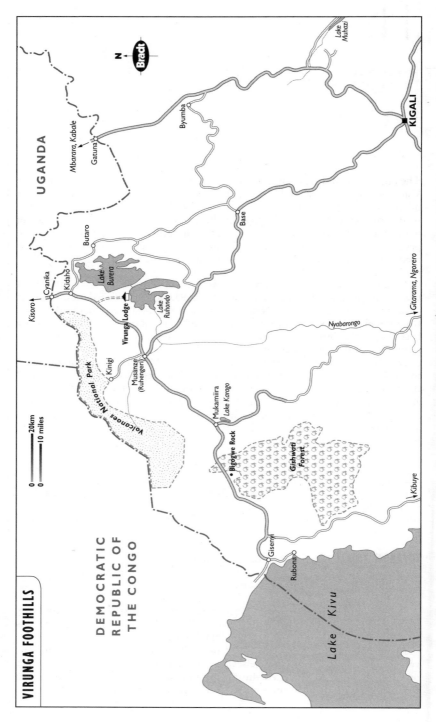

VIRUNGA FOOTHILLS

N

Bradt

UGANDA

Lake Muhazi

KIGALI

Mbarara, Kabale

Gatuna

Byumba

Base

Gitarama, Ngorero

Butaro

Cyanika

Kidaho

Lake Burera

Lake Ruhondo

Virunga Lodge

Nyabarongo

Kisoro

Kinigi

Musanze (Ruhengeri)

Volcanoes National Park

Mukamiira

Lake Karago

Bigogwe Rock

Gishwati Forest

Kibuye

DEMOCRATIC REPUBLIC OF THE CONGO

Gisenyi

Rubona

Lake Kivu

0 ____ 20km
0 ____ 10 miles

TO/FROM GISENYI The 62km drive between Musanze (Ruhengeri) and Gisenyi follows a fairly good (and by Rwandan standards unusually straight) surfaced road, and should take no longer than an hour and a quarter. Minibus-taxis between the two towns leave regularly and cost around Rfr800.

Driving from Musanze to Gisenyi, you pass (on the left) a surfaced road that goes first to Lake Karago (see page 198) and then continues southwards to join the Gitarama–Kibuye road, as shown on the map inside the front cover. It winds high up into the hills and the views are breathtaking – and you've plenty of time to admire them because the middle stretch (about 35km) is unsurfaced and so full of pot-holes that you can only drive very slowly. It passes through hamlets and beside tea plantations, so there is human interest too, but the main attraction has to be the wonderfully panoramic landscape. You could consider it as an alternative way of returning to Kigali from either Musanze or Gisenyi. Hikers can probably get lifts as transport goes to and from the tea plantations – and there is even the odd bus, though it's something of a miracle that the suspension survives the jolting.

TO/FROM UGANDA The border crossings between Uganda and Rwanda are covered more fully on page 36. Coming to Musanze straight from Kampala, the most efficient option is to catch a bus or minibus heading directly to Kigali, where you can pick up a minibus-taxi to Musanze.

Coming from the west of Uganda, you will have to pass through Kabale, from where you can either cross directly into Rwanda at the Katuna border post, or else continue within Uganda to Kisoro and cross at the Cyanika border post. If you have private transport, or are visiting Kisoro anyway, then the Cyanika route is the better option. Kisoro and Musanze lie approximately 40km from each other along a mostly tarred road. On public transport, you'll have to change vehicles at the border, and can expect to pay around Rfr500–600 for each leg.

Otherwise, given the poor state of the road between Kabale and Kisoro (as well as the limited amount of public transport), the most circuitous route between Kabale and Musanze on paper is almost certainly the most efficient in practice: that is to catch a minibus-taxi from Kabale to Kigali (you might need to change vehicles at the border), from where you can pick up another to Musanze. A variation on this would be to stop at Byumba on the Kabale–Kigali road, then travel along the back road to Base on the Musanze–Kigali road, but this will almost certainly entail spending a night in Byumba (see page 216).

WHERE TO STAY

All the accommodation options within Musanze currently fall into the budget or lower end of the mid-range category. Gorilla trackers seeking more comfortable accommodation are pointed towards the pair of smarter lodges situated close to the Volcanoes National Park headquarters at Kinigi, 12km from Musanze, or to the sumptuous Virunga Lodge near Lake Burera (covered later in the chapter). A new, luxury tented camp will be opening a short way out of town in mid 2007 (Ikoro, below).

Upmarket

Ikoro Tented Camp (10 tents) m 08 671572; e enquiries@elegantafrica.com; www.elegantafrica.com. Operated by Elegant Africa and due to open in mid 2007, this camp (in a woodland setting and with a view of the volcanoes) will have 10 luxury en-suite safari tents each with a private veranda. Materials and furnishings are being sourced locally. Facilities will include a restaurant, bar, lounge and internet access. It's located on the Musanze/Cyanika road about 1km past the turn-off to Kinigi and 200m beyond the Ituze Hotel. *US$100 per tent per night.*

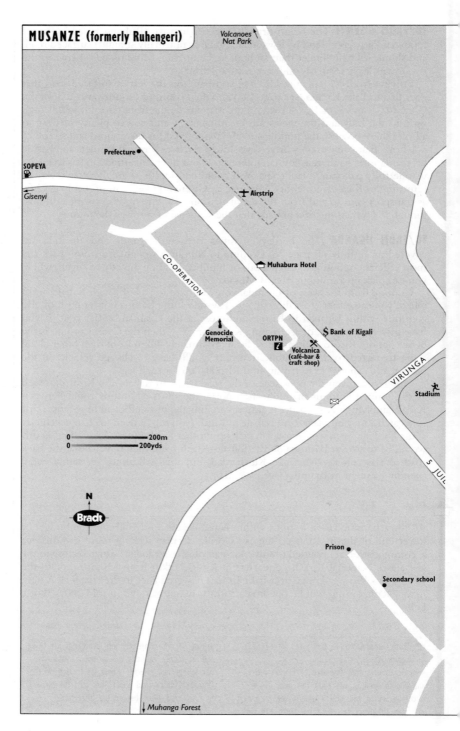

MUSANZE (formerly Ruhengeri)

Volcanoes
Nat Park

Prefecture

SOPEYA

Gisenyi

Airstrip

CO-OPERATION

Muhabura Hotel

Genocide
Memorial

ORTPN

Volcanica
(café-bar &
craft shop)

Bank of Kigali

VIRUNGA

Stadium

0 ———— 200m
0 ———— 200yds

N

Bradt

S JUIL

Prison

Secondary school

Muhanga Forest

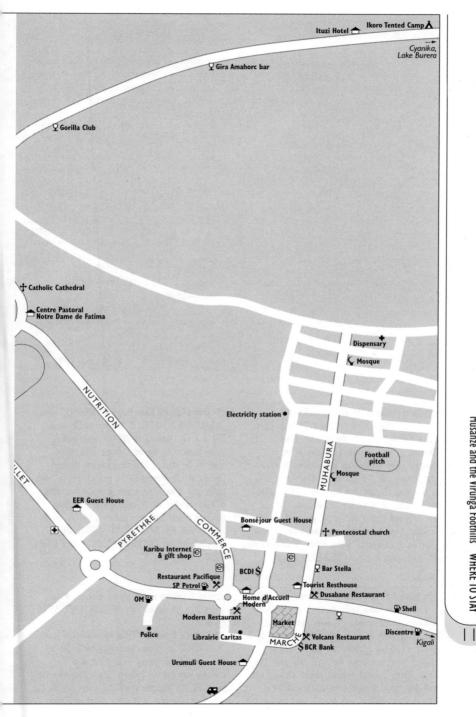

Ituzi Hotel · Ikoro Tented Camp

Cyanika,
Lake Burera

Gira Amahorc bar

Gorilla Club

Catholic Cathedral

Centre Pastoral
Notre Dame de Fatima

NUTRITION

Dispensary

Mosque

Electricity station

MUHABURA

Football
pitch

Mosque

EER Guest House

PYRETHRE

COMMERCE

Bonséjour Guest House

Pentecostal church

Karibu Internet
& gift shop

BCDI $

Bar Stella

Restaurant Pacifique
SP Petrol

Tourist Resthouse

Dusabane Restaurant

OM

Home d'Accueil
Modern

Shell

Modern Restaurant

Market

Discentre

Police

Librairie Caritas

MARCHE

Volcans Restaurant

Kigali

BCR Bank

Urumuli Guest House

Doug Teschner

This 2,643m peak is a pleasant hike, all the more attractive because it can be done easily in a day from Kigali without having to leave before dawn – and you're still back in town before dark. Also, as it's so close to the main road, you can get there by public transport. The hike involves 1,000m of ascent and takes two to four hours to the top (a four-to-seven-hour round trip of about 12km) for most people.

The 'mountain' is visible from the Kigali–Musanze road, on the right about an hour out of Kigali. It stands out as a hill that is bigger than the rest. You may wish to obtain a topographic map (Gakenke, map number 9) from the Ministry of Public Works in the Gikondo section of Kigali, but it is not necessary as long as visibility is good enough to see the mountain (which it almost always is).

To get there, drive for about 75 minutes out of Kigali. Then look for a village that includes a yellow building named (what else?) Mont Kabuye. Just after this village, a paved road leaves the main road on the right. There is a blue sign marked 'Hospital Nemba 1 km'. Take this road (which quickly becomes dirt) down and loop back left through 'town' to a soccer field on the right and a log bridge. Park here. The total distance from the main road is 0.8km. The guy in the house across the bridge will probably appear and offer to guard your car. If you like four-wheeling, you can cross the bridge and go as far as you are comfortable along this steep narrow road (maybe 1,500m at the very most).

Hikers should cross the bridge and follow the road, climbing steadily to its end (about 2km). After 30 minutes, look for a little shack on the right which (if open) will sell you warm Fanta and you may even be able to arrange for a child to carry some to the top. This is a good way to keep hydrated and support the local economy.

Where the road ends at a pipe, there is an obvious steep section of trail. Above this, there are multiple trails and it is not always easy to pick the best one, but you can easily

Mid-range

🏠 **Hotel Muhabura** (15 rooms) ✆/f 546296; m 08 322313/501541; muhabura12@yahoo.fr or bosco742004@yahoo.fr. The smartest hotel in Musanze is this venerable establishment set in compact green grounds on the outskirts of town along Avenue du 5 Juillet in the direction of Gisenyi. It is a very pleasant and reasonably priced set-up with 2 types of room: spacious en-suite dbls with hot bath and shower and larger apts with similar facilities. A good bar and restaurant serves a wide selection of continental dishes inside or outdoors for Rfr3,000 upwards. *Rfr15,000/20,000 dbl/apt.*

🏠 **Centre Pastoral Notre Dame de Fatima** (35 rooms) ✆ 546780/4; f 546783; e cpndefatima@yahoo.fr. This is a new (opened in 2004) modern-looking hostel situated on the edge of the town centre opposite the stadium and alongside an affiliated Catholic church. Although a bit institutional for some tastes, and a touch overpriced, it is the best option in Musanze after the Muhabura, with very clean rooms, a decent bar and restaurant, and an on-site internet café. *Rfr10,000/12,000 sgl/dbl using common showers; Rfr15,000/17,000 en-suite sgl/dbl; Rfr30,000 apt with TV.*

Budget

🏠 **Home d'Accueil Moderne** (8 rooms) ✆ 546525; f 546904. For some years the pick of the cheaper places scattered around the town centre, this welcoming small lodge is situated on Avenue du 5 Juillet diagonally opposite the market and less than 5 mins' walk from the main taxi park. The clean, freshly painted en-suite rooms all have nets and hot water, a good courtyard restaurant is attached, the staff is very friendly and helpful, safe

parking is available, and it's no problem if you arrive with US dollars only. *Rfr4,000/5,000/6,000 sgl/dbl/twin.*

🏠 **Centre d'Accueil de l'Eglise Episcopale** (30 rooms) ✆ 546856/7; e eerguesthouse@yahoo.fr. Set in large grounds on Avenue du 5 Juillet near the junction with Rue de Pyrèthre, about 1km from the taxi park, this peaceful church-run lodge has the only swimming pool in Musanze (filled with clean readjust on smaller trails if you lose the main one. The best route goes right at the top of the steep section and stays just to the right of the ridge, passing by the local water supply and eventually passing a school (prominently visible from below) in a big clearing. Above the school, the trail follows the right side of the ridge to a T-Junction. Turn left and enjoy the short flat stretch before turning right and heading steeply back up the very scenic ridge through farmlands and by houses with the mountain prominently visible above. If the sky is very clear, views of the volcanoes will appear off to the left.

After a while, the trail switches over to the left side of the ridge and soon reaches a flattish place on the ridge proper. Turn right after 50m for a scenic rest on rocks in a eucalyptus grove. You're about two-thirds of the way to the top. After your rest, continue up the steepening ridge toward the summit cone. A short steep section up a grassy patch leads to a rocky trail, which slabs off to the left and eventually swings around the peak to reach the pass on the left (north) side of the summit.

At the pass, leave the main trail by turning right on a smaller one. You're now 15 minutes from the top. Follow this vague path up the ridge, through new eucalyptus trees, to nearly the top. The precise but somewhat indistinct summit (visible en route from a prior false top) is reached by leaving the path for the final 20m. If it is very clear, you can see all the Virunga volcanoes and Lake Ruhondo to the north. Just down on the other side of the summit, there is a pine forest which offers shade on a sunny day.

As in all places in Rwanda, expect to be followed by a pack of children, although I have found that each time we go (I have done it five times), there are fewer, as they seem to be getting used to visitors.

Descend the same way, or pick another. The valley off to the right (looking down) is very beautiful, but it adds at least an hour to the descent.

water in 2006) and offers a range of budget accommodation. The welcome is usually friendly, the communal ablutions are clean and have hot showers, and a limited selection of meals is available. Camping is normally permitted in the church grounds for a nominal charge. *Rfr5,000 twin using common showers; Rfr15,000 en-suite apt; Rfr1,000 dorm bed.*

⌂ **Hotel Ituze** (9 rooms) ☎ 547014/64; m 08 630071. Situated alongside the Cyanika road, about 3km out of town past the turning to Kinigi, this rather basic but very welcoming hotel has a nice feel and lies well away from the bustle of the town, but it's only a realistic option with private transport. Inexpensive local meals are available. *Rfr3,500 sgl using common shower; Rfr4,000/5,000 en-suite twin/dbl with cold water only.*

⌂ **Tourist Resthouse** (6 rooms) ☎ 546635; m 08 520758. Centrally located on Rue de Muhabura, the friendly little lodge is a relative of the popular Skyblue Hotel in Kabale (Uganda), which means the staff speak English. The en-suite rooms are clean but cramped, and come with nets and sporadic hot water, but they feel a little overpriced for what they are. *R4/6,000 sgl/twin.*

⌂ **Bon Séjour Guesthouse** (5 rooms) Tucked away on a side road about 500m north of the taxi park, this place has scruffy but adequate en-suite rooms with cold water only and ³/₄ bed. *Rfr4,000.*

⌂ **Hotel Urumuli** (6 rooms) ☎ 546820 Conveniently located along a back road close to the market and literally around the corner from the new taxi park, this small hotel has rather poky en-suite rooms with nets, flaking paint and no hot water. *Rfr3,500 dbl.*

HOMESTAYS It's now possible for small numbers of people to stay in Rwandan homes in the Musanze area and join in local activities. See *Community-based Tourism* box on page 185. At present the main operator for homestays is Amahoro Tours – for details see *Practicalities* on page 186.

A NEW VERSION OF AN ANCIENT TALE Ruganzu II Ndori was one of the greatest of Rwanda's warrior kings. One source puts his reign at 1510-1543, another at 1600-1624, so.... who knows! His father, Ndahiro II, had catastrophically lost the Royal Drum, Rwoga, in battle, causing a time of great hardship for Rwanda: for 11 years the land was tortured by drought, sorghum withered in the ground, cows were barren and women conceived only sickly children. Considering the family cursed, the powerful abiiru (dynastic ritualists) banished Ruganzu from the kingdom – but after Ndahiro's death chiefs traced him and returned him to power.

Immediately rain began to fall on the parched land, sorghum grew fresh and sweet, cows produced rich milk and many calves, and woman became pregnant with fine, healthy sons. Ruganzu introduced the last of the Royal Drums, Karinga, to replace the lost Rwoga. He chose an adoptive Queen Mother from another clan; she was a poet and created a new form of dynastic poem. Ruganzu's conquests were many and much praised.

One day – so the ancient stories relate in various ways – the king and his entourage were visiting a part of Rwanda that today is just off to the right of the Kigali-Musanze road where it crosses the River Base. A sign to Nemba Hospital is nearby – as is a large rock known as 'Bagenge's Rock'.

Bagenge was the local chief in whose home the King was lodging for the night – and he had spent all that day in a state of great anxiety. The cause for his concern was the great rock, which was well known for moving about at night and relentlessly crushing anything that came within its path, whether mice, children, men, cattle or possibly even kings. Bagenge knew that death or injury to the King risked returning Rwanda to its previous state of drought and disaster.

He prepared a great feast, the greatest that the region had seen for some years, and the smell of the spit-roasted meats and pungent spices caused many a nearby villager's mouth to water. There was wine too, in great abundance, and banana beer; and after the feast dancers leaped and drummed and chanted in the firelight. Bagenge's aim was to entertain the King and his entourage until they fell deeply asleep, so that none would wander off and fall victim to the rock.

But kings sleep less than ordinary men. In the quiet of the night Ruganzu awoke. He wanted to feel air fresh upon his face and to plan new conquests in a silence unbroken by the snores of his attendants. He strolled off along the soft mud path and stood in the open, above the valley, looking upwards at the stars.

The ground shook, a shadow blotted out the starlight and the great rock lurched ominously towards the King. Ruganzu raised his staff threateningly and stood his ground. Disconcerted by such courage, the rock hesitated. Gently the King spoke (for he was wise, and knew that soft words hold the greatest power).

'Greetings, my subject. I hail you and I accept the offering you bring: the offering of your size and strength, to use for the good of my kingdom. Guard this village well. Protect the children who play in your shadow. Comfort the weary traveller who leans against you. Shelter the plants growing around your base. Remain in this spot for ever, the friend of all who live nearby. Perform this task well, my subject, and many centuries from now men will still remember you and tell this tale.'

As you will see, if you visit Bagenge's Rock today, it has indeed performed its task well and stayed peacefully in the same spot. All the same, if you wander the paths by night, keep your ears alert for the rumble of a sudden stealthy movement, because Rwanda is a Republic now and the power of kings is very much reduced …

CAMPING **Ikoro Tented Camp** (opening mid 2007, details under *Up-market*, above) will also have dedicated camping sites with their own washing (hot showers) and cooking facilities.

✖ WHERE TO EAT AND DRINK

As with hotels, there is plenty of choice when it comes to eating out in Musanze. The most extensive and expensive menu, inevitably, is at the **Muhabura Hotel**. The food is pretty good here – a selection of grills, stews and mild curries at around Rfr3,000 upwards for a heaped plate – and so is the ambience on the semi-shaded balcony. Beers and other drinks are only slightly more expensive than at the local bars and restaurants in town.

AMAHORO COMMUNITY-BASED TOURISM ASSOCIATION

Michael Grosspietsch & Christiane Gorka

It's on the same road that leads you to the gorillas, somewhere hidden on the left side, just a normal house that looks like many others in Rwanda. But once you enter the property, you'll find Alfonsine, the president of the Handicrafts Association, a member of the Amahoro Community-based Tourism Association (ACOTA), sitting in her bamboo chair, her youngest child probably holding on to her knees, the two older ones playing around somewhere with the neighbour's children. Other artisans will also be there, already busy at their work with the banana leaves. An old woman creates a ball, an orphan makes mats, one man is working on a chair, another is finishing off a suitcase. They will produce anything you like if you give them some time. Fidèle, who speaks French, explains how to work with the banana leaves and which ones to use. He cuts them in little pieces and hands them over. Now it's your turn. And before you know it, you'll find yourself sitting in between the other locals, busily making your own little mat.

Community-based tourism is the kind of tourism that doesn't isolate you from the local people and allows you to interact with them as much as you wish. Spend a day canoeing and fishing on the twin lakes Burera and Ruhondo and catch your own supper; cook with the family you are staying with overnight and participate in their daily life. Visit an orphanage where smiling children take you around. They dance for you and dance with you; they make you join in their children's games and teach you some words of Kinyarwanda. Or you can take part in local banana beer brewing, a traditional activity of great social importance in village life, and see the different steps of production. Sit down with the brewing families at the end of the day and talk about everything under the sun, sipping your own banana beer.

These and many other activities await you in the area around Musanze (Ruhengeri) and Gisenyi. Other ACOTA members, for example, will show you their agricultural work and introduce you to exotic fruits and plants such as passion fruit, sugar cane or vanilla. You can learn about traditional herbal medicine, or admire the fascinating skills of brick makers or bee-keepers. In the evening, enjoy your local food while traditional dancers invite you to participate in a cultural show of dancing and drumming…

ACOTA is a local initiative supported by the Musanze-based tour operator *Amahoro Tours* (www.amahoro-tours.com) and the German NGO *Sustainable Development through Tourism* (www.sd-tourism.org). Its main goal is to help a variety of local community groups to access the tourism market in ways that benefit their livelihood. If you're visiting the gorillas, try to spend some extra time in this beautiful area and experience traditional Rwanda. Meet its people and share their lives. And help to make a difference!

The **Home d'Accueil Moderne** has a popular courtyard restaurant serving a fair selection of grilled and fried meals in the Rfr1,000–2,000 range (great fish and chips). The courtyard restaurant in the **Hotel Urumuli** is similar in standard and price: the whole tilapia (a freshwater fish), chicken and goat kebabs are all recommended and excellent value. The **Tourist Resthouse** also has an inviting menu, dominated by stews rather than grills.

Scattered around town are at least a dozen local restaurants serving local food for around Rfr1,000 per plate – the **Modern** (roughly opposite the Home d'Accueil Moderne) is a cut above the rest. A pleasant new café-bar is the **Volcanica**, opposite the Bank of Kigali. And there are plenty of grocers with a range of cans, jars, packets, bottles and so forth.

Most of the above restaurants serve alcoholic drinks, but more dedicated drinking holes include the **Stella Bar** opposite the Tourist Resthouse, and the **Gorilla Club** and **Gira Amahoro Bar** on the Cyanika Road.

PRACTICALITIES

FOREIGN EXCHANGE The branch of the **Bank of Kigali** close to the Muhabura Hotel, **Banque Commerciale du Rwanda** behind the market and **BCDI** north of the market all offer foreign exchange facilities. They will probably not accept travellers' cheques – cash is safer. The **Bank of Kigali** has Western Union too.

For travellers who arrive from Uganda, there are no private forex bureaux in Musanze, so try to obtain some Rwandan francs when you cross the border. Otherwise, assuming that you have US dollars or euros cash, most of the hotels will sort you out at a rate fractionally lower than the street rate in Kigali, which is probably a safer bet than trying to change money on the street or in the market.

ORTPN The ORTPN office in Musanze town is on the first floor of the municipal buildings on Avenue du 5 Juillet; look out for the signpost opposite the Bank of Kigali, about 300m south of the Muhabura Hotel. A second ORTPN office is situated 12km out of town at the Volcanoes National Park headquarters in Kinigi. At the time of writing, depending on availability, last-minute gorilla-tracking permits can be booked through either of these offices. To make such a booking, pop in at around 17.00 on the day before you want to track, since this is when the next day's bookings are radioed through from the main booking office in Kigali. This situation might change during the lifespan of this edition.

OTHER FACILITIES There are a few **internet** cafés dotted around town, charging the usual rates of around Rfr500 per hour – try Karibu Internet (also a well-stocked gift shop) or the nameless café around the corner on Rue de Commerce. The only **bookshop** is the Librairie Caritas 100m west of the market. There is a clean **swimming pool** at the Centre d'Accueil de l'Eglise Episcopale; a nominal fee is charged to travellers staying at other hotels.

Next to the Fina Bank is a women's co-op named **Ituze** which does tie-&-dye, batik etc. The **Volcanica** café-bar opposite the Bank of Kigali also has a craft shop, offering stylish, contemporary hand-made products; and on the right of the Cyanika road just beyond the Ituze Hotel is **Fecar Inganzo**'s handicrafts workshop (see box opposite).

In and around the central market are a variety of small stalls and businesses – tailors, cobblers, people ironing clothes with old coal-filled irons, etc. In fact a new market is due to open not far from the centre in mid 2006, in a triangular plot with shops and stalls around the edge and open space in the middle, which may or may not replace the old one. Anyone will direct you there.

Fecar Inganzo, founded in 2002, is a federation of artisans from the 11 districts of former Ruhengeri Province (now North Province). It has a total membership of 5,557, almost 50% women. The project is set in an area over-dependent on agriculture, where it is crucial to provide alternatives to farming as well as activities that will help to conserve the environment and wildlife, particularly the mountain gorillas.

The government's Vision 2020 emphasises the role of higher education, IT, telecommunications, financial and management services and top-of-the-market tourism in the economic development of Rwanda; but there's still a need for the kind of grass-roots assistance that will enable rural populations to become active players in their country's new economy.

The development of local handicrafts is highly relevant to the promotion of tourism; it demonstrates pride in a unified Rwandan cultural heritage; it can generate an income extra or alternative to that from the lessening yields of farming; and it is one of the areas in which women's skills have equal recognition to men's. Moreover the handicrafts provide tourists with the souvenirs they so happily buy; and which, back in their owners' homes, demonstrate Rwandan skills to a wider audience.

Despite this, handicrafts producers in rural areas are perceived to have relatively low status. They remain trapped by poverty and are generally unaware of how to produce their wares in an organised, business-like, market-aware and market-appropriate way.

The Fecar Inganzo project aims to provide producers – the wood-carvers, carpenters, tailors, potters, weavers, basket-makers, metal-workers and other artists – with market and business information and training. It will develop sustainable livelihoods for rural artisan households, based on the principles of Fair Trade. It will foster their sense of pride in themselves and encourage recognition of their contribution to Rwandan culture and economic development. It will do this by supporting, developing and promoting the unique and most valuable asset that the artisan groups have to offer: their traditional craft-making skills.

Come to visit our workshop and see what we've already achieved! Look for our sign on the right-hand side of the road to Cyanika, about five minutes' drive from the centre of Musanze. The director of Elegant Africa (see page 179) in Musanze has already bought furniture from Fecar Inganzo, saying that he found the standard particularly good compared with that of most other carpenters in the area. You may well spot some of our products in the new Tented Camp that he plans to open nearby in 2007.

For more information about Fecar Inganzo contact Elaine Gardner on **e** *emgardner1@yahoo.co.uk.*

Musanze has two tour operators. **Highland Gorilla Tour & Travel** (m *08 414488;* **e** *ngyiroger@yahoo.fr; www.shyiradiocese.org.rw*), situated in the same building as the Centre d'Accueil de l'Eglise Episcopale, can also arrange car hire; and **Amahoro Tours** (*Market Street; PO Box 87 Musanze;* ↘ *546877;* m *08 687448;* **e** *info@amahoro-tours.com; www.amahoro-tours.com*) is the main agent for homestays in the area (see box on page 185), as well as involving visitors in local activities of their choice (canoeing, fishing, dancing, drumming, traditional medicine, bee-keeping, local cuisine...).They can also arrange gorilla visits and all the normal tourist programmes. This is a new and developing enterprise, so check the helpful website or email for the latest information.

Most people who visit Musanze see it purely as a base from which to track gorillas (see *Chapter 12*). But several local points of interest make for worthwhile day or overnight excursions from Musanze, notably the little-visited Lakes Karago, Burera and Ruhondo. For visitors seeking upmarket accommodation, the Virunga Lodge at Lake Burera and a pair of lodges at Kinigi are far more alluring than anything on offer in Musanze itself.

You might also want to ask ORTPN about the new Buhanga Eco-Park (✪ S 01°34.061, E 029°38.169; 1,628m), which lies 8km outside of Musanze – head out of town past the post office until you reach the Nyakinama College, turn right on to a rough dirt track after another 500m, and you'll reach the park after another 500m or so. Consisting of a small patch of forest dominated by spectacular dragon trees, this culturally significant site (see box *Ryangombe and the Buhanga Forest* on page 195) is under development as a nature trail, with a bar and possibly a hotel. If it's open by the time you visit Rwanda, it should be well worth seeing.

KINIGI More rustic sprawl than village, Kinigi is situated at an altitude of around 2,200m on the eucalyptus-strewn southern footslopes of the Virungas. It is of interest primarily as the site of the Volcanoes National Park headquarters (✪ S 01°25.783, E 029°35.717), the meeting point for gorilla tracking and other activities undertaken in the park, all of which require a check-in at 07.00. That aside, Kinigi is a pretty enough spot, offering great views of the volcanoes as well as some pleasant low-key walking opportunities, though somewhat compromised by the conspicuous absence of indigenous vegetation on the densely cultivated volcanic soils. Two of the three top hotels servicing the national park are situated in or close to Kinigi, and while neither is in the same class as Virunga Lodge on Lake Burera, they are both more affordable and more conveniently located for gorilla tracking. It is also permitted to camp at the park headquarters.

Getting there and away Kinigi lies 12km outside Musanze along a rather rough dirt track signposted to the left of the Cyanika Road about 300m past the Centre Pastoral Notre Dame de Fatima. Allow at least 20 minutes, better 30, for the drive to the park headquarters. There is no public transport but vehicle rentals can be arranged through the ORTPN office in Musanze, or at the taxi park near the market.

Where to stay

Mountain Gorilla's Nest (40 rooms) ⚋/f 546331; mobile: 08 305798; e mgorillanest@yahoo.com; ✪ S 01°26.365, E 029°34.729. Situated at an altitude of 2,295m between Kinigi and the Volcanoes National Park boundary, this smart new lodge lies in neat grounds enclosed by an intrusive circle of tall Antipodean eucalyptuses that block what would otherwise be a great view of the ragged edged rim of Sabinyo. Functional rather than characterful, the motel-style en-suite dbl rooms are bright and spacious, with telephone and hot water, and there are also apts with a fridge, TV (local stations only) and sitting room. Facilities include a good restaurant charging around Rfr4,000–5,000 for a 3-course dinner, a 9-hole golf course, and traditional music and dancing displays by request. *US$80/120 sgl/dbl*

room or *US$120/140 sgl/dbl apt, inc a hearty pre-gorilla-trek b/fast.*

Kinigi Guest House (11 rooms) ⚋ 547156; m 08 533606/516146; e asoferwa@rwanda1.com or beatrice_mukangenzi@yahoo.fr; www.rwanda-gorillas.com). Situated in peaceful green gardens just 300m from the park headquarters, this likeably low-key lodge is run by the charity ASOFERWA (see box opposite) and its en-suite wooden chalets have an almost Swiss appearance. There are comfortable public areas, a good restaurant and bar, and the view of the volcanoes is superb. *US$40/50 dbl/twin; US$60 VIP dbl; US$10 per bed in a 4-berth dorm. All rates b&b.*

Campsite near the ORTPN park office – details from ORTPN (see page 61).

If you spend the night close to the entrance to Rwanda's Volcanoes National Park prior to gorilla-tracking, you may choose to stay at the attractive and friendly Kinigi Guest House (see opposite) – which is run by the non-profit women's association ASOFERWA or Association de Solidarité des Femmes Rwandaises (Kigali office: ☏ 586394; f 584413; e asoferwa@rwanda1.com). Profits from the Guest House are ploughed back into ASOFERWA's programme.

This body was set up in August 1994 to help those left vulnerable and struggling as a result of the genocide, of whom many were women and children: widows, orphans, teenage mothers, traumatised women, victims of AIDS (through rape) and other forms of physical and moral violence, the old and handicapped, women in detention centres with their babies, and minors in re-education centres accused of genocide. All of these feature in ASOFERWA's work.

Among the multiple and urgent needs in 1994, ASOFERWA's first task was to provide shelter and other basic requirements for widows and for children being cared for by an older sibling. This was carried out within the framework of the 'Peace Villages' constructed throughout Rwanda under the national resettlement and rehousing programme. A village consists of 100 to 150 houses and a population of 600 to 1,200. Widows rehoused under this scheme were asked, in return, to take in orphans and care for them; while ASOFERWA helped them to set up income-generating schemes (agriculture, handicrafts, livestock, small kiosks or boutiques...). These also benefit the surrounding community, as do the villages' educational and medical facilities.

The work quickly expanded and international funding agencies gave support and sponsorship. Orphans have been found homes, women's groups set up, schools and training centres opened, young people given practical skills, a tannery, a modern dairy farm and a literacy training centre established. ASOFERWA also still works with mothers in prison and with minors accused of genocide, whether in prison, during their re-education or after their return to their community. In one area a mobile medical team cares for the psycho-social needs of rape victims.

The needs are still great; but speak to any of ASOFERWA's active and dedicated team and you'll be in no doubt that they're equal to the task. Someone at the Guest House will gladly give you more information. And, if you have any clothing or other practical items that you don't want to take back home with you after your stay, you could ask at Reception whether they may be useful for the people involved in any of the projects.

LAKE BURERA The largest and most beautiful of the lakes in the vicinity of Musanze, and overlooked by what is arguably the best tourist lodge anywhere in Rwanda, Burera (aka Bulera) has been almost entirely neglected by travellers until recently. With a private vehicle, however, the dirt road that loops around Burera's eastern shore makes for a superb day outing, while adventurous backpackers could happily spend several days exploring the lake using a combination of motorcycle-taxis, boats, and foot power. No budget accommodation exists anywhere on the lake shore, but the area is dotted with small villages where it shouldn't be a problem to get permission to pitch a tent, and there is talk of the Episcopal Church property on the Musangabo Peninsula being made into a guesthouse – check with the church's guesthouse in Musanze for further details.

Lake Burera is visually reminiscent of Uganda's popular Lake Bunyonyi – not too surprising when you realise that these two bodies of water lie no more than 20km apart as the crow flies. Burera's eccentric shape is defined by the incredibly

11

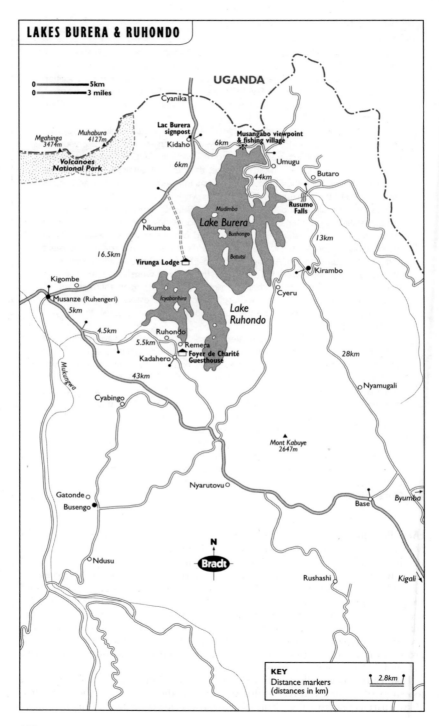

LAKES BURERA & RUHONDO

UGANDA

0 ▭▬▬ 5km
0 ▭▬▬ 3 miles

Cyanika

Mgahinga 3474m
Muhabura 4127m

Volcanoes National Park

Lac Burera signpost

Kidaho

Musangabo viewpoint & fishing village

6km

Umugu

Butaro

6km

44km

Nkumba

Mudimba

Lake Burera

Bushongo

Rusumo Falls

13km

Batutsi

16.5km

Virunga Lodge

Kirambo

Kigombe

Icyabanhira

Lake Ruhondo

Cyeru

Musanze (Ruhengeri)

5km

4.5km

Ruhondo

5.5km

Remera

Kadahero

Foyer de Charité Guesthouse

28km

Nyamugali

43km

Mukungwa

Cyabingo

Mont Kabuye 2647m

Gatonde

Busengo

Nyarutovu

Base

Byumba

N

Bradt

Ndusu

Rushashi

Kigali

KEY
Distance markers
(distances in km)

2.8km

190

steep hills that enclose it. The slopes which fall towards the lake are densely terraced and intensively cultivated: very little natural vegetation remains among the fields of plantains, potatoes, beans and other crops, while the most common tree is the Australian eucalyptus. The stunning and distinctive scenery around the lake is enhanced by the outlines of the Virunga Mountains, the closest of which towers 10km away on the western horizon.

Getting around

By road For travellers with their own transport, the circuit around the lake is straightforward enough. The road is mostly in good shape, and likely to present no problems provided that your vehicle has reasonable clearance (a 4x4 would be advisable during the rainy season). The full round trip from Musanze covers about 150km, 90km of which are on dirt, and realistically takes a minimum of five hours to complete. Better, arguably, to leave after breakfast, carry a picnic lunch, and make a day of it, stopping along the way to enjoy the views and rustic villages.

To follow the circuit, head out of Musanze along the surfaced road towards Cyanika, passing the turn-off for Virunga Lodge to your right after 16km, then continuing for another 6km to Kidaho, where you need to turn right into a dirt road signposted 'Lake Burera'. After about six relatively flat kilometres along this track, the lake becomes visible to the right: on the shore you'll see a small fishing village (so far as can be ascertained, also called Kidaho) and dozens of small boats used to ferry locals around the lake.

A few hundred metres past this village, a side road leads around the small Musangabo peninsula, where a platform (and potentially soon a guesthouse) run by the Episcopal Church offers stunning views in all directions. The church also operates a motorboat that can do the one-hour return trip to the Rusumo Falls for Rfr3,000 per party or the two-hour round trip to the bridge between Lakes Burera and Ruhondo for Rfr5,000.

The largest centre on the eastern shore of the lake is Butaro, which maps would suggest is only about 10km from Musangabo. In reality, the two are divided by a spectacular 44km stretch of road which hugs the cultivated contours about 100–200m above the lake shore. En route, the road passes through the small market village of Umugu. Butaro itself lies a couple of kilometres off the main road; about 50m from the junction, the attractive Rusumo Falls (not to be confused with their namesake on the Tanzania border) tumble over a cliff to the fields next to the lake.

After Butaro, the road veers away from the lake, and the views are few and far between, which leaves you with the option of returning the way you came (65km of which 50 are on dirt) or pushing on to complete the circuit (85km of which 41 are on dirt). Assuming that you decide to sally forth, the next main settlement you will reach, after 13km, is Kirambo (also referred to as Cyeru, the district for which it is the headquarters). Here, you can either turn left along a side road which leads to the village of Ruyange in a cultivated river valley at the southern tip of Lake Burera (a 20km round trip), or else continue straight ahead towards Base on the main Kigali–Musanze road. Base lies 28km past Kirambo, and is almost equidistant between Kigali and Musanze.

By public transport For travellers without a vehicle, the absence of public transport along parts of this circuit makes it inaccessible or challenging, depending on how you see these things. For a day trip to Burera, it is easy enough to get as far as Kidaho – any Cyanika-bound minibus-taxi can drop you there, though you will probably be expected to pay the full fare of around US$1 – from where a motorcycle-taxi to Musangabo peninsula will cost less than US$1. With an early

'We have always lived in the forest. Like my father and grandfathers, I lived from hunting and collecting in this mountain. Then the Bahutu came. They cut the forest to cultivate the land. They carried on cutting and planting until they had encircled our forest with their fields. Today, they come right up to our huts. Instead of forest, now we are surrounded by Irish potatoes!' – Gahut Gahuliro, a Mutwa born 100 years earlier on the slopes of the Virungas, talking in 1999.

The Batwa (singular Mutwa) Pygmies are the most ancient inhabitants of interlacustrine Africa, and easily distinguished from other inhabitants of the region by their unusually short stature and paler, more bronzed complexion. Semi-nomadic by inclination, small egalitarian communities of Batwa kin traditionally live in impermanent encampments of flimsy leaf huts, set in a forest clearing, which they will up and leave when food becomes scarce locally, upon the death of a community member, or when the whim takes them. In times past, the Batwa wore only a drape of animal hide or bark cloth, and had little desire to accumulate possessions – a few cooking pots, some hunting gear, and that's about it.

The traditional Batwa lifestyle is based around hunting, undertaken as a team effort by the male members of a community. In some areas, the favoured modus operandi involves part of the hunting party stringing a long net between a few trees, while the remainder advances noisily to herd small game into the net to be speared. In other areas, poisoned arrows are favoured: the hunting party will move silently along the forest floor looking for potential prey, which is shot from a distance, then they wait until it drops and if necessary deliver the final blow with a spear. Batwa men also gather wild honey, while the women gather edible plants to supplement the meat.

Today, the combined Batwa population of Rwanda, Burundi, Uganda and the eastern DRC is estimated at around 100,000 people. As recently as 2,000 years ago, however, East and Southern Africa was populated almost solely by Batwa and related hunter-gatherers, whose lifestyle differed little from that of our earliest common human ancestors. Since then, agriculturist and pastoralist settlers, through persecution or assimilation, have marginalised the region's hunter-gatherers to a few small and today mostly degraded communities living in habitats unsuitable to agriculture or pasture, such as rainforest interiors and deserts.

The initial incursions into Batwa territory were made when the first Bantu-speaking farmers settled on the forested montane escarpment of the Albertine Rift, some time before the 16th century, and set about clearing small tracts of forest for subsistence agriculture and posture. This process of deforestation was greatly accelerated in the early 20th century. By the 1930s, the few substantial tracts of highland forest remaining in the region had all been gazetted as forest reserves by the colonial authorities. In one sense, this move to protect the forests was of direct benefit to the Batwa, since it ensured that what little remained of them would not be lost to agriculture. But the legal status of the Batwa was altered to their detriment – true, they were still permitted to hunt and forage within the reserves, but, where formerly these forests had been recognised as Batwa communal land, they were now government property.

Another 50 years would pass before the Batwa were faced with the full ramifications of having lost all legal entitlement to their ancestral lands in the colonial era. In the 1970s and 1980s, the Batwa communities resident in most of the region's conservation areas were evicted, a move backed by international donors who also insisted that hunting and other forest harvesting – the traditional subsistence activities of the Batwa – should be criminalised. Adding insult to injury, while compensation was awarded to non-Batwa farmers who had settled within protected areas after they were gazetted and illegally cleared forest to make way for cultivation, the evicted Batwa received compensation only if they had destroyed part of the forest reserve in a similar manner.

In the early 1990s, Rwanda's last forest-dwelling Batwa were evicted from the Gishwati Forest Reserve to make way for a World Bank project intended to protect the natural forest. The World Bank later concluded that the project had failed, with more than half of the original forest having been cleared for pasture prior to 1994, and it admitted that the treatment of indigenous peoples had been 'highly unsatisfactory'. Since 1998, returned refugees have been settled in the remaining forest, resulting in further destruction, but the former Batwa residents of Gishwati are mostly still landless.

Today, more than 40% of Batwa households in Rwanda are landless, and none has legal access to the forest on which their traditional livelihood depends. Indeed, most Batwa now eke out a marginal living from casual wage labour on other peoples' farms, porterage, simple craftwork (particularly pottery), and singing and dancing at festivals – many are in essence forced to live as beggars. Furthermore, with Batwa men no longer able to fulfil their traditional roles as hunters and providers, many have turned to alcohol and drug (or spousal) abuse, leading to the imminent collapse of Batwa cultural values.

Locally, the Batwa are viewed not with sympathy, but rather as objects of ridicule. The extent of local prejudice against them can be garnered from a set of interviews posted on the Ugandan website www.edrisa.org. The Batwa, report some of their Bakiga neighbours: 'smoke marijuana … like alcohol … drink too much … make noise all night long … eat too much food … cannot grow their own food and crops … depend on hunting and begging … don't care about their children … the man makes love to his wife while the children sleep on their side' – a collection of circumstantially induced half-truths and outright fallacies that make the Batwa come across as the debauched survivors of a dysfunctional hippie commune!

Prejudice against the Batwa is not confined to their immediate neighbours. The 1997 edition of Richard Nzita's otherwise commendable *People and Cultures of Uganda* contrives, in the space of two pages, to characterise the pygmoid peoples of Uganda as beggars, crop raiders and pottery thieves – even cannibals! Conservationists and the Western media, meanwhile, persistently stigmatise the Batwa as gorilla hunters and poachers – this despite the strong taboo against killing or eating gorillas that informs every known Batwa community. Almost certainly, any gorilla hunting that might be undertaken by the Batwa today will have been instigated by outsiders.

This much is incontestable: The Batwa and their hunter-gatherer ancestors have inhabited the forests of the Albertine Rift for countless millennia. Their traditional lifestyle places no rigorous demands on the forest and could be cited as a model of that professed holy grail of modern conservationists: the sustainable use of natural resources. The Batwa were not major participants in the deforestation of the region, but they have certainly been the main human victims of this loss. And Batwa and gorillas cohabited the same forests for many millennia prior to their futures both being imperilled by identical external causes in the 20th century. As Jerome Lewis writes: 'They and their way of life are entitled to as much consideration and respect as other ways of life. There was and is nothing to be condemned in forest nomadism … The Batwa … used the environment without destroying or seriously damaging it. It is only through their long-term custody of the area that later comers have good land to use.'

Quotes from Lewis and Gahuliro are sourced from Jerome Lewis's exemplary report *Batwa Pygmies of the Great Lakes Region*, downloadable at www.minorityrights.org/admin/Download/Pdf/Batwa%2520Report.pdf.

start, you should also have time to catch a boat-taxi from the fishing village next to the peninsula to the lake shore below Butaro and the Rusumo Falls, and to return the same way. The boat-taxi takes 30–60 minutes in either direction, and costs around US$1.25. It should also be straightforward and affordable to hire a boat privately, either to go to the falls or else just to explore the lake.

Beryl Hutchison writes: 'I made the journey to Lake Burera by minibus and got to the peninsula by bicycle taxi. It was such a beautiful and tranquil place. There were no motorised boats so I hired a pirogue. I was told that the journey to Rusumo Falls takes about four hours and although the boatman was willing I decided against it. Instead we had a row round the lake and then got out of the pirogue and walked through the shambas to the Ugandan border.'

Lake Burera could also be explored more extensively by boat, an option suitable only for those with a pioneering spirit. The obvious place to start a trip of this sort would be Musangabo, though boats are the main form of transport throughout the area, so it should be easy enough to hire a boat and paddler anywhere. In addition to Rusumo Falls, there are at least four large islands in the southern half of the lake: Mudimba, Munanira, Bushongo and Batutsi. In theory, it should be possible to boat to the south of Lake Burera, hike across the narrow strip of hilly terrain that separates it from Lake Ruhondo, and then pick up another boat to the Foyer de Charité on the southern shore of that lake (see *Lake Ruhondo* below). We've never heard of a traveller who attempted this, so drop us a line to let us know how it goes!

On foot Keen walkers might also think about exploring the area over a few days. I've not heard of anybody doing this, so it would be uncharted territory, and would probably be practical only if you have a tent and are prepared to ask permission to camp at the many villages and homesteads along the way. It would probably be advisable to carry some food (though fish and potatoes should be easy to buy along the way). It is difficult to imagine that any serious security concerns are attached to hiking in this Uganda border area; you'll come across loads of local pedestrians for company, and travellers are still something of a novelty in this rural region.

The road to the east of the lake can effectively be viewed as an unusually wide hiking trail: it offers great views the whole way, is used by very few vehicles, and follows the contours for most of its length. The most beautiful stretch for hiking is the 44km between Musangabo and Butaro (which can also be covered by boat), and you would be forced to walk the 13km between Butaro and Kirambo. From Kirambo, there is a limited amount of public transport to Base, where it is easy to find a lift on to Musanze or Kigali.

⌂ Where to stay

⌂ **Virunga Lodge** (8 rooms) ☎ 502452 or (UK) +44 0870 8708480; m 08 536908; e salesrw@volcanoessafaris.com or salesuk@volcanoessafaris.com; www.volcanoessafaris.com; ✣ S 01°26.694, E 029°44.517. Boasting one of the most stunning locations in Africa, this recently opened lodge lies on a 2,175m hilltop overlooking Lakes Burera and Ruhondo to the southeast and with views stretching northwest to embrace four of the Virunga Volcanoes – a panoramic overview of this magnificent volcanic landscape. If you're after organic bush chic rather than transatlantic luxury, this is also arguably the finest lodge anywhere in Rwanda: accommodation in spacious stone-and-wood chalets with 2 dbl beds each, superb views from the private verandas, and an eco-friendly ethos underscored by the use of solar power and biodegradable toilets. This is an excellent base for gorilla tracking, with the one caveat being that the distance from Kinigi enforces a very early start – but the staff are used to this and organise early wake-up calls, showers and b/fast as a matter of course. The lodge lies about 30 mins' drive from Musanze, turning right off the Cyanika Road after 16km at Nyaragondo junction (✣ S 01°25.073, E 029°43.509). US$465/700 sgl/dbl inc all meals, alcoholic and non-alcoholic drinks, laundry, massage, activities around the lodge and all government taxes.

A NEW VERSION OF AN ANCIENT TALE None could shoot an arrow so far and straight as Ryangombe, the greatest warrior and hunter of his time. None could run so fast or stalk so silently. The sun dimmed its rays in respect when he was taking aim and the rain paused as he pursued his quarry. He defended the forest against farmers who would fell trees to make space for their crops, and the branches murmured their thanks as he rested in their shade. Women competed for his favours, opponents feared him, storytellers throughout the realm extolled his exploits and his name was lauded far and wide. So powerful was Ryangombe that he challenged even the mighty King Ruganzu, who ruled Rwanda almost seven centuries ago.

Ryangombe's favourite hunting-ground was the Buhanga Forest, in the volcano foothills not far from Musanze: a place of ancient trees, dark ravines and thrusting rocks, where sunlight throws patterns on the leafy floor and butterflies bask on mossy logs. Birds swoop and perch among the branches and small creatures scuttle in the undergrowth. In this forest is the sacred pool called *Gihanga*, empty in the rainy season but full to overflowing in the dry season, where Rwanda's early monarchs would come to bathe and drink the water.

It was on a dark, dark day here in the Buhanga Forest that Ryangombe faced his final opponent – no king or fellow warrior but a wild and angry buffalo, which burst upon him from the shelter of the trees. Its horns tore into his flesh and the forest floor was reddened by his blood. His companions, seeing their hero slain and wishing to be at his side in the higher world, taunted the buffalo until it gored them also and trampled their limbs with its hooves. The bodies of the young men lay beneath the great tree *Umuvumu*, still in the forest today, until Imana raised them to their final home on the slopes of Karisimbi. If you climb the mountain nowadays, you may – if your spirit is fair and you know how to listen with your heart – still hear their voices carried on the breeze as they talk and laugh together.

After Ryangombe's death, traditional healers from throughout the Great Lakes region would journey to the spot in Buhanga Forest where he fell. From the trees in that place they would take a branch back to their homelands, and use it as the base to build a shrine – *Ingoro* – from which to worship him and send prayers to their gods.

Sit quietly in Buhanga Forest today and you can sense its ancient history. Kings and healers and legendary heroes have walked its paths and felt its power. And – who knows – that sudden rustle that you hear behind you may even be the soft and stealthy footfall of Ryangombe as he stalks some ghostly prey.

LAKE RUHONDO Separated from Lake Burera by a 1km-wide strip of land (thought to be an ancient lava flow from Mount Sabinyo), Lake Ruhondo is, like the more northerly lake, an erratically shaped body of water whose shore follows the contours of the tall, steep hills that characterise this part of Rwanda. In common with Lake Burera, Ruhondo's shores are densely cultivated, and little natural vegetation remains, but it is nevertheless a very beautiful spot, offering dramatic views across the water to the volcanically formed cones of the Virunga Mountains looming on the horizon. Ruhondo is also an easy target for an overnight excursion, since good accommodation is available – though availability should be confirmed in advance.

The lake is most accessible from the southwest, where the Foyer de Charité guesthouse has a superb location on a hilltop overlooking the lake, with sweeping views across to the volcanoes in the northwest, and potentially stupendous sunsets. Several footpaths lead down the steep slopes below the mission to the

Traditionally the most popular spirit among the Bakiga of southwest Uganda and neighbouring parts of Rwanda is that of a respected rainmaker called Nyabingi, who – possibly in the mid to late 18th century – was murdered by a rival medium at her home in Mukante in the Bufundi Hills of the Rwanda-Uganda border area. After the death of Nyabingi, legend has it, her attendants were visited by numerous ill or barren Bakiga villagers, who would make sacrifices to the late rainmaker's spirit, which would cure their ailment if it approved of the items offered. Over subsequent decades, the spirit possessed a succession of Bakiga mediums, mostly but not always women, who would be blessed with Nyabinga's powers of healing, rainmaking and curing infertility.

Several Nyabingi mediums incited local uprisings against colonialism. The first such rebel was Queen Muhumusa, of mysterious origin, but possibly a former wife of the late Rwandan King Rwabuguri Kigeri. In 1909, Muhumusa was imprisoned by the German authorities in Rwanda after threatening that her son Ndungutse would capture the throne and boot the colonists out of his kingdom. Upon her release in 1911, the Queen crossed the border into Uganda and settled at Ihanga Hill near Bubale, 12km from present-day Kabale on the Kisoro Road. She then announced that she had come in search of a cave wherein was secured a sacred drum which, she claimed, would call up a limitless stream of calves when beaten by her and her son. As the news of the magic drum spread though Kigezi, hundreds of young Bakiga men joined in the quest for its location, hoping for a share of the spoils, and Muhumusa received wide support from local chiefs.

The Christian Muganda chiefs installed by the British in southwest Uganda regarded the growing cult surrounding Muhumusa to be evil and insurrectionist, and refused to have anything to do with it. This angered Muhumusa, who attacked the home of one such chief, burning it to the ground, killing several people, and threatening to impale her victim on a sharpened pole, along with any other disrespectful chiefs she could capture. The colonial authorities responded to this affront by attacking Muhumusa's residence with 50 troops and a cannon. At least 40 of the medium's followers were killed on the spot and buried in a mass grave, and several more died of wounds after fleeing the battle site. Muhumusa was captured and imprisoned in Mbarara, where she remained until her death in 1945. The British authorities then proceeded to criminalise the Nyabingi cult through the Witchcraft Ordinance of 1912.

lake shore, a knee-crunching descent and lung-wrenching ascent. At the lake, it is easy to negotiate a fee to take a pirogue to one of the islands, or to the hydro-electric plant on the opposite shore, where a small waterfall connects Lake Ruhondo with Lake Burera.

Getting around The best route to the Foyer de Charité starts on the main Kigali road about 5km south of Musanze. Coming from Musanze, you need to turn left along a dirt road signposted for Remera which initially leads through a marshy area dotted with traditional brickmaking urns, before following a cultivated river valley. After 2.8km, take a left fork, then almost 2km after that turn right to cross a bridge over the river. The road is flat until this point, but now it starts to ascend gently, with the lake becoming visible to the left about 2.5km past the bridge. Several footpaths lead from this viewpoint to the lake shore, an easier ascent than the one from the Foyer de Charité. Beyond the viewpoint, the road continues to climb for 3km to the village of Kadahero, where a left turn leads after about 200m to the mission.

This is all straightforward enough provided that you have a vehicle, ideally a 4x4, and that – if driving along the tar from Kigali – you don't inadvertently take

In order to help win over local converts, the earliest Christian missionaries to Rwanda and southwest Uganda used words associated with the Nyabingi cult in their sermons and descriptions of Christian rituals. The Virgin Mary was portrayed as a spiritual icon similar to but more powerful than Nyabingi, and many locals adopted the Mother of Jesus as a substitute for the traditional spirit associated with healing and fertility. By the 1930s, the Nyabingi cult, if not completely dead, had gone so far underground as to be undetectable – while it became increasingly common for locals to claim having seen the Virgin Mary at sites of worship formerly associated with Nyabingi.

At least one former Nyabingi shrine has more recently been adopted by a nominally Christian cult. The Nyabugoto Caves near the small town of Kunungu in southwest Uganda were in times past occupied by a renowned medium who regularly cured barren Bakiga women. In the late 1970s, it was reported that a local woman called Blandina Buzigye witnessed a large rock formation in this cave transform into the Virgin Mary before her eyes. It was in the same Ugandan cave, ten years later, that a former prostitute called Credonia Mwerinde founded a fertility cult that mutated into the doomsday movement whose entire membership was locked inside a blazing church by the leaders in a shocking massacre that attracted world headlines in March 2000.

Oddly enough, the term Nyabingi found its way across the Atlantic to Jamaica, where admirers of the rebellious Queen Muhumusa incorporated what are known as nyabinghi chants into their celebrations. Sometimes abbreviated to bhingi, the chants and dances were originally performed to invoke 'death to the black or white oppressors' but today they are purely ceremonial. Three differently pitched drums are used to create the nyabinghi beat, which – popularised in the late 1950s by the recording artist Count Ossie – has been a huge rhythmic influence on better-known secular Jamaican genres such as ska and reggae. Nyabinghi is also the name of a fundamentalist but strictly pacifist Rastafarian cult which regards the late Ethiopian emperor Haile Selassie as having been an earthly incarnation of God. Indeed, according to some Rastafarian cultists in Jamaica, the neglected Nyabingi spirit abandoned its home in the Rwanda-Uganda border area in 1937 and relocated to Ethiopia, where it took possession of Haile Selassie during the Italian Occupation. The present whereabouts of the spirit is unknown.

an earlier road signposted for Remera (this road does lead to the mission, but it's longer and rougher). There is no public transport, however, and hitching might prove to be frustrating. One option would be to catch public transport towards Musanze as far as the turn-off to Remera, then to walk the final 10km to the mission (the last 6km would be steep going with a rucksack). The alternative is to hire a motorcycle-taxi from Musanze – the going rate is around Rfr1,500–2,000 one-way – and arrange to be collected at a specified time.

Where to stay

Foyer de Charité (45 rooms) ↘ 547024; m 08 510659; f 547025; e vdprw@yahoo.fr. Established as a religious retreat in 1968, this mission was renovated in 1995 after it had been damaged during the genocide, and, although it remains first and foremost a religious retreat, lay visitors are very welcome most of the time. Comfortable guest rooms with wash basins are available, as are communal solar-heated showers, inexpensive and filling meals, and cold beers and sodas. There is little in the way of formal entertainment (the beautiful singing at evening mass in the chapel might qualify I suppose), but it's a lovely place to relax for a couple of days, and there's plenty of room for exploration on the surrounding roads. It is essential to make contact in advance, as the mission closes to lay visitors for special religious events – which probably add up to around 100 days annually. *Room rates are*

negotiable, but expect to pay around
Rfr6,000/9,000 sgl/dbl.

⌂ **Homestay** By the time you read this, it's

possible that Amahoro Tours (see page 187) will
have organised homestay facilities on an island in
Lake Ruhondo.

MUSANZE CAVE AND NATURAL BRIDGE
The impressive Musanze Cave lies in the grounds of a school about 2km from the town centre off the Gisenyi road. The main cave, reportedly 2km long, has an entrance the size of a cathedral, and is home to an impressive bat colony. The large ditch out of which the cave opens is littered with pockmarked black volcanic rubble, and at the opposite end there is a natural bridge which was formed by a lava flow from one of the Virunga volcanoes.

Legend has it that Musanze Cave was created by a local king, and that it has been used as a refuge on several occasions in history. There are plans to develop it as a tourist attraction – but meanwhile it's advisable not to enter. It was the site of a massacre during the genocide; local people consider it a tomb and don't take kindly to tourists scrambling about inside. Please respect this: either view from a distance or go with a local guide.

To get to Musanze Cave from the town, follow Avenue du 5 Juillet past the Hotel Muhabura towards Gisenyi. Just short of 2km from the town centre, you'll see the large steel *Entrepots Opravia Musanze* to your left. Turn right directly opposite this building, following a curved dirt track which after about 100m leads to a football field and school. The cave lies in a ditch on the opposite side of the football field.

LAKE KARAGO
This small lake is less impressive than the two larger lakes which lie to the east of Musanze, but it is also a lot more accessible on public transport, and sufficiently attractive that it served for years as the site of the president of Rwanda's holiday home. Lake Karago makes for a pleasant rustic excursion from Musanze, the main attraction being the characteristically mountainous Rwandan landscape around the lake and a set of rapids along the river that runs into the lake. There were also quite a few birds around when we visited, notably pelicans and herons.

Lake Karago lies 1.5km from Mukamiira, a small junction town on the main road between Musanze and Gisenyi. Regular *matatus* cover the 20km between Musanze and Mukamiira, where you need to turn left at the main junction towards Ngororero. The walk from Mukamiira to the first viewpoint over the lake takes about 15 minutes. From here, several footpaths lead to the shore, a 10–20-minute descent, depending on how muddy it is and which path you use.

Although Lake Karago can easily be visited as a day trip out of Musanze, there is a welcoming but very basic guesthouse in Mukamiira should you feel moved to spend the night. It is signposted *Bar Restaurant Chambres*, and lies alongside the Gisenyi road about 500 from the Ngororero junction. Single rooms cost US$2.50 (a fair reflection of the quality of the accommodation); hot bucket showers are provided, meals are prepared to order, and the fridge is stocked high with beers and sodas.

For the continuation of the road after Lake Karago, see page 179.

12

Volcanoes National Park

This 160km² national park (in French *Parc des Volcans*) protects the Rwandan sector of the Virunga Mountains, a range of six extinct and three active volcanoes which straddles the borders with Uganda and the DRC. The Volcanoes Park is part of a contiguous 433km² trans-frontier conservation unit that also includes the Virungas National Park and Mgahinga National Park, which protect the DRC and Ugandan sectors of the Virungas respectively. The three national parks are managed separately today (that's if the word 'managed' can be applied to any park in the DRC at the time of writing). Prior to 1960, however, the Volcanoes and Virungas Parks together formed the Albert National Park.

Under Belgian colonisation, the Albert National Park was established by the decree of 21 April 1925, in the triangle (considered a gorilla sanctuary) formed by the Karisimbi, Mikeno and Visoke volcanoes. At the time of its creation it was the first national park in Africa to be known as such. The *Institut du Parc National Albert* was created by decree on 9 July 1929. A further decree on 12 November 1935 determined the final boundaries of the Albert National Park, then covering 809,000ha. About 8% of the park lay in what is now Rwanda and today constitutes the Volcanoes National Park, while the rest was in the Congo. At the time of independence, Rwanda's new leaders confirmed that they would maintain the park (the gorillas were already well known internationally), despite the pressing problem of overpopulation.

Ranging in altitude from 2,400m to 4,507m, the Volcanoes National Park is dominated by the string of volcanoes after which it is named. This chain of steep, tall, free-standing mountains, linked by fertile saddles which were formed by solidified lava flows, is one of the most stirring and memorable sights in East Africa. The tallest mountain in the chain, and the most westerly part of the national park, is Karisimbi (4,507m) on the border with the DRC. Moving eastwards, the other main peaks within the national park are Visoke (aka Bisoke) on the DRC border; Sabinyo at the juncture of Rwanda, Uganda and the DRC; and Gahinga (aka Mgahinga) and Muhabura (aka Muhavura) on the Uganda border.

The Volcanoes National Park is best known to the outside world as the place where, for almost 20 years, the American primatologist Dian Fossey undertook her pioneering studies of mountain gorilla behaviour. It is largely thanks to Fossey's single-mindedness that poaching was curtailed while there were still some gorillas to save. For her dedication, Fossey would pay the ultimate price: her brutal – and still unsolved – murder at the Karisoke Research Centre in December 1985 is generally thought to have been the work of one of the many poachers with whom she crossed swords in her efforts to save her gorillas.

Three years after her death, Fossey's life work was exposed to a mass audience with the release of *Gorillas in the Mist*, a cinematic account of her life filmed on location in the Volcanoes Park. *Gorillas in the Mist* drew global attention to the plight of the mountain gorilla, and generated unprecedented interest in the gorilla tourism programme that had been established in the park some ten years earlier. In 1990, the

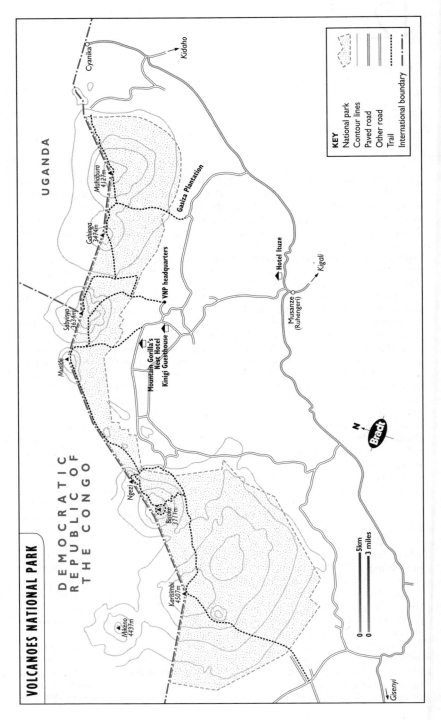

VOLCANOES NATIONAL PARK

DEMOCRATIC
REPUBLIC OF
THE CONGO

UGANDA

Cyanika

Kidaho

Muhabura
4127m

Gasiza Plantation

Gahinga
3474m

Sabyinyo
3634m

VNP headquarters

Hotel Ituze

Musanze
(Ruhengeri)

Kigali

Mountain Gorilla's
Nest Hotel
Kinigi Guesthouse

Muside

Ngezi

Bisoke
3711m

Karisimbi
4507m

Mikeno
4437m

Gisenyi

N

KEY
National park
Contour lines
Paved road
Other road
Trail
International boundary

5km
3 miles
0
0

Volcanoes Park was the best organised and most popular gorilla sanctuary in Africa, and gorilla tourism was probably Rwanda's leading earner of tourist revenue.

The wheels came off in February 1992, when the park headquarters were attacked, two park employees were killed, and the research centre established by Dian Fossey had to be evacuated. The park reopened to tourism in June 1993, but it was evacuated in April 1994 because of the genocide. In late 1995, it once again reopened to tourism, only to close again a few months later. Gorilla tracking was finally resumed on a permanent basis in July 1999, since when the number of tourists visiting the Virungas has increased rapidly. More details of gorillas and gorilla-tracking follow later in this section.

Gorillas and golden monkeys aside, primates are poorly represented by comparison with other forests in Rwanda and western Uganda. Little information is available regarding the current status of other large mammals, but 70-plus species have been recorded in Uganda's neighbouring Mgahinga National Park, most of which probably also occur in the larger Rwanda section of the Virungas. Elephant and buffalo are still quite common, judging by the amount of spoor encountered on forest trails, but are very timid and infrequently observed. Also present are giant forest hog, bushpig, bushbuck, black-fronted duiker, spotted hyena, and several varieties of small predator. Recent extinctions, probably as a result of deforestation, include the massive yellow-backed duiker and leopard.

A bird checklist for Volcanoes National Park compiled in 1980 totalled 180 species. About 15 previously unrecorded species were noted during a 2004 biodiversity survey, but it is possible that several other forest specialists have vanished since 1980. A local speciality is the vulnerable swamp-dwelling Grauer's rush warbler, while at least 16 Albertine Rift endemics are present, including handsome francolin, Ruwenzori turaco, Ruwenzori double-collared sunbird, Ruwenzori batis, strange weaver, dusky crimson-wing, collared apalis, red-faced woodland warbler and Archer's ground robin.

Gorilla tracking remains the most popular activity here, with a total of up to 40 permits issued daily, eight for each of the five habituated troops. But Volcanoes National Park is not just about mountain gorillas. Tourists who previously came for just one night can now stay for four or five and still not run out of things to do. Trekking, walking and climbing are now well organised, from a two-day ascent of Karisimbi to a non-strenuous nature walk to a cluster of crater lakes, but the most exciting innovation is that tourists can now visit a habituated troop of the near-endemic golden monkey.

GETTING THERE AND AWAY

The normal base for visiting the Volcanoes Park is Musanze (formerly Ruhengeri), which can easily be reached on public transport from Gisenyi, Kigali or Uganda. With a private vehicle, it is possible to drive to Musanze from Gisenyi or Kigali on the day you track (you need to be at the ORTPN office in Kinigi, by the park entrance, by 07.00), but this isn't a reliable option using public transport. There is no public transport between Musanze and the park headquarters at Kinigi. Details of arranging transport to tie in with gorilla-tracking are included under the gorilla-tracking section on page 204.

WHERE TO STAY AND EAT

There is no accommodation within the national park and overnight camping is forbidden. Check with ORTPN about camping possibilities nearby. For those on

Straddling the borders of Uganda, Rwanda and the DRC, the Virungas are not a mountain range as such, but a chain of isolated freestanding volcanic cones strung along a fault line associated with the same geological process that formed the Rift Valley. Sometimes also referred to as the Birunga or Bufumbira Mountains, the chain comprises six inactive and three active volcanoes, all of which exceed 3,000m in altitude – the tallest being Karisimbi (4,507m), Mikeno (4,437m) and Muhabura (4,127m).

The names of the individual mountains in the Virunga chain reflect local perceptions. Sabinyo translates as 'old man's teeth' in reference to the jagged rim of what is probably the most ancient and weathered of the eight volcanoes. Muhabura is 'the guide', and anecdotes collected by the first Europeans to visit the area suggest that its perfect cone, topped today by a small crater lake, still glowed at night as recently as the early 19th century. Gahinga is variously translated as meaning 'pile of stones' or 'the hoe', the former a reference to its relatively small size, the latter to the breach on its flank. Of the other volcanoes that lie partially within Rwanda, Karisimbi – which occasionally sports a small cap of snow – is named for the colour of a cowry shell, while Visoke simply means watering hole, in reference to the crater lake near its peak.

The vegetation zones of the Virungas correspond closely to those of other large East African mountains, albeit that much of the Afro-montane forest below the 2,500m contour has been sacrificed to cultivation. Moist broad-leaved semi-deciduous forest dominates up until the 2,800m contour, whilst the slopes at altitudes of 2,800–3,200m, where an average annual rainfall of 2,000mm is typical, support bamboo forest interspersed with stands of tall hagenia woodland. At higher altitudes, the cover of Afro-alpine moorland, grassland and marsh is studded with giant Lobelia, Senecios and other outsized plants similar to those found on Kilimanjaro and the Ruwenzori. Above 3,600m, biodiversity levels are very low and the dominant vegetation consists of a fragile community of grasses, mosses and lichens. A total of 1,265 plant species identified across the range to date includes at least 120 that are endemic to the Albertine Rift.

The most famous denizen of the Virungas is the mountain gorilla, which inhabits all six of the extinct or dormant volcanoes, but not – for obvious reasons – the more active ones. The Virungas also form the main stronghold for the endangered golden monkey, possibly the last one now that their only other confirmed haunt, the more southerly Gishwati Forest, has been cleared to cover less than 1% of its original extent. Recent estimates based on dung surveys tentatively place the buffalo population at close to 1,000, while the total number of elephants might be anything from 20 to 100. Other typical highland forest species include yellow-backed duiker, bushbuck and giant forest

a restricted budget, the best option is to overnight in Musanze (see page 179), but smarter and more convenient accommodation is available near the park headquarters at Kinigi (see page 188) or at the superior but more distant Virunga Lodge overlooking Lake Burera (see page 194). It is also possible to stay in Gisenyi or even Kigali the night before you trek, but this is not so realistic as it used to be now that the assembly time has shifted from 08.00 to 07.00 – you'd need to allow at least two hours for the drive from Kigali and 90 minutes from Gisenyi, and would most likely be late in the event of a breakdown or puncture.

NON-GORILLA ATTRACTIONS

Several non-gorilla-related hikes are now offered to visitors. The ascent of **Karisimbi** is a two-day excursion costing US$150; ORTPN will provide guides but trekkers should have suitable clothing and camping equipment. A shorter hog. The mountains' avifauna is comparatively poorly known, as evidenced by sightings of 36 previously unrecorded species during a cross-border biodiversity study undertaken in early 2004, bringing the total checklist for the Virungas to 294, including 20 Albertine Rift endemics.

Still in their geological infancy, none of the Virunga Mountains is more than two million years old and two of the cones remain highly active. The most dramatic volcanic explosion of historical times was the 1977 eruption of the 3,465m Mount Nyiragongo in the DRC, about 20km north of the Lake Kivu port of Goma. During this eruption, a lava lake that had formed in the volcano's main crater back in 1894 drained in less than one hour, emitting streams of molten lava that flowed at a rate of up to 60km per hour, killing an estimated 2,000 people and terminating only 500m from Goma Airport.

In 1994, a new lake of lava started to accumulate within the main crater of Nyiragongo, leading to another highly destructive eruption on 17 January 2002. Lava flowed down the southern and eastern flanks of the volcano into Goma itself, killing at least 50 people. Goma was evacuated, and an estimated 450,000 people crossed into the nearby Rwandan towns of Gisenyi and Musanze for temporary refuge. Three days later, when the first evacuees returned, it transpired that about a quarter of the town – including large parts of the commercial and residential centre – had been engulfed by the lava, leaving 12,000 families homeless. The lava lake in Nyiragongo's crater remains active, with a diameter of around 50m, and, although there has been no subsequent eruption, the crater rim still glows menacingly above Gisenyi's nocturnal skyline.

Only 15km northwest of Nyiragongo stands the 3,058m Mount Nyamuragira, which also erupted in January 2002. Nyamuragira is probably the most active volcano on the African mainland, with 34 eruptions recorded since 1882, though only the 1912–1913 incidence resulted in any fatalities. Nyamuragira most recently blew its top on 26 July 2002, spewing lava high into the air, along with a large plume of ash and sulphur dioxide, and destroying large tracts of cultivated land and forest.

It is perhaps worth noting that these temperamental Congolese volcanoes pose no threat to visitors to the mountain gorillas, as the relevant cones are all dormant or extinct. That might change one day: there is a tradition among the Bafumbira people that the fiery sprits inhabiting the crater of Nyamuragira will eventually relocate to Muhabura, reducing both the mountain and its surrounds to ash. Another Bafumbira custom has it that the crater lake atop Mount Muhabura is inhabited by a powerful snake spirit called Indyoka, which lives on a bed of gold and need only raise its head to bring rain to the surrounding countryside.

option (costing US$50) is the ascent of **Mount Visoke** to its crater lake at 3,711m; the upward climb takes about two hours. For the less energetic, walks of about two and a half hours (US$30) to the nearer **crater lakes** and in the forest are thoroughly enjoyable and will be particularly rewarding to birdwatchers!

It is also possible to visit **Dian Fossey's tomb** and the adjacent gorilla cemetery at the former Karisoke Research Camp. This trek costs US$50 per person and involves a 30-minute drive from the park headquarters to the trailhead then a 10-minute stroll to the park boundary. From here, the ascent through the forest takes anything from 90 minutes to three hours, depending on your fitness and how often you stop to enjoy the scenery, while the descent takes 1–2 hours. Fossey's old living quarter – which she nicknamed the mausoleum – is now a ruin, while several other landmarks in the camp are signposted.

In addition to the fees listed above, all activities attract a daily park entrance fee of US$25. All arrangements for these activities can be made through the ORTPN

12

offices, whether in Kigali, Musanze or Kinigi (if you want to pay by MasterCard, that can only be done in Kigali). Note that all hikes depart from the park headquarters at Kinigi at around 07.30 (check-in time 07.00), the same departure time as for gorilla tracking, which means that visitors can undertake only one activity per day within the park.

GORILLA TRACKING

Tracking mountain gorillas in the Virungas is a peerless wildlife experience, and one of Africa's indisputable travel highlights. It is difficult to describe the simple exhilaration attached to first setting eyes on a wild mountain gorilla. These are enormous animals: the silverbacks weigh about three times as much as the average man, and their bulk is exaggerated by a shaggily luxuriant coat. And yet despite their fearsome size and appearance, gorillas are remarkably peaceable creatures, certainly by comparison with most primates – gorilla-tracking would be a considerably more dangerous pursuit if these gentle giants had the temperament of vervet monkeys, say, or baboons (or, for that matter, humans).

More impressive even than the gorillas' size and bearing is their unfathomable attitude to their daily human visitors, which differs greatly from that of any other wild animal. Anthropomorphic as it might sound, almost everybody who visits the gorillas experiences an almost mystical sense of recognition: we regularly had one of the gorillas break off from chomping on bamboo to study us, its soft brown eyes staring deeply into ours, as if seeking out some sort of connection.

Equally fascinating is the extent to which the gorillas try to interact with their visitors, often approaching them, and occasionally touching one of the guides in apparent recognition and greeting as they walk past. A photographic tripod raised considerable curiosity in several of the youngsters and a couple of the adults – one large female walked up to the tripod, stared ponderously into the lens, then wandered back off evidently satisfied. It is almost as if the gorillas recognise their daily visitors as a troop of fellow apes, but one too passive to pose any threat – often a youngster will put on a chest-beating display as it walks past tourists, safe in the knowledge that they'll accept its dominance: something it would never do to an adult gorilla. (It should be noted here that close contact with humans can expose gorillas to fatal diseases, for which reason the guides try to keep their tourists at least 5m away – but the reality is that there is little anybody can do to stop the gorillas from flouting rules of which they are unaware.)

The magical hour with the gorillas is relatively expensive and getting there – have no illusions – can be hard work. The hike up to the mountain gorillas' preferred habitat of bamboo forest involves a combination of steep slopes, dense vegetation, slippery underfoot conditions after rain, and high altitude. For all that, the more accessible gorilla groups can be visited by reasonably fit adults of any age, and in 20 years of African travel we have yet to meet anybody who has gone gorilla-tracking and regretted the financial or physical expense.

PERMITS Eight permits per day are issued for each of the five habituated groups in the Volcanoes Park. At the time of writing, three habituated groups stay within tracking range on a permanent basis, while two others spend most of their time in the Volcanoes Park but occasionally cross the border into Uganda or the DRC. This means that up to 40 permits can be issued daily, depending on the movement of the gorillas. Trackers are not allocated a specific group in advance but the guides make a concerted effort to match people to a group based on their apparent fitness – Sabinyo and Group Thirteen being the least demanding hikes and Susa the most challenging.

The little-known golden monkey *Cercopithecus kandti* (sometimes treated as a distinctive race of the more widespread blue monkey *C. mitis*) is listed as 'endangered' by the World Conservation Union, so it's a rare treat for visitors to be able to view a newly habituated group of about 15 in the Volcanoes National Park. Visits can be arranged through any ORTPN office; they last for one hour and are for a maximum of six people; the cost is US$75 (plus a US$25 park entrance fee).

Endemic to the Albertine Rift, the golden monkey is characterised by a bright orange-gold body, cheeks and tail, contrasting with its black limbs, crown and tail-end. It was previously found in the Gishwati Forest, which since the return of the post-genocide refugees has become too degraded; and there may be a small population somewhere in the Nyungwe Forest; but it is thought that the only viable population is on the Virunga volcanoes. Within this restricted range it is the numerically dominant primate, and reasonably common – the number of individuals protected within Volcanoes National Park is a matter of conjecture, but a 2003 survey estimated a population of 3–4,000 in its smaller neighbour, Uganda's Mgahinga National Park.

In early 2002, ORTPN approached the Dian Fossey Gorilla Fund International (DFGFI) to discuss the possibility of habituating the golden monkeys for purposes of tourism. The DFGFI welcomed the chance to learn more about this little-studied monkey and to help promote tourism in the park. First, two possible groups were selected for habituation – they are in areas of the park that would be suitable as part of a nature trail for tourists. Field assistants were then trained in habituation and data collection techniques, and work could begin.

The first few months were terribly frustrating. Dense vegetation (bamboo) made approaching the groups very difficult and the monkeys would flee at the first sight of humans. In time, the researchers were able to refine their techniques and determine at what time of day the monkeys were most active, which made them easier to locate. Gradually the monkeys came to accept the presence of the observers for longer and longer periods. Meanwhile the researchers were gathering more and more data about their diet, habitat use, social structure and behavioural ecology, all of which must be understood if the project is to succeed in the long term.

The first group was 'opened to the public' in summer 2003 and has delighted visitors. It's a very different experience from gorilla-viewing, where the huge creatures are entirely visible as they react and interact; the golden monkeys in their bamboo thicket are smaller, nimbler and can be harder to spot. However, they will become bolder with time, and eventually the second (and larger) group should also be habituated for tourism. The benefits of this project are mutual; for tourists, the pleasure of observing a rare species of monkey; for researchers, the satisfaction of learning more about a little-known species; and for the endangered golden monkeys, far less threat of extinction, as they are studied, protected and better understood.

A gorilla-tracking permit effectively costs US$375 (including the US$25 park entrance fee). It can be bought in advance through the ORTPN office in Kigali or tour operators in Kigali and abroad. Depending on availability, permits can also be bought on the spot at Musanze or Kinigi, but there is no guarantee a permit will be available on any given day and procedures may change, so you are strongly advised to check this beforehand with ORTPN in Kigali – see box *Booking a gorilla permit* on page 45. Either way, it is advisable for independent travellers to visit or ring the ORTPN office in Musanze or Kinigi the afternoon before they intend to

The largest living primates, gorillas are widespread residents of the equatorial African rainforest, with a global population of perhaps 100,000 concentrated mainly in the Congo Basin. Until 2001, all gorillas were assigned to the species *Gorilla gorilla*, split into three races: the western lowland gorilla *G. g. gorilla* of the western Congo Basin, the eastern lowland gorilla *G. g. graueri* in the eastern Congo, and the mountain gorilla *G. g. beringei* living in highland forest on the eastern side of the Albertine Rift. The western race was formally described in 1847, but the eastern races were only described in the early 20th century – the mountain gorilla in 1903, a year after two individuals were shot on Mount Sabinyo by Oscar von Beringe, and the eastern lowland gorilla in 1914.

The conventional taxonomic classification of gorillas has been challenged by recent advances in DNA testing and fresh morphological studies suggesting that the western and eastern gorilla populations, whose ranges lie more than 1,000km apart, diverged some two million years ago. For this reason, they are now treated as discrete species: *G. gorilla* (western) and *G. beringei* (eastern). One distinct western race – the Cross River gorilla *G. g. dielhi* of the Cameroon-Nigeria border region – fulfils the IUCN criteria for 'Critically Endangered', since it lives in five fragmented populations, only one of which is protected, with a combined total of fewer than 200 individuals. In 2000, the Cross River gorilla and mountain gorilla shared the dubious distinction of being placed on a shortlist of the world's 25 most endangered primate taxa.

The status of the western gorilla is relatively secure, since it is far more numerous in the wild than its eastern counterpart, and has a more extensive range spanning half-a-dozen countries. Recent estimates place the total population of western gorillas at around 80,000, but numbers are in rapid decline, largely due to hunting for bushmeat and the lethal ebola virus. The fate of the eastern gorilla – still split into a lowland and a mountain race – is far less certain. In the mid 1990s, an estimated 17,000 eastern lowland gorillas remained in the wild, but is widely thought that the population has halved – or worse – since the outbreak of the ongoing civil war in the DRC. Rarer still, but more stable, is the mountain gorilla, which has just 700 individuals confined to two ranges: the border-straddling Virunga Volcanoes and Bwindi National Park in Uganda.

The first study of mountain gorilla behaviour was undertaken in the 1950s by George Schaller, whose pioneering work formed the starting point for the more recent research initiated by Dian Fossey in the 1960s. The brutal – and still unsolved – murder of Fossey at her research centre in December 1985 is generally thought to have been the handiwork of one of the many poachers with whom she crossed swords in the Virungas. Fossey's acclaimed book *Gorillas in the Mist* remains perhaps the best starting point for anybody who wants to know more about mountain gorilla behaviour, while the eponymous movie, a posthumous account of Fossey's life, drew global attention to the plight of the mountain gorilla.

The mountain gorilla is distinguished from its lowland counterparts by several adaptations to its high-altitude home, most visibly a longer and more luxuriant coat. It is

go tracking in order to confirm arrangements. Through June to September, when demand is high, permits for specific days can sell out well in advance, so be sure to book as far ahead as possible.

Trackers are required to check in at the park headquarters at Kinigi at 07.00, where they can enjoy a complimentary cup of tea or coffee (and if necessary make use of the last clean flush toilets they'll see for a few hours) before being allocated to one of the five habituated groups. A briefing is held at around 07.30 after which you must drive to the appropriate trailhead, so that the actual tracking generally starts at 08.15–08.30.

on average bulkier than other races, with the heaviest individual gorilla on record (of any race) being the 220kg dominant silverback of Rwanda's Sabinyo Group. Like other gorillas, it is a highly sociable creature, moving in defined troops of anything from five to 50 animals. A troop typically consists of a dominant silverback male (the male's back turns silver when he reaches sexual maturity at about 13 years old) and sometimes a subordinate silverback, as well as a harem of three or four mature females, and several young animals. Unusually for mammals, it is the male who forms the focal point of gorilla society; when a silverback dies, his troop normally disintegrates. A silverback will start to acquire his harem at about 15 years of age, most normally by attracting a young, sexually mature female from another troop. He may continue to lead a troop well into his 40s.

A female gorilla reaches sexual maturity at the age of eight, after which she will often move between different troops several times. Once a female has successfully given birth, however, she normally stays loyal to the same silverback until he dies, and she will even help to defend him against other males. (When a male takes over a troop, he generally kills all nursing infants to bring the mothers into oestrus more quickly, a strong motive for a female to help preserve the status quo.) A female gorilla has a gestation period similar to that of a human, and if she reaches old age she will typically have raised up to six offspring to sexual maturity. A female's status within a troop is based on the length of time she has been with a silverback: the alpha female is normally the longest-serving member of the harem.

The mountain gorilla is primarily vegetarian, with bamboo shoots being the favoured diet, though they are known to eat 58 different plant species in the Virungas. It may also eat insects, ants being a particularly popular protein supplement. A gorilla troop will spend most of its waking hours on the ground, but it will generally move into the trees at night, when each member of the troop builds itself a temporary nest. Gorillas are surprisingly sedentary creatures, typically moving less than 1km in a day, which makes tracking them on a day-to-day basis relatively easy for experienced guides. A troop will generally only move a long distance after a stressful incident, for instance an aggressive encounter with another troop. Gorillas are peaceable animals with few natural enemies and they often live for up to fifty years in the wild, but their long-term survival is critically threatened by poaching, deforestation and exposure to human-borne diseases.

It was previously thought that the Virunga and Bwindi gorilla populations were racially identical, not an unreasonable assumption given that a corridor of mid-altitude forest linked the two mountain ranges until about 500 years ago. But recent DNA tests indicate the Bwindi and Virunga gorillas show sufficient genetic differences to suggest that they have formed mutually isolated breeding populations for many millennia, in which case the 'mountain gorilla' should possibly be split into two discrete races, one – the Bwindi gorilla – endemic to Uganda, the other unique to the Virunga Mountains. Neither race numbers more than 400 in the wild, neither has ever bred successfully in captivity, and both meet several of the criteria for an IUCN classification of 'Critically Endangered'.

HABITUATED GROUPS The most difficult to reach of the permanent groups is the **Susa Group**, which lives on the slopes of Mount Karisoke. Consisting of 39 individuals, including four silverbacks and several youngsters, this is the second-largest group of mountain gorillas in the world (there is a larger research group) and it was the one originally studied by Dian Fossey. A visit to the Susa Group is delightfully chaotic and totally unforgettable, with gorillas seemingly tumbling out of every bush and bamboo stand. The Susa Group is the first choice of most fit visitors, but be under no illusions about the severity of the hike. The ascent from the car park to the forest boundary is gaspingly steep, and will take the best part of an hour. On a good day, it will take no more than 20 minutes to reach the gorillas from the boundary; on a bad day you might be looking at two hours or more in either direction and it has been known to take as long as seven hours to locate the group in the dry season (the record from the previous day will give an indication of how deep in the gorillas are, as they generally don't move too far in one day).

A far less strenuous prospect is the **Sabinyo Group**, whose permanent territory lies within the Volcanoes Park, on a lightly forested saddle between Mount Sabinyo and Mount Gahinga. Depending on exactly where the gorillas are, the walk from the car park to the forest boundary is flat to gently sloping, and will typically take 20–30 minutes. Once in the forest, the gorillas might take anything from ten minutes to an hour to reach, but generally the slopes aren't too daunting. The Sabinyo Group consists of 11 individuals, with two silverbacks. Although it is less numerically impressive than the Susa Group, the Sabinyo Group does seem more cohesive and one gets a clearer impression of the group structure and interaction. What's more, the dominant male Guhondo is the heaviest gorilla (of any race) ever measured, at 220kg.

Group Thirteen spends most of its time on the same saddle as the Sabinyo Group, but its territory does cross into neighbouring countries, so it is not permanently in the Volcanoes Park. When it is around, however, it is normally just as easy to reach as the Sabinyo Group. Group Thirteen's name dates to when it was first habituated, and numbered 13 gorillas, but today it numbers 17 individuals with one silverback. As with the Sabinyo Group, this means you get a good feel for group structure and interaction. Group Thirteen seems to be a favourite of many of the guides, probably because its silverback is more relaxed and approachable than those in other groups.

The other two groups are the **Amahoro Group**, numbering 14 and generally to be found on the slopes of Mount Visoke, and the more recently habituated **Umubano Group**, with eight individuals. Both of these groups have one silverback and the hikes to reach them are intermediate in difficulty between those of Susa and Sabinyo.

TRANSPORT No public transport connects Musanze to the park headquarters at Kinigi, 13km from town, nor does it from Kinigi to any of the car parks from where one enters the forest to start tracking. Individual travellers may be able to beg lifts with other tourists, but for larger transport-less groups the only option is to hire a vehicle and driver for the morning. ORTPN in Musanze can advise on this and Highland Gorilla Tour & Travel (see page 187) can arrange vehicle hire. In the rainy season you'll probably need a 4x4; in the dry season an ordinary *taxi-voiture* should be adequate and will cost far less. The going rate for a 4x4 from/to Musanze is around US$60 for the round trip; tour operators in Kigali can organise it as a day trip from Kigali for around US$150, or less if several of you share a vehicle. If you spend the night beforehand at the Mountain Gorilla's Nest, the Kinigi Guest House or the ORTPN Campsite, all quite close to the Kinigi park office, you stand a reasonable chance of hitching a lift up there from the main road; but you'll still need transport in the morning to reach the start of the trek. Whatever method you choose, make sure that it's reliable – if you don't turn up at the appointed time you risk invalidating your permit and having to pay again.

PHYSICAL PREPARATION Depending on which group you visit, and your own level of fitness, the trek to see the gorillas might amount to anything from the proverbial stroll in the park to genuinely exhausting – the guides have on occasion had to carry tourists down! The main obstacles are the steep slopes that characterise the Virungas, particularly en route to the Susa Group. Once in the forest, the slopes aren't as steep, and the pace is slower, but bending and crawling through the thick vegetation can be tiring, particularly after rain when everything is muddy underfoot.

Don't underestimate the tiring effects of being at high altitude. The trekking takes place at elevations of between 2,500m and 3,000m above sea level, not high enough for altitude sickness to be a concern but sufficient to knock the breath out of anybody – no matter how fit – who has just flown in from a low altitude. For this reason, visitors who are spending a while in Rwanda might think seriously about leaving their gorilla-tracking until they've been in the country a week or so, and are better acclimatised. Most of Rwanda lies at above 1,500m, and much of the country is higher – a couple of days at Nyungwe, which lies above 2,000m, would be good preparation for the Virungas. Likewise, if you are coming from elsewhere in Africa, try to plan your itinerary so that you spend your last pre-Rwanda days at medium to high altitude: for example, were you flying in from Kenya, a few days in Nairobi (2,300m) or even the Maasai Mara (1,600m) would be far better preparation than time at the coast.

If you are uncertain about your fitness, avoid visiting the Susa Group, but rather ask if you can be allocated to the party for Group Thirteen or the Sabinyo Group, both of which are reached by reasonably easy hikes on flattish terrain. Once on the trail, take it easy, and don't be afraid to ask to stop for a few minutes whenever you feel tired. Guides will generally cut you a walking-stave if you ask, or there may be some at the park office that previous trackers have left behind. Drink plenty of water, and carry some quick calories – biscuits and chocolate can both be bought at supermarkets in Musanze. The good news is that, in 99% of cases, whatever exhaustion you might feel on the way up will vanish with the adrenalin charge that follows the first sighting of a silverback gorilla!

WHAT TO WEAR AND TAKE Be prepared to walk a long distance in steep, muddy conditions, possibly with rain overhead, before you encounter any gorillas. Put on your sturdiest walking shoes. Ideally, wear thick trousers and a long-sleeved top as protection against vicious stinging nettles. It's often cold when you set out, so start off with a sweatshirt or jersey (which also help protect against nettles). The gorillas are thoroughly used to people, so it makes little difference whether you wear bright or muted colours. Whatever clothes you wear to go tracking are likely to get very dirty as you slip and slither in the mud, so if you have pre-muddied clothes you might as well wear them. When you're grabbing for handholds in thorny vegetation, a pair of old gardening gloves are helpful. If you feel safer with a walking-stick, pack a folding one.

Carry as little as possible, ideally in a waterproof bag of some sort. During the rainy season, a poncho or raincoat might be a worthy addition to your daypack, while sunscreen, sunglasses and a hat are a good idea at any time of year. You may well feel like a snack during the long hike, and should certainly carry enough drinking water – at least one litre, more to visit the Susa Group. Bottled water is sold in Musanze. Especially during the rainy season, make sure your camera gear is well protected – if your bag isn't waterproof, seal your camera and films in a plastic bag (for further details about photographing gorillas see the box *Photographic tips* on pages 74–5).

Binoculars are not necessary to see the gorillas. In theory, birdwatchers might want to carry binoculars, though in practice only the most dedicated are likely to make use of them – the trek up to the gorillas is normally very directed, and walking up the steep slopes and through the thick vegetation tends to occupy one's eyes and mind.

You may need to show your passport or some other form of identification when you check in; find out about this from ORTPN beforehand.

Mountain gorillas are the focus of several conservation organisations. The five international organisations currently working in Rwanda are listed alphabetically with a summary of their activities:

DIAN FOSSEY CONSERVATION PROGRAMME (*www.gorillas.org*) Formerly the Dian Fossey Gorilla Fund, the London-based DFCP manages 20 projects designed to integrate traditional conservation and research with economic development and education. These include:

- *Beekeepers*, who are supported to develop modern sustainable honey farms at the edge of, rather than inside, the park boundary.
- *Fresh water in village schools* using local engineering technology to provide water cisterns. Water collection is one of the main causes of encroachment in the gorilla habitat, and children living close to the forest often miss school to collect water for their families.
- *Training in sustainable agriculture* for farmers in areas adjacent to gorilla habitat.
- *Tree planting* to alleviate environmental degradation, since most fuel used in households comes from wood.
- *Virunga Wildlife Clubs* in schools, which organise field trips, tree planting and environment-week activities, and a *Conservation Network* that links local organisations in the Virunga region.

DIAN FOSSEY GORILLA FUND INTERNATIONAL The Atlanta-based DFGFI funds and operates the **Karisoke Research Centre** (www.gorillafund.org; select 'Karisoke Research Centre'), originally established by Dr Dian Fossey in 1967. Although the research centre was destroyed during the 1990s, staff continue to monitor three gorilla groups and carry out daily anti-poaching patrols from a base outside the park. DFGFI aims to strengthen research and protection efforts through education, local capacity building, and support to a Geographic Information Systems unit based within the national university.

INTERNATIONAL GORILLA CONSERVATION PROGRAMME (*www.mountaingorillas.org*) IGCP is a joint initiative of three organisations, the *African Wildlife Foundation, Fauna and Flora*

REGULATIONS AND PROTOCOL Tourists are permitted to spend no longer than one hour with the gorillas, and it is forbidden to eat, urinate or defecate in their presence. It is also forbidden to approach within less than 5m of the gorillas, a rule that is difficult to enforce with curious youngsters (and some adults) who often approach human visitors. Smoking is forbidden anywhere within the national park boundary ('it's unhealthy for the animals', according to one rather earnest guide, which seems to be taking concerns about passive smoking to stratospheric absurdity – more genuine justifications are litter, fire and annoying other tourists).

Gorillas are susceptible to many human diseases, and it has long been feared by researchers that one ill tourist might infect a gorilla, resulting in the possible death of the whole troop should they have no immunity to that disease. For this reason, you should not go gorilla-tracking with a potentially airborne infection such as flu or a cold, and are asked to turn away from the gorillas should you need to sneeze.

To the best of our knowledge, no tourist has ever been seriously hurt by a habituated gorilla, but there is always a first time. An adult gorilla is much stronger than a person, and will act in accordance with its own social codes. Therefore it is vital that you listen to your guide at all times regarding correct protocol in the presence of gorillas.

International and the *World Wide Fund for Nature*. IGCP's overall goal is the sustainable conservation of the world's remaining mountain gorillas and their habitat. IGCP aims to enhance communication and cooperation between protected-area authorities through regional meetings, training programmes, cross-border patrols and communications networks; and advises governments on environmental policy and legislation enforcement. IGCP provides training and support for park staff, and has established a Ranger Based Monitoring programme throughout the Virunga region.

MOUNTAIN GORILLA VETERINARY PROJECT (*www.mgvp.org*) MGVP provides veterinary care to the mountain gorillas. The project's vets monitor the health of individual gorillas in both the research and tourist groups, and are able to intervene in emergency situations, such as a gorilla becoming trapped by a life-threatening snare. Since disease transmission from humans is a serious threat to the gorillas' survival, MGVP also monitors the health of government and project staff working in the park, and organises seminars addressing health and hygiene issues. The MGVP receives funding from the Morris Animal Foundation and is affiliated to the Maryland Zoo in Baltimore, USA.

WILDLIFE CONSERVATION SOCIETY (*www.wcs.org/international/Africa/rwanda*) With strong historic links to the mountain gorillas, WCS's major programme in Rwanda is now the Nyungwe Forest Conservation Project, although it is still involved with the Volcanoes and Akagera National Parks. WCS is also implementing training programmes in monitoring and research with its partners, including the ORTPN (Office Rwandais du Tourisme et des Parcs Nationaux). It provides direct support to the management of parks and wildlife, and supports ORTPN in tackling immediate threats.

In addition, the volcanoes fall within the focus of WCS's Albertine Rift Project (*www.albertinerift.org*). The objective of this programme is to improve conservation by providing information for park managers, building capacity to better manage these areas, and encouraging collaboration across national boundaries. Biological and socio-economic surveys are used to identify priority conservation areas and to plan measures to alleviate poverty in the communities that border them.

TOURISM AND CONSERVATION

Over the two decades following the European discovery of mountain gorillas, at least 50 individuals were captured or killed in the Virungas, prompting the Belgian government to create the Albert National Park in 1925. This protected what are now the Congolese and Rwandan portions of the Virunga mountains, and was managed as a cohesive conservation unit.

The gorilla population of the Virungas is thought to have been reasonably stable in 1960, when a census undertaken by George Schaller indicated that some 450 individuals lived in the range. By 1971–73, however, the population had plummeted to an estimated 250. This decline was caused by several factors, including the post-colonial division of the Albert National Park into its Rwandan and Congolese components, the ongoing fighting between the Hutu and Tutsi of Rwanda, and a grisly tourist trade in poached gorilla heads and hands – the latter used by some sad individuals as ashtrays! Most devastating of all perhaps was the irreversible loss of almost half of the gorillas' habitat between 1957 and 1968 to local farmers and a European-funded agricultural scheme.

In 1979, Amy Vedder and Bill Webber initiated the first gorilla tourism project

The first of these took place at the Mountain Gorilla's Nest Hotel (Kinigi) in June 2005, when the naming of 29 gorillas was followed by a celebration party with traditional music and dancing. On the same day, a Gorilla Fundraising Gala was held at the Kivu Sun Hotel in Gisenyi.

The 2006 ceremony is due on June 17, when 12 gorillas will be named, again to the accompaniment of traditional music and dance. Visitors are most welcome to attend these events, which will take place annually in June and raise valuable funds for the protection of the mountain gorillas; tour operators will fit it into your itinerary by request. As well as the naming, there is the opportunity to 'adopt' (sponsor) a gorilla and/or to make general donations to the animals' welfare.

THE TRADITIONAL NAMING CEREMONY The birth of a child in Rwanda is a big event for the whole family and neighbourhood. The naming of the child is traditionally the chance to welcome him or her into their world. During the ceremony, the baby is carried outside and shown to the public, and young children suggest names for this infant who has recently joined them. The parents then select one of the names. It's a lively gathering, accompanied by plenty of food, drink and, of course, dancing.

In the past few decades the tradition has also been applied to young mountain gorillas, with the park guides taking on the role of proposing the names – which are based on the behaviour, circumstances and background of the infants or their mother.

For more information, tickets and details of sponsorship contact ORTPN (details on page 61) or check www.rwandatourism.com.

in Rwanda's Volcanoes Park, integrating tourism, local education and anti-poaching measures with remarkable success. Initially, the project was aimed mainly at overland trucks, who paid a paltry – by today's standards – US$20 per person to track gorillas. Even so, gorilla tourism raised up to ten million US dollars annually by the mid 1980s, making it Rwanda's third-highest earner of foreign revenue. The mountain gorilla had practically become the national emblem, and was officially regarded as the country's most important renewable natural resource. To ordinary Rwandans, gorillas became a source of great national pride: living gorillas ultimately created far more work and money than poaching them had ever done. As a result, a census undertaken in 1989 indicated that the local mountain gorilla population had increased by almost 30% to 320 animals.

Gorilla tourism came to an abrupt halt in 1991, when the country erupted into the civil war that culminated in the 1994 genocide. The civil war also raised considerable concern about the survival of the gorillas. Researchers and park rangers were twice forced to evacuate the Volcanoes Park, land mines were planted by various military factions, and the Virungas were used as an escape route by thousands of fleeing refugees. Remarkably, however, when researchers were finally able to return to the park, it was discovered that only four gorillas could not be accounted for. Two of the missing gorillas were old females who most probably died of natural causes; the other two might have been shot, but might just as easily have succumbed to disease. It is also encouraging to note that the war has had no evident effect on breeding activity, a strong indication that it was less disruptive to the gorillas than had been feared.

But in this most volatile part of Africa little can be taken for granted. Just as Rwanda started to stabilise politically, the DRC descended into anarchy. For years, eastern Congolese officials, who lived far from the capital, received no formal salary and were forced to devise their own ways of securing a living, leading to a level of corruption second to none in the region. At least 16 gorillas were killed in three separate incidents in the DRC between 1995 and 1998, since when the Congolese part of the Virungas was effectively closed to tourists and researchers alike prior to re-opening in 2005. Under the circumstances, it is remarkable to learn that the latest gorilla count – undertaken in 2003 – shows a continued increase to at least 380 individuals in the Virungas.

While concern about the fate of a few gorillas might seem misplaced in the context of a war that claimed a million human lives, it is these self-same gorillas which give Rwanda a real chance of rebuilding the lucrative tourist industry that was shattered by the war. It will do this in an environment in which increasing concern is being voiced about the ramifications of habituating gorillas for tourists. There is, for instance, the issue of health: humans and gorillas are genetically close enough for there to be a real risk of a tourist passing a viral or bacterial infection to a habituated gorilla, which might in turn infect other members of its group, potentially resulting in all their deaths should they have no resistance to the infection.

Another concern is that habituating gorillas to humans increases their vulnerability to poachers. During 1995, seven habituated mountain gorillas died as a result of poaching: four members of the Kyaguliro Group in Uganda's Bwindi National Park were speared to death, while the famous silverback Marcel in the DRC was shot dead, together with one adult female. In both cases, an infant was removed: the one captured at Bwindi is now assumed to be dead; the one taken from the Volcanoes Park was confiscated at the Ugandan border and returned to the troop from which it was taken. These incidents were thought to be linked to one dealer's attempts to acquire an infant gorilla, and did not appear to signal the start of a trend. Then, in May 2002, two females were shot and two babies stolen in Rwanda's Volcanoes Park; in October 2002 an infant was taken by – but subsequently rescued from – poachers.

Given the above, a reasonable response might be to query the wisdom of habituating gorillas in the first place. The problem facing conservationists is that gorillas cannot be conserved in a vacuum. At current prices, the authorities can potentially earn US$15,000 daily in tracking permits alone, much of which can be pumped back into the protection and management of the Volcanoes Park. There are also the broader benefits of job creation through tourism in and around the Virungas. And even in terms of pure conservation, habituation has many positive effects, allowing researchers and rangers to monitor the gorillas on a daily basis, and to intervene when one of them is ill, injured or in a snare. As a gorilla researcher based in Musanze once put it, tourism for all its negatives is probably the only thing that will save the Volcanoes Park – and by default save the gorillas.

For post-genocide Rwanda, struggling to re-establish a reputation as a viable tourist destination, things would be ten times worse without the mountain gorillas. It is the gorillas that will bring back the tourists, who will also spend money in other parts of the country, thereby providing foreign revenue and creating employment well beyond the immediate vicinities of the mountain gorilla reserves. Tourism is probably integral to the survival of the mountain gorilla; the survival of the mountain gorilla is certainly integral to the growth of Rwanda's tourist industry. This symbiotic situation motivates a far greater number of people to take an active interest in the fate of the gorillas than would be the case if gorilla tourism were to be curtailed.

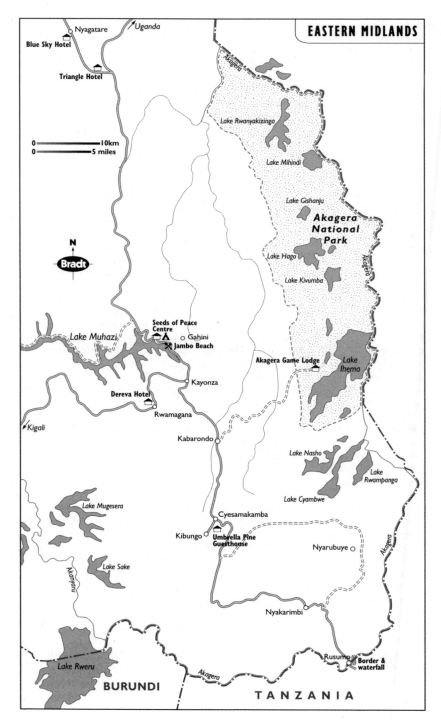

Uganda

Nyagatare

Blue Sky Hotel

Triangle Hotel

Akagera

Lake Rwanyakizinga

Lake Mihindi

0 ————— 10km
0 ————— 5 miles

Lake Gishanju

Akagera National Park

N
Bradt

Lake Hago

Lake Kivumba

Akagera

Seeds of Peace Centre

Lake Muhazi

Gahini

Jambo Beach

Akagera Game Lodge

Lake Ihema

Kayonza

Dereva Hotel

Rwamagana

Kigali

Kabarondo

Lake Nasho

Lake Rwampanga

Lake Cyambwe

Lake Mugesera

Cyesamakamba

Kibungo

Umbrella Pine Guesthouse

Nyarubuye

Akanyaru

Lake Sake

Nyakarimbi

Akagera

Lake Rweru

Rusumo

Border & waterfall

Akagera

BURUNDI

TANZANIA

13

Eastern Rwanda

East of Kigali, the highlands of the Albertine Rift descend towards the western rim of the Lake Victoria Basin, a relatively flat and low-lying region marked by a distinctly warmer and more humid climate than the rest of Rwanda. Geographically, the most significant feature of eastern Rwanda is probably the Akagera River, which forms the border with Tanzania and feeds the extensive complex of lakes and marshes protected within Akagera National Park – the most important attraction in eastern Rwanda, covered in the next chapter.

Akagera aside, the east of Rwanda lacks any major tourist attractions. Other landmarks include the Rusumo Falls on the Tanzania border and Lake Muhazi, both of which are diverting enough if you are in the area, but not really worth making a major effort to reach, although the drive along the northern shore of Lake Muhazi is attractive. The area of rolling hills and cattle farming in the far northeast near the Uganda border offers far-reaching views – but this is an area for strolling and people-watching rather than any great excitement. The handful of towns that dot the region are uniformly on the dull side, although some have lively markets and the breezy highland town of Byumba in the northeast is surrounded by extensive tea plantations.

The main roads through eastern Rwanda are surfaced and covered by the usual proliferation of minibus-taxis. Accommodation options are limited by comparison with those in other parts of the country, but all the main towns have at least one reasonably comfortable – and reasonably priced – hotel. Because it lies at a lower altitude than the rest of the country, the Tanzania border area is the one part of Rwanda where malaria is a major rather than a minor risk, particularly during the rainy season.

THE BYUMBA ROAD

RWANDA NA GASABO The first substantial right turn off the main Kigali–Byumba road, about 25km out of Kigali, takes you on a winding route to Rwanda Na Gasabo or the original Rwanda hill. This is where (allegedly) the first of the ancient kings, travelling to Rwanda from the northeast, stopped at the top and set up his kingdom. It's high, with a flat top and a view in all directions. After leaving the main road, continue for a short distance to a cluster of houses where there's a sharp left turn on to a narrow road that climbs steeply. Just follow this upwards and you'll reach the top of the hill. (A 4x4 is advisable, particularly after rain.) People are generally around, so ask directions if you're unsure. The view is spectacular. There are plans to develop this site for tourism (reconstructed dwellings, interpretation boards...) but at present it's peaceful.

Legends abound! The ancient King Gihanga (see box on page 226) is said to have left two of his cows here; their names were Rugira and Ingizi. One day another king went hunting and threw a branch after an animal; the tip sank into the ground and took root, becoming a species found nowhere else in Rwanda. The great trees planted as the gateway to his land are still standing, after many centuries. Then again, there was a magic earthenware pot in the court; it would fill with water of its own accord to signify that rain was on the way. Also the monarch had a very special group of royal drummers, whose drumming awakened him in the morning and sent him to sleep at night. And so on. You may well meet someone up there who will tell you other tales.

LAKE MUHAZI (NORTHWESTERN SHORE) About five minutes further up the Kigali–Byumba road after the Gasabo turning, another right turn at ✪ S 01°45.753, E 030°07.788, signposted for the village of Rwesero, is the start of a beautiful (but sometimes rough) road that follows the northern bank of Lake Muhazi and emerges on the main road flanking Akagera Park. The road offers a succession of tranquil, watery views (and numerous birds), with the possibility of stopping for a meal or drink at one of the resorts near Rwesero. Allow a half-day for this road, including stops – you can do it in less, but it's a shame to hurry and the surface is sometimes quite rutted. The road also crosses several small creeks on rough wooden 'bridges' so is best done in the dry season and certainly in a 4x4. It may well become impassable in a couple of places when the lake rises: ask about this. Hitching could be difficult; transport comes in from either end but doesn't necessarily go the whole way through.

This part of the lake was much studied by the Germans as they explored their new territory. Writing in 1907, a Doctor Mildbraed rather crossly commented:

> The west end of Lake Muhasi terminates in a papyrus swamp, and therefore promised rich spoils for zoological treasure-hunters. We were all the more keenly disillusioned to find the fauna far more meagre in character in this great water basin – the first we had explored in Africa – than we had been led to suppose in Germany. In spite of the luxurious vegetation at this part of the lake, the most diligent search was needed before we found a few sponges and polypi attached to some characeous plants.

Very soon after leaving the main road you cross a small iron bridge; then, after about 25 minutes (or longer if you stop to look at birds and enjoy the lakeside views), you'll come to two simple places to eat or sleep, wonderfully located at the water's edge within a few hundred metres of Rwesero. The first place on the right as you come from Kigali is the **Café-Resto Hakurya y'i Gasabo** (S 01°47.545, E 030°10.160, 1,444m), which has a very slow bar/restaurant, a camping area, and three small, en-suite double rondawels for Rfr5,000 each – unfortunately, there is no telephone reception in the area, so it's not possible to make an advance reservation. The **Rwesero Beach Resort** also has a bar/restaurant, along with a picnic place and camping, and is probably the better option for day trippers seeking a lakeside snack or drink. Both places have boats, so you can fish on the lake – or cross to the opposite bank and camp there. There's plenty of birdlife around too, including pied and malachite kingfishers and fish eagle, and otters are sometimes seen in the area.

BYUMBA The sprawling town of Byumba, which lies about 75km north of Kigali, some 3km off the main road to Kibale (Uganda), is the sixth largest in Rwanda (population 66,500) and the highest settlement of note, perched at an altitude of 2,220m above the Mulindi Valley. Blessed with rich volcanic soils, Byumba lies at the heart of Rwanda's burgeoning tea industry, which has assumed a growing economic importance in recent years and now creates employment for around 60,000 people. More than 10 million kilograms of tea is exported from Rwanda yearly, much of it to the UK and Pakistan, with annual earnings of up to US$20 million accounting for more than 30% of state revenue since 2004. Byumba offers nothing in the way of tourist attractions, though the neat green tea plantations that blanket the surrounding countryside are very pretty – you could well spend a couple of days here just walking and enjoying the expansive views – and the dirt road connecting it to Base is one of the most scenic in the country.

There is plenty of transport to Byumba from Kigali and the Gatuna border with Uganda. The 42km road between Byumba and Base, notable for spectacular views of the tea estates around Base, is serviced by at least one bus daily, leaving Byumba in the early morning and returning from Base later in the day. There don't seem to be any minibus-taxis along this route, but hitching isn't impossible. On the Kigali–Byumba road about 10km outside Kigali is the rather surprising Highland Flowers Rose Farm, growing high-quality roses for sale locally and for export to Europe.

The **Hotel Urumuli** (✆ *564322/3*) was the pick of the accommodation in Byumba prior to its closure at the end of 2005. It's not clear when or whether it will re-open, but assuming that it does, the solidly built, semi-circular en-suite rooms with hot water should cost around Rfr8,000–10,000. It's at the top of the long main street, about 2km from the public taxi park but served by private minibuses – Okapicar, Gasabo, Ataco, etc. For now, the most appealing alternative is the **Centre Diocésain de Formation et de Conférence** (✆ *564375*; ⊛ S 01°35.167, E 030°03.410), which lies about 500m back towards the taxi park and has 13 en-suite rooms at Rfr4,000/6,000/7,000 single/double/twin. Food and drinks are available, but the rooms can get busy with church guests, so try to book ahead. An alternative is the **Ikaze Bagenzi Bar Restaurant Amacumbi** (m *08 528047*), which has basic singles for around Rfr2,000, a room sleeping four in bunk beds for Rfr7,500 and an en-suite double for Rfr6,000. There are showers, running water and flush toilets. It's about 300m from the minibus station and can be reached by walking downhill past the bakery, turning right when you reach an open area used as a market and then left at the next junction. The **Banque Commerciale du Rwanda**, 100m from the minibus station, changes US$ cash and theoretically travellers' cheques; it also has Western Union.

THE NYAGATARE ROAD

RWAMAGANA One of several unremarkable small towns in eastern Rwanda, Rwamagana is of interest to travellers primarily as a base from which to explore Lake Muhazi and possibly Akagera National Park, though it does boast a couple of marginally interesting colonial buildings including a large church. The market is currently being rebuilt. The town lies about 60km from Kigali, no more than an hour's drive along a good surfaced road covered by regular minibus-taxis, some of which are 'express' while others also serve villages nearby. In Kigali they leave from the Nyabugogo bus station and call at Remera bus station en route. On your return you may also be dropped off at Kigali's central bus station in Avenue de Commerce.

The **Dereva Hotel** (✆ *567244*; m *08 322228/527093/468352*; *www.derevahotel.com*; ⊛ S 01°56.831, E 030°26.336, 1,534m), set in large green grounds alongside the main road, offers what are probably the most commodious lodgings in this part of Rwanda. The clean rooms, though a little gloomy, are very reasonably priced at Rfr4,000/5,000 for a single/double using common showers, Rfr6,000/7,000 for an en-suite with nets and hot showers, or Rfr7,000/8,000 for a suite-like apartment. The attached restaurant serves large meals in the Rfr2,000–4,000 range. If the Dereva is full you could try the much shabbier **Ikambere** (✆ *567372*), where an en-suite double (cold water) costs US$5.

As you pass through Rwamagana coming from Kigali, look out for some new buildings on the left of the main road at the Kigali end of town. These are part of a project run and financed by Projet Rwa/020 of Lux-Development (✆ 567380); it includes the development and promotion of local handicrafts and trains young people to produce them. It also markets the work of craftspeople throughout Kibungo province. You can generally watch the items (patchwork, tie & dye, beadwork, bags made from sisal and – improbably! – from bottle-tops, leatherwork and so on) being made. The young trainees are helped to work together in groups after their training. The crafts shop on the premises is run by the association 'IAKI', meaning *Inter-Association des Artisans de Kibungo*, so carries a range of local objects.

KAYONZA This small, rather scruffy settlement is situated 78km from Kigali, at the junction (01°53.975, E 030°30.454) of the main north–south road connecting Kagitumba on the Rwanda border to Rusumo on the Tanzania border. Kayonza is, if anything, even less remarkable than Rwamagana, though once again it serves as a possible base for exploring Lake Muhazi and Akagera National Park and is readily accessible from Kigali on public transport (minibuses leave from Nyabugogo bus station). Volunteers working in Kayonza reckon there is some good walking to be had by heading out of town in the general direction of Akagera National Park.

The few basic hotels at the Kayonza junction are either closed or barely functional – at present you'd do better to stay in Rwamagana or to continue on to Muhazi, Nyagatare or Kibungo.

LAKE MUHAZI (EASTERN SHORE) In common with most lakes in Rwanda, Muhazi is an erratically shaped body of water whose shores follow the contours of the surrounding hills. Roughly 60km long but nowhere more than 5km wide, Muhazi is a classic 'flooded valley' type of lake, its serpentine shape broken by numerous tendrils stretching northward or southward along former tributaries. It is a pretty spot, not as beautiful perhaps as the lakes around Ruhengeri, but – at least for travellers dependent on public transport – with the added virtue of easy accessibility. The birdlife here is highly rewarding, and the lake harbours an unusually dense population of spotted-necked otter, though no other large mammals are found in the area.

The eastern tip of Lake Muhazi lies beside the surfaced Nyagatare road, about 8km north of Kayonza. Here, opposite the turn-off to the small hillside town of Gahini, is the **Seeds of Peace Centre** (Episcopal Church; *office* ✆f 567422; m 08 652792; e *gahini@rwanda1.com*; 01°50.502, E 030°28.496; 1,460m) which is well organised for tourism, with boating, swimming, birdwatching, a restaurant offering fresh lake fish, camping, a picnic place and two reconstructed traditional dwellings. It also has rondavels, each with two bedrooms, bathroom, kitchen and lounge: the charge is Rfr20,000 for a full apartment or Rfr17,000 for one room, all inclusive of breakfast. A new double-storey block with conventional hotel rooms and a smart restaurant is scheduled to open in 2006. Profits from this and the Gahini Guest House (see below) go back into the diocese for its work in the local community.

Across the road and up a steepish hill is Gahini, an attractive little town set high above the lake. The friendly **Gahini Guest House** (Episcopal Church; *office* ✆f 567422; e *gahini@rwanda1.com*) has an en-suite double at Rfr6,000, single/double with shared facilities at Rfr4,000/5,000, and capacious dormitories (bunk beds) at Rfr1,000 per person. A few hundred metres further along the road towards Rwamagana is the **Jambo Pleasure Beach**, a similar (but currently smaller) lakeside resort with a restaurant and camping space but no rooms.

A NEW VERSION OF AN ANCIENT TALE The monarch Ruganzu II Ndori was so great and famous a king that the mountains, rocks and forests of Rwanda were proud when he passed among them. One day, one of the rocks boasted to an eagle flying overhead that the king and his entourage had walked across it that same morning.

'Krarrk!' croaked the eagle in mocking disbelief. 'With my keen eyes I can spot the smallest mouse as it slips into its hole or the thinnest snake coiled in the shadows. Yet I see no sign that the king has passed your way.'

The rock scratched its weather-beaten head and thought deeply. Then it devised a plan. The next time King Ruganzu approached, it softened itself slightly so that his footsteps left an impression on its surface. Now the eagles and the crows and the skimming bee-eaters could see clearly that the king had walked upon the rock.

Word got around, and other rocks soon adopted the same tactic. If you visit Rwanda today, you may still see various traces of Ruganzu's footprints. Then one of the more ambitious rocks thought: 'If I create a jug, and fill it with beer, the monarch can drink his fill when he passes and I will become the chief rock within his kingdom.'

Carefully it formed itself into a jug, and filled that jug with cool, refreshing banana beer, and the king and all his courtiers drank their fill. But then some other rocks nearby saw what was happening and were jealous; they quickly made bigger and better jugs, and filled some of them with sorghum beer too so that the monarch had a choice.

Today, if you visit the old district of Murambi, you can still see half-a-dozen of these jugs, and if you're *very* lucky you may even catch a fleeting, aromatic scent of ancient beer. The region is called *Rubona rwa Nzoga* (Rubona of the beer); and the local tradition is that whatever time a guest may arrive at a house, the hosts will always have a jug of beer ready and waiting to quench his thirst.

Of course rocks in several other parts of Rwanda eventually copied the idea and made their own jugs too.... but they never matched the quality or quantity of Murambi's beer, which remained the monarch's favourite throughout his reign.

Murambi was incorporated into Kayonza District in 2006. Minibus-taxis go to Kiramuruzi (between Gakenke and Kiziguro on the Akagera National Park map on page 230), from where Rubona rwa Nzoga is about 30 minutes' walk. But don't expect exact replica jugs...

NYAGATARE This scattered town of 8,500 souls is the administrative centre of the sizeable but thinly populated Nyagatare District, which extends over the most northeasterly corner of Rwanda to the borders with Uganda and Rwanda. Prior to 2006, Nyagatare was also the capital of the now-defunct Umutara Province, much of which lay within the north of Akagera National Park and the adjacent Mutara Wildlife Reserve before these areas were de-gazetted in 1997 to accommodate returned refugees. Set along the eastern bank of the forest-fringed Muvumba River, Nyagatare must originally have lain just outside the boundary of the Mutara Wildlife Reserve. Set at a relatively low altitude of 1,355m, it retains something of a dusty frontier feel, surrounded by rolling hills whose cover of scrubby acacias and tall cactus-like euphorbia trees is far closer in appearance to Akagera than any other settled part of Rwanda.

It would be an act of febrile distortion to describe Nyagatare as any sort of travel magnet. All the same, if you are seeking a wholly un-touristy experience, you could do worse than spend a night or two here. The surrounding area is great walking country – ask (and take note of) local permission and advice, fill up your water bottle and then just stroll off across fields, plains, hillsides… It's a wonderfully clear, open panorama (unlike in much of the rest of Rwanda with its jutting hills

Eastern Rwanda **THE NYAGATARE ROAD**

13

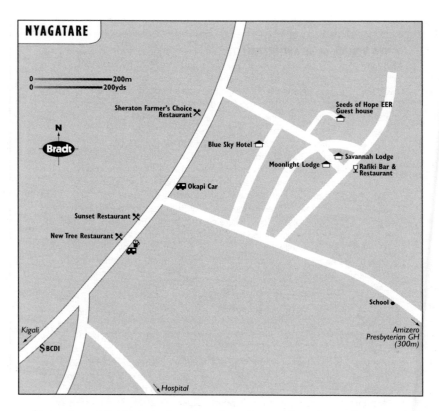

0 ————————— 200m
0 ————————— 200yds

Sheraton Farmer's Choice Restaurant ✗

Seeds of Hope EER Guest house 🏠

N

Bradt

Blue Sky Hotel 🏠

🏠 **Savannah Lodge**

Moonlight Lodge 🏠

🍷 **Rafiki Bar & Restaurant**

🚗 **Okapi Car**

Sunset Restaurant ✗

New Tree Restaurant ✗

School ●

Kigali

💲 **BCDI**

Amizero Presbyterian GH (300m)

↘ *Hospital*

and intensive cultivation), fresh and gently green at moister times of year, parched and tinder dry just before the rainy season. For wildlife enthusiasts, local farmers claim that antelope and zebra often cross the border of Akagera to graze peacefully amongst their cattle, while the riparian woodland along the river as it passes the small town centre offers some potentially rewarding birdwatching. Also, in Nyagatare as in all of Rwanda, you can while time away pleasantly by people-watching and engaging in conversation – thanks to its proximity to Uganda and high population of returned refugees, this is one part of Rwanda where English is far more widely spoken than French.

With its relatively dry climate and infertile soils, this northeastern corner of Rwanda was very thinly settled prior to the gazetting of Akagera in 1935. It remains one of the few parts of the country dominated by pastoralism rather than agriculture: you won't travel far here without coming across herds of cattle – mostly the long-horned Ankole – plodding from clump to clump of bristly scrub. And as one might expect of an area so recently settled, there's a pioneering feel about the hamlets and villages of Umutara, which were built (often with foreign funds) to accommodate the returning refugees. Squatting defiantly on the empty plains, these are the houses of a child's pictures: plain and single-storied, with a small square window on either side of the front door. In fact they're dotted all over Rwanda, but the open landscapes here make them more visible.

Getting there and away Nyagatare lies about 175km from Kigali along a (mostly good) surfaced road via Rwamagana and Kayonza. The drive should take up to three hours in a private vehicle, branching left from the main roads continuing to the Uganda border about 3km before you reach the town centre. Regular minibus-taxis run to Nyagatare from Kigali, costing Rfr1,300 per person. Most minibus-taxis leave from the Nyabugogo bus station, but if you prefer to leave from the city centre, there's an Ataco Express departure hourly from 07.00 to 16.00, and you can also pick up direct transport from the Remera taxi park on the east side of Kigali. Regular public transport also connects Nyagatare to the Uganda border and Kayonza. The GPS (Blue Sky Hotel) is 01°17.340, E 030°19.655.

Where to stay

Blue Sky Hotel (35 rooms) 565244; sat: 0808 666660. This prominent multi-storey hotel stands a block back from the main road and consists of 2 wings divided by a small plot that the owner hopes to buy soon to develop as a swimming pool and open-air bar. The old wing is rather scruffy but the sgl rooms (with ³/₄ bed) are priced accordingly, whereas the much smarter but cheaply fitted rooms in the new wing feel a touch overpriced for what you get. In the evenings the bar is companionably busy with local people and the restaurant serves a good-value buffet – although b/fast is a touch measly. Other facilities include a sauna and massage room. *Rfr3,000 using common showers or Rfr5,000 en-suite (old wing); Rfr10,000 en-suite sgl (³/₄ bed) or 15,000 twin/dbl (new wing).*

Centre Spirituel Amizero (17 rooms) 565051. Situated in nice gardens about 1km from the main road and taxi park, this out-of-town Presbyterian resthouse is the best overall option in Nyagatare, but it's not so convenient for those without a private vehicle. The en-suite brick-faced rooms all have nets, TV and (usually) hot water, and an inexpensive restaurant is attached. *Rfr5,300/9,000 twin/dbl; Rfr1,000 per dormitory bed.*

Seeds of Hope Guesthouse (20 rooms) 567422; m 08 835718; e gahini@rwanda1.com. Situated in large grounds just around the corner from the Blue Sky, this friendly but rather basic and rundown guesthouse, run by the Episcopal Church, offers the best value in the town centre. The restaurant looks rather forlorn and under-stocked so you are probably better eating elsewhere. *Rfr5,000 en-suite twin; Rfr3,000 twin with shared bathroom; Rfr1,000 dormitory bed.*

Savanna Lodge (8 rooms) The pick (just about) of a trio of very basic lodges clustered to the southeast of the Blue Sky, this offers basic accommodation in small sgl rooms using shared facilities. *Rfr3,000.*

Triangle Hotel (20 rooms) Situated on the corner of the turn-off to Nyagatare on the main Kigali–Uganda road, this place has basic rooms with mosquito nets using shared facilities, but no phone or restaurant. It's probably OK if you're stuck or broke. *Rfr4,000 dbl.*

Where to eat The best option is probably the **Blue Sky Hotel**, which serves a good evening buffet for Rfr1,000 excluding meat or Rfr1,500 inclusive of meat, and will soon open a smarter hotel in the new wing. Otherwise, a good half-dozen eateries are scattered around town, serving the usual *mélanges* of meat, rice and vegetables, including the **Sunset**, **New Tree** and winningly named **Sheraton Farmers' Choice Restaurant**.

Practicalities The tiny main street offers – surprisingly – a photo laboratory, post office, filling station, dry cleaners, barber, general store and a sign-writer who also sells (rather gaudy) local paintings. The best option for foreign exchange is the BCDI on the main road, but it will probably accept cash only. There is no internet service.

THE RUSUMO ROAD

KIBUNGO The largest town in the southeast of Rwanda (population 48,500), Kibungo sprawls westward from the main Rusumo Road about 25km south of Kayonza. It is the administrative centre of the recently created Ngoma District, a region suffering not only from the aftermath of the genocide, but also from several

13

From mountain gorillas to elephants, Rwanda is blessed with its fair share of impressive wild beasts. But it is also a major stronghold for what is unquestionably the most imposing of Africa's domestic creatures: the remarkable long-horned Ankole breed of cattle associated with the pastoralist peoples of Uganda and Rwanda border areas.

Sometimes referred to as the Cattle of Kings thanks to their association with the royal lineages of Uganda and Rwanda, Ankole cattle come in several colours, ranging from uniform rusty-yellow to blotched black-and-white, but they always have a long head, short neck, deep dewlap and narrow chest, and the male often sports a large thoracic hump. What most distinguishes Ankole cattle from any familiar breed, however, is their preposterous, monstrous horns, which grow out from either side of the head like inverted elephant tusks, and in exceptional instances can reach a length up to 2.5m – dimensions unseen on any Rwandan or Ugandan tusker since the commercial ivory poaching outbreak of the 1980s.

The ancestry of Ankole cattle has been traced back to Eurasia as early as 15000BC, but the precursors of the modern long-horned variety originate in Ethiopia, where the humpless Egyptian longhorn (as depicted on ancient Egyptian pictographs) and humped Asian zebu were crossed about 4,000 years ago to form a long-horned, humped breed known as the Ethiopian sanga. A number of credible oral traditions indicate that the sanga was introduced to northwest Uganda in mediaeval times, probably as part of the same wave of southward migration from Ethiopia associated with the foundation of the legendary Bacwezi Kingdom in Uganda circa AD1350.

Hardy, and capable of subsisting on limited water and poor grazing, these introduced cattle were ideally suited to local conditions, except that they had no immunity to tsetse-borne diseases, which forced the pastoralists who tended them to keep drifting southward. The outsized horns of the modern cattle are probably a result of selective breeding subsequent to their ancestors' arrival in southern Uganda about 500 years ago, at around the time the Ankole Kingdom was founded near modern-day Mbarara. Although the long horns were bred primarily for aesthetic reasons, the artificial process of breeding might have involved an element of natural selection. When threatened by large predators such as hyena or lion, it is customary for Ankole cattle to form a tight circle with horns facing outward, and it has also been noted how the calf often walks closely in front of its mother, protected by her horns.

Both in Uganda and Rwanda, pastoralists traditionally value cows less for their individual productivity than as status symbols: the wealth of a man would be measured

debilitating rainfall failures over recent years, so that it has often been dependent on outside food aid. It is a convenient base from which to explore Akagera National Park if you don't fancy paying to stay at the upmarket game lodge or camping in the park itself, and it also forms a possible springboard for a half-day trip to the Rusumo Falls. Otherwise, Kibungo is no more distinguished than other towns in this part of Rwanda, with its main focal point being a small grid of scruffy roads lying 3km west of the altogether more dynamic junction suburb known as Cyesamakamba (or Cyamakamba).

Getting there and away Kibungo lies 100km from Kigali along a good surfaced road, branching southward at the main traffic circle in Kayonza after 75km. The drive should take no more than two hours. Regular minibus-taxis connect Kigali to Kibungo – Ataco has departures from the city centre hourly between 06.45 and 17.45 – and there is also plenty of minibus-taxi transport on to Rusumo. The main taxi park in Kibungo is at Cyesamakamba more-or-less opposite the Umbrella Pine by the size and quality of his herd, and the worth of an individual cow by its horn size and, to a lesser extent, its coloration. In Rwanda, the noblest cow is the *inyambo*, which has an even deep blackish- or brownish-red hide, large lyre-shaped horns, and long hooves. Other long-horned cows of any coloration are called *ibigarama*, while stockier short-horned cows are referred to as *inkuku* – which may or may not be a pejorative derived from the widespread Bantu word for chicken!

Traditionally, the closely related pastoralist cultures of Rwanda and Uganda were as deeply bound up with a quasi-mystical relationship to cattle as the Maasai are today. Like Eskimos and their physical landscape, this abiding mental preoccupation is reflected in the 30 variations in hide coloration that are recognised linguistically by the Bahima of Ankole, along with at least a dozen peculiarities of horn shape and size. The Bahima day is traditionally divided up into 20 periods, of which all but one of the daylight phases is named after an associated cattle-related activity. And, like the Maasai, Rwandan and Ugandan pastoralists traditionally looked down on any lifestyle based around fishing or agriculture – and they also declined to hunt game for meat, with the exception of buffalo and eland, which were sufficiently bovine in appearance to make for acceptable eating.

In times past, the diet of the pastoralists of Uganda and Rwanda did not, as might be expected, centre on meat, but rather on blood tapped from the vein of a living cow, combined with the relatively meagre yield of milk from the small udders that characterise the Ankole breed. Slaughtering a fertile cow for meat was regarded as akin to cannibalism, but it was customary for infertile cows and surplus bullocks to be killed for meat on special occasions, while the flesh of any cow that died of natural causes would be eaten, or bartered for millet beer and other fresh produce. No part of the cow would go to waste: the hide would be used to make clothing, mats and drums, the dung to plaster huts and dried to light fires, while the horns could be customised as musical instruments.

Today, neither Rwanda nor Ankole is as defiantly traditionalist as, say, Ethiopia's Omo Valley or Maasailand, and most rural Bahima today supplement their herds of livestock by practising mixed agriculture of subsistence and cash crops. But the Ankole cattle and their extraordinary horns, particularly common in eastern Rwanda, pay living tribute to the region's ancestral bovine preoccupations. Meanwhile, on a more prosaic note, this hardy breed – first farmed in the USA in the 1960s, where they are most often called Watusi cattle, a name no longer used in Rwanda – is of growing interest to international stock farmers because its meat has the lowest cholesterol levels of any commercial breed.

Hotel, but Ataco also has a terminal in the town centre proper. The GPS for Cyesamakamba junction is 02°08.091, E 030°33.448 and for the town centre (Snack Bar et Logement Juru) it's 02°09.283, E 030°32.778.

🏠 Where to stay and eat

🏠 **Motel Umbrella Pine** (8 rooms) ☎ 566269. Situated in Cyesamakamba 200m south of the main traffic circle, this simple but attractive, friendly and hard-working little place has been a reliable bet for some years now. There are shortcomings – dodgy plumbing, water shortages during the dry season – but the staff are so willing that it's worth a try. The rooms have hot water and nets, and the restaurant not only serves good, inventive meals (under Rfr3,000) but can rustle up a picnic if you

need it for visiting Akagera. The hotel can be hard to spot, tucked away behind a petrol station on the right coming from Kigali. *Rfr5,600/8,260 en-suite sgl/dbl b&b.*

🏠 **Centre St Joseph** (20 rooms) ☎ 566303. Situated 100m from the feeder road to Kibungo, close to the Stella Taxi Express office, this attractive Catholic-run guesthouse offers good, clean en-suite rooms (cold water) as well as good, inexpensive local fare, and both soft and alcoholic drinks at the outdoor

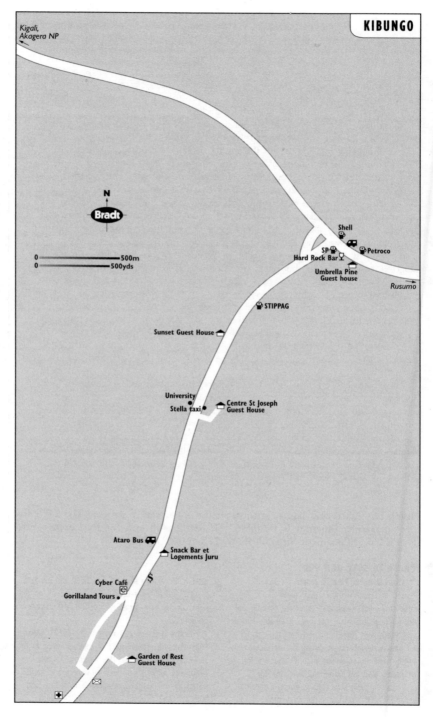

KIBUNGO

Kigali,
Akagera NP

N

Bradt

0 ————————— 500m
0 ————————— 500yds

Shell

SP
Hard Rock Bar
Petroco

Umbrella Pine
Guest house

Rusumo

STIPPAG

Sunset Guest House

University
Stella taxi
Centre St Joseph
Guest House

Ataro Bus
Snack Bar et
Logements Juru

Cyber Café
Gorillaland Tours

Garden of Rest
Guest House

bar/restaurant. *Rfr2,500/5,000/7,000 sgl/dbl/suite; Rfr1,500 dormitory bed.*

🏠 **Sunset Guesthouse** (5 rooms) ✆ 566767. Also situated alongside the feeder road about 700m from the junction, this low-key new guesthouse consists of a converted homestead set in a small quiet garden. The en-suite rooms have large beds and are very good value, but there is no restaurant or bar, and the nearest eateries are back around the junction. *Rfr5,000 dbl.*

🏠 **Garden of Rest Guesthouse** (4 rooms) ✆ 566396; m 08 467815;

e gardenofrest2005@yahoo.fr. This appealing small resthouse is situated in Kibungo proper, 100m downhill of the main surfaced road through town, and it offers comfortable en-suite accommodation in clean, tiled dbl rooms with netting and en-suite shower. The outdoor bar and restaurant looks good too. *Rfr5,000 dbl.*

✗ **Snack Bar et Logement Juru** (8 rooms) ✆ 566432; m 08 566286. This is the most central option in Kibungo, but it is very scruffy and the depressing rooms seem wildly overpriced. *Rfr5,000/8,000 sgl/dbl.*

Practicalities There is a post office and small bank on the main road, but no facilities for foreign exchange. The internet café opposite the bank appeared to be non-operational in early 2006, but that might change. Right next door to this, Gorillaland Car Hire (✆ 08 304891) might be worth contacting for transport to Akagera. A couple of other bars and restaurants are dotted around the junction, serving chilled beers, goat kebabs and other local fare – the food isn't comparable to that of the Umbrella Pine, but it is a lot cheaper.

NYAKARIMBI If you are heading to Rusumo, it's definitely worth stopping at this large village, which straddles the road from Kibungo about 20km before the Rusumo border crossing. This part of Rwanda is noted for its distinctive cow-dung 'paintings' – earthy, geometric designs which are mostly used to decorate the interiors of houses. In Nyakarimbi, however, a couple of the houses have cow-dung paintings on their outer walls, and about 2km south of the town there's a craft co-operative. This is where most of the geometric paintings and pottery you see in Kigali originate from, but it's more fun (and cheaper) to buy them at source, especially as the people who run the co-operative aren't at all pushy. The sign outside reads 'Ishyirahamwe Association Kakira – Art "Imigongo"' and shows geometric patterns. A small brochure, available in the workshop, explains (in more or less these words):

In olden times, there was Kakira, son of Kimenyi, King of Gisaka in Kibungo province (southeastern Rwanda). Kakira invented the art of embellishing houses and making them more attractive. To decorate the inside walls, cow dung was used, in patterns with prominent ridges. Then the surfaces were painted, in red and white colours made from natural soil (white from kaolin, red from natural clay with ochre), or else in shining black made from the sap of the aloe plant – ikakarubamba – mixed with the ash of burned banana skins and fruits of the solanum aculeastrum plant. It was the art of mixing together the soil, fire, raw materials from the cow and medicinal art that is the source of this work.

Kakira's knowledge was disappearing, due to the increasing use of industrial materials (paint); and so a women's association was created to maintain Kakira's work. After the 1994 genocide, most of the women, now widows, restarted their work together. Since 2001, the association has benefited from better promotion. Previously the women made no more than 20 pieces a month; now it is much more as orders have increased. Today, the Kakira Association makes 'Imigongo' art: modelled and painted tiles, panels, tables and other objects.

Coloured tiles cost US$16, black-and-white tiles US$6 – and they're beautiful, with very intricate patterns. Working hours are Monday to Saturday, 07.30–12.30 and 14.00–18.00. Kakira products can be ordered from the workshop or via Mr

13

A NEW VARIATION ON A TRADITIONAL TALE The great King Gihanga ruled a part of Rwanda in the early 12th century – or perhaps the late tenth. Some historians say that he was the first of the royal dynasty, others claim that many kings preceded him. That's the trouble with oral history – the facts are elusive, and who knows whether or not any of this story is true! Anyway, it's certain that Gihanga had many wives and many children.

One day, his favourite daughter Nyirarucyaba lost her temper with a wife who was not her mother, scratching at the woman's face and tearing her hair until she screamed in pain. To lose control was considered very shameful and all the courtiers had seen what happened, so the king had no choice. He banished Nyirarucyaba, sending her to the deep forest where only wild beasts live. She wept pitifully but he would not yield, although his heart was torn.

After many days alone, the girl heard a rustling in the leaves and a snapping of branches – and crouched to the ground in fear. But it was a young man who had, like her, been cast into exile. Now, together, they began to contact the animals around them. There was one that seemed friendly, despite its great size and ugly voice. By day it munched the forest grasses and by night they kept warm against its soft hide.

In time it gave birth to a young one, with wet matted skin and shaky legs, which nuzzled under its mother and sucked at her teats. They saw that it drank a white liquid and learnt that it was milk. Now they had food indeed! They shared the milk with the calf and grew strong and healthy. In time they bore children of their own and the cow had many more calves.

Meanwhile the king had fallen sick with an illness that robbed him of all strength and joy. Doctors could find no cure. Finally three of the court's wisest men, so old that their hair was white and thin upon their heads, recognised it as grief, and took it upon themselves to speak. They told him Nyirarucyaba was still alive – and at once he sprang from his couch and dispatched hunters to the forest to search for her. They found her beside a stream, her children at her side and many cattle grazing nearby. Her return to her delighted father was a time of great celebration at the court.

The cattle came too, with their rich supply of milk. The courtiers gained a taste for it, and grew fat and strong. One day – it was summer, and the grasses around the huts carried much pollen – one of the king's grandchildren asked him the name of the precious beasts. At that moment he sneezed explosively – 'Ha-ha-ha-inkaaah!' – and all heads nodded wisely. The king had spoken. From that time on, the cow has been called 'inka' in Kinyarwanda.

Emmanuel Bugingo (☏ *08594372;* e *bugingemmanuel@yahoo.fr*; ⊕ 02°16.165, E 030°41.812; 1,609m).

RUSUMO FALLS The Rusumo border with Tanzania, 60km southeast of Kibungo (⊕ 02°22.798, E 030°46.999, 1,320m), is also the site of Rwanda's most impressive waterfall. Rusumo Falls isn't particularly tall, and it couldn't be mentioned in the same breath as the Victoria or Blue Nile Falls, but it is a voluminous rush of white water nevertheless, as the Akagera River surges below the bridge between the two border posts. The Rwandan officials don't appear to have any objection to tourists wandering into No Man's Land and on to the bridge to goggle at the spectacle, though they may or may not ask to see a passport first. At present you can photograph the falls from the bridge, but nothing else in the immediate vicinity. It's best to ask permission anyway.

It's here at Rusumo that the German Count von Götzen, later to become Governor of German East Africa, entered Rwanda in 1894. He then travelled across the country to Lake Kivu, visiting the Mwami at Nyanza en route. Later, in 1916, when the Belgians were preparing to wrest the territory from the Germans, Belgian troops dug a trench and mounted artillery at the spot where one can see the falls today, in order to dislodge the German troops ensconced on the other bank who were guarding the only negotiable crossing. More recently, in 1994, Rusumo Bridge served as the funnel through which an estimated 500,000 Rwandans – half of them within one 24-hour period – fled from their home country to refugee camps around Ngala and elsewhere in northwest Tanzania. Journalists reporting on the exodus described standing on the bridge and counting the bloated bodies of genocide victims tumbling over the waterfall at a rate of one or two per minute.

TRAVELLING FROM KIGALI TO MWANZA (TANZANIA)

Izzie Robinson

We managed it in two days, but be warned – the second day is a long day. Also we could have just been lucky…

Getting from Kigali to the Tanzania border at Rusumo Falls involved getting up early and locating a minibus. We bought three tickets to accommodate our bags, and when that seat was sold to someone (who then practically sat on my lap) our fellow passengers complained and helped us keep our breathing space. We were most grateful and this proved to be the last comfortable minibus ride for a long while.

The journey to Rusumo was not a long one and there weren't even many roadblocks. We only got asked once if we had any weapons in our bags. We passed through Rwandan immigration, walked across the bridge and up the hill to the Tanzanian post. We hadn't been sure about this border so we had got our visas in advance in Kigali. As it was Tanzanian visas were available there.

Then we looked round for some transport. Nothing! After a little wait, a car pulled up and we negotiated a price with the driver to take us to Ngara. The journey only took a couple of hours, so we were there in good time to find accommodation and buy some fruit from the market. We also tried to get a seat on the Mwanza bus, but it turned out that the bus was broken. A helpful man suggested we buy seats on the Kahama-bound bus and try to get on to Mwanza from there.

We stayed in a cheap little hostel which was clean and pleasant, and we were even offered a wake-up call at 5am. It didn't materialise but it's the thought that counts. We headed off in the dark and managed to get the front two seats next to the driver – a good move for our first experience of Tanzanian minibuses. After cramming in as many people as humanly possible and then some, our bags were then rammed into the back space. We reckon this was the moment when the coffee pot we'd carried all the way from Ethiopia broke into a million pieces!

As dawn broke, we set off at speed, passing small barefoot children shivering on the way to school. We got to Kahama by 11am and there we learnt there was no bus to Mwanza, but if we went to Shinyanga we could continue from there. We shrugged and bought a ticket. To get to Shinyanga we travelled on a proper bus as opposed to a minibus, giving us slightly more room.

In Shinyanga we found a bus going to Mwanza (yay!) but it was empty and we ended up sitting miserably in the sun for hours and hours waiting to go. Up to that point the roads had been OK, but the stretch to Mwanza was painfully slow as we crawled in and out of large crater pot-holes. It was after dark by the time we got to Mwanza, where we had to walk around with our bags trying to find a room. But at least we got there.

13

So far as travel practicalities go, the surfaced road between Kibungo and Rusumo is in reasonable condition, and can be covered in an hour. Regular minibus-taxis service the route. About 200m back from the Rusumo border, the basic **Amarembo Hotel** has a Tanzanian contact number (0746 693 3030) a total of 11 rooms at Rfr2,000/3,000 single/double, a decent restaurant serving a tasty buffet lunch and dinner, and a great balcony offering a view across the facing rooftops to the Kagera River and surrounding papyrus beds. It gets busy with cross-border traffic. There's also an 'Anarembo Taxi Express' running between the hotel and Kigali: Rfr1,800 one way.

14

Akagera National Park

Named after the river which runs along its eastern boundary, Akagera National Park is Rwanda's answer to the famous savanna reserves of Kenya, Tanzania and the like. In contrast to the rest of the country, the area is relatively warm and low-lying, and its undulating plains support a cover of dense, broad-leafed woodland interspersed with lighter acacia woodland and patches of rolling grassland studded evocatively with stands of the superficially cactus-like *Euphorbia candelabra* shrub. To the west of the plains lies a chain of low mountains, reaching elevations of between 1,600m and 1,800m. The eastern part of the park supports an extensive wetland: a complex of a dozen lakes linked by extensive papyrus swamps and winding water channels fed by the mighty Akagera River.

In terms of game-viewing, it would be misleading to compare Akagera to East Africa's finest savanna reserves. Poaching has greatly reduced wildlife populations in recent years, and what was formerly the north of the park has been settled by returned refugees. The intense human pressure on Akagera is reflected in the fact that much of the northern and western territory (together with the adjoining 300km^2 Mutara Wildlife Reserve) was de-gazetted in 1997, reducing its total area by almost two-thirds from around 2,500km^2 to 1,085km^2. Even after this concession to local land requirements, the lakes that remain within the national park are routinely used to water domestic cattle – indeed, the long-horned Ankole cow is far and away the most commonly seen large mammal in Akagera.

For all that, Akagera is emphatically worth visiting. There are plenty of animals around, with the likes of buffalo, elephant, zebra, giraffe, hippo and various antelope all reasonably visible, and they aren't as skittish as one might expect. The lakes support some of the highest concentrations of hippo you'll find anywhere in Africa, as well as numerous large crocodiles, while lion, leopard and black rhino are still present in small numbers. And the birdlife is phenomenal – the checklist of 550 species includes the sort of rarities that will have ardent birdwatchers in raptures alongside a surprising density of raptors and some of Africa's most impressive concentrations of big waterbirds.

As big an attraction as the animal life is the sensation of being in a genuinely off-the-beaten-track chunk of bush: this is one African game reserve where you can still drive for hours without passing another vehicle, never knowing what wildlife encounter might lie around the next corner. Akagera is also among the most scenic of savanna reserves, with its sumptuous forest-fringed lakes, tall mountains and constantly changing vegetation.

Akagera is a good game reserve. It could, with improved management and a bit of time, once again become a truly great one. Equally, it could well be that Akagera will simply not be able to withstand the clamour for land from outside its already reduced boundaries. Which way it goes, one senses, will depend largely on its ability to generate serious tourist dollars and employment opportunities. Rwanda's population has doubled in the last 20 years and it is set to double again over the

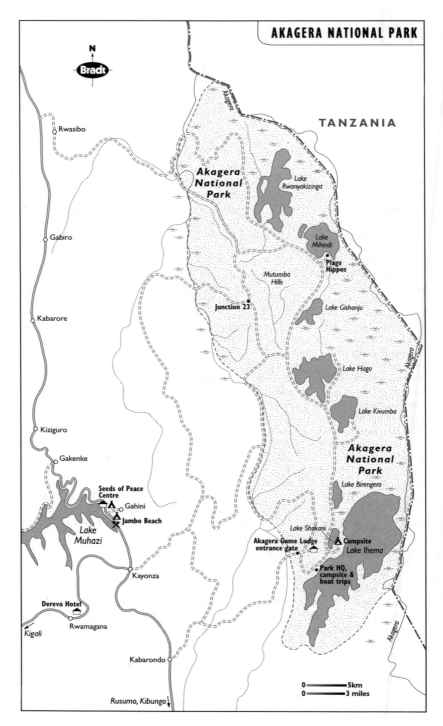

N
Bradt

TANZANIA

Rwasibo

Akagera
National
Park

Lake
Rwanyakizinga

Gabiro

Lake
Mihindi

Plage
Hippos

Mutumba
Hills

Kabarore

Junction 23

Lake Gishanju

Lake Hago

Lake Kivumba

Kiziguro

Gakenke

Akagera
National
Park

Lake Birengero

Seeds of Peace
Centre

Gahini

Jambo Beach

Lake
Muhazi

Lake Shakani

Akagera Game Lodge
entrance gate

Campsite
Lake Ihema

Kayonza

Park HQ,
campsite &
boat trips

Dereva Hotel

Kigali

Rwamagana

Kabarondo

0 ————— 5km
0 ————— 3 miles

Rusumo, Kibungo

The Belgian colonisers were concerned about nature conservation. From 1920 onwards (and earlier, in the Congo) conservation measures were put into practice and became the object of various legislative and administrative decrees. It was the decree of 26 November 1934 that created the Parc National de la Kagera, on about 250,000ha. The park included – which was extremely rare before 1960 – a Strict Natural Reserve and an adjoining area where certain human activities were tolerated. It came under the jurisdiction of the Institut des Parcs Nationaux du Congo Belge et du Ruanda-Urundi, which was also responsible for the three parks (Albert, Garamba and Upemba) in the Belgian Congo. (In fact 8% of the Albert Park was also in Rwanda; now representing the Volcanoes Park in the northwest.) Kagera was renamed Akagera after independence, when the new Republic's leaders announced their intention of maintaining the park (and the Volcanoes Park) despite population pressure. Akagera's borders were altered – a few thousand hectares were retroceded to local communities while almost 20,000ha of the lacustrine zone to the south were incorporated. In 1975, 26 elephants were transported, first by helicopter and then by truck, from Bugesera, which was to be developed for agriculture. In November 1984, Rwanda held an official celebration of the park's 50th anniversary.

next 20. The pressure on Akagera will only increase with time; yet in the context of this rapid population growth, forsaking a vast tract of not particularly arable game reserve to grazing will not address the heart of the land issue but merely alleviate a short-term problem.

The survival of Akagera is not simply an esoteric conservation concern, but one that has implications for the country's development as a whole. Prior to the civil war, Rwanda's fledgling tourist industry was one of its three main sources of foreign revenue. If Rwanda is to rebuild that industry, and to develop a self-contained tourist circuit of its own, then it desperately *needs* Akagera. For, without a savanna reserve of Akagera's ilk, the country seems destined to attract nothing but pit-stop cross-border gorilla tourism, tourists spending one or two nights in one small part of the country as an extension of a safari elsewhere in East Africa. It's to be hoped that the facilities of the very new Akagera Game Lodge inside the park may help to rebuild Akagera's tourism.

If you visit Akagera, you won't regret it – it's a lovely, untrammelled slice of African bush. No less important, perhaps, you'll be doing Rwanda a favour.

NATURAL HISTORY

Akagera is notable for protecting an unusually wide diversity of habitats within a relatively small area. Prior to the civil war, it was regarded as one of the few African savanna reserves to form a self-sustaining ecological unit, meaning that its resident large mammals had no need to migrate seasonally outside of the park boundaries. Whether that is still the case today is an open question: roughly two-thirds of the original park was degazetted in 1997, and, while some of this discarded territory is still virgin bush, it is probably only a matter of time before it will all be settled, putting further pressure on Akagera's diminished wildlife populations.

The modern boundaries of the park protect an area of 1,085km², stretching along the Tanzania border for approximately 60km from north to south, and nowhere wider than 30km. The eastern third of the park consists of an extensive network of wetlands, fed by the Akagera River, and dominated by a series of small-to-medium-sized lakes. Lake Ihema, the most southerly of the lakes to lie within the revised park boundaries, is also the largest body of open water, covering about 100km^2. The lakes are connected by narrow channels of flowing water and large expanses of seasonal and perennial papyrus swamps. The eastern wetlands are undoubtedly the most important of the habitats protected within the park: not only do they provide a permanent source of drinking water for the large mammals, but they also form an important waterbird sanctuary while harbouring a number of localised swamp dwellers.

Akagera's dominant terrestrial habitat is dense broad-leafed woodland, though pockets of acacia woodland also exist within the park, while some of the lake fringes support a thin belt of lush riparian woodland. Ecologically, the savanna of Akagera is in several respects unique, a product of its isolation from similar habitats by the wetlands to the east and mountainous highlands of central Rwanda to the west. The flora shows strong affinities with the semi-arid zones of northern Uganda and Kenya, but the fauna is more typical of the Mara-Serengeti ecosystem east of Lake Victoria. Akagera's geographical isolation from similar habitats is emphasised by the natural absence of widespread plains animals such as rhino and giraffe, both of which were subsequently introduced and thrived in their adopted home. Much of the bush in Akagera is very dense, but there are also areas of light acacia woodland and open grassland, notably on the Mutumba Hills and to the northeast of Lake Rwanyakizinga.

MAMMALS While Akagera's considerable scenic qualities and superb birdlife are largely unaffected by the recent years of turmoil, the large mammal populations have suffered badly at the hands of poachers. Having said that, we arrived at Akagera expecting the worst, and were pleasantly surprised at how much wildlife there still is. It is the classic 'bad news, good news' scenario. The populations of all large mammals (except perhaps hippo) are severely depleted in comparison with ten years ago, while a few high-profile species, if not already locally extinct, appear to be heading that way. The good news, however, is that most large mammals are still sufficiently numerous to form a viable breeding population; furthermore, with adequate protection, these numbers are likely to be supplemented by animals crossing into the park from unprotected parts of neighbouring Tanzania which still support plenty of big game. Akagera, in short, is a damaged but salvageable game reserve.

Extirpated species include the **African wild dog**, probably a victim not of poaching but, in common with many other African reserves, of a canine plague which would have been introduced into the population through contact with domestic dogs. Of the larger predators, **spotted hyena** and **leopard** are still around, but infrequently observed (though you might well come across hyena spoor, particularly the characteristic white dung).

The future of the park's **lion** hangs in the balance. Prior to 1994, the park supported an estimated 250 individuals, including a couple of prides that were uniquely adapted to foraging in the swamps, and others specialised in climbing trees. During the civil war, large numbers of lion were hunted out by the army to protect the presidential cattle herds; more recently they have been poisoned by cattle herders living outside the park. The situation today is open to conjecture. After a few years without any confirmed sightings, a female with three cubs was observed in the north of the park in the year 2000. More recent published estimates have placed the population at anywhere from 15 to 60 individuals, but local sources are less optimistic, placing the total number of resident lions at fewer than 10. That said, given the tenacity of this regal feline, and its tendency to wander long distances, it is one species that could naturally replenish itself through individuals crossing over from Tanzania.

Smaller predators are well represented. Most likely to be encountered by day are various **mongooses** (we saw dwarf, banded and black-tailed mongooses), while at night there is a chance of coming across viverrids such as the lithe, heavily spotted and somewhat cat-like **genet**, and the bulkier black-masked **civet**. Also present, but rarely seen, are the handsome spotted **serval cat** and the dog-like **side-striped jackal**.

One of the most common terrestrial mammals is the **buffalo** and, while the population is nowhere near the estimated 8,000 that roamed the park in the 1980s, it is probably still measurable in thousands. **Hippo**, too, are present in impressive numbers: on some of the lakes there must be at least a dozen pods of up to 50 animals, and the total population probably exceeds 1,000. The handsome **impala** is probably the most common and habitat-tolerant large mammal in the park, and of the 11 antelope species which occur in Akagera (see box *Antelope of Akagera* on pages 234–5), only the aquatic **sitatunga** is immediately endangered and unlikely to be seen by visitors. Small herds of **Burchell's zebra** are regularly encountered in open areas.

Also very common are three savanna primates: the dark, heavily built **olive baboon** (boldly resident around the game lodge), the smaller and more agile **vervet monkey**, and the tiny wide-eyed **bushbaby** (the latter a nocturnal species likely to be seen only after dusk). The forest-dwelling **silver monkey**, although listed for Akagera, is probably now very rare, possibly even locally extinct, due to habitat loss following the reduction in the park's area. For the same reason, it is debatable whether Africa's largest swine, the **giant forest hog**, still occurs in Akagera. The smaller **bushpig**, a secretive nocturnal species, is present but rarely encountered, while the diurnal **warthog** is very common and often seen trotting off in family parties, stiff tail held high.

Two large mammal species that don't occur there naturally were introduced to the park prior to the civil war. The first of these is the **Maasai giraffe**, which was introduced from the Magadi region of southern Kenya in January 1986. The original herd of two males and four females produced its first offspring in 1988 and has since multiplied to a population of around 60 head, which tends to stick to patches of acacia woodland close to the park headquarters and game lodge.

In 1957, Akagera became the recipient of Africa's first **black rhino** translocation, when a herd comprising five females and one male was flown across from the bordering Karagwe region of Tanzania, to be supplemented by another male a year later. The rhino prospered in the dense bush and by the early 1970s had colonised most of the park – one individual is known to have strayed south almost as far as the Rusumo Falls – and by the end of that decade the population comfortably exceeded the half-century mark. Then came the wholesale rhino poaching of the 1980s: by the end of that decade no more than a dozen individuals survived, and it was long thought that the remainder were shot in the civil war. The occasional unverified rhino sighting was reported by visitors in the years that followed, but it was only in early 2004 that veterinary surgeon Claudia Schoene was able to confirm the presence of a nine-year old female in the north. Plans are under way for this lone survivor – now named Patricia – to be joined by a translocated male from Kenya or South Africa.

Although the **African elephant** used to occur naturally in Akagera, the last recorded sighting of the original population was on the shores of Lake Mihindi in 1961. The present-day herd is descended from a group of 26 youngsters that was translocated to Akagera in 1975, part of an operation to clear all the elephants from the increasingly densely populated Bugesera Plains to the south of Kigali. Up to 100 adult elephants were shot in the process, while a young American filmmaker Lee Lyon was killed by one of the survivors upon its release into Akagera. By the late 1980s an estimated 45 individuals roamed Akagera and, although population

ANTELOPE OF AKAGERA

The 11 antelope species in Akagera range from the eland, the world's largest antelope, through to the diminutive common duiker. The most common, however, is the **impala** *Aepeceros melampus*, a slim handsome antelope which bears a superficial similarity to the gazelles, but belongs to a separate family. Chestnut in colour, the impala has diagnostic black and white stripes running down its rump and tail, and the male has large lyre-shaped horns. It is one of the most widespread antelope species in East and southern Africa, normally seen in large herds in woodland habitats, and common in the woodland around and between the lakes of Akagera.

The **Defassa waterbuck** *Kobus ellipsiprymnus defassa* is a large, shaggy brown antelope with a distinctive white rump. The male has large lyre-shaped horns, thicker than those of the impala. The waterbuck inhabits practically any type of woodland or grassland provided that it is close to water, and it is probably the most common large antelope after impala in the far south of Akagera.

Very common in the north of the park and in the Mutumba Hills, the **topi** or **tsessebe** *Damaliscus lunatus* is a large, slender dark-brown antelope with striking yellow lower legs. It has a rather ungainly appearance, reminiscent of the hartebeest and wildebeest, to which it is closely related, and is often seen using an anthill as a sentry point. Oddly, the herds of topi in northern Akagera seem to be far larger than those found in the Serengeti ecosystem.

Similar in size to a topi, but far more handsome, the **roan antelope** *Hippotragus equinus* has, as the Latin name suggests, a horse-like bearing. The uniform fawn-grey coat is offset by a pale belly, and it has short decurved horns and a light mane. After the civil war, roan were thought to be very rare in Akagera (a 1998 estimate places the population at below 20) but they are now on the recovery, with some sources placing the population at around 150.

Much larger still is the **common** or **Cape eland** *Taurotragus oryx*, which attains a height of up to 1.75m and can weigh as much as 900kg. The common eland is light-brown in colour, with faint white vertical stripes, and a somewhat bovine appearance accentuated by the relatively short horns and large dewlap. In Akagera, small herds are most likely to be seen on the open grassland of the Mutumba Hills, where the population is thought to exceed 50.

growth was stunted by poaching during the civil war, the current population of at least 100 is probably the largest the park has supported in 50 years.

BIRDS Akagera is, after Nyungwe, the most important ornithological site in Rwanda, with a checklist of 550 species recorded before its area was reduced in 1997 (now probably closer to 525 species). What's more, these two fine birding destinations complement each other to such an extent that very few birds recorded in Rwanda aren't found at one or other site. In addition to being the best place in Rwanda to see a good selection of savanna birds and raptors, Akagera is as rich in waterbirds as anywhere in East Africa, and one of the few places where papyrus endemics can be observed.

Among the more colourful and common of the savanna birds are the gorgeous lilac-breasted roller, black-headed gonolek (easily picked up by its jarring duets), little bee-eater, Heuglin's robin-chat and brown parrot. Less colourful, but very impressive, are the comical grey hornbill and noisy bare-faced go-away bird. The riparian woodland around the lakes hosts a number of specialised species, of which Ross's turaco, a bright-purple, jay-sized bird with a distinctive yellow mask, is the most striking.

A trio of smaller antelope are also mainly confined to the Mutumba Hills. The largest of these is the **Bohor reedbuck** *Redunca redunca*, a light-fawn animal with moderately sized rounded horns; reedbucks are almost always seen in pairs, and in Akagera are rather skittish.

The smaller **oribi** *Ourebia ourebi* is a tan grassland antelope with short straight horns and a small but clearly visible circular black glandular patch below its ear. It is the commonest antelope on the Mutumba Hills, typically seen in parties of two or three, and has a distinctive sneezing alarm call.

The **klipspringer** *Oreotragus oreotragus* is a goat-like antelope, normally seen in pairs, and easily identified by its dark, bristly grey-yellow coat, slightly speckled appearance and unique habitat preference. Klipspringer means 'rock jumper' in Afrikaans and it is an apt name for an antelope which occurs exclusively in mountainous areas and rocky outcrops.

The only small antelope found in thicker bush is the **common duiker** *Sylvicapra grimmia*, an anomalous savanna representative of a family of 20-plus small hunchbacked antelopes associated with true forests. Generally grey in colour, the common duiker has a distinctive black tuft of hair sticking up between its small straight horns. It is common in all bush areas, though it tends to be very skittish.

A widespread resident of thick woodland and forest, the pretty **bushbuck** *Tragelaphus scriptus* is a medium-sized, rather deer-like antelope. The male is dark brown or chestnut, while the much smaller female is generally pale red-brown. The male has relatively small, straight horns, while both sexes have pale throat patches, white spots and sometimes stripes. The bushbuck tends to be secretive, but might be seen anywhere in Akagera except for open grassland.

Similar in appearance to the bushbuck, and a close relation, the semi-aquatic **sitatunga** *Tragelaphus spekei* is a widespread but infrequently observed inhabitant of west and central African swamps. The male, with a shoulder height of up to 125cm (much taller than a bushbuck) and a shaggy fawn coat, is unmistakable, while the smaller female might be mistaken for a bushbuck except for its more clearly defined stripes. The status of the sitatunga within Akagera is uncertain; it is certainly still present, but mostly restricted to inaccessible swampy areas.

A notable feature of Akagera's avifauna is the presence of species such as the crested barbet, Arnot's (white-headed black) chat and Souza's shrike, all of which are associated with the *brachystegia* woodland of southern Tanzania and further south, but have colonised the mixed woodland of Akagera at the northernmost extent of their range. More noteworthy still is the red-faced barbet, a localised endemic of savannas between Lake Victoria and the Albertine Rift. Finally, the savanna of Akagera is one of the last places in Rwanda where a wide range of large raptors is resident: white-backed and Rüppell's griffon vultures soar high on the thermals, the beautiful bateleur eagle can be recognised by its wavering flight pattern and red wing markings, while brown snake eagles and hooded vultures are often seen perching on bare branches.

Most of the savanna birds are primarily of interest to the dedicated birder, but it is difficult to imagine that anybody would be unmoved by the immense concentrations of water-associated birds that can be found on the lakes. Pelicans are common, as is the garishly decorated crowned crane, the odd little open-bill stork and the much larger and singularly grotesque marabou stork. Herons and egrets are particularly visible and well-represented, ranging from the immense goliath heron to the secretive black-capped night heron and reed-dwelling purple heron. The lakes also support a variety of smaller kingfishers and shorebirds, and a

Perhaps the most eagerly sought of all African birds, the shoebill is also one of the few that is likely to make an impression on those travellers who regard pursuing rare birds to be about as diverting as hanging about in windswept railway stations scribbling down train numbers. Three factors combine to give the shoebill its bizarre and somewhat prehistoric appearance. The first is its enormous proportions: an adult might stand more than 150cm (5ft) tall and typically weighs around 6kg. The second is its unique uniform slatey-grey coloration. Last but emphatically not least is its clog-shaped, hook-tipped bill – at 20cm long, and almost as wide, the largest among all living bird species. The bill is fixed in a permanent Cheshire-cat smirk that contrives to look at once sinister and somewhat inane, and when agitated the bird loudly claps together its upper and lower bill, rather like outsized castanets.

The first known allusions to the shoebill came from early European explorers to the Sudan, who wrote of a camel-sized flying creature known by the local Arabs as Abu Markub – Father of the Shoe. These reports were dismissed as pure fancy by Western biologists until 1851, when Gould came across a bizarre specimen amongst an avian collection shot on the Upper White Nile. Describing it as 'the most extraordinary bird I have seen', Gould placed his discovery in a monotypic family and named it *Balaeniceps Rex* – King Whale Head! Gould believed the strange bird to be most closely allied to pelicans, but it also shares some anatomic and behavioural characters with herons, and until recently it was widely thought to be an evolutionary offshoot of the stork family. Recent DNA studies support Gould's original theory, however, and the shoebill is now placed in a monotypic subfamily of the Pelecanidae.

The life cycle of the shoebill is no less remarkable than its appearance. One of the few birds with an age span of up to 50 years, it is generally monogamous, with pairs coming together during the breeding season (April to June) to construct a grassy nest of up to 3m wide on a mound of floating vegetation or a small island. Two eggs are laid, and the parents rotate incubation duties, in hot weather filling their bills with water to spray over the eggs to keep them cool. The chicks hatch after about a month, and will need to be fed by the parents for at least another two months until their beaks are fully developed. Usually only one nestling survives, probably as a result of sibling rivalry.

The shoebill is a true swamp specialist, but it avoids dense stands of papyrus and tall grass, which obstruct its take-off, preferring instead to forage from patches of low floating vegetation or along the edge of channels. It consumes up to half its weight in food daily, preying on whatever moderately sized aquatic creature might come its way, ranging from toads to baby crocodiles, though lungfish are especially favoured. Its method of hunting is exceptionally sedentary: the bird may stand semi-frozen for several hours before it lunges down with remarkable speed and power, heavy wings stretched backward, to grab an item of prey in its large, inescapable bill. Although it is generally a solitary hunter, the shoebill has occasionally been observed hunting co-

prodigious number of fish eagles, whose shrill duet ranks as one of the most evocative sounds of Africa.

On a more esoteric note, the papyrus swamps are an excellent place to look for a handful of birds restricted to this specific habitat: the stunning and highly vocal papyrus gonolek, as well as the more secretive and nondescript Caruthers's cisticola and white-winged warbler. Akagera used to be regarded as one of the best places in Africa to see the shoebill, an enormous and unmistakable slate-grey swamp-dweller whose outsized bill is fixed in a permanent Cheshire-cat smirk (see box above). A useful birding report on Akagera can be sourced online at www.worldtwitch.com/rwanda_uganda_des.htm.

operatively in small flocks, which splash about flapping their wings to drive a school of fish into a confined area.

Although the shoebill is an elusive bird, this is less a function of scarcity than of the inaccessibility of its swampy haunts. Nevertheless, *BirdLife International* recently classified it as near-globally threatened, and it is classed as CITES Appendix 2, which means that trade in shoebills, or their capture for any harmful activity, is forbidden by international law. Estimates of the global population vary wildly. In the 1970s, only 1,500 shoebills were thought to persist in the wild, but this estimate has subsequently been revised to 10–15,000 individuals concentrated in five countries – Sudan, Uganda, Tanzania, Congo and Zambia. Small breeding populations also occur in Rwanda and Ethiopia, and vagrants have been recorded in Malawi and Kenya.

The most important shoebill stronghold is the Sudd Floodplain on the Sudanese Nile, where 6,400 individuals were counted during an aerial survey undertaken over 1979–82, followed by the inaccessible Moyowosi-Kigosi Swamp in western Tanzania, whose population was thought to amount to a few hundred prior to a 1990 survey that estimated the population to be greater than 2,000. Ironically, although Uganda is the easiest place to see the shoebill in the wild, the national population probably amounts to fewer than 1,000 birds.

Outside of Uganda, Akagera National Park is potentially one of the most accessible shoebill haunts anywhere in Africa. In the 1980s, the local shoebill population was estimated at around 15–20 pairs, and there is no particular reason to think this has changed greatly in the interim – shoebills are not hunted as food, they pose no threat to cattle herders, and the inaccessible swamps they inhabit were largely unaffected by the 1997 reduction in Akagera's area. Sadly, however, little effort has been made to establish the current status of shoebills in Akagera, or to make the bird's habitat accessible to tourists by boat. All the same, the rangers say that one pair is occasionally seen in the papyrus beds fringing Lake Birengiro, and (more encouragingly perhaps) ornithologists Dave Sargeant and Nigel Moorhouse observed a solitary shoebill on the northern shore of Lake Ihema on a day trip from Kigali in June 2003.

The major threat to the survival of the shoebill is habitat destruction. The construction of several dams along the lower Nile means that the water levels of the Sudd are open to artificial manipulation. Elsewhere, swamp clearance and rice farming pose a localised threat to suitable wetland habitats. Lake Opeta, an important shoebill stronghold in eastern Uganda, has been earmarked as a source of irrigation for a new agricultural scheme. A lesser concern in some areas is that shoebills are hunted for food or illegal trade, while in others local fishermen often kill the shoebills in the belief that seeing one before a fishing expedition is a bad omen. As is so often the case, tourism can play a major role in preserving the shoebill and its habitat: a classic example being Uganda's Mabamba Swamp, where the local community has already seen financial benefits from ornithological visits from nearby Entebbe.

REPTILES The **Nile crocodile**, the world's largest reptile and a survivor from the age of the dinosaurs, is abundant in the lakes. Some of the largest wild specimens you'll encounter anywhere are to be found sunning themselves on the mud-banks of Akagera, their impressive mouths wide open until they slither menacingly into the water at the approach of human intruders. Not unlike a miniature crocodile in appearance, the **water monitor** is a type of lizard which often grows to be more than a metre long and is common around the lakes, tending to crash noisily into the bush or water when disturbed. Smaller lizards are to be seen all over, notably the colourful rock agama, and a variety of snakes are present but, as ever, very secretive.

DANGEROUS ANIMALS Although it is technically forbidden to leave your vehicle except at designated lookout points, the guides in Akagera seem to enforce this rule somewhat whimsically. Bizarrely, some guides seem to be unduly nervous about approaching elephant and buffalo in a vehicle but are dangerously blasé about trying to sneak up on the same animals on foot. It's probably worth noting that, whatever your guide might say, it is extremely foolhardy to leave the vehicle in the presence of elephant, buffalo or lion.

Hippo and crocodile are potentially dangerous, and claim far more human lives than any terrestrial African animal. For this reason, you should be reasonably cautious when you leave the car next to a lake, particularly at dusk or dawn or in overcast conditions, when hippos are most likely to come out of the water to graze. The danger with hippos is getting *between* them and the water; you have nothing to worry about when they are actually in the water. Special caution should be exercised if you camp next to a lake – don't wander too far from your site after dark, and take a good look around should you need to leave your tent during the night (if there are hippo close by, you'll almost certainly hear them chomping at the grass). Crocs are a real threat only if you are daft enough to wade into one of the lakes.

The most dangerous animal in Akagera is the malaria-carrying anopheles mosquito. Cover up after dark – long trousers and thick socks – and smear any exposed parts of your body with insect repellent. Many tents come with built-in mosquito netting. This will protect you when you sleep, provided that you don't hang a light at the entrance to your tent, which will ensure that a swarm of insects enter it with you. Incidentally, never leave any food in your tent: fruit might attract the attention of monkeys and elephants, while meat could arouse the interest of large predators.

Not so much a danger as a nuisance are tsetse flies, which are quite common in dense bush and can give a painful bite. Fortunately, the pain isn't enduring (though people who tend to react badly to insect bites might want to douse any tsetse bite in antihistamine cream) and there is no risk of contracting sleeping sickness during a short stay in Akagera. Insect repellents have little effect on these robust little creatures, but it's worth noting that they are attracted to dark clothing (especially blue).

FURTHER INFORMATION

An accurate useful fold-out colour map is sold at the ORTPN office in Kigali, as well as at the gate. The numbered junctions shown on the map help with navigation, though not all junctions are still numbered on the ground. The map costs around Rfr2,000 and includes some descriptive material about the park on the flip. Also for sale at the gate, the coffee-table book *Akagera: Land of Water, Grass and Fire* by Jean-Pierre Vande Weghe, first published in 1990 and subsequently reprinted but never updated, presents an alluring picture of Akagera as it must once have been – it's historically fascinating, but likely to create false expectations of a visit to the park today, and is ultimately a rather depressing testament to human destructivity.

GETTING THERE AND AWAY

In a private vehicle, Akagera can be reached from Kigali in a long two hours, and from Kibungo or Rwamagana in about one hour. The only usable entrance gate, 500m from the new Akagera Game Lodge, is reached via a 27km dirt road which branches from the main surfaced road at Kabarondo, 15km north of Kibungo. This dirt road is in fair condition, passable in any vehicle except perhaps after rain. Within the park, however, a 4x4 is advisable, though any vehicle with good clearance should be OK in the dry season.

Reaching Akagera on public transport is more problematic. Any minibus-taxi travelling between Kayonza and Kibungo can drop you at the junction, from where the only realistic option is a motorbike-taxi (assuming that you can find one). Inside the park, unless you're staying at the Game Lodge, no walking is permitted with or without a guide, and no vehicle is available for game drives.

WHERE TO STAY

Akagera Game Lodge (60 rooms) ☎ 657805; m 08 611491; f 567806; e akagelodge@rwanda1.com; ✪ S 01°52.314, E 030°42.911, 1,610m. Re-opened in 2003 on the site of the former Akagera Hotel, this smart lodge lies in wooded hilltop grounds offering a superb view over Lake Ihema into the hills of Tanzania. Originally under South African management but recently taken over by a local entrepreneur, the lodge is dated somewhat by the rather monolithic and angular 1970s architecture, but it is otherwise very pleasantly decorated and the en-suite twin or dbl rooms are comfortable and presentable in a motel-like way. Facilities include a good and surprisingly affordable à la carte restaurant, a swimming pool, conference facilities and tennis courts, and the overall level of service is impressively professional given the remote locale. For those wanting to do an early morning game drive (recommended), the filling b/fast normally starts at 06.00 and can be served at 05.30 by request. Walks and game drives accompanied by guides can be arranged. *Rfr44,250/56,050 sgl/dbl; Rfr73,750/85,550 suite; all rates b&b.*

▲ Camping For the self-sufficient, this is allowed at various locations in the park, and costs US$10 pp per night for non-residents, US$5 for foreign residents, or Rfr2,000 for Rwandans. Contact ORTPN or ask at the date for further details.

FEES

The fee structure for Akagera is rather confusing so bear with us! First up, a one-off entrance fee of US$10 (non-residents), US$5 (foreign residents) or Rfr1,000 (Rwandans) is charged to all visitors and covers the full duration of their stay. In addition, the park levies a one-off vehicle fee of Rfr2,000–10,000 (locally registered vehicles) or US$10–50 (foreign registered vehicles), depending on the size and type of vehicles, with the highest fees applying to trucks and buses. To this must be added a game viewing fee of US$20/30/50 (non-residents) US$15/20/25 (foreign residents) or Rfr2,500/3,000/5,000 (Rwandans) for one/two/three days. Note that this fee is charged per calendar day (as opposed to per 24 hours, so you pay for two days if you do an afternoon and morning game drive either side of an overnight stay) but that visits of longer than three days are treated as a three-day visit (in other words, you pay nothing more to stay on for a fourth day or longer). No fees are levied simply for staying at the game lodge. Regular visitors can buy annual permits – for foreigners these cost US$60 (one person), US$100 (couple), US$150 (family).

ACTIVITIES

BOAT TRIPS Boat trips are generally available on Lake Ihema, and are worthwhile. Book in advance via ORTPN in Kigali – see page 61. Close encounters with outsized crocodiles and large pods of hippo are all but guaranteed, and you'll also pass substantial breeding colonies of African darter, cormorant and open-bill stork. Other waterbirds are abundant: the delicate and colourful African jacana can be seen trotting on floating vegetation, fish eagles are posted in the trees at regular intervals, jewel-like malachite kingfishers hawk from the reeds, while pied

14

Placed by some authorities in the same family as the closely related sparrows, the weavers of the family Ploceidae are a quintessential part of Africa's natural landscape, common and highly visible in virtually every habitat from rainforest to desert. The name of the family derives from the intricate and elaborate nests – typically but not always a roughly oval ball of dried grass, reeds and twigs – that are built by the dextrous males of most species.

It can be fascinating to watch a male weaver at work. First, a nest site is chosen, usually at the end of a thin hanging branch or frond, which is immediately stripped of leaves to protect against snakes. The weaver then flies back and forth to the site, carrying the building material blade by blade in its heavy beak, first using a few thick strands to hang a skeletal nest from the end of a branch, then gradually completing the structure by interweaving numerous thinner blades of grass into the main frame. Once completed, the nest is subjected to the attention of his chosen partner, who will tear it apart if the result is less than satisfactory, and so the process starts all over again.

All but 12 of the 113 described weaver species are resident on the African mainland or associated islands, with some 21 represented within Rwanda alone. All but five of the Rwandan species are placed in the genus Ploceus (true weavers), which is among the most characteristic of all African bird genera. Most of the Ploceus weavers are slightly larger than a sparrow, and display a strong sexual dimorphism. Females are with few exceptions drab buff- or olive-brown birds, with some streaking on the back, and perhaps a hint of yellow on the belly.

Most male Ploceus weavers conform to the basic colour pattern of the 'masked weaver' – predominantly yellow, with streaky back and wings, and a distinct black facial mask, often bordered orange. Five Rwandan weaver species fit this masked weaver prototype more-or-less absolutely, and a similar number approximate it rather less exactly, for instance by having a chestnut-brown mask, or a full black head, or a black back, or being more chestnut than yellow on the belly. Identification of the masked weavers can be tricky without experience – useful clues are the exact shape of the mask, the presence and extent of the fringing orange, and the colour of the eye and the back.

The golden weavers, of which only one species is present in Rwanda, are also brilliant yellow and/or light orange with some light streaking on the back, but they lack a mask or any other strong distinguishing features. The handful of forest-associated Ploceus weavers, by contrast, tend to have quite different and very striking colour patterns; and,

kingfishers hover high above the water to swoop down on their fishy prey. Of greater interest to enthusiasts will be the opportunity to spot marsh specialists such as blue-headed coucal and marsh flycatcher.

GAME DRIVES Unless you're staying in the Game Lodge, game drives are available only if you have a private vehicle, ideally a 4x4. Guides are provided at no extra charge (though a tip will be expected) and, while most of them have limited knowledge, they will help you to find your way around and will probably be better at picking up game in the thick bush. The game-viewing circuit is in essence limited to one main road running northwards from the park headquarters at Lake Ihema. Most of the lakes are passed by this road, or can be approached using a short fork. North of Lake Hago, the road branches into two main forks, one of which heads west into the Mutumba Hills, the other continuing along the lake route. These roads reconnect at Lake Rwanyakizinga.

The possibilities for game drives are restricted by the fact that the park can only be entered near Lake Ihema and the Game Lodge. In a long half-day, you could although sexually dimorphic, the female is often as boldly marked as the male. The most aberrant among these is Vieillot's black weaver, the males of which are totally black except for their eyes, while the black-billed weaver reverses the prototype by being all black with a yellow facemask.

Among the more conspicuous Ploceus species in Rwanda are the black-headed, Baglafecht, slender-billed, yellow-backed and Vieillot's black weavers – for the most part gregarious breeders forming single- or mixed-species colonies of hundreds, sometimes thousands, of pairs. The most extensive weaver colonies are often found in reed beds and waterside vegetation, such as can be seen around the lakes of Akagera. Few weavers have a distinctive song, but they compensate with a rowdy jumble of harsh swizzles, rattles and nasal notes that can reach deafening proportions near large colonies. One more cohesive song you will often hear seasonally around weaver colonies is a cyclic 'dee-dee-dee-Diederik', often accelerating to a hysterical crescendo when several birds call at once. This is the call of the Diederik cuckoo, a handsome green-and-white cuckoo that lays its eggs in weaver nests.

Oddly, while most East African Ploceus weavers are common, even abundant, in suitable habitats, seven highly localised species are listed as range-restricted, and four of these – one Kenyan, one Ugandan and two Tanzanian endemics – are regarded to be of global conservation concern. Of the other three, the strange weaver Ploceus alienus – black head, plain olive back, yellow belly with chestnut bib – is an Albertine Rift endemic restricted to a handful of sites in Rwanda and Uganda, notably Nyungwe National Park.

Most of the colonial weavers, perhaps relying on safety in numbers, build relatively plain nests with a roughly oval shape and an unadorned entrance hole. The nests of more solitary weavers are often more elaborate. Several weavers, for instance, protect their nests from egg-eating invaders by attaching tubular entrance tunnels to the base – in the case of the spectacled weaver, which inhabits riverine woodland in Akagera, this tunnel is sometimes twice as long as the nest itself. The Grosbeak weaver (a peculiar larger-than-average brown-and-white weaver of reed beds, distinguished by its outsized bill and placed in the monospecific genus Amblyospiza) constructs a large and distinctive domed nest, which is supported by a pair of reeds, and woven as precisely as the finest basketwork, with a neat raised entrance hole at the front. By contrast, the scruffiest nests are built by the various species of sparrow- and buffalo-weaver, relatively drab but highly gregarious dry-country birds which are poorly represented in Rwanda.

realistically travel from the entrance as far north as the Mutumba Hills and back. To head further north requires the best part of a day, with the option of using the exit-only route north of Lake Rwanyakizinga emerging on the main tar road to the Uganda border. The tracks in the far north are very indistinct, and should be attempted only in the company of a guide. Once back on the main road, the guide can be dropped at Kayonza or Kabarondo junctions with enough money to make his way back to the headquarters by motorbike-taxi.

Starting from the entrance gate, a hilly road through very thick scrub leads over about 5km to **Lake Ihema**. It is on a humid and mosquito-plagued island near the eastern shore of Ihema that Henry Stanley, the first European to enter modern-day Rwanda, set up camp on the night of 11 March 1876, only to turn back into what is now Tanzania the next day after he was repulsed from the lake's western shore. Today, Defassa waterbuck are common residents around Ihema, as are some reportedly aggressive buffaloes. The park headquarters at the lake are worth stopping at to look for hippos, crocodiles and waterbirds – possibly even shoebill, which has been identified reliably on the northern lakeshore. Baboons hang

14

around the headquarters, and a pair of the localised Arnot's chat is resident. This is also where boat trips can be arranged.

About 4km north of Lake Ihema, a road forks through more thick scrub to the small **Lake Shakani**, a scenic camping spot and home to large numbers of hippo. The bush here is rattling with birdlife (look out for the brilliant scarlet chest of the black-headed gonolek) and impala are rather common. Unfortunately the lake is also a popular place to water cattle. About 8km north of this, **Lake Birengiro** is a shallow, muddy body of palm-fringed water which supports huge numbers of waterbirds, notably pelicans, storks, the odd long-toed plover and at least one pair of shoebill. The best of the lakes for general game viewing, however, is **Lake Hago**, about 15km further north and encircled by a decent track. This is where elephant are most likely to be seen, as well as small herds of buffalo and zebra, and it must support several hundred hippo.

South of Lake Hago, the vegetation is mostly very dense, and animals are difficult to spot, though you can be reasonably confident of seeing baboons, vervet monkeys and impala. This all changes when you turn left at Junction 23, to ascend towards the **Mutumba Hills** through an area of park-like woodland whose large acacias are favoured by giraffe. Eventually the woodland gives way to open grassland and easily the best game viewing in the park. Here, you can be certain of seeing the delicate oribi and reedbuck, as well as the larger topi. With luck, you'll also encounter eland, zebra and (in the wet season) large herds of buffalo.

North of the Mutumba Hills, the vegetation is again very thick, and animals can be difficult to spot, though impala, buffalo and zebra all seem to be present in significant numbers. The papyrus beds around **Lakes Gishanju** and **Mihindi** form the most accessible marshy areas in the park, and are worth taking slowly by anybody who hopes to see papyrus-dwellers. The **Plage Hippos** (Hippo Beach) on Lake Mihindi was, oddly, about the one place in Akagera where we stopped next to open water and *didn't* see any hippos, but it's a pretty spot, and would make for an ideal picnic site.

Heading further north, **Lake Rwanyakizinga** is another favoured spot with elephants, and the open plains to the west of the lake are excellent for plains animals such as warthog, zebra and herds of 50-plus topi. This little-visited part of Akagera is one that is inhabited by lion – and a solitary and secretive rhino. Having looked around this area, your options are either to head back the way you came, or (more popular) to head cross-country out of the park along the route mentioned earlier in this section.

Appendix I

LANGUAGE

Words in Kinyarwanda are spelt phonetically here, to make their pronunciation easy. The letters 'r' and 'l' (and their sounds) are often interchanged, also sometimes 'b', 'v' and 'w'. When a word ends in 'e', pronounce it as the French 'é'. Pronounce 'i' as 'ee' rather than 'eye'.

English	French	Kinyarwanda
COURTESIES		
good day/hello	*bonjour*	*muraho*
good morning	*bonjour*	*mwaramutse*
good afternoon	*bonjour*	*mwiriwe*
good evening	*bonsoir*	*mwiriwe*
sir	*monsieur*	*bwana*
madam	*madame*	*mubyeyi*
how are you?	*ça va?*	*amakuru?/bitese?*
I'm fine, thank you	*ça va bien, merci*	*amakuru/meza/égo*
please	*s'il vous plaît*	*mubishoboye*
thank you	*merci*	*murakoze*
excuse me	*excusez moi*	*imbabazi*
goodbye (morning)	*au revoir*	*mwiliwe*
goodbye (afternoon)	*au revoir*	*mwilirwe*
goodbye (evening)	*au revoir*	*muramukeho*
goodbye (for ever)	*au revoir/adieu*	*murabeho*
BASIC WORDS		
yes	*oui*	*yégo*
no	*non*	*oya*
that's right	*c'est ça*	*ni byo*
maybe	*peut-être*	*ahali*
good	*bon*	*byiza*
hot	*chaud*	*ubushyuhe*
cold	*froid*	*ubukonje*
and	*et*	*na*
QUESTIONS		
how?	*comment?*	*bite?*
how much?	*combien?*	*angahe?*
what's your name?	*quel est votre nom?*	*witwande?*
when?	*quand?*	*ryali?*
where?	*où?*	*hehe?*
who?	*qui?*	*nde?/bande?*

English	French	Kinyarwanda

FOOD/DRINK

beans	*haricots*	*ibihyimbo*
beer	*bière*	*byeri*
butter	*beurre*	*amavuta*
bread	*pain*	*umugati*
coffee	*café*	*ikawa*
eggs	*oeufs*	*amagi*
fish	*poisson*	*amafi*
meat	*viande*	*inyama*
milk	*lait*	*amata*
potatoes	*pommes de terre*	*ibirayi*
rice	*riz*	*umuceli*
salad	*salade*	*salade*
soup	*potage*	*isupu*
sugar	*sucre*	*isukali*
tea	*thé*	*icyayi (chai)*
tomatoes	*tomates*	*inyanya*
drinks	*boissons*	*ibinyobura*
water	*eau*	*amazi*

SHOPPING

bank	*banque*	*ibanki*
bookshop	*librairie*	*isomero*
chemist	*pharmacie*	*farumasi*
shop	*magazin*	*iduka*
market	*marché*	*isoko*
battery	*pile/batterie*	*bateri*
film	*filme*	*filime*
map	*carte*	*ikarita*
money	*argent*	*amafaranga*
soap	*savon*	*isabuni*
toothpaste	*dentifrice*	*umuti w'amenyo*

POST

post office	*poste (PTT)*	*iposta*
envelope	*enveloppe*	*ibahasha*
letter	*lettre*	*urwandiko*
paper	*papier*	*urupapuro*
postcard	*carte postale*	
stamp	*timbre*	*tembri*

GETTING AROUND

bus	*bus*	*bisi*
bus station	*gare routière*	*aho bisi ihagarara*
taxi	*taxi*	*tagisi*
car	*voiture*	*imodoka*
petrol station	*station d'essence*	*aho kunyweshereza essence*
plane	*avion*	*indege*
far	*loin*	*kure*
near	*près*	*hafi*
to the right	*à droit*	*i buryo*

English	French	Kinyarwanda
to the left	*à gauche*	*i bumoso*
straight ahead	*tout droit*	*imbere*
bridge	*pont*	*ikiraro*
hill	*colline*	*agasozi*
lake	*lac*	*ikiyaga*
mountain	*montagne*	*umusozi*
river	*fleuve*	*uruzi*
road	*route*	*umuhanda*
street	*rue*	*inzira*
town	*ville*	*umudugudu*
valley	*vallée*	*umubanda*
village	*village*	*akadugudu*
waterfall	*chute*	*isumo*

HOTEL

bed	*lit*	*igitanda*
room	*chambre*	*icyumba*
key	*clef/clé*	*urufunguzo*
shower	*douche*	*urwiyu hagiriro*
bath	*baignoire*	*urwogero*
toilet/WC	*toilette*	*umusarane*
hot water	*l'eau chaude*	*amazi ashushye*
cold water	*l'eau froide*	*amazi akonje*

MISCELLANEOUS

dentist	*dentiste*	*umuganga w'amenyo*
doctor	*médecin*	*umuganga*
embassy	*ambassade*	*ambasade*
tourist office	*bureau de tourisme*	*ibiro by ubukererarugendo*

TIME

minute	*minute*	*idakika*
hour	*heure*	*isaaha*
day	*jour*	*umunsi*
week	*semaine*	*icyumweru*
month	*mois*	*ukwezi*
year	*an/année*	*umwaka*
now	*maintenant*	*ubu/nonaha*
soon	*bientôt*	*vuba*
today	*aujourd'hui*	*none*
yesterday	*hier*	*ejo hashize*
tomorrow	*demain*	*ejo hazaza*
this week	*cette semaine*	*iki cyumweru*
next week	*semaine prochaine*	*icyumweru gitaha*
morning	*matin*	*igitondo*
afternoon	*après-midi*	*ni munsi*
evening	*soir*	*umugoroba*
night	*nuit*	*ijoro*
Monday	*lundi*	*ku wa mbere*
Tuesday	*mardi*	*ku wa kabili*
Wednesday	*mercredi*	*ku wa gatatu*

English	French	Kinyarwanda
Thursday	*jeudi*	*ku wa kane*
Friday	*vendredi*	*ku wa gatanu*
Saturday	*samedi*	*ku wa gatandatu*
Sunday	*dimanche*	*ku cyumweru*
January	*janvier*	*Mutarama*
February	*février*	*Gashyantare*
March	*mars*	*Werurwe*
April	*avril*	*Mata*
May	*mai*	*Gicuransi*
June	*juin*	*Kamena*
July	*juillet*	*Nyakanga*
August	*août*	*Kanama*
September	*septembre*	*Nzeli*
October	*octobre*	*Ukwakira*
November	*novembre*	*Ugushyingo*
December	*décembre*	*Ukuboza*

AFRICAN ENGLISH
Philip Briggs

Although a high proportion of Rwandans were raised in Kenya, Uganda or Tanzania and so speak English as a second language, not all get the opportunity to use it regularly, and as a result they will not be as fluent as they could be. Furthermore, as is often the case in Africa and elsewhere, an individual's pronunciation of a second language often tends to retain the vocal inflections of their first language, or it falls somewhere between that and a more standard pronunciation. It is also the case that many people tend to structure sentences in a second language similar to how they would in their home tongue. As a result, most Rwandans, to a greater or lesser extent, speak English with Bantu inflections and grammar. The above considerations aside, I would venture that African English – like American or Australian English – is over-due recognition as a distinct linguistic entity, possessed of a unique rhythm and pronunciation, as well as an idiomatic quality quite distinct from any form of English spoken elsewhere. And learning to communicate in this idiom is perhaps the most important linguistic skill that the visitor to any African country where English is spoken can acquire. If this sounds patronising, so be it. There are regional accents in the UK and US that I find far more difficult to follow than the English spoken in Africa, simply because I am more familiar with the latter. And precisely the same adjustment might be required were, for instance, an Australian to travel in the American south, a Geordie to wash up in my home town of Johannesburg, or vice versa.

The following points should prove useful when you speak English to Africans:

- Greet simply, using phrases likely to be understood locally: the ubiquitous sing-song 'How-are-you! – I am fine', or if that draws a blank try the pidgin Swahili 'Jambo!' It is important always to greet a stranger before you plough ahead and ask directions or any other question. Firstly, it is rude to do otherwise; secondly, most Westerners feel uncomfortable asking a stranger a straight question. If you have already greeted the person, you'll feel less need to preface a question with phrases like 'I'm terribly sorry' or 'Would you mind telling me' which will confuse someone who speaks limited English.
- Speak slowly and clearly. There is no need, as some travellers do, to take this too far, as if you are talking to a three-year-old. Speak naturally, but try not to rush or clip phrases.
- Phrase questions simply, with an ear towards Bantu inflections. 'This bus goes to Huye?' might be more easily understood than 'Could you tell me whether this bus is going to Huye?' and 'You have a room?' is better than 'Is there a vacant room?' If you are not

understood, don't keep repeating the same question more loudly. Try a different and ideally simpler phrasing, giving consideration to whether any specific word(s) – in the last case, most likely 'vacant' – might particularly obstruct easy understanding.

- Listen to how people talk to you, and learn from it. Vowel sounds are often pronounced as in the local language (see Kinyarwanda pronunciation above), so that 'bin', for instance, might sound more like 'been'. Many words, too, will be pronounced with the customary Bantu stress on the second-last syllable.

- African languages generally contain few words with compound consonant sounds or ending in consonants. This can result in the clipping of soft consonant sounds such as 'r' (important as eem-POT-ant) or the insertion of a random vowel sound between running consonants (so that pen-pal becomes pen-I-pal and sounds almost indistinguishable from pineapple). It is commonplace, as well, to append a random vowel to the end of a word, in the process shifting the stress to what would ordinarily be the last syllable eg: pen-i-PAL-i.

- The 'l' and 'r' sounds are sometimes used interchangeably (hence Lake Burera/Bulera and Rue Karisimbi/Kalisimbi), which can sometimes cause confusion, in particular when your guide points out a lilac-breasted roller! The same is to a lesser extent true of 'b' and 'v' (Virunga versus Birunga), 'k' and 'ch' (the Rwandan capital, spelt Kigali, is more often pronounced 'Chigari') and, very occasionally, 'f' and 'p'.

- Some English words are in wide use. Other similar words are not. Some examples: a request for a 'lodging' or 'guesthouse', is more likely to be understood than one for 'accommodation', as is a request for a 'taxi' (or better 'special hire') over a 'taxi-cab' or 'cab', or for 'the balance' rather than 'change'.

- Avoid the use of dialect-specific expressions, slang and jargon! Few Africans will be familiar with terms such as 'feeling crook', 'pear-shaped' or 'user-friendly'.

- Avoid meaningless interjections. If somebody is struggling to follow you, appending a word such as 'mate' to every other phrase is only likely to further confuse them.

- We've all embarrassed ourselves at some point by mutilating the pronunciation of a word we've read but not heard. Likewise, guides working in national parks and other reserves often come up with innovative pronunciations for bird and mammal names they come across in field guides, and any word with an idiosyncratic spelling (eg: yacht, lamb, knot).

- Make sure the person you are talking to understands you. Try to avoid asking questions that can be answered with a yes or no. People may well agree with you simply to be polite or to avoid embarrassment.

- Keep calm. No-one is at their best when they arrive at a crowded bus station after an all-day bus ride. It is easy to be short tempered when someone cannot understand you. Be patient and polite; it's you who doesn't speak the language.

- Last but not least, do gauge the extent to which the above rules might apply to any given individual. It would be patently ridiculous to address a university lecturer or an experienced tour guide in broken English, equally inappropriate to babble away without making any allowances when talking to a villager who clearly has a limited English vocabulary. Generally, I start off talking normally to anybody I meet, and only start to refine my usage as and when it becomes clear it will aid communication.

248

Appendix 2

WEBSITES

For up-to-the-minute news reports from Rwanda and elsewhere in Africa the most comprehensive site is probably **www.allafrica.com**. Follow links to Rwanda. The website of the Rwandan newspaper *The New Times* has a range of local news items not picked up elsewhere: **www.newtimes.co.rw**. A good site for checking the latest currency exchange rate (not all include the Rwandan franc) is **www.xe.com**. Conditions in Rwanda – as elsewhere in Africa – may change, so as a precaution, before travelling, always check the Foreign Office website **www.fco.gov.uk/travel**, or that of the US State Department: **www.travel.state.gov**.

Four comprehensive websites on Rwanda are **www.rwandemb.org** (set up by the Rwandan Embassy in Washington, DC); the well organised **www.rwandagateway.org**; that of the Rwandan Embassy in London, **www.ambarwanda.org.uk**; and that of ORTPN (the Rwanda Tourist Board): **www.rwandatourism.com**, which provides impressive 'virtual tours' of many of the country's attractions. All have numerous links and between them cover a wide range of topics, including Rwanda's history, geography, politics, development, genocide trials, economy, business potential and tourism. On the whole the essentials are up to date although some sections haven't been touched for a while at the time of writing. Another (self-explanatory) tourism site is **www.rwanda-golf.com**.

For more-or-less current phone numbers (and sometimes addresses) of hotels and other businesses in Rwanda, try **www.rwandaphonebook.com**; it's a kind of condensed Yellow Pages. (All Rwanda land-line phone numbers now have six digits; if you come across one with only five, try adding 5 at the beginning and it will probably work.)

The website of KIST (Kigali Institute of Science and Technology) generally has some interesting details of small-scale development and appropriate technology: **www.kist.ac.rw**. Its associated site **www.rwandainformation.org** is good on statistics. The site of the UN International Criminal Tribunal for Rwanda, **www.ictr.org**, has details of the current status of genocide criminals and the trials in progress. Human Rights Watch on **www.hrw.org** carries news of Rwanda, as does the Amnesty International site **www.amnesty.org**.

Finally, just doing a general internet search under 'Rwanda' will throw up a huge range of miscellaneous information, some of it reasonably up to date and some more than a decade old. You really need to aim for something specific, such as 'Rwanda+gorillas' or the name of specific activities, otherwise it's hard to sift the good from the bad. And for specific out-of-print books on Rwanda (and any other subject under the sun), try the unmatchable **www.usedbooksearch.co.uk**.

Appendix 3

FURTHER READING
HISTORICAL BACKGROUND

Reader, John *Africa: A Biography of the Continent* Hamish Hamilton, 1997. This award-winning book, available as a Penguin paperback, provides a compulsively readable introduction to Africa's past, from the formation of the continent to post-independence politics – the ideal starting point for anybody seeking to place their Rwandan experience in a broader African context.

Fegley, Randall (compiler) *Rwanda – World Bibliographical Series volume 154* Clio Press, 1993. This selective, annotated bibliography contains over 500 entries covering a wide range of subjects including Rwanda's history, geography, politics, literature, travellers' accounts, flora and fauna. Its preface and introduction give a condensed but useful (although somewhat dated) overview of Rwanda from early times until just before the genocide.

Kagame, Alexis *Un abrégé de l'ethno-historie du Rwanda* and *Un abrégé de l'histoire du Rwanda de 1853 à 1972*, Editions Universitaires du Rwanda, Butare, 1972 and 1975. These works are now out of print (and there are no English translations) but the seriously interested should try to track down secondhand copies. Drawing on oral tradition, Kagame describes the country and its people from several centuries before the arrival of the Europeans (in the first book) through to the first decade of colonisation (in the second).

NATURAL HISTORY
Field guides (mammals)

Kingdon, Jonathan *The Kingdon Field Guide to African Mammals* Academic Press, 1997. This is my first choice: the most detailed, thorough and up to date of several field guides covering the mammals of the region. The author, a highly respected biologist, supplements detailed descriptions and good illustrations of all the continent's large mammals with an ecological overview of each species. Essential for anybody with a serious interest in mammal identification.

Stuart, Chris & Tilde *The Larger Mammals of Africa* Struik, 1997. This useful field guide doesn't quite match up to Kingdon's, but it's the best of the rest, and arguably more appropriate to readers with a relatively casual interest in African wildlife. It's also a lot cheaper and lighter!

Stuart, Chris & Tilde *Southern, Central and East African Mammals* Struik, 1995. This excellent mini-guide, compact enough to slip into a pocket, is remarkably thorough within its inherent space restrictions. Highly recommended for one-off safari-goers, but not so good for forest primates, which limits its usefulness in Rwanda.

Dorst, J & Dandelot, P *Field Guide to the Larger Mammals of Africa* Collins, 1983 and Haltenorth, T & Diller, H *Field Guide to the Mammals of Africa including Madagascar* Collins, 1984. Formerly the standard field guides to the region, these books are still recommended in many travel guides. In my opinion, they have largely been superseded by subsequent publications, and now come across as very dated and badly structured – with mediocre illustrations to boot.

Estes, Richard *The Safari Companion* Green Books (UK), Russell Friedman Books (SA), Chelsea Green (USA). This unconventional book might succinctly be described as a field guide to mammal behaviour. It's probably a bit esoteric for most one-off visitors to Africa, but a must for anybody with a serious interest in wildlife.

Field guides (birds)

Stevenson, Terry & Fanshawe, John *Field Guide to the Birds of East Africa* T & A D Poyser, 2002. The best bird field guide, with useful field descriptions and accurate plates and distribution maps. It covers every species found in Rwanda as well as in Uganda, Kenya, Tanzania and Burundi. For serious birdwatchers, this is *the* book to take.

Van Perlo, Ber *Illustrated Checklist to the Birds of Eastern Africa* Collins, 1995. This is the next best thing to the above (and is cheaper and lighter), since it illustrates and provides a brief description of every species recorded in Uganda and Tanzania, along with a distribution map. I don't know of any bird found in Rwanda but not in Tanzania or Uganda, and I found that distribution details can normally be extrapolated from the maps of neighbouring countries. Be aware that the descriptive detail is succinct and many of the illustrations are misleading

Williams, J & Arlott, N *Field Guide to the Birds of East Africa* Collins, 1980. As with the older Collins mammal field guides, Williams' was for years the standard field guide to the region, and is still widely mentioned in travel literature. Unfortunately, it feels rather dated today: less than half the birds in the region are illustrated, several are not even described, and the bias is strongly towards common Kenyan birds.

Zimmerman et al *Birds of Kenya and Northern Tanzania* Russell Friedman Books, 1996. This monumentally handsome hardback tome is arguably the finest field guide to any African territory. The geographical limitations with regard to Rwanda are obvious, but its wealth of descriptive and ecological detail and superb illustrations make it an excellent secondary source. A lighter and cheaper but less detailed paperback version was published in 1999.

Others

Fossey, Dian *Gorillas in the Mist* Hodder & Stoughton, 1983. Enjoyable and massively informative, Fossey's landmark book is recommended without reservation to anybody going gorilla-tracking in the Parc des Volcans.

Goodall, Jane *Through A Window* Houghton Mifflin, 1991. Subtitled *My Thirty Years with the Chimpanzees of Gombe*, this is one of several highly readable books by Jane Goodall about the longest ongoing study of wild primates in the world. Set in Tanzania, this is nevertheless obvious pre-trip reading for anybody intending to track chimps in Nyungwe.

Kingdon, Jonathon *Island Africa* Collins, 1990. This highly readable and award-winning tome about evolution in ecological 'islands' such as deserts and montane forests is recommended to anybody who wants to place the natural history of Nyungwe and the Virungas in a continental context.

Mowat, Farley *Woman in the Mists* Futura, 1987. An excellent biography of the controversial Dian Fossey, one which leans so heavily on her own journals that parts are almost autobiography.

Stuart, Chris & Tilde *Africa's Vanishing Wildlife* Southern Books, 1996. An informative and pictorially strong introduction to the endangered and vulnerable mammals of Africa, this book combines coffee-table production with an impassioned and erudite text.

BACKGROUND TO THE GENOCIDE

Prunier, Gérard *The Rwanda Crisis – History of a Genocide* Hurst & Company, 1998. This painstakingly researched history of the Rwandan genocide, full of personal anecdotes and individual stories, describes with icy clarity the composition of the time bomb that began ticking long before its explosion in 1994. Prunier presents the genocide as part of a deadly logic, a plan hatched for political and economic motives, rather than the result of ancient hatred. He helps the reader to understand not only Rwanda's genocide but also the complexities of modern conflict in general.

Melvern, L R *A People Betrayed – the Role of the West in Rwanda's Genocide* Zed Books, 2000; and *Conspiracy to Murder: The Rwandan Genocide* Verso 2004. Linda Melvern's investigative study of the international background to Rwanda's genocide, *A People Betrayed*, contains a full account of how the tragedy unfolded. Documents held in Kigali, and previously unpublished accounts of secret UN Security council deliberations in New York, reveal a shocking sequence of events, and the failure of governments, organisations and individuals who could – had they opted to do so – have prevented the genocide. Melvern's equally powerful sequel, *Conspiracy to Murder*, continues the investigation, drawing on a vast amount of new material including documents abandoned by the *génocidaires* when they fled from Rwanda.

Dallaire, Lt Gen Roméo *Shake Hands with the Devil: the failure of humanity in Rwanda* Arrow Books, 2004. Dallaire was force commander of the UN Assistance Mission for Rwanda at the time of the genocide. This angry, moving and deeply human book describes the impossible situation he faced, caught up in a nightmare of killing and terror and yet denied the men and the operational freedom he needed in order to quell it. We see the unfolding of the genocide, in all its aspects, from the perspective of probably the one man who, had he been better heeded and supported, could have lessened its effects.

Gourevitch, Philip *We wish to inform you that tomorrow we will be killed with our families* Picador, 1998. Subtitled 'Stories from Rwanda', this winner of the *Guardian* First Book Award is war reporting of the highest order. Blending starkly factual narrative with human anecdotes and observations, Gourevitch paints on a broad canvas and the picture he creates is unforgettable. He shows us 'little people' caught up in unstoppable horrors – and reaching great heights of heroism.

Rwanda – Death, Despair and Defiance African Rights, London, 1995. This 1,200-page compilation by the UK organisation African Rights is a painfully thorough and detailed account of the genocide and its effect on Rwanda's people – the careful preparations, the identities of the killers and their accomplices, the massacres, the attacks on churches, schools and hospitals, and the aftermath. Victims tell their own stories and those of their families, and the horror and immensity of the slaughter are highlighted by the simplicity of their narratives. The impact is powerful, sometimes overwhelming. The index enables the reader to discover easily what happened in any particular area or village.

Leave None to Tell the Story African Rights Watch, 1999. Another painfully comprehensive account, full of personal testimonies based on Rwandan government records, this shows how ordinary administrative structures and practices were turned into mechanisms of murder. It describes the opposition to the killing and how it was crushed, while survivors relate how they resisted and escaped. Using diplomatic and court documents, the survey shows what might have been the result had the international reaction been swifter and more determined.

Barnett, Michael *Eyewitness to a Genocide: The United Nations and Rwanda* Cornell University, 2002. Tracing the history of the UN's involvement with Rwanda, Barnett argues that it did bear some moral responsibility for the genocide. A clear and factual study, also covering the warnings raised by the genocide and the question of whether it is possible to build wholly moral institutions.

Keane, Fergal *Season of Blood – a Rwandan Journey* Penguin, 1995. Keane's prose – sometimes so precisely balanced that it verges on poetry – is always impeccable. Here he blends factual narrative and analysis with spontaneous emotion in such a way that the reader is both moved and informed in a single phrase. As a BBC correspondent, he was travelling around Rwanda – among the killers and among the victims – as the genocide spread countrywide. His reports at the time brought home the extent of the human tragedy and their essence is preserved in this book, which won the 1995 Orwell Prize.

Sibomana, André *Hope for Rwanda* Pluto Press, 1999. In this very personal account, subtitled *Conversations with Laure Guilbert and Hervé Deguine*, the speaker describes the unfolding of the genocide, and his own experiences, with impressive fairness, clarity and lack of accusation. A touching and informative book by a remarkable man.

MISCELLANEOUS

Lewis, Jerome & Knight, Judy *The Twa of Rwanda* World Rainforest Movement (UK), 1996. The Twa are the smallest 'ethnic' group in Rwanda. This report, published by the World Rainforest Movement in co-operation with the International Work Group for Indigenous Affairs (Denmark) and Survival International (France), traces their history, highlights their current impoverished situation, quotes their opinions about their past and future, and allows them to express their fears and aspirations. It also shows the dilemma faced by African governments as they try to build national unity while still respecting cultural diversity.

Halsey Carr, R & Howard Halsey, A H *Land of a Thousand Hills* Viking, 1999. Rosamond Halsey Carr moved to Rwanda as a young bride in 1949 and has stayed for over 50 years. She watched the decline of colonialism, the problems of independence and the growing violence. When the genocide started she was evacuated by the American Embassy but returned four months later, and began turning an old pyrethrum drying-house on her flower plantation into a home for genocide orphans, which still functions today. This very readable and moving book chronicles the extraordinary life of an extraordinary woman, in the country she loved and made her home.

Stassen, Jean-Philippe *Déogratias* Aire Libre, Dupuis (Belgium) 2000. If you can read at least some French, this 80-page *bande dessinée* (graphic novel) tells the story of a young Hutu who killed during the genocide and how this, together with drink, destroyed him. With skill and humanity, the creator succeeds in 'telling the untellable' and producing a powerful document.

http://philipbriggs.wordpress.com A blog by Philip Briggs that provides an interactive update service for Bradt readers and other travellers, volunteers and service providers in Rwanda.

WIN £100 CASH!
READER QUESTIONNAIRE

Send in your completed questionnaire for the chance to win
£100 cash in our regular draw

All respondents may order a Bradt guide at half the UK retail price – please
complete the order form overleaf.

(Entries may be posted or faxed to us, or scanned and emailed.)

We are interested in getting feedback from our readers to help us plan future Bradt
guides. Please answer ALL the questions below and return the form to us in order
to qualify for an entry in our regular draw.

Have you used any other Bradt guides? If so, which titles? . . . .
. . . .

What other publishers' travel guides do you use regularly? . . . .
. . . .

Where did you buy this guidebook? . . . .

What was the main purpose of your trip to Rwanda (or for what other reason did
you read our guide)? eg: holiday/business/charity etc. . . . .
. . . .

What other destinations would you like to see covered by a Bradt guide?
. . . .

Would you like to receive our catalogue/newsletters?

YES / NO (If yes, please complete details on reverse)

If yes – by post or email? . . . .

Age (circle relevant category) 16–25   26–45   46–60   60+

Male/Female (delete as appropriate)

Home country . . . .

Please send us any comments about our guide to Rwanda or other Bradt Travel
Guides. . . . .
. . . .
. . . .
. . . .

Bradt Travel Guides
23 High Street, Chalfont St Peter, Bucks SL9 9QE, UK
✆ +44 (0)1753 893444 f +44 (0)1753 892333
e info@bradtguides.com
www.bradtguides.com

CLAIM YOUR HALF-PRICE BRADT GUIDE!

Order Form

To order your half-price copy of a Bradt guide, and to enter our prize draw to win £100 (see overleaf), please fill in the order form below, complete the questionnaire overleaf, and send it to Bradt Travel Guides by post, fax or email.

Please send me one copy of the following guide at half the UK retail price

Title	Retail price	Half price
...	....	....	....

Please send the following additional guides at full UK retail price

No	Title	Retail price	Total
...	....	....	....
...	....	....	....
...	....	....	....

Sub total ....
Post & packing ......
(£1 per book UK; £2 per book Europe; £3 per book rest of world)
Total ....

Name ....

Address..

Tel .... Email ....

☐ I enclose a cheque for £. .... made payable to Bradt Travel Guides Ltd

☐ I would like to pay by credit card. Number: ....

Expiry date: ... / ... 3-digit security code (on reverse of card) .....

☐ Please add my name to your catalogue mailing list.

☐ I would be happy for you to use my name and comments in Bradt marketing material.

Send your order on this form, with the completed questionnaire, to:

Bradt Travel Guides RWA/3
23 High Street, Chalfont St Peter, Bucks SL9 9QE
✆ +44 (0)1753 893444   f +44 (0)1753 892333
e info@bradtguides.com   www.bradtguides.com

Bradt Travel Guides

www.bradtguides.com

Africa

Africa Overland	£15.99
Benin	£14.99
Botswana: Okavango, Chobe, Northern Kalahari	£15.99
Burkina Faso	£14.99
Cape Verde Islands	£13.99
Canary Islands	£13.95
Cameroon	£13.95
Eritrea	£12.95
Ethiopia	£15.99
Gabon, São Tomé, Príncipe	£13.95
Gambia, The	£13.99
Ghana	£13.95
Johannesburg	£6.99
Kenya	£14.95
Madagascar	£14.95
Malawi	£13.99
Mali	£13.95
Mauritius, Rodrigues & Réunion	£13.99
Mozambique	£12.95
Namibia	£14.95
Niger	£14.99
Nigeria	£15.99
Rwanda	£14.99
Seychelles	£14.99
Sudan	£13.95
Tanzania, Northern	£13.99
Tanzania	£16.99
Uganda	£13.95
Zambia	£15.95
Zanzibar	£12.99

Britain and Europe

Albania	£13.99
Armenia, Nagorno Karabagh	£13.99
Azores	£12.99
Baltic Capitals: Tallinn, Riga, Vilnius, Kaliningrad	£12.99
Belgrade	£6.99
Bosnia & Herzegovina	£13.99
Bratislava	£6.99
Budapest	£7.95
Cork	£6.95
Croatia	£12.95
Cyprus see North Cyprus	
Czech Republic	£13.99
Dubrovnik	£6.95
Eccentric Britain	£13.99
Eccentric Cambridge	£6.99
Eccentric Edinburgh	£5.95
Eccentric France	£12.95
Eccentric London	£12.95
Eccentric Oxford	£5.95
Estonia	£12.95
Faroe Islands	£13.95
Hungary	£14.99
Kiev	£7.95
Latvia	£13.99
Lille	£6.99
Lithuania	£13.99

Ljubljana	£6.99
Macedonia	£13.95
Montenegro	£13.99
North Cyprus	£12.99
Paris, Lille & Brussels	£11.95
Riga	£6.95
River Thames, In the Footsteps of the Famous	£10.95
Serbia	£13.99
Slovenia	£12.99
Spitsbergen	£14.99
Switzerland: Rail, Road, Lake	£13.99
Tallinn	£6.99
Ukraine	£13.95
Vilnius	£6.99

Middle East, Asia and Australasia

Georgia	£13.95
Great Wall of China	£13.99
Iran	£14.99
Iraq	£14.95
Kabul	£9.95
Maldives	£13.99
Mongolia	£14.95
North Korea	£13.95
Oman	£13.99
Palestine, Jerusalem	£12.95
Sri Lanka	£13.99
Syria	£13.99
Tasmania	£12.95
Tibet	£13.99
Turkmenistan	£14.99

The Americas and the Caribbean

Amazon, The	£14.95
Argentina	£15.99
Bolivia	£14.99
Cayman Islands	£12.95
Costa Rica	£13.99
Chile	£16.95
Chile & Argentina: Trekking	£12.95
Eccentric America	£13.95
Eccentric California	£13.99
Falkland Islands	£13.95
Peru & Bolivia: Backpacking and Trekking	£12.95
Panama	£13.95
St Helena, Ascension, Tristan da Cunha	£14.95
USA by Rail	£13.99

Wildlife

Antarctica: Guide to the Wildlife	£14.95
Arctic: Guide to the Wildlife	£15.99
British Isles: Wildlife of Coastal Waters	£14.95
Galápagos Wildlife	£15.99
Madagascar Wildlife	£14.95
Southern African Wildlife	£18.95
Sri Lankan Wildlife	£15.99

Health

Your Child Abroad: A Travel Health Guide	£10.95

Index

accommodation 65–6
airlines 35–6, 62
Akagera National Park 229–42, *230*
   activities 239–42
   antelope 234–5
   birds 234–6
   boat trips 239
   dangerous animals 238
   further information 238
   game drives 240–2
   getting there and away 238–9
   history 231–8
   mammals 232–4
   natural history 231
   park fees 239
   Plage Hippos 242
   reptiles 237
   shoebill sightings 237, 242
   where to stay 239
Albertine Rift Endemics 135, 137, 140, 175, 201, 203
Amahoro Community–Based Tourism 185
Amahoro Island 164
Ankole cattle 222–3
antelope 234–5
area codes 74
arts 29–32
Arusha (Tanzania) 19
ASAR 107
ASOFERWA 189
Astrid, Queen 127
Astrida *see Huye*
at a glance 2
ATMs 62

background information 3–22
Bagenge's Rock 184
banana beer 132
bananas 118–9
banking hours 62
Batwa 6–7, 8, 13, 29, 30, 31, 107, 125, 192–3

becoming involved 77–80
begging 71
Belgian rule 11–15
bicycle-taxis 65
Bigugu, Mount 147, 151
biking 64
bilharzia 54–5
binoculars 42
Birengiro, Lake 242
Birunga Mountains *see Virunga Mountains*
Bisesero 165
Bizimungu, President Pasteur 18, 19
boat transport 64
book shops 61
bribery 71
budgeting 43–5
buffalo 233, 238
Bufumbira Mountains *see Virunga Mountains*
Bugarama Hot Springs 150, 159
Buhanga Forest 188, 195
Bukavu 159
bureaucracy 71
bureaux des change *see forex bureaux*
Burera, Lake 189–94, *190*
Burton, Sir Richard 4–5
Burundi 17, 36
Butare *see Huye*
Byumba 216–7

camping 41
Caplaki 102, 107
cattle 222–3, 226
Centre Marembo 79
chameleons 142–3
cheese 67
chimpanzees 148–9, 150, 175
Christianity 25–6
Classé, Bishop Léon 13
climate 2, 35
clothing 41–2
coffee 68

communications 72–6
Congo, Democratic Republic of 36
COPABU 131, 133
credit cards 43, 45
cricket 105
currency 2
Cyamudongo Forest 150
Cyangugu 154–59, *156*

dance 29
Dancing Pots 30, 107
Dian Fossey Gorilla Fund 205, 210
diarrhoea 51–2
distance table 64
DRC *see Congo, Democratic Republic of*
drinks 67–8
driving 37, 39, 62–4
DSTV 76

Eastern Rwanda *214*, 215–228
eating out 66
ebola 56
education 13, 27–9
elections 20
electricity 2
elephant 233–4
email 73–4
embassies, foreign (in Rwanda) 72
embassies, Rwandan (abroad) 39–40
ENGALYNX 80
English 69
exchange rate 54

famines 12
fauna 4–6
fax 74
Fecar Inganzo 187
federal map 22
first–aid kit 51
flag 21
flights, domestic 62
flights, international 35–6
football 32–4
foreign exchange 62
forex bureaux 43
Fossey, Dian 199, 200, 203, 206
French 69
further reading 251–4

Gacaca courts 20
general information 1–80
genocide 18–19, 20, 25, 133, 155, 161, 165,
    212–3, 227

Genocide Memorial Day 61
genocide memorials 19, 103–4, 113–4, 134,
    162, 164, 165
geography 2, 3
German east Africa 9–11
getting around 62–5
Gikongoro 134
giraffe 233
Gisakura Tea Estate 144, 145–6
Gisenyi 165–76, *168–9*
Gishanju, Lake 242
Gishwati Forest 174–6
Gisozi 103
Gitarama 15, 115–7, *116*
Goma 174
gorilla, mountain 206–13
    conservation 211–3
    conservation organisations 210–11
    discovery of 10
    during the genocide 212–3
    ecology 206–7
    food 207
    naming ceremony 212
    nesting 207
    permits 54, 204
    protocol
    range
    silverbacks 207
    taxonomy 206–7
    tourism 211–3
    tracking 204–10
Government of National Unity 18
Grant, Captain James 4

Habyarimana, President Juvenal 16, 17
Hago, Lake 242
Halsey Carr, Rosamond 125, 172, 174
handicrafts 32
Harroy, Jean–Paul 14
Health & safety 47–58
hippo 233, 238
history 6–22
hitching 64
HIV/AIDS 21, 47, 57
homestays 183
human statistics 2
Hutu 6, 8, 11, 13–19, 25, 29
Huye 22, 77, 127–34, *126*, *129*
    accommodation 128–30
    banks 131
    book shops 131
    cathedral 133
    excursions 133–4

Huye *continued*
  genocide 133
  getting around 128
  getting there and away 127
  handicrafts 131
  market 131
  national museum 131–3
  nightlife 130
  post office 130
  restaurants 130
  Ruhande Arboretum 131

identity cards 13, 17
Ihema, Lake 232, 241
Ihema, Lake 9
Ihururiro Group 78
Ikuvuguto National Dairy 124
Imana 25–6
Imbabazi Orphanage 172–3, 174
immunisations 47
independence, build–up to 14–15
insect bites 53
insurance 51
International Criminal Tribunal 19
International Peace Marathon 110
internet 46, 73–4
Intore dancers 29, 124
investing in Rwanda 80
itinerary planning 46

Kabgayi 117–20
Kabuye, Mount 182–3
Kagame, President Paul 15, 16, 18, 19, 21,
  34
Kagera River 5
Kakira Association 225
Kamageri's Rock 121
Kamembe *see Cyangugu*
Kandt, Richard 102, 151
Karago, Lake 198
karate 33
Karisoke 199, 200
Kayibanda, President Grégoire 14, 15, 16,
  115
Kayonza 218
Kibeho 134
Kibungo 221–5, *224*
Kibuye 161–5, *162*
Kigali 45, 83–114,*84–5, 88–9, 93, 96*
  accommodation 87–95
  airport 85–6
  Amahoro Stadium
  arts 104

Kigali *continued*
  banks 100
  bookshops 106
  buses 113
  cash withdrawals 100
  city tour 102
  entertainment 104
  flights to 83–6
  foreign exchange 86
  forex bureaux 100
  Genocide Memorial 103–4
  getting around 86–7
  getting there and away 83
  handicrafts 107–9
  internet 101
  Kandt's House
  library 106
  map 86
  markets 108, 109
  museums 102
  nightlife 99–100
  Nyabugogo 109, 111–2
  Nyamirambo 95, *96*, 109
  ORTPN office 86
  post office 100
  restaurants 97–9
  road connections 86
  shopping 101
  sport 104–5
  telephone, public 101
  tour operators 110–1
    minibus–taxis 111–2
  walks 109
Kinigi 188
Kinyarwanda 69, 243–6
Kivu, Lake 153–76
Kubijega 120, 121

language 69, 243–7
lion 232, 238
literature 29
Livestock for Life 78
Livingstone, Dr David 5
Logiest. Colonel Guy 15
luggage 40

magazines 73
Makwaza, Mount 134
malaria 48–9, 238
markets 67
Mecklenburg, Duke of 10, 11, 40, 166
media 72–6
meningitis 56

Mihindi, Lake 242
minibus–taxis 65
mobile phones *see telephone, cell*
money 43–5, 62
monkeys 140–41, 175, 202, 205, 233
mosquitoes 53
motos 65
Mountain Gorilla's Nest 188
MRND party 16, 18
MTN 101
Muhazi, Lake 216, 218
Musanze & the Virunga Foothills 177–98,
    178
Musanze 22, 54, 70, 177– 88, *180–1*
Musanze Cave 198
Museveni, President Yoweri (Uganda) 16,
    21
music 29
Musinga, Mwami (King) 12–13, 120
Muslims 25

Napoleon's Island 164
National Museum of Rwanda, 131–3
Ndaba Falls 165
Ndadaye, President Melchior (Burundi) 17
newspapers 73
Nile River 4–5, 146–7, 151
Ntarama 113–4
Ntaryamira, President Cyprien (Burundi)
    17
Nyabingi Cult 196–7
Nyabisindu *see Nyanza*
Nyagatare 219–21, *220*
Nyakabuye 150
Nyakarimbi 225–6
Nyamata 83, 113
Nyamuragira, Mount 203
Nyanza 9, 120–5, *122*
Nyiragongo, Mount 175, 203
Nyungwe Forest National Park 135–52,
    136
    accommodation 144
    activities 144–52
    Bigugu Trail 147
    biodiversity 135, 137
    birds 139–41
    camping 143–4
    chimpanzee tracking 150
    coloured trails 145
    eating 143–4
    flora 138
    further information 142
    getting there and away 143

Nyungwe Forest National Park *continued*
    Gisakura 145–6
    Kamiranzovu Trail 147
    mammals 139, 140–41
    monkeys 140–41
    park fees 144
    source of the Nile 151
    Uwinka 143, 145
    waterfall trail 145

Oakdale Demonstration Farm 124
oral history and traditions 7–8, 25–6, 29,
    122, 160, 184, 195, 196–7, 219, 222, 226
ORTPN 45, 61, 86
overland borders 36–7

packing 40–43
Parc des Volcans *see Volcanoes National Park*
PARMEHUTU party 14, 15
passport 39
people and culture 25–34
permits, gorilla tracking 45
place names 69
planning and preparation 35–46
politics 2
Pope John Paul II, 25
post 76
prehistory 6–9
prickly heat 56
provinces 22
public holidays 61
public transport 64–5
Pygmies *see Batwa*

rabies 57
radio 76
rail 64
RANU party 16
religion 25–6
restaurants 66
rhino 233
road accidents 58
Road to Huye, the 115–25
RPF party 18, 19
Ruanda–Urundi 9–15
Rubona 173–4
Rubona rwa Nzoga 219
Rudahigwa, Mwami (King) 13, 15, 120, 123
rugby 34
RUGO 77
Ruhango 120
Ruhengeri *see Musanze*
Ruhondo, Lake 195

7-16 Travel
$2.50

Rusizi Falls 159
Rusumo Falls 226–8
Rusumo Falls 9
Rwabugiri, Mwami (King) 9
Rwamagana 217–8
Rwanda na Gasabo 215
Rwanyakizinga, Lake 242
Rwesoro 216
Rwigima, Major–General Fred 16, 17
Ryangombe 195
Ryangombe Cult 26
RYICO 79

satellite phones 76
Schaller, George 206, 211
schistosomiasis *see bilharzia*
security 39
Seeds of Peace Centre 218
self–drive *see driving*
Shakani, Lake 242
shoebill 236–7, 242
shopping 76
skin infections 55
sleeping bag 42
snakebite 57
solar ovens 31
Speke, John Hanning 4–5, 123
sport 32–4
Stanley, Henry Morton 5, 9, 241
sunstroke 56
SURF 79

Tanzania 36–7, 227
taxis 65
telephone 2, 74–5
cell 75, 102
television 76
theft 58, 71
thrombosis, deep vein 54–5
ticks 53
time 2
tour operators 37–9, 110–1
tourist information 61

travel clinics 49–51
travellers cheques 43, 54
travelling in Rwanda 61–80
tsetse flies 53
Tutsi 6, 8, 11, 13–19, 25, 29
Twa *see* Batwa

Uganda 36–7
United Nations 14, 18, 19

vaccinations 47–8
vegetation 3
Viaki Crafts Village 133
Virunga Lodge 194
Virunga Mountains 175, 202–3
visas 39
Volcanoes National Park 199–213, *200*
    acclimatisation 209
    accommodation 179–85, 188, 194, 201
    activities 202–4
    Amahoro Group 208
    clothing
    crater lakes 203
    Dian Fossey's tomb 203
    getting there and away 201, 208
    golden monkeys 205
    gorilla tracking 204–10
    Group Thirteen 208, 209
    Karisimbi trek 202
    preparation 208–9
    regulations
    Sabinyo Group 208, 209
    Susa Group 207, 209
    tracking permits 45, 204–6
    Umubano Group 208
    Visoke trek 203
von Beringe 10
von Götzen, Count 9, 10, 226

weaver birds 240–1
websites 46, 249
when to visit 35
women travellers 72